T0389445

European Perceptions of China and Perspectives on the Belt and Road Initiative

East and West

CULTURE, DIPLOMACY AND INTERACTIONS

Edited by

Chuxiong George Wei (*Hong Kong Shue Yan University*)

VOLUME 11

The titles published in this series are listed at *brill.com/ewcd*

European Perceptions of China and Perspectives on the Belt and Road Initiative

Edited By

Stephen Rowley

BRILL

LEIDEN | BOSTON

Library of Congress Cataloging-in-Publication Data

Names: Rowley, Stephen, editor.
Title: European perceptions of China and perspectives on the Belt and Road
    Initiative / edited by Stephen Rowley, Sun Yat-sen University.
Description: Leiden ; Boston : Brill, [2021] | Series: East and West :
    culture, diplomacy and interactions, 2467-9704 ; volume 11 | Includes
    bibliographical references and index. | Summary: "European Perceptions
    of China and Perspectives on the Belt and Road Initiative is a collection
    of fourteen essays on the way China is perceived in Europe today. These
    perceptions - and they are multiple - are particularly important to the
    People's Republic of China as the country grapples with its increasingly
    prominent role on the international stage, and equally important to
    Europe as it attempts to come to terms with the technological, social
    and economic advances of the Belt and Road Initiative. The authors
    are, on the whole, senior academics specializing in such topics as
    International Relations and Security, Public Diplomacy, Media and
    Cultural Studies, and Philosophy and Religion from more than a dozen
    different European countries and are involved in various international
    projects focused on Europe-China relations"– Provided by publisher.
Identifiers: LCCN 2021023307 (print) | LCCN 2021023308 (ebook) |
    ISBN 9789004469839 (hardback) | ISBN 9789004469846 (ebook)
Subjects: LCSH: Yi dai yi lu (Initiative : China)–Foreign public opinion,
    European. | Public opinion–Europe. | East and West. | China–Foreign
    public opinion, European. | China–Foreign relations–Europe. |
    Europe–Foreign relations–China.
Classification: LCC DS740.5.E85 E87 2021 (print) | LCC DS740.5.E85 (ebook) |
    DDC 303.48/25104–dc23
LC record available at https://lccn.loc.gov/2021023307
LC ebook record available at https://lccn.loc.gov/2021023308

Typeface for the Latin, Greek, and Cyrillic scripts: "Brill". See and download: brill.com/brill-typeface.

ISSN: 2467-9704
ISBN: 978-90-04-46983-9 (hardback)
ISBN: 978-90-04-46984-6 (e-book)

Contents

List of Graphs, Figures and Tables

Figures

Graphs

Tables

Notes on Contributors

Neville Chi Hang Li
is Lecturer at Lingnan University. He received his PhD in Politics, Languages and International Studies from the University of Bath in 2017. His research interests focus on Security Studies, Politics and International Relations in Asia-Pacific and Media and Political Communication.

Mario Esteban
is Associate Professor at the Centre for East Asian Studies of the Autonomous University of Madrid and Senior Analyst at Elcano Royal Institute. His research interests are focused on the international relations of East Asia, EU-East Asia Relations, and the domestic and international politics of China. His work has been published in academic journals such as *The China Quarterly, The Journal of Contemporary China, Journal of Current Chinese Affairs, African and Asian Studies, The Chinese Political Science Review, and The European Journal of East Asian Studies.*

David J. Galbreath
is Professor and Dean of the Faculty of Humanities and Social Sciences at the University of Bath, UK.
His most recent publications include:
– *Contemporary European Security,* with Jocelyn Mawdsley and Laura Chappell (2019, Routledge).
– *Routledge Handbook for Defence Studies* with John Deni (*2019, Routledge*).
– 'Evolving Dynamics of Societal Security and the Potential for Conflict in Eastern Ukraine', *Europe-Asia Studies* 2020, with Tetyana Malyarenko *DOI:* 10.1080/09668136.2019.1705964.
– *Defence Studies: A Reader* with Alex Neads (Routledge 2020).

Irina Golubeva
is Associate Professor of Intercultural Communication at the University of Maryland Baltimore County, USA, and Co-Director of the *Intercultural Leadership Certificate Program.* She specialises in the development of intercultural competence; the internationalisation of higher education; and the conceptualization of intercultural citizenship. She worked for ten years with international students as the International Admissions Coordinator and Head of the International Office at her previous institution in Hungary.

Olexiy Haran

was Dean and organizer of the Faculty of Social Sciences at the re-born University of Kyiv-Mohyla Academy (UKMA), the oldest Ukrainian University founded in 1615 and re-established in 1991. Since 2002, he has also served as Research Director at the Democratic Initiatives Foundation, one of the leading Ukrainian analytical and sociological centres. His recently edited book is *Constructing a Political Nation: Changes in the Attitudes of Ukrainians during the War in the Donbas* (2017).

Youssef Elhaoussine

is a researcher from France with a scientific and marketing background. Initially, he worked in China as a production manager before turning to an academic career in teaching and research in B2B Branding. His research interest also includes the Belt and Road Initiative. Currently, Elhaoussine is Assistant Professor at the Beijing Normal University – Hong Kong Baptist University United International College in China.

Ivana Karaskova

lectures at Charles University, Czech Republic and is a China Research Fellow at the Association for International Affairs (AMO), where she founded and now leads MapInfluenCE projects, mapping China's influence in Central Europe, and is a member of China Observers in Central and Eastern Europe (CHOICE), which is a collaborative international platform bringing together China experts from 17 CEE countries. Currently (until February 2021), she is a Europe-China Policy Fellow at MERICS in Berlin, Germany. She is a member of the China expert pool at the European Center of Excellence for Countering Hybrid Threats (Hybrid CoE) in Helsinki. She has presented her research to Members of the European Parliament and US Congress.

Kaspars Klavins

is one of the leading scholars in Latvia on the topics of Islamism, contemporary Islamic philosophy, Medieval history and Korean history, culture and spirituality. Prof. Klavins is the author of 14 scientific monographs, a number of chapters in different books and fundamental historical source publications, as well as the author of many scientific articles (including articles in English, French and German). He has written on medieval history, the history of modern ideas, conflict resolution, German studies, ecology, Arab culture, Islamic civilization and Korean spirituality.

Dominik Mierzejewski

is Professor and Chair of the Center for Asian Affairs at the University of Lodz (a university-based think-tank) and Professor in the Department of Asian Studies. His central area of research is China foreign policy and the role of local government involvement. He is co-author of *China's Selective Identity. State, Identity and Culture* (Palgrave, 2019) and author of *China's Provinces and the Belt and Road Initiative* (Routledge, 2021).

Csaba Moldicz

is an Associate Professor in the Department of International Relations, Faculty of International Business and Management, Budapest Business School, Hungary. His main research field is the economic integration process of the European Union and China with a special focus on the Central and European region. He is currently the Head of Research at the Oriental Business and Innovation Group, which was founded by the Budapest Business School and the Central Bank of Hungary in 2016.

Mariana Nicolae

teaches soft skills at the Bucharest University of Economic Studies and the University of Bucharest. She is the founding director of the Master in International Business Communication (www.mibcom.ase.ro). She was a Fulbright senior scholar, a Fulbright ambassador for higher education institutions and participated as an expert evaluator in the Framework Programme FP7 of the European Union. At present she is a volunteer in several NGOs through which she spreads her deep conviction that education is the only viable way forward for the world.

Jean-Paul Rosaye

is a Professor at Artois University in France. He is the author of more than sixty publications, mainly on the history of ideas in a European context. He has also published several monographs on the idealist ascendancy from the late Victorian period to the beginning of the 20th century. His French translation of F. H. Bradley's metaphysical treatise *Appearance and Reality* has just been published by the French philosophical editor Hermann (Apparence et réalité. Essai de métaphysique).

Stephen Rowley

is currently Professor of English at Sun Yat-sen University where he is Director of the Centre for European Studies in the School of International Studies, and a member of the 'One Hundred Talents Programme'. He is author of more than fifty publications in literature, language, pedagogy and intercultural studies, and has published a novel, a book of short stories and a volume of poetry. Stephen Rowley was formerly Vice-President of the University of Artois (France).

Rubén Ruiz-Ramas

is Assistant Professor in the Department of Political Science and Administration, UNED (Madrid, Spain). Since 2019, Ruiz-Ramas is also Vice Dean for International Relations and Erasmus at the Faculty of Political Science and Sociology. Previously, he was Research Associate at the City University of London and Research Fellow at the School of International Studies of Sun Yat-sen University (Guangdong, China).

Greg Simons

is Associate Professor and researcher at the Humanitarian Institute at Ural Federal University in Russia; a researcher at the Institute for Russian and Eurasian Studies (IRES) at Uppsala University in Sweden; a lecturer and leading researcher in the Department of Communication Science at the Business Technology Institute at Turiba University in Riga, Latvia. His research interests include: changing political dynamics and relationships; mass media; public diplomacy; political marketing; crisis management communications; media and armed conflict; and the Russian Orthodox Church. He also researches the relationships and connections between information, politics and armed conflict more broadly, such as the GWOT and Arab Spring.

Max Roger Taylor

is a trained political scientist with a research focus on EU-China diplomacy. He is particularly interested in the practical promotion of the EU's values with China in closed-door diplomatic dialogues, at the micro-level. His doctoral research has involved participation in numerous policy engagement activities with practitioners including Track I and II EU-China dialogues. Dr Taylor received his PhD from the University of Bath in 2019.

Erik Vlaeminck

holds a PhD in Russian from the University of Edinburgh. In 2018, he was a visiting scholar at Tyumen State University (Russia) where he participated in a research project on cultural relations and public diplomacy in Siberia. Erik's current research interest is the role of public diplomacy and (international) cultural relations in Russian foreign policy. As an external consultant, he has contributed to commissioned studies for clients such as the British Council. Erik is the author of several peer-reviewed articles and book chapters as well as the co-editor of two monographs.

Introduction

Stephen Rowley

1   China's Image in the West

As an individual, it is usually enlightening to know what other people think about one as it helps principally either to justify one's behavior or to question it, and if one feels that the other's point of view is objective and accurate, then to take appropriate measures to modify one's opinion or action. This is a process of self-exploration, or as the philosopher Paul Ricoeur succinctly expressed it: "the shortest route from self to self is through the other".[1] If this is generally sound policy on an individual level – even if the discovery of other people's views of oneself usually arises accidentally or in a moment of heated debate – it is arguably even more important on a national and international level. To know how a country is perceived abroad will potentially have vital repercussions in the international arena. The perception of others is not just informative, it may also be instructive to the point of changing a nation's foreign policy and dictate how it relates to other countries. It is essential therefore, not to error in gauging this perception.

This book – *European Perceptions of China and Perspectives on The Belt and Road Initiative* – has grown out of the desire of a country, the People's Republic of China (or PRC), to know how it is perceived by other countries in order to understand international response and consequently, to gauge the validity of its actions. This is in many ways a very laudable approach to international relations. Within the academic sphere, Sun Yat-sen University has taken up the challenge to investigate China's image in Europe as part of its contribution to the strengthening of the multiple soft power enterprises the country has undertaken in recent years.

One of the motivations behind these soft power enterprises is the feeling that, historically, China has been the victim of a 'bad press' over a lengthy period of time. Chinese migration to the US in the nineteenth century was fraught with many problems which, apart from purely racist sentiment, would be qualified today as arising from a collision of cultures, resulting in the introduction of the Chinese Exclusion Act (only repealed after WWII – when China was an ally – in 1949). Shortly after that, China replaced the Soviet Union as

---

1   See Jean-Paul Rosaye's remarks on this issue in this same volume.

America's new Cold War enemy and future adversary in WWIII, as fantasized in various works of fiction, the most influential being Singer and Cole's meticulously documented *Ghost Fleet*.

Racial hatred in great part engendered the construction of a negative stereotype, the cruel, misogynistic Chinese despot whose power-crave can only be satisfied with world domination. Europe played a strong hand in building this image, with Shiel's early novel, *The Yellow Danger* (1898), being the template for the construction of this stereotypical war fiction.[2] The image was of course reinforced by the *Fu Manchu* books and films which gave a personification to mass English-speaking audiences which until then had associated China with the sordid opium dens pervading the more established literature of Dickens and Wilde.

Both England and France have indulged these fantasies, although the former's role has been greater. Commentators have provided various reasons for Europe's need to construct such a negative stereotype of the Chinese: the Opium Wars; the Boxer Rebellion; religion and the experiences of missionaries; the obvious need to justify the imperialist carving up of China; or more simply a feeling of superiority. 1949, and the establishment of a communist state which later saw China on 'the other side' during the Korean and Vietnamese wars, certainly strengthened the need for a negative cultural stereotype.

A more recent development has of course been generated by the repercussions of the COVID-19 pandemic on Europe-China relations (the latest publication of the European Think-tank, Network on China, represents an excellent pan-European country analysis in this light – see their "Special Report", April 2020). One offshoot of the pandemic is a growing wariness of dependence on China, especially for critical goods within the medical field. The shortage of everyday medicines like Paracetamol has created calls to relocate production to Europe and this is coupled with a greater wariness, intensified by deteriorating US-China relations.

The impact of the virus in the US has been used to justify the dismantling of US-China relations by the Trump administration and helped to further exacerbate the 'China bashing' which, after a brief interlude at the beginning of his presidency, has again become rife in Washington circles. The ground had of course been prepared well before the COVID outbreak. American

---

2   In his article The "Yellow Peril" Mystique: Origins and Vicissitudes of a Racist Discourse (2000), Lyman explores the stereotype within an American context. For a more detailed commentary see Tchen and Yeats (2014), Yellow Peril! An Archive of Anti-Asian Fear. Frayling (2014) gives an in-depth study within the British context in his The Yellow Peril: Dr Fu Manchu and the Rise of Chinaphobia.

commentators and government assistants or strategists, such as Steve Bannon (until his dismissal), had stoked anti-Chinese feeling well before Trump's "China virus" rhetoric. Arguably the most influential of these would be Peter Navarro and his series of publications – *Death by China*, *The Coming China Wars*, *Crouching Tiger*, etc – which resort to fiercely adversarial and confrontational terms in connection with the PRC and only augment deep-seated American anxiety as regards Chinese intentions. The so-called leader of the 'free world' has attempted to influence European allies with its fears of the growing challenge to American primacy and, to a certain extent, has succeeded – as several of the essays here reflect.

Leaving aside sensationalist literature involving China, the notion of a perceived threat which the PRC would pose to the West is of an extremely complex nature and should not be the subject of reckless rhetoric. Twenty years have passed since Yee and Storey edited a volume of essays on this perceived threat and whilst it is arguable that the latter has augmented, both economically and militarily, as the Chinese nation has developed further, nevertheless, this threat remains very much as the authors defined it twenty years ago: simply "a matter of perception".[3]

Whilst economic issues remain understandably highly prominent in this context of appraising the BRI – and again there are many volumes which take a single focus approach, although we note in passing the excellent publication by Brill entitled *The Belt and Road Initiative: Law, Economics and Politics*, which takes an intriguingly threefold approach – it was not the reason for the early genesis of this volume despite the fact that several of the contributors here do focus upon it. This book's essential objective was to gauge China's image in Europe at a time when the BRI is no longer in its infancy. Such an undertaking often implies a retracing of historical factors which have contributed to the relations between the PRC and Europe, or a more institutional approach, like that found in the volume edited by Christiansen, Kirchner and Wissenbach, entitled *The European Union and China*. Other recent books do examine China's image, although they do so from an English-speaking perspective (a notable exception to this would be the Sinologist Gregory Lee's *China Imagined: From European Fantasy to Spectacular Power*, which nevertheless has its roots in a historical Anglo-French perspective – given Lee's own remarkably singular background). There have been other multi-faceted approaches to Europe – China relations which would be closer in approach to this work, some of which

---

3   "... a China threat, real or imagined, is only a matter of perception", *The China Threat: Perception, Myth and Reality*, p.17.

have a specific perspective without neglecting the broader European view (and here I am thinking of the 2019 report produced by the French Centre for Asian Studies (IFRI) entitled "China's Belt and Road and the World: Competing Forms of Globalisation").

The essential contribution therefore of this volume is to show how China is perceived in individual European countries by analysing media contents, opinion surveys and other sources of information in non-English speaking European countries. In doing so, this book fills an important intellectual gap as it draws upon findings from at least ten different European countries, as well as from Europe as a whole, and underlines the links to the growing importance of China's ever-increasing role on the world scene, as illustrated by the advance of the Belt and Road Initiative. Several of the contributors here have noted the pervasive role of American media (tv and film especially) in the unconscious shaping of European opinion on China – an influence which tacitly accepts the assumption that Western countries share, or would like to share, the same system of values as the US. It is a system which is perceived as being at odds with Chinese values, and certainly provides a nebulous but fruitful area for further academic investigation.

As indicated above, there is a long history to the reception of China in Europe and this book cannot hope to present an extensive and exhaustive study of this vast field. However, the advent of the One Belt, One Road Initiative – known also as the Silk Road Initiative or simply now as the Belt and Road Initiative (BRI) – is of particular interest to the PRC as the country tries to fathom the diverse reactions to this initiative which represents a colossal project to connect almost two-thirds of the world's population across seventy countries. The success of the project depends in great part on the image projected, and in this case, the residual image remaining from numerous endeavours to undermine a nation. It was inevitable therefore that this book would devote considerable space to this popular subject, from both international relations and media perspectives, whilst at the same time introducing various general aspects of mutual interest, as well as more philosophical considerations.

This volume did not start out life as another book on the economic, political or geopolitical impact of the BRI, of which there are already many. Think-tanks in particular are frequently solicited to contribute analyses in these spheres and several of the chapters here make direct reference to the latter, in particular the significant work of Spanish think-tanks (see the contribution of Mario Esteban, for example). A lot of the initial work on the BRI stemmed from a consideration of its economic impact and implications for international relations but has since broadened in scope to include the inevitable geopolitical implications and more recently, cultural issues which illustrate China's increasing use of its enormous soft power leverage.

This book is the fruit of work carried out largely at the Centre for European Studies at Sun Yat-sen University's Zhuhai campus. In December 2017, an international conference was held on this campus and foreign scholars were invited to present papers on the subject of 'China: a European Perspective'. Fourteen scholars from different European universities attended along with eight local specialists. In all, sixteen European countries were represented at the conference, along with our Chinese hosts, and in all, twenty-two papers were read. This book has partly grown out of that conference: a number of articles were selected for publication whilst other scholars who did not attend the conference were invited to contribute. Whilst it is not exhaustive, the range of the articles presented here is nevertheless very wide in scope. The intention is not to change the image of China in Europe – that has to be left to policy makers, if it is deemed relevant – but to give accurate accounts of the existing situation and to outline the (recent) historical and sometimes philosophical issues which have contributed to the construction of the present situation. The fact that the majority of references to China (mainly outside the economic sector) in the Western media are on the whole negative or at least extremely guarded – and this view is supported in particular by the way China is perceived to have dealt with the coronavirus crisis – in itself engenders essential questions which both China and the West have to address.

The book has been divided into three sections which reflect mainly current concerns and interests, with a majority of the chapters focusing on international relations and the reception of the Belt and Road Initiative in Europe. The latter reception is, as one might expect, somewhat mixed, with former Eastern bloc countries on the whole a tad more welcoming as regards the project. Western European countries have shown a very cautious, if not suspicious, approach but we can also witness in several countries a genuine desire to keep an open mind and to see what may be gained through collaborative action, dominated of course by economic investment.[4]

The first and main section here contains seven chapters and examines closely the implications for international relations between Europe and the PRC of both the Belt and Road Initiative in particular, and the image of China more generally. The two are often surprisingly linked whilst both are

---

4   The situation in Europe has to be qualified by the fact that several former Soviet bloc countries demonstrate a hypersensitivity to the term 'communist' and this leads to a notable suspicion of all initiatives undertaken by the PRC. As is frequently pointed out here, it is a suspicion which reflects the gulf between elites and 'the man in the street'.

extremely important in the eventual overcoming of stereotyped responses based essentially on ignorance, their own traumatic political experience, or an unwillingness to engage in cross-cultural exchanges. In this light, knowing oneself through the eyes of others will also help to change perceptions and contribute to shifts, both internally and externally, and hopefully bring both parties to an enhanced level of mutual understanding. Knowing the 'other' can only benefit all concerned parties and the timetable should be advanced for Europe to develop similar undertakings and not be satisfied with clichés and negative stereotypes concerning the world's undoubted second power (still on the rise) which has so much to contribute in the international arena. Talk of a 'hostile nation' for example, is not helpful (see press coverage in Britain of the Hinckley Point debate or more recent remarks on Huawei's present and future 5G role in the UK). 'Demonisation' is not a recent construct (the term can be found in early writings on The Boxer Rebellion for example) and is both reductive, counter-productive, and leads in the end to friction and conflict through a misunderstanding of intentions and an ignorance of history.

Certain articles could have been accommodated in at least two sections as their content may be seen to overlap. For example, Greg Simon's article, 'China's Public Diplomacy Versus Mainstream Media's Narrative: A Challenge in Image and Reputation Management' belongs to both international relations, through its very dense and rich literature review, and to the image of China in the Swedish media, which is more the focus of the second part of his study. Choices have been made on the dominant thread of each author's contribution.

The First Section begins with a collaborative article by Professor David Galbreath of Bath University and is co-written with Neville Chi Hang Li and Max Roger Taylor, researchers from the same university. In many ways, the article may be said to set the tone for the rest of the volume. The authors have chosen an evocative title – 'Stuck between a Rock and a Hard Place: Europe and the "New Chinese Century"' – which examines a European continent faced with the emergence of this "new Chinese century" which looms ahead, whilst the former is simultaneously flanked by the respective needs and influences of both Russia and the United States. The impending choice facing Europe is therefore of the utmost importance and sensitivity.

The chapter is divided into three sections where the authors look first of all at the emerging relations with China (since 1989); it then focuses on the US and Russian factors which they suggest are frequently omitted from the equation; and then ends by taking into consideration the reverberations of a Europe minus Great Britain and the implications of this for the EU-China relationship.

The authors highlight the relative lack of political agreements in EU-China relations although they do underline the significant cooperation on climate change and environmental issues. Any future relationship between the two may well be tempered by what has been described as the 'Dragon-Bear' connection – closer developments between China and Russia – which may well go beyond a "relationship of convenience" to become a working alliance which would have inevitable repercussions as regards the EU and PRC (President Xi Jinping's state visit to Moscow at the beginning of June 2019, followed by the joint Sino-Russian military maneuvers in July, point to the validity of the researchers' findings – and perhaps fears). The authors feel therefore that it is important for Europe to maintain its research on China and to promote the Mandarin language abroad, both factors which can only lead to a better understanding, particularly if the US becomes less engaged in Europe and the China-Russia relationship becomes more tepid.

This article is followed by Mario Esteban's 'Spain's Views of China: The Economy is the Key'. Esteban's analysis of Sino-Spanish relations relies heavily upon numerous comprehensive and credible opinion polls and interviews which point, rather like other conclusions in this section, to the economy as being the key to reaching above and beyond what are otherwise described as stereotyped and ambivalent attitudes. The author probes beneath the surface of the latter to discover that, in fact, there is a divide between what the government, media, and elites think of China on the one hand, and what the public at large thinks.

Generally speaking, China's image in Spain fares much better than that of countries that one would normally envisage as having traditionally closer ties with Spain, and society's elites see China as a fountain of opportunity, especially if the BRI can provide the opening for greater Chinese investment in the country. There are however reasons why that investment would be limited, and perhaps even contradictory, in the sense that Spain would be seeking Chinese help to turn its ports into Mediterranean hubs that can reach across the Atlantic. There have already been steps taken in this direction but China seems much keener to invest in an Algerian hub whose ports would of course then be in competition with their Spanish counterparts.

The Spanish public seems to be much more wary of cooperation with China and Esteban demonstrates that this is in great part because of an erroneous public appreciation of the part China already plays in the Spanish economy. The man in the street would tend to see Chinese investment and the flood of Chinese products as a major threat to Spain. This discrepancy between the opinion of the elite and that of the people could in great part be bridged by the positive arrival of the Belt and Road Initiative. This should be true, not just for the image of China in Spain, but for that in Europe as a whole.

China's current relations with Ukraine would seem to be at a delicate point and this is reflected in the following chapter by Olexiy Haran entitled 'Kyiv-Beijing Relations in the Context of the Ukrainian-Russian Conflict: Interests, Concerns and Images'. These relations are relatively complex and rest upon factors which are maintained in a tenuous balance by the two countries. This essay captures the situation by tracing the evolution of bilateral relations which have traversed two revolutions in Ukraine, as well as hostile Russian activity in Crimea and the Donbas. The relations have been understandably colored by Ukraine's bitter disappointment concerning the inactivity of the great powers regarding the issue of Russian aggression. By summarizing recent historical events, Haran gauges to what extent Ukrainians view other countries today and concludes, through statistical analysis, that the image of China in Ukraine has reached a certain neutrality, which might be even slightly positive.

There are several reasons for this situation which Haran examines before looking pointedly at future prospects between the two countries. Despite a delicate balancing act which must take into consideration the sensibilities of Russia on the one hand and Japan on the other, as well as the pull of the European Union, Haran's conviction – like Esteban's, and that of other contributors - is that it is the economy which must play a pivotal role. There is consequently a call for increased Chinese investment in Ukraine – and the BRI provides a welcome opportunity in this light – whilst the latter must remain wary in order not simply to become a Chinese food or raw materials base. The author's stance is to assess future relations between China and Ukraine from a guardedly optimistic perspective. Haran is perfectly aware of the implications of the China-Russia *rapprochement* and offers valuable insights by highlighting Ukraine's present situation in comparison to contemporary Chinese preoccupations with Taiwan, Tibet and Xinjiang.

From Ukraine we move to Poland and Dominik Mierzejewski's article 'Sino-Polish Relations: From Socialist Brothers to the Post-Cold War Period's Reconfigurations'. Poland, like several other members of the former Soviet bloc, has over the years adapted a pragmatic but nevertheless cautious approach to its relations with the PRC. In constructing his essay on these relations, Mierzejewski engages in a tri-fold analysis before reaching his thoughtful conclusions. He initially explores what we mean by collective memory – essential to an understanding of the Polish approach – before presenting Sino-Polish interpretations of the 1950s when The Soviet Union's role was preponderant. His final pathway leads him to discuss how an interpretation of historical documents leads us to an appraisal of contemporary bilateral relations. The cataloguing of Sino-Polish developments over the years is extremely meticulous and provides an excellent example of how the past can come to shed light on the present situation in the region, which is extended to include the whole of Central Europe.

Mierzejewski insists upon the very pragmatic nature of the Polish stance but he also issues a stern warning and strong recommendation that certain Central and Eastern European countries be treated as equals in any future developments involving aid between nations. He completes his essay with a call for a workable relationship between Poland and China which would take into consideration the reality of relations with, and between, the superpowers and he cautions against falling into what he refers to as a "South-South narrative".

The relationship between Central Europe and China – especially with the arrival of the BRI – is also the focus of Csaba Moldicz's article 'German and Hungarian Views on The Belt and Road Initiative – a Power Game Balance in Central Europe?' which examines the quest for a balance of power which has arisen from the divergent approaches of Germany and Hungary to the growing international presence of China. Hungary appears to be caught between a traditional reliance on German industry and its current need to attract Chinese investment to the region.

Moldicz argues that there is a clear conflict between German hesitancy – and even suspicion of China's growing influence in Central Europe, which is reflected at both political and economic levels where decisions are tinted by a fear of technological transfer and the sobering prospect that China's ultimate goal might be a weakening of European bonds – and Hungary's more welcoming stance. The author nevertheless takes into consideration many pertinent Hungarian arguments which diverge from the German viewpoint and he is notably enlightening on the issue of why China initiated the BRI in the first place ("China's economic and political rise needs a spatial dimension too"). Generally speaking, Hungary's view is less ambivalent than Germany's – according to Moldicz – with emphasis put on repositioning the Central European region at the heart of the world economy. From this point of view, Chinese investment in the region represents a lifeline and real hope for the future.

This article is followed by that of a former Research Fellow at Sun Yat-sen University, Rubén Ruiz-Ramas. In his article entitled 'Transnational Organized Crime and Foreign Direct Investment in Spain: What Could the Government-Supported Chinese FDI Learn from the Russian Precedent?', the author looks closely at the relationship between FDI (Foreign Direct Investment), TOC (Transnational Organised Crime), and the effect of both on bilateral relations between Spain and China, as well as the image of China in Spain. He begins by first looking at China's FDI in the EU and its acceptance within strategic sectors. He then turns his focus to Spain's economic activity and the way in which this has shaped perceptions of the Chinese – particularly the way in which more illicit procedures have created what Ruiz-Ramas calls a "matrix of stereotypes".

Ruiz-Ramas's method of investigation is to scrutinize TOC in Spain, demonstrating in the process the role of Russian/Post-Soviet illegal activity and its knock-on effect as far as current attitudes to Chinese activity are concerned. The author is extremely meticulous in his examination of police operations in Spain and this examination leads him to compile his own tables which he presents to the reader as a statistical basis to draw implicit conclusions. Towards the end of his essay he returns to the Russian precedents of Lukoil and Gazprom before concluding that the resulting stereotyping of the Chinese in Spain has created concern at governmental level whilst both parties are keen to allay fears and attract more Chinese investment to Spain. Like Esteban, Ruiz-Ramas observes that there is a notable divergence between the elite's perception of the situation and that of the 'man in the street' but hope remains that trust can be built in order for there to be advances at both national and international levels.

Another former Research Fellow at Sun Yat-sen Univeristy, Youssef Elhaoussine is the author of an essay – 'Know Better, Like Better: An Appraisal of the Effect of the Belt and Road Initiative on Chinese Brand Image in France' – which is deceptively simple in that it addresses the question of whether or not the more we know about a culture makes us more receptive to the commercial products of that culture and bestows upon them a more positive brand image for the consumer. As the reader might anticipate, the author's answer to this question is an obviously positive one. However, the importance of proving – through statistical analysis – that this is indeed the case, is a necessary stage in the promotion of Chinese products in Europe. In this light, Elhaoussine's contribution is significant as he establishes the empirical truth of what may otherwise be considered as a mere assumption.

Elhaoussine initially devised a questionnaire which he then sent simultaneously to French nationals living in China and French nationals living in France. The cultural awareness of the former, gained through their exposure to another culture, indeed makes them more receptive to the positive brand image of Chinese products, as opposed to the stereotypical images acquired from the negativity (low cost/poor quality) generated in the 80s and 90s which they were associated with and which, for the most part, their counterparts remaining in France continue to see as still valid and appropriate.

The importance of this relatively simple outcome serves as a strong recommendation to those in charge of BRI policy, with particular reference to the

'Made in China' brand evaluation. In other words, Chinese economic dynamism must be accompanied by, even preceded by, the use of soft power to convey a deeper knowledge and understanding of Chinese civilisation and traditions. As Rosaye later argues too, the BRI cannot be a purely economic undertaking. Elhaoussine supports this argument with a detailed literature review which makes the simplicity of the outcome as legitimate and significantly applicable, as it is limpid.

Section Two of the book contains five articles which focus upon media communications in various European countries, from Sweden to Belgium and across to former Eastern bloc countries (Hungary, Romania and the Czech Republic). In certain cases, a specific population segment – such as students, for example – is examined in order to explore stereotypes and to suggest ways to change negative perceptions which have become engrained in cultural clichés.

The first article in this section by Ivana Karaskova from Charles University, Prague, and entitled 'China's Image in the Czech Republic: Media Reflection of Elite Policies', is both broad in its scope and deep in its analysis of Czech media. Karaskova's investigation of the image of China in the Czech Republic is constructed upon empirical data gathered over a significant period of time (2010–2017) and using an equally significant number of media outlets (42). As the author rightly points out, such an academic study has been missing, not just in the Czech Republic, but within the wider context of the region of Central and Eastern Europe where she sees the possibility of extending her research to a much broader platform.

Karaskova's investigation is thorough, and far-reaching in scope and points to the conclusion that media channels remain somewhat at odds with the official discourse of governmental and other elites. The latter – as we find in other countries – would prefer a more positive reception of China within the public at large. There is an attempt to promote this by underlining the advantages of an improved relationship with the PRC. These advantages would of course be essentially economic.

Influencing public opinion in a positive way is certainly a major undertaking, especially if the media has already embarked upon the portrayal of the PRC as an entity embracing opposite values and preferences which they feel the new Czech Republic stands for or should stand for. Whilst there has been a multiplication of references to China in recent years – corresponding to its rise as the world's second economic power – these references do not, once again, reflect the position of political elites. This discrepancy leads the author to conclude that the approach taken so far has not produced the results that the elites might have initially desired, and therefore a more pertinent line should be followed in order to reflect a more accurate and objective image of China, at least as far as the general public is concerned.

This article is followed by Erik Vlaeminck's evocatively entitled study: 'China's Image in Belgian Media: Between Fascination and Fear'. This contribution in many ways typifies the microanalytical approach which has much wider applications. As its title suggests, it focuses upon a country, Belgium, and after examining relevant theory, analyses the cases of exemplary French and Flemish-language newspapers over a given period of time, to delineate the representation of China and ascertain whether or not this representation differs in the respective newspapers and cultures under scrutiny. The author himself does underline the implicit limitations of his undertaking but also indicates future useful paths of exploration for the researcher.

Vlaeminck's conclusions are enlightening in that one suspects that the binary equation of fear and fascination is not confined to Belgium but is rather indicative of a northern/southern or Anglo-Saxon/Latin difference of approach to the acceptance or rejection of China's Belt and Road Initiative within Europe as a whole. The results are encouraging for the Chinese initiative in that the latter's soft power influence may be seen to be increasing.

'Exploring Public Perceptions of, and Interactions with, the Chinese in Hungary' by Irina Golubeva, is the third article in this section and in her well-constructed essay, the author looks at the situation in Hungary following the 16+1 Summit which was held in Budapest in November 2017. Her objective was not to analyze the possibilities for economic and cultural cooperation arising from the Belt and Road Initiative, but as a specialist of intercultural communication, to set about examining how the Chinese are perceived in Hungary, given that a greater knowledge of the 'other' can only bring about more fruitful future exchanges and cooperation between the two countries, which China understands as a fundamentally integral part of the BRI.

Before undertaking her study of a sample of almost 400 adult respondents, fairly evenly balanced in terms of gender, Golubeva gives a background survey of work that has already been undertaken with various native populations, and she simultaneously reinforces her work with intercultural theory. She studies an adequate sample, although the results may seem to be somewhat stereotypical and possible to forecast beforehand in that they bear a strong similarity to results already carried out in studies in the US.[5] This in itself may have

---

5 There is a tendency in the West to view Chinese society as 'programmed', with the stereotype of Chinese people as adhering to the traits of obedience, conformity, self-effacement, and so on. These in turn are seen to lead to a lack of creativity (Chinese technological prowess would suggest an obvious paradox here). By advancing this model, we in the West are neglecting

its significance in that it is a distinct possibility that US cinema and Western-influenced media in Hungary may have pre-shaped the answers to the questions asked. Consequently, as Golubeva points out, the questions arising from her study are: why is this the case and what can be done about it? The author envisages this work as part of a larger project which will address the serious questions of valid and viable intercultural exchange between Hungarians and the growing number of Chinese who take up either temporary or permanent residency in Hungary. Upon the improvement of the Hungarian perception of the Chinese will depend the volume and success of all other future projects, especially those related to the Belt and Road Initiative.

Before embarking upon her admittedly narrower (in scope), but nevertheless important study – 'China – A View from Romania Beyond Perceptions and Stereotypes' – Mariana Nicolae evokes several salient facts in the history of China, amongst which we find the role of religion, which inevitably has its particular significance to a Romanian public. In several of the articles in this book, religion is a recurring cultural benchmark. Nicolae asks herself the question why, despite a shared ideology in the 20th century and a genuine interest in Chinese culture, Romania has not wholeheartedly embraced the Belt and Road Initiative. She suggests that the term 'communist' is an inevitable stumbling block, given the Romanian experience, but this in itself would seem insufficient to account for Romanian reticence.

To shed light on this situation, as professor at the Bucharest University of Economic Studies, Nicolae carried out a survey using 121 students of International Business and Economics attending her university. The respondents, in their twenties, showed a gender bias of roughly 4 to 1 in favor of the female sex. Whilst any generalization must be used with the utmost caution given the relatively small size of the sample, nevertheless, there are certain pointers which these pragmatic students of business reveal in their answers. Perhaps the most telling is that almost 50% of respondents see China primarily as a communist country, so the "anathema" of this terminology remains part of a marked legacy which does indeed prove to have its influence amongst these young adults who might otherwise be considered as open-minded and extremely eager to forge greater economic ties.

Nicolae follows her survey with a note on several recent books and events which should have drawn the countries closer together despite the impeding

---

are own cultural grooming – even before Hofstede it was recognised that all culture is a form of mental programming. To the Chinese model we oppose the liberal Western tradition for which the US is generally taken to be the guiding light. Such stereotypes do not bear much scrutiny. The challenge lies in bringing the two together.

role of a Westernized media which has shaped consciousness in the opposite direction. In her conclusion, the author laments this situation and calls upon the authorities in her country to give much more political and administrative support to efforts that would contribute to a better understanding between the two countries and subsequently lead to a greater volume of exchanges, especially in the light of the Belt and Road Initiative.

The longer essay closing this section: 'China's Public Diplomacy Versus Mainstream Media's Narrative: a Challenge in Image and Reputation Management' by Greg Simons, is a further example of the country profile studies – in this case Sweden – and analyses the situation at a given time, pointing to both questions and possibilities for the future. The initial question asked by the author is how the national image of China is communicated within a foreign media system, that of Sweden. Before going on to answer that question, Simons provides a useful exploration of what we actually mean by public diplomacy. Once he has examined the concept, he then discusses the Chinese approach to it which seems to be extremely pragmatic in that China's focus is upon economic development and consequently, whatever obstacles may bar the route, they must be overcome. Traditional media communication has become very expensive and increasingly less effective, so in matters of public diplomacy, China has come to rely more on internet-based information and communication in order to manage its media reputation.

The image of China in Sweden, Simons contends, is related to its image in the Western liberal world as a whole, to which Sweden of course adheres. Whilst China supports international institutions, it is seen to contest the Western liberal democratic system which means that its global role, and more specifically, increased future global role, is seen with a certain amount of fear and suspicion and the Belt and Road Initiative does not escape this mindset. Nevertheless, Simons is persuaded that Sweden does partly differ from the typical Western approach to BRI as its government, whilst remaining extremely cautious, follows a more wait-and-see policy in the expectation that Beijing will eventually provide signals as to its intentions and future policy.

The author's detailed analysis of the press covers a five-month period in 2017 and involves a meticulous scrutiny of five Swedish newspapers of differing political shades. His survey includes the XIX Congress of the Chinese Communist Party in October 2017 and the solidification of the power of President Xi Jinping which seems to have been subject to a unanimously negative treatment in the Swedish mass media. Despite China's message of public diplomacy – the creation of a more harmonious world through the use of its cultural soft power and the attraction of its new economic power, as seen through aspects of the BRI – Sweden remains aligned (not allied) to the global liberal political stance which is still US-centric in nature. In terms of economics, Sweden is keen to have a mutually beneficial relationship with China but remains cautious when it comes to international relations, and these views are very much present in the media that Simons examines.

The final section of this book brings together two essays which look at the broader picture of Sino-European encounters by initially stepping back from a focus on contemporary issues in an attempt to better understand how some of these issues – amongst them certain misconceptions as regards the Chinese – have taken root in Western societies.

The first of the two essays in this section, by Kaspars Klavins of the University of Latvia entitled: 'The Spiritual Roots of Typical European (and Western) Evaluations of China', provides an overview of both Western and Eastern thought by focusing on how the former has come to judge the latter through its own prism of values. It is a macro-evaluation of what is essentially an ethnocentric approach to cross-cultural encounters. The essay is particularly illuminating on the Jesuits' attempt at cross-cultural understanding through their own methodology and philosophy and focusses upon the prime role that religion has played over the centuries. In most cases, this role reposes on two totally different thought-systems and whilst Klavins is not judgmental in his approach, there is nevertheless the suggestion that, despite the West's intention to impose its philosophical mindset on China, the latter continues to embrace a more holistic approach which contributes to a healthier society.

Klavins paints a very broad *tableau* and his essay helps the reader to grasp the historical incomprehension at the heart of much negativity we find in contemporary commentary of China. He concludes his essay with a commendable call for mutual cultural dialogue between Europeans and Chinese today through a more profound respect of intellectual and philosophical traditions which must at last become enriching for both parties. The alternative is to continue on parallel antagonistic paths.

The essay which concludes this volume is a philosophical reflection by Jean-Paul Rosaye from Artois University, France and is a fittingly open-ended conclusion to what Sino-European encounters actually mean. The essay's title is: 'The Historical Foundation for a Speculative BRI as the Best Route to a Renewed Self', and in it, Rosaye argues that today, Europe finds itself at a crossroads of civilizations and must make a choice as to which direction it will follow. His argument is a very clear and concise account where he places the start of the present European crisis in the sixties which saw the beginning of a debate amongst intellectuals – French ones in particular – as to whether or not the Anglo-Saxon approach should be adopted, and their civilizational model embraced. The argument is pursued up to the present where it has been sharpened by the arrival of Donald Trump to the US presidency and the 'Brexit vote' which will take the United Kingdom out of the EU. The question posed today therefore is: which direction is best for Europe so that it may regenerate its infrastructures and revitalize its intellectual community? The arrival of the Belt and Road Initiative is set as a viable alternative, and what Rosaye calls "a speculative BRI" emerges as a possible theoretical path to take in order to bring about a very necessary European cultural renaissance. It is by embracing the Chinese initiative and coming to terms in a vital way with a new 'other', that a renaissance may take place. Or, as he puts it: "Only a speculative and intellectual exploration reconfigures thought genuinely and discards debilitating prejudices".

In order to illustrate his argument, Rosaye gives the intriguing examples of the evolution of the 'English' garden, through its French and Chinese 'stages', and the development of economic liberalism which has more to do with traditional Chinese thought than it may have been given credit for. Both are the results of cultural cross-fertilization, of what we would call now, intercultural exchange. One of the offshoots of this is that Europe once again finds itself at a crucial moment in its history and must once more decide upon the path best suited to the realization of its own potential. Whilst he does not clearly communicate his choice of model, saying that the Anglo-Saxon one is already inscribed in the European spirit, he nevertheless points to the importance to Europe of re-adjusting its perspectives on China today, in favor of a rich new silk road of cultural exchanges which will in turn serve as the catalyst to a European intellectual rebirth.

2   Conclusions

If one were to draw an overriding conclusion from the findings here, it would be that within Europe there is a striking discrepancy between the desires and policies of élites and the rather nebulous persuasions of the 'man in the street' who would almost always push for a different outcome to relations with China than the governments which decide upon public policy. There is inevitably a large amount of negative stereotyping still at work which the Chinese government must come to terms with if it is to make the Belt and Road Initiative more than an economic endeavour.

Due to its diversity, history and the absence of a central European policy towards China (which is further made difficult by China's penchant to deal with individual European countries rather than the EU as an entity), there is no uniform perception of China's image. There is of course a widely-accepted desire to embrace the PRC as an economic partner, as long as we are talking about a level playing field. Opening China's markets, protecting against product piracy and organized crime, along with human rights concerns and a fear of China's growing – and approaching – military might, are all shaping a European perception which for the time being wavers due to the internal forces which compose the EU.

Since 2018, with the BRI looming closer to Europe and becoming more visible in its economic and geopolitical advances,[6] there has been a spate of articles in the Western media – one thinks of the British press in particular[7] – which have reaffirmed the caution, even suspicion, on the part of the West to China's new Belt and Road Initiative and the colossal financial sums which the latter entails. Many take their cue from Hillary Clinton's memorable "new colonialism" or what is seen as Africa's vulnerability to debt distress which has led certain parties to talk about "predatory loan practices" or "debt-trap diplomacy". Rather than seeing a win-win situation, there is a dominant trend at the moment to see this Chinese initiative as a way of accommodating the country's excess capacity to produce goods and infrastructure. In a nutshell, the BRI is frequently perceived as nothing short of a masterplan which works primarily in China's interest.

China regularly attempts to refute the arguments and dissipate the fears – shown by the appearance of numerous articles in the English-speaking press in recent years, such as the one which appeared as October 25th, 2018 by a Chinese professor of international relations who lamented in *China Daily* that "Many western observers still view the Belt and Road Initiative as Beijing's means of shifting its excess capacity and influence outward".[8] This sentiment is part of an overall pattern of communication which suggests that Beijing is unhappy with the way the BRI is perceived in the West. However, argument alone will not suffice – especially if it emanates from *China Daily* which in itself is viewed by many western observers as a dubious source of objective information. China may require what Elhaoussine would term, a complete 'rebranding'. The multiplication of soft power initiatives would seem to be the obviously appropriate way forward. Whatever the means decided upon, this

---

6   As the BRI advances, in Western eyes the military threat of China increases, particularly with the construction of ports which could provide the PRC with military footholds where none existed before.

7   British hostility in the press has increased with the introduction of the Hong Kong Extradition Bill and the ensuing disturbances.

8   See Shi Yulong's article entitled BRI's image being tarred by false claims, China Daily, October 25, 2018.

book, and the Belt and Road Initiative as a whole, are part of a long and arduous quest to redress the balance and establish a more just, as well as a much more complex, image of the Middle Kingdom.

The essays here provide a snapshot of China's image in various European countries and simultaneously call for a new appraisal of current Sino-European relations. Numerous sectors are evoked to enhance cultural knowledge and awareness: language, history, philosophy, religion, technology, etc. Soft power endeavours must accompany – even precede – hard economic dealings. The BRI provides a great opportunity for a *rapprochement* which has an essentially economic impetus but whose outcome must be the less tangible dimension of increased understanding. By identifying problems and exploring causes and potential solutions, it is hoped that this volume will be seen as an important step along the road which will eventually lead to a better and more accurate perception of China, as well as contributing to this greater understanding between East and West.

Bibliography

Chaisse, J., and Gorski, J. (editors) (2018), The Belt and Road Initiative: Law, Economics and Politics, Leiden: Brill.

Christiansen, T. Kirchner, E., and Wissenbach, U. (2019), The European Union and China, London: Red Globe Press.

Ekman, A. (editor) (2019), China's Belt and Road and the World: Competing Forms of Globalisation, Etudes de l'Ifri, Ifri.

European Think-tank Network on China (ETNC) (2020), Special Report.

Frayling, C. (2014), The Yellow Peril: Dr Fu Manchu and the Rise of Chinaphobia, London, Thames and Hudson.

Lee, G. (2018), China Imagined, London: Hurst and Company.

Lyman, S.M. (2000), The "Yellow Peril" Mystique: Origins and Vicissitudes of a Racist Discourse, International Journal of Politics, Culture and Society, Vol.13, No.4 (Summer 2000), pp. 683–747, Springer.

Navarro, P. (2008), The Coming China Wars, New Jersey: Pearson Education.

Navarro, P. (2011), Death by China, New Jersey: Pearson Education.

Navarro, P. (2015), Crouching Tiger: What China's Militarism Means for the World, New York: Prometheus Books.

Ricœur, P. (1992), Oneself as Another. Translated by K. Blamey. Chicago: University of Chicago Press.

Singer, P.W. and Cole, A. (2016), Ghost Fleet, New York, Mariner.

Tchen, J.K.W., and Yeats, D. (editors) (2014), Yellow Peril! An archive of Anti-Asian Fear, London, Verso.

Yee, H., and Storey I. (editors) (2002), The China Threat: Perception, Myth and Reality, London, RoutledgeCurzon.

CHAPTER 1

'Stuck between a Rock and a Hard Place'

Europe, the EU and the New Chinese Century

David J Galbreath, Neville Chi Hang Li and Max Roger Taylor

1   Introduction[1]

The European relationship with China (People's Republic of China, PRC) today is one of cooperation through trade and global security initiatives such as the Iran Nuclear Deal or the Israeli-Palestinian crisis. Both the EU, as a trading bloc, and China are two of the top three largest markets in the world (the United States being the other). At the same time, as the Chinese economy continues to grow, and Chinese President Xi Jinping consolidates power, Europe and the EU are facing a crisis in Euroscepticism, with the UK and Brexit being the most severe deterioration in terms of membership. At the same time, both the United States and the Russian Federation, have become less predictable, and arguably, more bellicose. The 2016 Global Attitudes Survey showed that Chinese respondents play 'a more important role than 10 years ago', more than did respondents from the EU, US and even India.[2] The relationship between the global powers is changing and those changes will have an impact on the Europe-China relationship.

The title of this chapter is 'Stuck between a Rock and a Hard Place' because this represents the situation in which Europe finds itself in relation to China, and what some might call the 'New Chinese Century'. The so-called 'rock and hard place' for Europe are the US on one hand, and Russia on the other. The US has taken a hard line on relations with China – with significant impact – and on the way that Europe might seek to broaden or deepen its trade, having pressed the EU on numerous occasions to maintain the arms embargo that was put in place following the democracy protests in 1989 (often characterised by Tiananmen Square). Any time that the European Parliament has sought to overturn the embargo has been met with heavy lobbying on the part of the US. In addition to disagreements over human rights and trade dumping, the

---

1   The authors contributed equally to this work.
2   See Pew Research Centre, Spring 2016 Global Attitudes Survey (http://www.pewglobal.org/dataset/spring-2016-survey-data/ Date Accessed: 8 March 2018).

relationship is practical but retains a degree of resentment and suspicion. At the same time, following the 2014 occupation and then annexation of Ukraine's Crimean Peninsula (if not before that, in the 2008 Russo-Georgian War), many European countries feel threatened by a resurgent Russia. This threat perception has been heightened by the role of Russian troops and supplies in East Ukraine, as well as supporting the Bashar Al-Assad regime in Syria. The EU responded to the Crimea annexation with trade and financial sanctions while Russia used European sites for prospective targets in its *Zapad* military exercises in 2017. We argue here, that two outcomes would make conditions worse for Europe-China relations. The first is if the US-China relationship were to decline further; and the second is if China seeks to support Russia in its territorial ambitions in Europe and Eurasia.

This chapter will look at the changing Europe-China relationship with a particular focus on the changing dynamics between the US, EU and China. Where the economic relationships between the US and China still dominate their diplomatic relationships, and with the EU being China's largest trading partner, there are reasons why a straight forward economic analysis would miss the potential challenges to prospective positive Europe-China relations. Thus, this chapter will examine this relationship in three sections. The first section will focus upon Europe's relationship with China since 1989, with a specific look at how the literature has sought to conceptualise this relationship. The second section will look at exogenous factors of Europe's China policy between 'a rock and a hard place', suggesting that the literature often misses the US and Russian factors in Europe-China relations. The third section will look at endogenous challenges to the Europe-China relationship by focusing on the UK and its impending departure from the EU. The conclusion balances these two sets of factors to help discuss the prospective of Europe-China relations going forward.

2   Overview of EU-China relations

2.1   *Charting Europe-China Relations: From Colonialism to Cooperation*
Relations between Europe and China are historically framed by conflict and humiliation as the European colonial powers strongly contributed to the collapse of Imperial China in 1912, long impacting China's development thereafter (Guo, 2013: 59). The ruling Qing Dynasty, hampered by poor leadership and isolationism, was militarily and economically weaker than its European rivals by the 19th century. In this context, the First Opium War (1840–42) with the British Empire, triggered by China's prohibition of opium, led to defeat and

humiliating concessions including significant reparations, the leasing of Hong Kong and opening of ports to Britain (Chow, 2015: 10). China was defeated again in the Second Opium War (1857–60), after which Britain gained customs administration of Imperial China and was leased Kowloon (Guo, 2013: 59). The late 1800s were characterised by further humiliation, including the extraction of exclusive trading rights to substantial parts of China by Britain, France and Germany (along with Russia) following China's devastating loss in the Sino-Japanese war (1894–95) (Guo, 2013: 60).

Although this historical backdrop continues to impact political relations between China and Europe, recent decades have seen contemporary relations rapidly develop in scope and substance between the supranational European Union and China (Sachdeva, 2014: 427). Bilateral relations were formally established in 1975, not long in advance of China's historical opening to international markets through Deng Xiaoping's extensive economic reform programme, which introduced private enterprise and foreign investment to China's then closed command economy, initially through designated *special economic zones* (Dai, 2006: 5; Guo, 2013: 248–249; Lanteigne, 2013: 40). These (ongoing) reforms have effectively catalysed China's systemic rise, as breakneck growth rates – captured by total GDP quadrupling between 1978–2004 and real GDP averaging 9.3% between 1980–2015 – have engendered unrivalled foreign exchange reserves, immense foreign investment capacity and major trade surpluses with international partners, all of which have resulted in China's economic and military power being second only to the US (Lanteigne, 2013: 40–42; Li, 2009: 1–3; Wang, 2016: 315).

EU-China relations have progressed in parallel with these transformative developments, as witnessed by milestones such as the signing of a bilateral trade agreement in 1985; the first European Commission delegation inaugurated in 1988; and a slew of early cooperation programmes in sectors such as education and culture, science and agriculture (Dai, 2006: 5; EEAS, 2017a: 1; Men, 2011: 544–545). However, this positive trajectory of EU-China relations temporarily ceased with China's suppression of student protests at Tiananmen Square in 1989 (Dai, 2006: 5; EEAS, 2017a: 1). In response, relations were suspended by the EU and economic sanctions were introduced, most significantly an arms embargo, which remains in place, as of 2020.

Nevertheless, due to China's economic importance by this stage, relations largely normalised within three years and the remaining decade witnessed considerable developments to EU-China political relations (Dai, 2006: 5; EEAS, 2017a: 1). These included the establishment of a new bilateral political dialogue (1992) and more controversially, a human rights dialogue (1995), not to mention the first annual EU-China summit in 1998 (Dai, 2006: 5; EEAS, 2017a: 1; Yuan and Orbie, 2015: 343).

2.2   The Comprehensive Strategic Partnership: Deepening Relations in the Face of China's Systemic Rise

The launch of a Comprehensive Strategic Partnership in 2003 reflected another major landmark for EU-China relations, driven by a mutual desire to foster a political relationship comparable to the highly developed economic relationship (Farnell and Crookes, 2016: 3; Maher, 2016: 961). The strategic partnership features three thematic *pillars*: Political Dialogue; Economic & Sectoral Dialogue; and as of 2012, People-to-People Dialogue. These pillars collectively encompass more than 50 dialogues, while each pillar is topped by high-level dialogues and collectively, the annual summit (EEAS, 2015).

This mutual desire to further institutionalise and symbolically enhance political relations derived principally from shared strategic interests (Casarini, 2006: 7). To this end, the EU and China sought to cooperate as major powers to manage complex international challenges, surrounding areas like the global economy, transnational terrorism and climate change (Geeraerts, 2014: 4–5; Sachdeva, 2014: 427–428). Additionally, both sides promoted multipolarity and viewed the strategic partnership as a means of countering the assertive unipolarity of the Bush Administration (2000–08), which for China, threatened a containment strategy in the Asia-Pacific (Sachdeva, 2014: 428). Beyond this commonality, it is worth noting that from the EU side, the strategic partnership was also perceived as a means of speeding up China's domestic reform process and shaping its international conduct, in line with the prevailing norms and multilateral frameworks (Maher, 2016: 961).

Despite these common interests and ambitions, scholars tend to consider the outcomes of the strategic partnership to be "disappointing" (Farnell and Crookes, 2016: 4). Beyond positive collaboration on the Iran nuclear deal, each side has expressed contrasting positions on major international issues like development aid and crises such as those in Syria and Ukraine, which have had profound security implications for the EU (EU, 2016: 11; Fox and Godement, 2009: 9; Maher, 2016: 966, 970). Relatedly, the priorities of each side have diverged, with the EU beset by internal crises (i.e. the Eurocrisis, migration, Brexit) and a resurgent Russia, while China has sought to project its power globally, including regional/international efforts to counter US dominance.

In this respect, two key examples highlight how China's global power projection has directly impacted EU interests. Firstly, China created the 16+1 formation in 2011 (institutionalised in 2013), consisting of eleven EU member states (Bulgaria, Croatia, Czech Republic, Estonia, Hungary, Latvia, Lithuania, Poland,

Romania, Slovakia, Slovenia) and five EU accession candidates (Albania, Bosnia and Herzegovina, FYROM, Montenegro, and Serbia) from Central and Eastern Europe (CEEC, 2018; Fallon 2015: 145). While the EU member states involved have been eager to benefit from increased trade, investment in their infrastructure and scientific/cultural exchanges with China, the EU fears a "divide and conquer" (Turcsányi, 2014: 2) strategy designed to compromise unity at the EU level (Fallon, 2015: 145).

A second key example is reflected in China's highly ambitious Belt and Road Initiative (BRI), the sheer *global* scale of which has inherent implications for EU interests including the maintenance of existing global norms (EU, 2017). The project sees China investing hundreds of billions of USD in infrastructure to recreate the ancient silk road between Europe and China, through three multi-regional land routes (*the Silk Road Economic Belt*) and one sea route (*the Maritime Silk Road*), collectively encompassing at least 60 countries, equating to 64% of the world's population and 30% of its GDP (Du and Zhang, 2018: 191; Huang, 2016: 318–320; Wang, 2016: 22–25). Prominent EU concerns include issues such as the openness of projects to non-Chinese companies, the upholding of environmental and labour standards, risks of unsustainable debts for target states and the broader opacity of individual projects (*See*: EU, 2017).

2.3   *Bilateral Economic and Political Relations under the Strategic Partnership*

Irrespective of these international strategic divergences, at the bilateral level, the core economic relationship has continued to grow, with trade flows surpassing €1.5 billion daily as the EU constitutes China's biggest economic partner and China, the EU's second largest (EC, 2014; Geeraerts, 2014: 12). The success of EU-China economic relations lies in mutual interest. Historically, the EU has been attracted by the opportunities presented by China's market, while China has long recognised the capacity of EU expertise, technology and investment to contribute to its development (Farnell and Crookes, 2016: 4; Casarini, 2006: 11–12). Similarly, shared interests promise further expansion, as both sides face common challenges in areas like the management of global financial markets, job creation and ageing work forces (Farnell and Crookes, 2016: 4).

Nevertheless, EU-China economic relations are beset by significant ongoing tensions. Firstly, the EU has imposed anti-dumping measures on China amidst allegations of unfair trade practices, with prominent examples including solar panel and steel overcapacity (ECFR, 2016: 133). In conjunction with related concerns of widespread state aid to Chinese state-owned enterprises (SOEs), the EU has refused to grant China Market Economy Status (MES) at the World Trade Organisation (WTO) (Casarini, 2006: 16; Farnell and Crookes, 2016: 88).

This reflects a notable source of bilateral conflict, with consecutive EU-China summits being impeded as China maintains that the EU is obligated to grant it MES (Xinhua, 2017a).

Beyond this, notable tensions also surround trade and investment, as the EU attributes a €175 billion trade deficit and very low EU FDI to Chinese barriers to market access (EC, 2017a). These include discriminatory public procurement and the application of legislation to European companies versus favourable treatment for Chinese businesses, particularly SOEs, and concerns over intellectual property protection (EC, 2017b; Farnell and Crookes, 2016: 4). While ongoing negotiations for a *Comprehensive Investment Agreement* aim to redress these issues through investment protection, improved market access and regulation of SOEs, the negotiations have progressed slowly since 2014 (EC, 2014; 2017c; Farnell and Crookes, 2016: 110–111). Scholars attribute this pace to the profound challenges China faces in potentially undermining vested SOE interests along with fears over the possible political instability that could arise from economic liberalisation (Farnell and Crookes, 2016: 112–113).

In contrast, the political relationship remains comparatively underdeveloped. However, EU-China cooperation on environment and climate change represents a notable exception, built around strong common interest. The EU has sought to tackle global climate change, while China represents one of the largest emitters and has been eager to harness EU technology and investment to mitigate the negative by-products of its rapid economic growth, which also threaten political stability (Carrapatoso, 2015: 179–180; De Cock, 2011: 89; EEAS, 2017b). Bilateral environment and climate cooperation has taken the form of numerous cooperation programmes/projects in mainland China, built on the relevant sectoral dialogues, as well as intense cooperation in carbon emissions trading, wherein EU businesses are majority investors and bilateral collaboration has been instrumental in China launching its first nationwide system in 2017 (De Cock, 2011: 100–102; EC, 2017d; EEAS, 2017b; Farnell and Crookes, 2016: 179–180). At the multilateral level, the EU and China have become leaders in international climate mitigation, particularly in the face of US reticence, strongly aiding the signing of the historical Paris Agreement in 2016, as they effectively co-represented developing and developed countries (ECFR, 2016: 138).

Nonetheless, bilateral cooperation in these sectors has not been free of tension. The EU has been frustrated with China's reluctance to include non-state actors in cooperation programmes/projects, while there continues to be concerns on the EU side about the risks of compromising the EU's leadership in environmental technologies through technology transfers to aid China (Farnell and Crookes, 2016: 179–181; Scott, 2009: 218). More recently, the

European Commission published a Strategic Outlook on EU-China relations which makes this tension more apparent, calling on the EU to 'robustly seek [a] more balanced and reciprocal [condition] governing the economic relationship [with China]' (see EC, EU-China – A Strategic Outlook).

The lack of evolution in EU-China political relations arguably stems from a mutual lack of understanding concerning values (Crookes, 2013: 643). While the EU maintains that China should reform in line with its values, China rejects their proclaimed universality and considers them wholly Western constructs (Maher, 2016: 962–963; Men, 2011: 536). These dynamics are particularly sensitive for China, as it draws parallels with historical European colonialism. The conflict is particularly acute in the context of *human rights*, where both sides express very different interpretations of the value at the multilateral and bilateral levels (Shen, 2013: 170). Notably, the strength of bilateral economic relations between China and individual member states (including those connected to 16+1), frequently threaten or undermine EU unity in these forums (See: ECFR, 2016: 126–127; Reuters, 2017). The establishment of a third pillar of the strategic partnership in 2012, People-to-People Dialogue, represents an explicit attempt to build mutual understanding in EU-China political relations, as it boosts cooperation in the sectors of education and culture (Burnay, et al., 2014: 51; EC, 2018)

Ultimately, contemporary EUrope-China relations reflect a highly transactional partnership where the strongest areas of economic and political cooperation derive from mutual self-interest. In this sense, the relationship is somewhat hollow, as a core of substantial bilateral political understanding is yet to materialise, despite the ambitions of the strategic partnership or People-to-People Dialogue.

3   Europe's China Policy between the US and Russia

3.1   *US and China Relations and Their Effect on Europe*

Regarding the systematic rise of the PRC, there is a growing literature advocating the 'New Chinese Century'. The rapid economic development in China has been categorized as the 'Chinese model' (Jacques, 2009) and there appears to be a phenomenon of 'Sinomania' in the western world (Anderson, 2010) which flourished especially during the Obama administration. One of the major reasons is that all the global financial crises have originated from the western free market economy. Due to the semi-closed nature of the planned economy, or what Deng called the 'socialist market economy', China's economic development is to a large extent standalone as regards the economic catastrophe. The believers in this 'New Chinese Century' seem to pledge themselves to the belief that China will replace America and dominate the 21st century.

For Hung however, the rise of the Chinese has geopolitical and economic consequences for the world order (Hung, 2015). This section now examines how the rise of China challenges US hegemony, which inevitably forces the union of Western powers which hinders the Europe-China relationship. This reinforces our central argument that the Europe-China relationship is stuck between a rock and hard place, i.e. between America and Russia.

One of the major economic policies of China, i.e. the Belt and Road Initiative, not only affects the geopolitical climate in the Eurasia region, but also has more profound implications for the global world order. Beijing proposed the formation of the Asian Infrastructure Investment Bank (AIIB) in order to fund the building of infrastructure in the countries along the construction of the Belt and Road. The AIIB is well-known as a Chinese version of the World Bank which counters the US economic dominance, and this idea is not particularly new as similar international organizations exist such as the African Development Bank. What is different this time is that some US allies in Europe (e.g. the UK, France and Germany), which joined the AIIB (AIIB 2018b) as founding members, bring some hope that the international organization could in fact serve as a counterbalance to American power. Although the articles of agreement of the AIIB were ratified by most of the member states in 2015, there is still not a single approved project on infrastructure building as part of the Belt and Road Initiative in European countries (AIIB, 2018a). This is a result of the 'divide and conquer' strategy of the PRC that deliberately seized on bilateral agreements with individual EU states instead of going through the AIIB. It is reasonable to envisage that a grand project like the BRI will start to invest and build from East to West, as there are AIIB approved projects in countries like Azerbaijan, Georgia and Tajikistan that intersect Europe and Asia. Yet, a closer look at the bilateral deals that China has made with European countries shows there are in fact multiple bilateral projects. For example, the port project in Piraeus is regarded as the "dragonhead" of the BRI (Brînză, 2016). Beijing has also concluded deals on infrastructure projects with Poland and regards Poland as "the gate to Europe" (Xinhua, 2017b). It is also recognized that instead of going through an international agreement with the EU, Beijing's 'divide and conquer' strategy appears to be a well-calculated move to gain allies to support China in Europe and the international community (see Pachebo, 2018). European countries that have received significant amounts of Chinese bilateral investment – such as Hungary and Greece – have a record of blocking EU criticism on China's human rights conditions (Denyer, 2017; Smith, 2017; Benner and Weidenfeld, 2018).

Nevertheless, this is not to say that the EU-China relationship is well-secured, as we argue that the relationship is hugely affected by the US and Russia. After decades of US trade deficit with China, the Trump administration claims that the US will impose tariffs on Chinese imports. In January 2018, a safeguard tariff on solar cells and modules and residential washing machines was announced, based on the investigations of the US International Trade Commission (ITC) (EOP, 2018). In section 201, the document highlighted the unfair trade practices of Chinese imports as regards washing machines and solar panels. The ITC recommended a 20% and 30% tariff respectively on the first 1.2 million units of these imported goods. The cases indicated that it is not only the EU which is upset about the dumping of imported goods like solar panels (ECFR, 2016), but the US appears to take it more seriously and actively considers more severe anti-dumping measures against China.

In March 2018, President Trump announced his plan to impose a tariff on steel and aluminium, backed by Section 232 which justifies the safeguard practice as a national security exemption (US Department of Commerce, 2018). Even though both the US and China are members of the WTO, the international organization allows tariffs under the terms of national defence and security. Before deciding whether this is an act of protectionism, it is worth noting that China accepted the conditionality of economic reform in order to become a member of the WTO in 2001. According to the Chinese interpretation, China should have been automatically granted Market Economy Status (MES) for a fifteen-year period, on joining the WTO. However, after the EU refused to grant China MES in 2016 (Casarini, 2006: 16; Farnell and Crookes, 2016b: 88), the US then submitted a statement to the WTO against granting MES to China in 2017 (Lawder 2017). The impact of this is two-fold 1) the WTO must handle both EU and US opposition to granting China MES and 2) China may also submit the tariff disputes to the WTO. The review of both cases will take time and it is uncertain as to whether the investigations will take place simultaneously. However, it is certain that if China loses in the first case, the WTO is not required to review the second.

The economic disputes between the US and the PRC are also likely to affect the EU-China trade relationship, especially when the US is using the tariff exemption in exchange for the support of the West to isolate China. Larry Kudlow, the Director of the National Economic Council of the US, said explicitly that not only NAFTA members would get tariff exemptions, but that Europe and other US allies in Pacific Asia could also possibly be exempted (Moore, 2018). In response, Beijing retaliated by announcing its plan to impose tariffs on American imports including soybeans, automobiles and other chemical products (Helmore, 2018). At the moment of writing this chapter, some of the proposed tariffs from both sides have come into effect. However, it is too early to claim there will be an all-out trade war between the US and the PRC, or begin to evaluate how it would reshuffle the winners and losers in trade relations.

From a neoliberal perspective, a trade war will hurt everyone in terms of absolute gain, yet if a realist perspective is taken; it is about who can survive longer and gain a relative advantage in the international competition. The proposed tariffs by the US are just one of the many economic tactics available to the Trump administration to actively deal with a rising China. The American ban on the Chinese telecommunication company ZTE to prevent it buying hardware and software from US tech companies, as well as Trump's recent idea to re-join the Trans-Pacific Partnership (TTP), are also signs that the US-China relationship is worsening. This would force Europe to pick sides between the two and ultimately affect EU-China relations. In fact, in Beijing in April 2018, 27 ambassadors from EU countries expressed their deep concerns as regards the negative repercussions, e.g. subsidies of Chinese products/companies and safety concerning intellectual property, that the BRI would bring to the global free trade economy (Prasad, 2018).

Apart from the economic stand-off between the US and the PRC that may affect the EU-China relationship in a negative way, there are nevertheless some positive effects that bring the EU and China together. After Trump revealed his intention to withdraw from the Paris climate agreement, this stimulated a closer relationship between the EU and China on combating climate change (Boffey and Neslen, 2017). The Near-Zero Emission Coal (NZEC) projects in 2007, as well as a new joint project in 2017 to aid China to build up its emission trading system, are examples of the EU supporting the largest coal-burning country in the world to reduce greenhouse gas emissions. Due to the withdrawal of the US from the Paris agreement, the EU-China relationship will continue to flourish by actively combating climate change in the international community, reinforcing our argument that geopolitical factors need to be taken into account in the analysis of the EU-China relationship.

3.2   *Russia, China and 'Dragonbear'*

As we have seen, this working relationship between Europe and the PRC is challenged by several factors. Many of these factors are endogenous to the relationship, such as trade, climate change and human rights. However, the role of Russia in the EU-China relationship is an exogenous factor and one that we argue should be taken more seriously. The relationship between Russia and both Europe and the PRC has evolved over time. Where Cold War tension existed between the then Soviet Union and Western Europe on one hand, and the PRC on the other, the relationship of an independent Russia has continued to diverge between Europe and the PRC. Following the 2008 Russia-Georgia War, the EU-Russia relationship has continued to deteriorate, with further Russian military action in Ukraine and the seizing of Crimea to become part of the Russian Federation from 2014 onwards; the use of chemical weapons to poison former intelligence agents in the UK (2006 and 2018); and finally, Russian military aid and political support for Bashar al-Assad in Syria. These events have overshadowed cooperation over Iran, the Israeli-Palestinian conflict, and other areas such as the frozen conflict in Nagorno-Karabakh.

Perhaps the most worrisome issue for Europe is the increasing relationship between Russia and the PRC. This relationship can be looked at in two ways. The first is that the Russia-PRC relationship is one of practicalities in a largely US dominated world. If for example, we look at US-led invasions of Iraq; political interference in many countries with close links to the PRC and Russia; and growing hostility to a militarily strong China, we see that China and Russia have a common interest to limit US global power and question the basis for the rules of the international system even as the US seeks to rewrite them. In this scenario, the relationship between the PRC and Russia is limited by these common interests *vis-a-vis* the US but do not extend further.

However, there is a second way to look at the relationship between the PRC and Russia, which has been described by international security analyst, Velina Tchakarova, as 'DragonBear'.[3] This approach assumes – like the first – that there exists a practical relationship, but adds that Russia acts as a 'free rider' on the growing power of the PRC. However, in reading Tchakarova's work, one can distinguish a political relationship forming that goes beyond common interests in that Russia itself will be curtailed by the rise of the PRC while at the same time benefiting from a changing international system. The relationship becomes political in that the PRC and Russia work together to use regional and global institutions to check US power and reset the rules in their favour. Tchakarova argues that,

> ... the Dragonbear connection is especially strong in emerging organisations and institutions such as BRICS, SCO, NDB, AIIB, just to name a few. Last but not least, the cooperation between China and the Eurasian Economic Union (EAEU) within the framework of the new Silk Road initiatives called One Belt, One Road (OBOR) has strategic character. Both

---

3 See for instance https://medium.com/@vtchakarova/the-russia-china-alliance-what-does-the-dragonbear-aim-to-achieve-in-global-affairs-e09b1addıc4a.

countries have signed an agreement on integrating the EAEU and OBOR and thus consolidate the Eurasian landmass in the long term.[4]

She goes further to say that these arguments "point to an imminent Dragonbear alliance". And herein lies the key difference between the first and second views of the PRC and Russia relationship. A relationship of convenience on one hand, and an alliance on the other, denote two levels of intensity of cooperation that have different impacts on the international system, and more importantly for the EU and PRC relationship. At the end of the day, while China is Europe's biggest trading partner and sits several time zones away from Europe's borders, Russia borders many EU countries and has shown a revanchist's propensity towards its neighbours.

Overall, we see a divergence in the relationship between Europe and the PRC and Europe and Russia. While China is not a military threat to the European mainland and its ambitions do not set out to counter Europe specifically, Russia plays a different role. Furthermore, China is simply too economically and diplomatically powerful to be ignored, while Russia, with its reliance on exporting oil and natural gas, does not outweigh the perceived threat. A Europe-China relationship that makes Russia stronger *vis-à-vis* Europe is a potential spoiler that many Europe-China analysts might too readily ignore. Given that Europe is the PRC's largest importer, there is a need for European governments to keep their relationship with China separate from their relationship with Russia. Ideally, for Europe, China should keep its relationships separate as well.

4   The UK, EU and China after Brexit

Following the result of the United Kingdom European Union membership referendum in 2016, Britain triggered Article 50 of the Lisbon Treaty, confirming the UK's departure from the EU at the end of 2020. This initiated the two-year negotiation period for the UK exit plan as it would no longer remain in the single market and customs union. The Brexit letter states that the UK will trade with the EU on WTO terms if there is no Brexit withdrawal agreement after the transition period (May 2017). Since 2015, the UK-China relationship has been progressing in economic terms and has included a state visit by Xi Jinping which sealed a £30 billion trade deal (Prime Minister's Office 2015). That same

---

4   Ibid.

year, the UK became one of the founder members of the AIIB (AIIB, 2018b). Cooperation between the UK and China has been tightening through multiple projects ranging from agriculture to the nuclear industry (Innovate UK, 2017; UK Environment Agency, 2017). From the Chinese perspective, building a relationship with the UK was the stepping stone to the single market of the EU. Consequently, the result of the EU referendum leaves huge uncertainty as to whether the UK will retain single market access. The Chinese ambassador to the EU, Zhang, claims that even though there is an established basis of trade engagement between the UK and China, there would be no further discussion if a Brexit withdrawal agreement is not reached (Ministry of Foreign Affairs of the PRC, 2018).

The UK government has been actively shifting its rhetoric from European identity to that of a "Global Britain" whose future lies outside the EU (UK Cabinet Office 2018). Yet the key for the UK to move beyond Europe and build strong ties with a rising China still ironically relies on the collective economic asset of the single market of the EU. Although Prime Minister Theresa May visited Beijing on a trade mission in February 2018, the result was far from fruitful, contrasting with what the Cabinet Office had called the "Golden Era" of UK-China relations. There are, in fact, a number of flashpoints between the two in national security and human rights issues – a situation which is unlikely to improve with Brexit. For example, the Chinese refused to grant security access to the UK's Office for Nuclear Regulation (ONR) for the nuclear plant in Essex (Vaughan, 2017). There is also an international dispute on the legal power of the Sino-British joint-declaration on the issue of Hong Kong (Phillips, 2017). In 2014, The Occupy Movement raised doubts in the British parliament concerning the One Country, Two Systems policy in Hong Kong, as have multiple incidents that have seen British parliamentary representatives and human rights activists refused entry to Hong Kong (Phillips and Haas, 2017; Li, 2018). There is no doubt that great uncertainty exists between the UK, EU and China. Yet Brexit would leave the UK no choice but to be one of the most 'pro-China' 'European' states when compared to other Continental European countries. However, given the greater reliance on US foreign policy agenda-setting, this is unlikely to be the case. The UK also needs to maintain relatively close ties with the EU so as to remain a valuable trade partner to the Chinese. While from Beijing's perspective, a more disunited Europe could be an advantage for the divide and conquer strategy that has been effective in the bilateral agreements of the Belt and Road Initiative.

5   Conclusion

In this chapter, we have illustrated the current state of Europe's relations with China and how both the US and Russia impact on this relationship. The central research question is what impact these states have on the EU-China relationship. Relying on a combination of literatures and policy documents, we have argued that Europe is often between 'a rock and a hard place' which limits its relationship with China to its overwhelming economic basis. The first section has illustrated how this relationship developed, looking at the major issues and milestones in the EU-China relationship around trade and diplomacy and onwards towards the Belt and Road Initiative. The second section has paid particular attention to the EU as an alternative Western counterpart to the US in China's modernising global challenge. The focus has also been on the constraining nature of the EU's relationship with the US *vis-à-vis* China. The third section has looked at how China's seeming common cause with the Russian Federation is a further challenge to the EU-China relationship. In particular, by looking at the concept of 'Dragonbear', the chapter has explored the prospect of an alliance between China and Russia and what this means for a Europe that considers Russia a revanchist power on its border. While the prospects for 'Dragonbear' are arguably limited and are further asymmetric in favour of the PRC in this relationship, the chapter has stressed that the Russia factor should not be discounted altogether, especially as China seeks to build transport infrastructure to Europe through Russia.

The final section has examined the changing nature of Europe itself, and Brexit in particular. While the UK government seeks to radically renegotiate its relationship with Europe, the EU will remain its most important trading partner. With the UK maintaining that a Britain outside Europe is a more global Britain, the prospects for Chinese trade with, and investment in, Europe may well leave the UK outside this important economic relationship. Furthermore, as the country most closely linked to the tendencies of US foreign policy and the most bellicose in relation to Russia, there are reasons why Europe may find its relationship with China easier without the UK at the centre of EU trade and foreign policy.

Overall, the relationship between the EU and China is likely to continue to improve, especially if the US becomes less engaged in Europe and the China-Russia relationship cools. Furthermore, as stated, the fact that the UK is leaving important decision-making institutions in the EU suggests that the EU will be freer to change its relationship with China beyond trade. Importantly for Europe, China has the potential to be an important stabiliser in Africa and a potential constrainer of Russian foreign policy. Both of these outcomes would address Europe's major security concerns and would encourage a radical reorientation towards China and away from the US. While this does not appear to be in the interest of the US and some European countries (including the UK), political changes in the US and Europe make it more likely as time goes on. As a result, it is increasingly important that Europe maintain its research on China and on Europe-China relations, in addition to the promotion of Mandarin language proficiency going forward. After all, there are still some serious differences over values and morals that, if given the opportunity, could very easily disrupt the relationship between Europe and China. The better we understand one another, the more likely it is that these differences will not become a barrier to cooperation.

Bibliography

AIIB (2018a). Approved Projects Overview – AIIB [Online]. Available from: https://www.aiib.org/en/projects/approved/index.html [Accessed 21 April 2018].

AIIB (2018b). Members of the Bank – AIIB [Online]. Available from: https://www.aiib.org/en/about-aiib/governance/members-of-bank/index.html [Accessed 21 April 2018].

Anderson, P. (2010), Sinomania. London Review of Books.

Benner, T., and Weidenfeld, J. (2018), Europe, don't let China divide and conquer [Online]. Politico. Available from: https://www.politico.eu/article/europe-china-divide-and-conquer/ [Accessed 21 April 2018].

Boffey, D., and Neslen, A. (2017). China and EU strengthen promise to Paris deal with US poised to step away [Online]. Available from: http://www.theguardian.com/environment/2017/may/31/china-eu-climate-lead-paris-agreement [Accessed 21 April 2018].

Brînză, A. (2016). How a Greek Port Became a Chinese 'Dragon Head' [Online]. The Diplomat. Available from: https://thediplomat.com/2016/04/how-a-greek-port-became-a-chinese-dragon-head/ [Accessed 21 April 2018].

Burnay, M., Hivonnet, J., and Raube, K. (2014). 'Soft Diplomacy' and People-to-People Dialogue between the EU and the PRC. European Foreign Affairs Review 19 (3), 35–55.

Carrapatoso, A. (2011). Climate policy diffusion: Interregional dialogue in China-EU relations. Global Change, Peace and Security 23 (2), pp. 177–194.

Casarini, N. (2006). The evolution of the EU-China relationship: From constructive engagement to strategic partnership [Online]. European Union Institute for Security Studies. Available from: http://ftp.infoeuropa.eurocid.pt/database/000037001-000038000/000037834.pdf [Accessed 13 April 2018].

CEEC (2018). Cooperation between China and Eastern European countries [Online]. Available from: http://www.china-ceec.org/eng [Accessed 12 April 2018].

Chow, G.C. (2015). China's economic transformation. Chichester: John Wiley & Sons.

Crookes, P.I. (2013). Resetting EU–China relations from a values-based to an interests-based engagement. International Politics 50 (5), pp. 639–663.

Dai, X. (2006). Understanding EU-China relations: An uncertain partnership in the making [Online]. Centre for European Students, University of Hull, research paper 1/2006. Available from: https://pdfs.semanticscholar.org/22c2/a45586ba60281e0cfddb3271f4ccbdf9f534.pdf [Accessed 12 April 2018].

De Cock, G. (2011). European Union as a bilateral norm leader on climate change vis-a-vis China. European Foreign Affairs review 16, pp. 89–105.

Denyer, S. (2017). Europe divided, China gratified as Greece blocks E.U. statement over human rights [Online]. Washington Post. Available from: https://www.washingtonpost.com/news/worldviews/wp/2017/06/19/europe-divided-china-gratified-as-greece-blocks-e-u-statement-over-human-rights/ [Accessed 21 April 2018].

Du, J., and Zhang, Y. (2017). Does One Belt One Road initiative promote Chinese overseas direct investment? China Economic Review 47, pp. 189–205.

EC (2014). EU and China begin investment talks [Online]. European Commission. Available from: http://europa.eu/rapid/press-release_IP-14-33_en.htm [Accessed 12 April 2018].

EC (2016). International action on climate change: Bilateral cooperation with China [Online]. Available from: https://ec.europa.eu/clima/policies/international/cooperation/china_en [Accessed 21 April 2018].

EC (2017a). European Union, trade in goods with China [Online]. European Commission. Available from: http://trade.ec.europa.eu/doclib/docs/2006/september/tradoc_113366.pdf [Accessed 12 April 2018].

EC (2017b). China [Online]. European Commission, Directorate-General Trade. Available from: 3 [Accessed 13 April 2018].

EC (2017c). Speech by President Jean-Claude Juncker at the 12th EU-China Business Summit [Online]. European Commission. Available from: http://europa.eu/rapid/press-release_SPEECH-17-1526_en.htm [Accessed 12 April 2018].

EC (2017d). EU welcomes launch of China's carbon market [Online]. European Commission. Available from: https://ec.europa.eu/clima/news/eu-welcomes-launch-chinas-carbon-market_en [Accessed 13 April 2018].

EC (2018). EU-China High-Level People-to-People Dialogue – Detail [Online]. European Commission. Available from: http://ec.europa.eu/education/policy/international-cooperation/china_en [Accessed 13 April 2018].

EC (2019). EU-China – A strategic outlook 2019 [Online]. European Commission. Available from: https://ec.europa.eu/commission/sites/beta-political/files/communication-eu-china-a-strategic-outlook.pdf [Accessed 31 March 2020].

ECFR (2016). European Foreign Policy Scorecard 2016 [Online]. European Council on Foreign Relations. Available from: http://www.ecfr.eu/page/-/ECFR157 _SCORECARD_2016.pdf [Accessed 17 April 2018].

EEAS (2015). EU-China Dialogue Architecture [Online]. European External Action Service. Available from: https://eeas.europa.eu/delegations/china_en/18538/EU -China%20Dialogue%20Architecture [Accessed 10 April 2018].

EEAS (2017a). EU-China: Main events [Online]. European External Action Service. Available from: https://eeas.europa.eu/sites/eeas/files/eu-china_chronology_0.pdf [Accessed 10 April 2018].

EEAS (2017b). Environment and Climate Change [Online]. European External Action Service, Delegation of the European Union to China. Available from: http://eeas .europa.eu/delegations/china/eu_china/environment/index_en.htm [Accessed 13 April 2018].

EOP (2018). Section 201 Cases: Imported Large Residential Washing Machines and Imported Solar Cells and Modules [Online]. Available from: https://ustr.gov/ sites/default/files/files/Press/fs/201%20Cases%20Fact%20Sheet.pdf. [Accessed 21 April 2018].

EU (2016). Elements for new EU strategy on China [Online]. European Union. Available from: https://eeas.europa.eu/sites/eeas/files/joint_communication_to _the_european_parliament_and_the_council_-_elements_for_a_new_eu_strategy _on_china.pdf [Accessed 13 April 2018].

EU (2017). Belt and Road Forum – EU common messages [Online]. European Union. Available from: https://eeas.europa.eu/delegations/china_fi/26051/Belt%20and%20 Road%20Forum--EU%20common%20messagesb [Accessed 17 April 2018].

Fallon, T. (2015). The new silk road: Xi Jinping's grand strategy for Eurasia. American Foreign Policy Interests 37 (3), pp. 140–147.

Farnell, J., and Crookes, P. I. (2016). The politics of EU-China Economic Relations. London: Palgrave Macmillan.

Fox, J., and Godement, F. (2009). A power audit of EU-China relations [Online]. European Council on Foreign Relations. Available from: http://www.centreasia.eu/sites/ default/files/publications_pdf/a_power_audit_of_eu_china_relations_full_text _0.pdf [Accessed 13 April 2018].

Geeraerts, G. (2014). EU-China relations [Online]. Brussels Institute of Contemporary China Studies (BICCS). Available from: https://www.academia.edu/4776103/EU -_China_Relations [Accessed 13 April 2018].

Guo (2013). Chinese politics and government: Power, ideology and organisation. New York: Routledge.

Helmore, E. (2018). China threatens 'Trump country' with retaliatory tariffs ahead of midterms [Online]. Available from: http://www.theguardian.com/business/2018/ apr/06/china-us-tariffs-trump-country-midterms [Accessed 21 April 2018].

Huang, Y. (2016). Understanding China's Belt & Road Initiative: Motivation, framework and assessment. China Economic Review 40, pp. 314–321.

Hung, H. (2015). The China Boom: Why China Will Not Rule the World. New York: Columbia University Press.

Innovate UK (2017). Working with China on agriculture challenges: more time to apply [Online]. Available from: https://www.gov.uk/government/news/working-with -china-on-agriculture-challenges-more-time-to-apply [Accessed 23 April 2018].

Jacques, M. (2009). When China Rules the World: The End of the Western World and the Birth of a New Global Order. New York: Penguin Press.

Lanteigne, M. (2013). Chinese foreign policy: An introduction. New York: Routledge.

Lawder, D. (2017). U.S. formally opposes China market economy status at WTO [Online]. Reuters. Available from: https://www.reuters.com/article/us-usa-china-trade-wto/ u-s-formally-opposes-china-market-economy-status-at-wto-idUSKBN1DU2VH [Accessed 21 April 2018].

Li, N.C.H. (2018). 'One Country, Two Systems' under siege: Rival Securitizing Attempts on Democratization of Hong Kong. In: D. Johanson, T. Wu, and J. Li, (editors), New Perspectives on China's Relations with the World: National, Transnational and International. Bristol: E-International Relations Publishing.

Li, R. (2009). A rising China and security in East Asia. New York: Routledge.

Maher, R. 2016. The elusive EU–China strategic partnership. International Affairs 92 (4), pp. 959–976.

May, T. (2017). Prime Minister's letter to Donald Tusk triggering Article 50 [Online]. Available from: https://www.gov.uk/government/publications/prime-ministers- letter-to-donald-tusk-triggering-article-50 [Accessed 23 April 2018].

Men, J. (2011). Between human rights and sovereignty – An examination of EU–China political relations. European Law Journal 17(4), pp. 534–550.

Ministry of Foreign Affairs of the PRC (2018). Ambassador Zhang Ming's Interview with the Politico [Online]. Available from: http://www.fmprc.gov.cn/mfa_eng/wjb _663304/zwjg_665342/zwbd_665378/t1552225.shtml [Accessed 23 April 2018].

Moore, M. (2018). Larry Kudlow predicted Europe's exemption from Trump's tar- iff plan [Online]. New York Post. Available from: https://nypost.com/2018/03/11/ larry-kudlow-predicted-europes-exemption-from-trumps-tariff-plan/ [Accessed 21 April 2018].

Phillips, T. (2017). China 'humiliating' the UK by scrapping Hong Kong handover deal, say activists [Online]. Available from: http://www.theguardian.com/world/2017/ jul/01/china-humiliating-uk-hong-kong-handover-deal [Accessed 23 April 2018].

Phillips, T., and Haas, B. (2017). British Conservative party activist barred from enter- ing Hong Kong [Online]. Available from: http://www.theguardian.com/world/2017/ oct/11/british-conservative-party-activist-benedict-rogers-hong-kong [Accessed 23 April 2018].

Prasad, R. (2018). EU Ambassadors Condemn China's Belt and Road Initiative [Online]. Available from: https://thediplomat.com/2018/04/eu-ambassadors-condemn-chinas -belt-and-road-initiative/ [Accessed 21 April 2018].

Prime Minister's Office (2015). China State Visit will unlock more than £30 billion of commercial deals [Online]. Available from: https://www.gov.uk/government/news/ china-state-visit-will-unlock-more-than-30-billion-of-commercial-deals [Accessed 23 April 2018].

Reuters (2017). Greece blocks EU statement on China human rights at U.N [Online]. Available from: https://www.reuters.com/article/us-eu-un-rights/greece-blocks-eu -statement-on-china-human-rights-at-u-n-idUSKBN1990FP [Accessed 13 April 2018].

Sachdeva, G. (2014). EU–China and EU–India: A tale of two strategic partnerships. Strategic Analysis 38 (4), pp. 427–431.

Scott, D. (2009). Environmental issues as a 'strategic' key in EU–China relations. Asia Europe Journal 7 (2), pp. 211–224.

Shen W. (2013). EU-China Relations on human rights in competing paradigms: Continuity and change. In: T. Christianson, E. Kirchner and P. B. Murray, (editors). The Palgrave handbook of EU-Asia relations, pp. 165–180. London: Palgrave Macmillan.

Smith, H. (2017). Greece blocks EU's criticism at UN of China's human rights record [Online]. The Guardian. Available from: http://www.theguardian.com/world/2017/ jun/18/greece-eu-criticism-un-china-human-rights-record [Accessed 21 April 2018].

Turcsányi, R. (2014). Central and Eastern Europe's courtship with China: Trojan horse within the EU [Online]. European Institute for Asian Studies, EU-Asia at a Glance, January. Available from: http://www.eias.org/wp-content/uploads/2016/02/EU -Asia-at-a-glance-Richard-Turcsanyi-China-CEE.pdf [Accessed 17 April 2018].

UK Cabinet Office (2018). Building a global Britain [Online]. Available from: https://www .gov.uk/government/speeches/building-a-global-britain [Accessed 23 April 2018].

UK Environment Agency (2017). Second phase of assessment on new nuclear reactor for UK begins [Online]. Available from: https://www.gov.uk/government/news/ second-phase-of-assessment-on-new-nuclear-reactor-for-uk-begins [Accessed 23 April 2018].

US Department of Commerce (2018). Section 232 Reports [Online]. Available from: https://www.commerce.gov/news/press-releases/2018/02/secretary-ross-releases -steel-and-aluminum-232-reports-coordination [Accessed 21 April 2018].

Vaughan, A. (2017). Chinese firm behind Essex nuclear plant refuses to reveal security information [Online]. Available from: http://www.theguardian.com/environment/ 2017/oct/01/chinese-firm-behind-essex-nuclear-plant-refuses-to-reveal-security -information [Accessed 23 April 2018].

Wang, Y. (2016). The Belt and Road Initiative: What will China offer the world? Beijing: New World Press.

Xinhua (2017a). Full text of Chinese Premier Li's speech at 12th China-EU business summit [Online]. Available from: http://www.xinhuanet.com/english/2017-06/03/c_136337149.htm [Accessed 12 April 2018].

Xinhua (2017b). Poland, a gate to Europe in Belt and Road Initiative [Online]. Available from: http://www.xinhuanet.com/english/2017-05/12/c_136277691.htm [Accessed 21 April 2018].

Yuan, H., and Orbie, J. (2015). The social dimension of the EU-China relationship: A normative and pragmatic European approach? European Foreign Affairs Review 20 (3), pp. 337–355.

CHAPTER 2

Spain's Views of China

The Economy Is the Key

Mario Esteban

The Chinese authorities are well aware that a country's reputation and image are strategic assets for its standing inside the international community (Kurlantzick, 2007; Lampton, 2008; Li, 2009; Zheng and Zhang, 2007: 6–12). In addition, China's own population is paying increasing attention to how the country is judged abroad and this is a factor affecting China's vision of other countries, the popularity of Chinese political leaders and the legitimacy of the regime itself. Hence, China has invested a significant amount of resources in developing its public diplomacy, for example, by establishing numerous Confucius Institutes throughout the world since 2004.[1]

Analysing the image of China in Spain is relevant as Spain is the thirteenth biggest economy in the world, the fourth inside the Eurozone, one of the most influential political actors inside the European Union, and the ninth country in the Lowy Institute Global Diplomacy Index.[2]

This present article resorts to opinion polls (multiple editions of the Elcano Royal Institute Barometer from 2002 to 2017 and of the Barometer of the Image of Spain),[3] elite interviews of Spanish officials and business

---

1 Wu Jing and Lu Nuo, 2006: 孔子学院成为中国"软实力"的最亮品牌 [2006: The Counfucious Institute is the most brilliant brand of the Chinese "soft power"], Central government portal, http://www.gov.cn/jrzg/2007-01/01/content_485693.htm, 01 January 2007 (accessed 22 November 2018).

2 Global Diplomacy Index, Lowy Institute, https://globaldiplomacyindex.lowyinstitute.org/ (accessed 24 February 2020).

3 The Elcano Royal Institute Barometer (known by its initials BRIE in Spanish) is a periodic survey, conducted three times a year since 2002 using a sample of 1,200 people, representative of the Spanish general population. The BRIE is focused exclusively on the opinions, values and attitudes of the Spanish population towards international relations and Spanish foreign policy. For more information about the BRIE and access to all its editions and technical specifications see: http://www.realinstitutoelcano.org/wps/portal/rielcano_en/ publications/barometer-rielcano. The Barometer of the Image of Spain (known by its initials BIE in Spanish) is an annual on-line survey conducted in different countries since 2012 with over 400 people, focused exclusively on the opinions, values, and attitudes towards international relations and Spanish foreign policy. For more information about the BRIE and access

representatives,[4] and media analysis, to present and explain the evolution of Spain's views of China over the last few years.

1   Mutual Perceptions

An analysis of the polls conducted on mutual images between Spain and China, and in particular, the different editions of the Elcano Royal Institute Barometer, shows us that these images are asymmetric, ambivalent, and stereotyped. However, those conclusions should be nuanced in certain cases.

Mutual Spain-China perceptions are asymmetrical since the Chinese population values Spain much higher (average of 7.6 on a scale of 0 to 10) than the Spaniards value China (5.2). This situation is reflected in figures 2.1 and 2.2 using data up to November 2016 and March 2017 respectively. This higher assessment of Spain among the Chinese population must be qualified by other results: Germany and the United Kingdom (8.1), France (7.8), Italy (7.7), and the United States (7.6) score equal to or even higher than Spain. Japan, as a country that raises mixed feelings in China, obtains an evaluation of 6.2, higher than the 5.9 given to Spain by the Spaniards themselves. Hence it is safe to argue that part of this asymmetry lies in the tendency of Chinese people to give higher scores than Spanish people. Therefore, the relevant point here is that the Chinese value Spain as they value other advanced European countries whilst the Spaniards have a less positive view of China than of peer OECD countries, but more positive than of other non-OECD powers such as Russia, and non-OECD neighbors such as Morocco.

In addition, Spanish valuation of China is similar to the assessments made in other EU countries, although slightly lower – see Table 2.1.

Despite the limited appreciation shown by the Spaniards towards China, the latter is perceived as a great power at present (below the United States and somewhat above Germany – see Figure 2.3) and as the most empowered nation over the last few years – see Figure 4. For over half of interviewees in the last BRIE, China will be the most powerful country in 2050 (53%), whereas

---

to all its editions and technical specifications see: http://www.realinstitutoelcano.org/wps/portal/rielcano_es/observatorio-imagen-espana/barometro-imagen-espana/.

4   The interviews were conducted between January 2016 and September 2018 in the Prime Minister's Office, the Ministry of Economy and Business, the Ministry of Foreign Affairs and Cooperation, the Spanish Institute for Foreign Trade, the Embassy of Spain in Beijing, Spain Trade and Investment Office in Beijing, and the Spanish Confederation of Employers' Organizations.

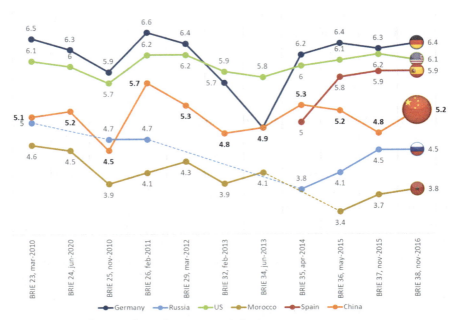

FIGURE 2.1   Evaluation of some key countries in Spain
             [a] Elcano Royal Institute Barometer, Elcano Royal Institute, http://www
             .realinstitutoelcano.org/wps/portal/rielcano_en/publications/barometer
             -rielcano, nd (accessed 22 November 2018).
             SOURCE: ELCANO ROYAL INSTITUTE BAROMETER.[a]

only 31% name the United States as being the most powerful country by the middle of the 21st century – see Figure 2.5. Therefore, in the eyes of the Spanish population, the United States of America remains the most influential power, but China is perceived as its heir in the medium-long term.

Part of the ambivalent image of China in Spain derives from this recognition of growing Chinese power. In a positive sense, China is more highly rated in Spain than other countries with much more cultural affinities to Spain, such as Mexico, Cuba or Venezuela, and significantly better than Morocco, Iran or Saudi Arabia – see Figure 6. In addition, despite the great international criticism that China receives for its perceived levels of corruption and opacity, Spaniards consider China to be less corrupt than Spain and other Mediterranean coun- tries – see Figure 2.7.

Regarding the well-being of Spain-China bilateral relations, the Spanish population views these links like those maintained with Western countries such as France, Germany, and the United States. That is, a complex relation- ship which has more positive than negative elements – see Figure 2.8.

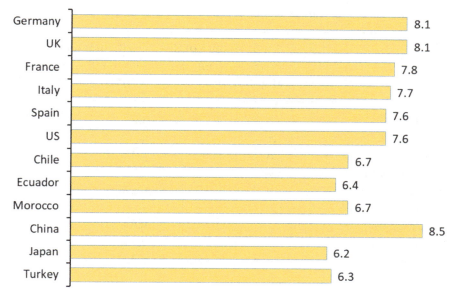

FIGURE 2.2   Evaluation of some key countries in China
           [a] Barometer of the Image of Spain, Elcano Royal Institute, http://www
           .realinstitutoelcano.org/wps/portal/rielcano_es/encuesta?WCM_GLOBAL
           _CONTEXT=/elcano/elcano_es/observatoriomarcaespana/estudios/resultados/
           barometro-imagen-espana-7, February-March 2017 (accessed 22 November 2018).
           SOURCE: BAROMETER OF THE IMAGE OF SPAIN, MARCH 2017.[a]

The rise of China as a global power worries Spaniards, and this concern is growing, but less so than other issues such as jihadist terrorism, drug trafficking or global warming – see Figures 2.9a and 2.9b. It is quite telling that both the percentage of the Spanish population that perceives the rise of China and globalization as a threat, is almost the same – see Figure 2.9a; and that the percentage of Spaniards who see the rise of China as no threat decreased significantly from 22 percent before the global financial crisis to less than 10 percent after it– see Figure 2.9b.

Where do these fears and ambivalence concerning China, evident in certain sectors of Spanish society, come from? The answer would appear to be from China's own power. Power is admired, but also feared. As regards Chinese power, the economic dimension is particularly relevant and Spanish people are especially concerned about the competition of Chinese goods, the relocation of productive activities to China, and more recently, Chinese investments abroad.

Already in 2005, before the international economic crisis hit Spain with great virulence, in one of his seminal works on Spain's perception of China,

TABLE 2.1   Valuation of China in some key countries

	6th Barometer of the Image of Spain May/Jun 2016	7th Barometer of the Image of Spain Feb/Mar 2017
Spain*	4.8	5.2
Germany	4.7	5.4
France	5.0	5.8
United Kingdom	5.2	5.8
Italy	--	6.2
Portugal	5.2	--
United States	5.5	6.5
Chile	--	7.3
Ecuador	--	7.8
Colombia	7.2	--
Peru	7.8	--
Morocco	7.6	7.5
China	8.3	8.5
Japan	--	3.5
Turkey	--	6.4
India	6.9	--

SOURCE: BAROMETER OF THE IMAGE OF SPAIN.[a] (*) IN THE CASE OF SPAIN, THE SOURCE IS THE ELCANO ROYAL INSTITUTE BAROMETER JAN. 2016 AND DEC. 2016.[b]

[a] Barometer of the Image of Spain, Elcano Royal Institute, http://www.realinstitutoelcano.org/wps/portal/rielcano_es/observatorio-imagen-espana/barometro-imagen-espana/, nd (accessed 22 November 2018).

[b] Elcano Royal Institute Barometer, Elcano Royal Institute, http://www.realinstitutoelcano.org/wps/portal/rielcano_en/publications/barometer-rielcano, nd (accessed 22 November 2018).

Javier Noya stressed that the possible outbreaks of Sinophobia among the Spanish population did not have political or social foundations, but were rooted "exclusively in the economic aspect, where fears and misgivings arise due to the threat posed by Chinese imports and the attractiveness of China as an investment destination" (Noya, 2005). At that time, economic competition with China was seen as one of the biggest problems faced by the European Union – see Figure 2.10 – and the Chinese economy was depicted more as a

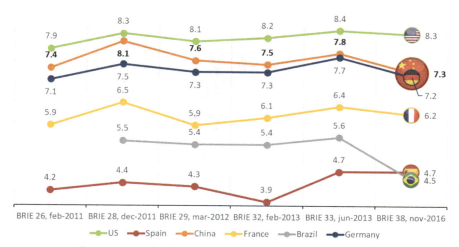

FIGURE 2.3   The international influence of some key countries in the eyes of the
Spanish people
ᵃ Ibid.

SOURCE: ELCANO ROYAL INSTITUTE BAROMETER.ᵃ

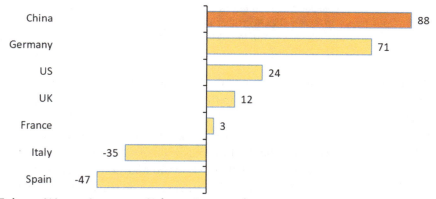

(Balance: % increasing power - % decreasing power)

FIGURE 2.4   The evolution of the power of some key countries in the eyes of the
Spanish people
ᵃ Elcano Royal Institute Barometer, Elcano Royal Institute, http://www
.realinstitutoelcano.org/wps/wcm/connect/c99b8c80465309d5a282bbc4d090bb2e/
26Oleada_Informe_Completo.pdf?MOD=AJPERES&CACHEID
=c99b8c80465309d5a282bbc4d090bb2e February-March 2011 (accessed 22
November 2018).

SOURCE: ELCANO ROYAL INSTITUTE BAROMETER, MARCH 2011.ᵃ

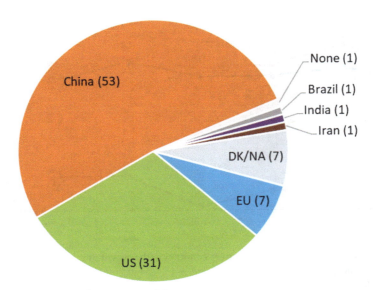

FIGURE 2.5   The most powerful country in 2050
            ᵃ Elcano Royal Institute Barometer, Elcano Royal Institute,
            http://www.realinstitutoelcano.org/wps/wcm/connect/
            564a22004331a87ebaa0fb5cb2335b49/24Oleada_Informe
            _Completo.pdf?MOD=AJPERES&CACHEID=564a22004331a87ebaa0fb5cb2335b49,
            June 2010 (accessed 22 November 2018).
            SOURCE: ELCANO ROYAL INSTITUTE BAROMETER, JUNE 2010.ᵃ

threat to Spanish companies, due to the low prices of Chinese products, than as an opportunity gained by access to the Chinese market – see Figure 2.11.

Over a decade later, we are exploring how new kinds of Spain-China economic relations – such as Chinese investment in Spain and the Belt and Road Initiative – are received in Spain, in order to determine the validity of that analysis. Qualitative data suggest that economic and political elites tend to have more positive views of China than the Spanish society at large, where indifference or concern tend to be more prevalent.

2   Is Chinese FDI Well Received in Spain?

Spain is a late and modest destination for Chinese investment. Up to 2008, Spain received hardly any Chinese investment at all. In the last eight years, however, flows of Chinese investment have increased to EUR 4 billion, according to the Spanish Ministry of Economics, and EUR 3 billion if one accepts the figures provided by the Rhodium Group. In both instances we have quite

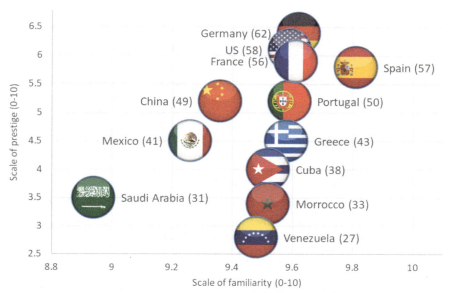

FIGURE 2.6   Reputation of some key countries in Spain
        ª Elcano Royal Institute Barometer, Elcano Royal Institute,
        http://www.realinstitutoelcano.org/wps/wcm/connect/
        73037a0048b71bdd9f479fc2d8a74536/36BRIE_Informe
        _Junio2015.pdf?MOD=AJPERES&CACHEID=73037a0048b71bdd9f479fc2d8a74536,
        Abril-May 2015 (accessed 22 November 2018).
        SOURCE: ELCANO ROYAL INSTITUTE BAROMETER, JUNE 2015.ª

modest figures when compared with the EUR 10 billion of assets of Spanish companies acquired by Chinese firms in Latin America (Esteban, 2015: 55–59). The amount of Chinese investment in Spain is quite unremarkable also when compared with Chinese investment in other European countries, and with the foreign direct investment received by Spain from other countries. According to the Rhodium Group figures, Spain is the ninth most important target country for Chinese FDI in Europe, and the statistics offered by the Spanish Ministry of Economics make China the tenth largest investor in Spain, with a 2.65% share of Spain's stock of inward foreign direct investment as of 31 December 2015 (Pérez, 2018: 44).

There is a clear difference between the perceptions and attitudes towards Chinese investments by the Spanish government and the media, and by public opinion at large. Both the governments of the Spanish Socialist Party (PSOE) and the Popular Party (PP), which have alternated in power since 1982, have tried to attract Chinese investments, especially in the aftermath of the global financial crisis in 2008. From the Spanish government's point of view, leaving

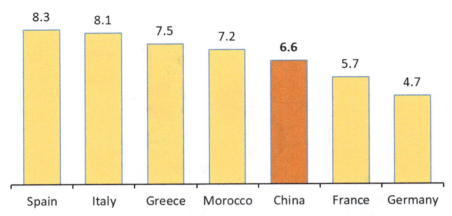

FIGURE 2.7   Level of corruption of some key countries in the eyes of the Spanish people
             a Elcano Royal Institute Barometer, Elcano Royal Institute, http://
             www.realinstitutoelcano.org/wps/wcm/connect/
             e53113804ea555429fa7ffb5284b5e68/32BRIE_Informe
             _Febrero2012.pdf?MOD=AJPERES&CACHEID
             =e53113804ea555429fa7ffb5284b5e68, February 2013 (accessed 22 November 2018).
             SOURCE: ELCANO ROYAL INSTITUTE BAROMETER, FEB. 2015.[a]

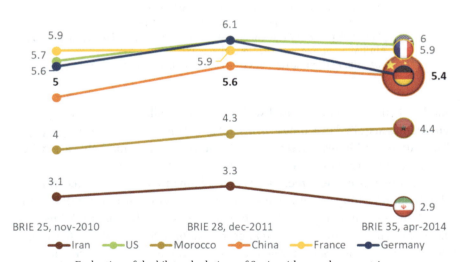

FIGURE 2.8   Evaluation of the bilateral relations of Spain with some key countries
             a Elcano Royal Institute Barometer, Elcano Royal Institute, http://
             www.realinstitutoelcano.org/wps/portal/rielcano_en/publications/barometer
             -rielcano, nd (accessed 22 November 2018).
             SOURCE: ELCANO ROYAL INSTITUTE BAROMETER.[a]

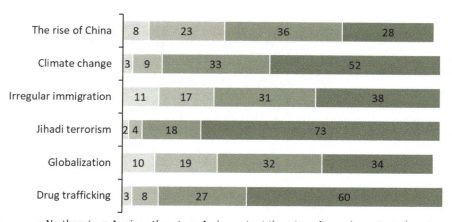

FIGURE 2.9A   Threats to Spain's security
               [a] Elcano Royal Institute Barometer, Elcano Royal Institute, http://
               www.realinstitutoelcano.org/wps/portal/rielcano_es/encuesta?WCM_GLOBAL
               _CONTEXT=/elcano/elcano_es/barometro/oleadabrie36, June 2015 (accessed 22
               November 2018).
               SOURCE: ELCANO ROYAL INSTITUTE BAROMETER, JUNE 2015.[a]

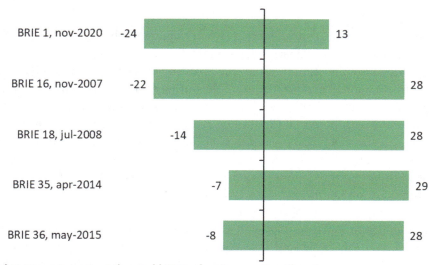

(+) % A very important threat; (-) % No threat or a minor threat

FIGURE 2.9B   How threatening is the rise of China for Spain?
               [a] Elcano Royal Institute Barometer, Elcano Royal Institute, http://
               www.realinstitutoelcano.org/wps/portal/rielcano_en/publications/barometer
               -rielcano, nd (accessed 22 November 2018).
               SOURCE: ELCANO ROYAL INSTITUTE BAROMETER.[a]

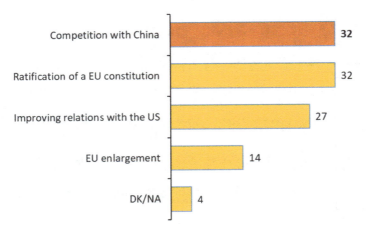

FIGURE 2.10   The most pressing issues for the EU
              a Elcano Royal Institute Barometer, Elcano Royal Institute, http://www
              .realinstitutoelcano.org/wps/wcm/connect/004c940047e222ef92cada
              076e8e26e4/10%C2%AAOleada_Informe_Completo.pdf?
              MOD=AJPERES&CACHEID=004c940047e222ef92cada076e8e26e4, November
              2005 (accessed 22 November 2018).
              SOURCE: ELCANO ROYAL INSTITUTE BAROMETER, NOVEMBER 2005.ᵃ

aside investment in strategic sectors, when it comes to Chinese investments in Spain the attitude is: "the more investment, the better".

With this conviction in mind, the Spanish government has developed a series of concrete actions. For example, during every visit of senior Spanish officials to China, apart from seeing their Chinese counterparts, there is also a meeting with potential Chinese investors interested in Spain. Consistent with this strategy is also the fact that, according to the Spanish trade promotion office, ICEX, between 2014 and 2016 China is the place where Spanish officials have given the most briefings on Spain's Golden Visa program. This promotion of Spanish assets to Chinese investors also applies to the high-technology sector. ICEX has organized trade missions for Spanish aerospace companies to make contact with the Commercial Aircraft Corporation of China, and this facilitated the acquisition of the engineering firm Aritex by the Aviation Industry Corporation of China in April 2016 for EUR 167 million.

Although the government has not undertaken a thorough and exhaustive analysis of all Chinese investments in Spain, the general feeling in the administration is that most of the 126 Chinese firms that were based in the country before 30 June 2016, have had a positive or very positive experience. According to the interviewed officials, this is particularly true with firms that

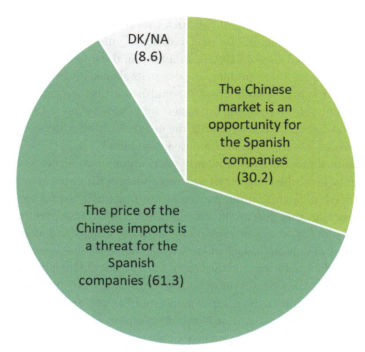

FIGURE 2.11   China and the Spanish companies
              [a] Elcano Royal Institute Barometer, Elcano Royal Institute,
              http://www.realinstitutoelcano.org/wps/wcm/connect/
              21e3340047e216d091bfd9076e8e26e4/8BRIE_Informe_Completo
              .pdf?MOD=AJPERES&CACHEID=21e3340047e216d091bfd9076e8e26e4,
              February 2005 (accessed 22 November 2018).
              SOURCE: ELCANO ROYAL INSTITUTE BAROMETER, FEBRUARY 2005.[a]

have generated a large number of jobs[5] or have helped Spanish firms to penetrate the Chinese market in the fields of agriculture, food and beverages, and
distribution.

By contrast, there are a few, but well-known, negative cases, such as the purchase of the Edificio España skyscraper by Wanda Group, which was not able
to have its renovation project approved by the Madrid City Council and eventually sold the building to a Spanish group. Another example is the dismissal

---

5 A representative from the Ministry of the Economy of Spain claimed that total Spanish FDI
   in China generated 30,674 jobs whereas Chinese investment in Spain generated less than
   20,000 jobs Investment trends and records in Spain, ICEX España Exportación e Inversiones,
   http://www.investinspain.org/invest/wcm/idc/groups/public/documents/documento/
   mde1/ndeo/~edisp/doc2015414726.pdf,February 2020 (accessed 24 February 2020).

from the board of the NH Hotel Group of two HNA Group executives, despite HNA being the largest shareholder, due to a conflict of interest once this Chinese company purchased Carlson Hotels. In addition, the opening of an ICBC office in Madrid has also been problematic due to its alleged involvement in illicit activities such as money laundering. A Spanish court is investigating this issue involving not only ICBC Spain, but also ICBC Luxembourg – ICBC's European unit. These cases have damaged both the image of Chinese investors in Spain and of Spain as a destination for Chinese investment.[6]

On the one hand, there are two frequently cited arguments in favor of Chinese investments. First, the coupling of the availability of Chinese capital and the financial needs of Spanish firms, particularly during the Eurozone crisis. Second, the synergies that potentially emerge when the Chinese partner facilitates access to the Chinese consumer market. On the other hand, concerns expressed usually focus on the lack of knowledge that the Chinese investors have of the Spanish legal system and the lack of transparency in their firms.

However, despite the strong consensus in favor of Chinese investments that exists among government and media actors, Spanish public opinion has a different view. The 37th Elcano Royal Institute Barometer, conducted in November 2015, shows that most Spanish citizens perceive Chinese investment with hesitancy, especially when compared with investment from other countries such as Germany, the United States and France – see Figure 2.12.

3   From Which Countries Would You Like Spain to Receive More or Less Investments?

As can be observed, Spaniards are generally in favor of inward foreign direct investment, especially if it comes from Germany, the United States or France. However, the attitude is different *vis-à-vis* China. One quarter of those interviewed think that China's investments in Spain should be reduced. This is a striking figure given that the country that generates the second most negative sentiment, Japan, was only viewed as such by 9% of interviewees.

These numbers are more easily understood when one looks at the 34th Elcano Royal Institute Barometer, conducted in November-December 2013, which shows that a large percentage of Spaniards (concretely 34%) believe

---

6 Other significant disinvestments by Chinese companies in Spain, such as the sales of Campofrío, Naturgas Energía or a 20% stake in the Osborne Group by WH Group Limited, China Three Gorges, and Fosun respectively, should be understood in a wider corporate strategic framework and have raised no criticism in Spain.

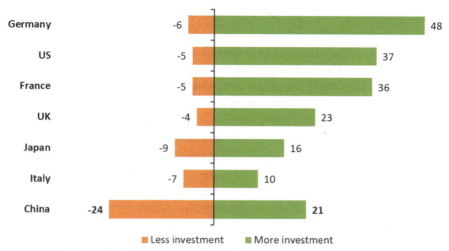

FIGURE 2.12 From which countries would you like Spain to receive more or less investments?
ᵃ Elcano Royal Institute Barometer, Elcano Royal Institute, http://
www.realinstitutoelcano.org/wps/portal/rielcano_es/encuesta?WCM_GLOBAL
_CONTEXT=/elcano/elcano_es/barometro/oleadabrie37, January 2016 (accessed
22 November 2018).
SOURCE: ELCANO ROYAL INSTITUTE BAROMETER, JANUARY 2016.ᵃ

that China is the biggest investor in Spain, while only 17% think it is Germany, 10% France and 8% the United States. In reality, China is only the tenth biggest investor in Spain with 2.65% of the total stock of FDI received by Spain before 31 December 2015 (Pérez, 2018: 44).

What then explains this desire for proportionally less Chinese investment? This is not about people purely focusing on recent inward FDI flows, since China has never been one of the five main origins of Spain's inward FDI and it is far behind the flows from many OECD countries. More research needs to be done on this topic but two plausible explanations are that companies from non-OECD countries generate less trust in Spain than OECD companies; along with the envy and rejection generated in some sectors of Spanish society by the economic success of the Chinese community in the context of the deep economic crisis that the country has gone through between 2009 and 2014.

4 Spanish Perceptions of BRI and Actions Taken

Although the BRI is barely known or paid attention to by the Spanish public, it has attracted considerable attention from the political and economic elites in

Spain. Both the Spanish government, and the larger Spanish companies, have shown interest in being involved in China's BRI, since they regard it as an economic opportunity more than as a geostrategic risk. There are three sectors in which expectations concerning potential opportunities for Spanish companies are particularly high: construction and management of large infrastructures; cultural tourism; and food exports. Businesses in these sectors have already started to position themselves to grasp potential opportunities. The general understanding among the interviewed officials and business representatives is that these business opportunities might emerge both in Spain and China, as well as in third countries. This was reflected during Xi Jinping's visit to Spain in November 2018 in point number 4 of the joint declaration and the signature of a memorandum of understanding for cooperation in third markets, 2018.[7]

Correspondingly, other effects likely related to the BRI, are the increase of the stake of Hutchison Whampoa in the port of Barcelona and the acquisition by COSCO of a 51% stake in Noatum, the biggest Spanish port terminal operator. By contrast, overseas business opportunities in third countries are mostly expected to be available for the larger Spanish construction and engineering firms.

There is not much interest in the BRI outside business, academic and think-tank circles. Hence, no opinion poll has been conducted in Spain on this topic. The actors that see more opportunities are construction companies, which are keen to obtain contracts in third countries along the Belt and Road, and firms in the tourism and agribusiness sectors (Serra, 2016).

A number of ministries and official institutions have allocated some of their researchers to follow developments within the BRI and the Spanish government has begun to include BRI-related topics in the official agenda concerning China. Through various events and information seminars in Spain and China, the Government has started to promote the idea that the BRI presents business opportunities for several sectors of the Spanish economy. In June 2016 for instance, the Spanish trade office in Beijing organised a Silk Road seminar for Spanish companies specialising in building and managing infrastructures. This is one of the reasons why Spain relatively quickly became a founding member of the Asian Infrastructure Investment Bank (AIIB), which it has always perceived as a key pillar of the BRI.

---

7 Declaración conjunta de la República Popular China y el Reino de España sobre el fortalecimiento de la Asociación Estratégica Integral en un Cambio de Época, Ministerio de Asuntos Exteriores, Unión Europea y Cooperación, https://www.lamoncloa.gob.es/presidente/actividades/Documents/2018/281118-Declaración%20Conjunta%20España%20-%20China.pdf, 28 November 2018 (accessed 24 February 2020).

Spanish public agencies such as the trade office in Beijing and some semi-public organizations like *Casa Asia* and the Spain-China Council, have organised, or helped to organise, several events related to the BRI, both in Spain and China. Some of them have involved the participation of high-level officials. For instance, the then Spanish Foreign Minister, José García-Margallo, closed the Second Silk Road Forum organised in Madrid in October 2015 and showed great enthusiasm about the new business opportunities that the BRI might bring, declaring that: "Spain is committed to the New Silk Road project". Along the same lines, the Spanish Prime Minister, Mariano Rajoy, attended the first Belt and Road Cooperation Forum and the Minister of Foreign Affairs, Josep Borrell, attended the second.

On the other hand, some of the BRI related opportunities, such as Chinese interest in investing in Mediterranean ports, are questioned because of potential risks. Although Spain hosts the two busiest cargo ports in the Mediterranean Sea, Algeciras and Valencia, and COSCO spent EUR 203 million in June 2017 to buy a 51% stake in Noatum, the $3.3 billion deal to build a deep-sea port in Cherchell illustrates that China has chosen Algeria, not Spain, as its maritime platform in the Western Mediterranean. If this operation materializes successfully, this new port would compete in the medium term with Spanish ports for traffic on the long transoceanic routes and would reduce the role of Spanish ports as redistribution platforms for North Africa.

As businesses and the government have increased their interest in the BRI, the Spanish media have also started to cover the initiative. Most of the coverage focuses on the economic side of the project, but the geopolitical and geostrategic dimensions have slowly come to the fore. The Catalan newspaper *La Vanguardia*, for example, devoted a whole issue of its monthly magazine to the BRI, cautioning as to how this Chinese initiative may exacerbate geopolitical tensions in Eurasia and the multiple difficulties of all sorts that it would have to overcome to be successful.[8] Nevertheless, this piece on the BRI implications for Spain is adamant about advocating for Spain's active participation in this project (Rios, 2016). Interestingly, thus far there have been very few op-eds on the topic, and those that have been published tend to judge the BRI in a positive light. Internationally recognised figures such as Javier Solana, Ana Palacio, and former president José Luis Rodriguez Zapatero, have

---

8 Rodríguez, A., China, la nueva ruta de la seda, La Vanguardia Dossier Nº60, https://www.lavanguardia.com/vanguardia-dossier/20160315/40442029836/china-nueva-ruta-seda-vanguardia-dossier.html, 15 March 2016 (accessed 22 November 2018).

all welcomed the BRI as a Chinese endeavour to bring China and Europe closer together.[9]

In conclusion, the image of China in Spain is both stereotyped and ambivalent. China enjoys a better image in Spain than some Latin-American countries with more cultural affinities to Spain and much better than other non-OECD countries like Morocco, Iran, Russia and Saudi Arabia. On the other hand, the Spanish population has a significantly better image of the traditional partners of Spain than of China and shows some concern about the rise of the latter, and in particular about the implications for the Spanish economy. In that regard, there is a gap between the attitudes favoured by political and economic elites and society at large. The political and economic elites tend to emphasize the opportunities brought by the development of the Chinese economy, for example, through direct investment and the Belt and Road Initiative, whereas society at large tends to be more indifferent or to perceive the Chinese economy as a threat.

Bibliography

Esteban, M. (editor) (2015), China in Latin America: Repercussions for Spain, Madrid: Elcano Royal Institute.

Kurlantzick, J. (2007), China's Charm: How China's Soft Power is Transforming the World? New Haven: Yale University Press.

Lampton, D. M. (2008), The Three Faces of Chinese Power: Might, Money, and Minds, Berkeley: University of California Press.

Li, M. (editor) (2009), Soft Power: China's Emerging Strategy in International Politics, Plymouth: Lexington Books.

Noya, J. (2005), Sombras chinescas: un análisis de la imagen de China en España, Análisis del Real Instituto Elcano 121.

Nye, J. S. (2004), Soft Power: The Means to Success in World Politics, New York: Public Affairs Press.

---

9 Palacio, A., Reactivemos la ruta de la seda, El País, https://elpais.com/elpais/2014/05/07/opinion/1399478370_834777.html, 9 May 2014 (accessed 22 November 2018); Solana, J., El desafío de la nueva ruta de la seda, El País, https://elpais.com/elpais/2015/03/25/opinion/1427315633_973822.html, 7 April 2015 (accessed 22 November 2018); Zapatero describe como "oportunidad para Europa y Asia" el tren España-China, Expansión, http://www.expansion.com/agencia/efe/2015/06/18/20854948.html, 18 June 2015 (accessed 22 November 2018).

Pérez, S. (coordinator) (2018), China: De país emergente a líder mundial, Boletín Económico ICE 3097, 44.

Rios, X. (2016), España y la ruta de la seda, Vanguardia Dossier 60, pp. 90–95.

Serra, J. (2016), La estrategia China de «Una Franja, Una Ruta», posibles consecuencias para España, y oportunidades para las empresas españolas, Boletín Económico ICE 3072, pp. 39–48.

Zheng, Y., and Zhang, C. (2007), "Soft Power in International Politics and China's Soft Power" (国际政治中的软力量以及对中国软力量的观察), World Economics and Politics (世界经济与政治) 7, pp. 6–12.

CHAPTER 3

Kyiv-Beijing Relations in the Context of the Ukrainian-Russian Conflict

Interests, Concerns and Images

Olexiy Haran

1   Introduction

When the Soviet Union collapsed and Ukraine gained its independence in 1991, most diplomatic efforts of the new state were devoted to maintaining a delicate balance between Russia and the West while officially proclaiming the country's aim "to return to Europe". Despite these priorities, the Ukrainian elite hoped that relations with the PRC, an emerging economic giant, would have great potential. Kyiv considered that it could be attractive to Beijing given Ukraine's role in the post-Soviet space, its transit potential, military-industrial complex, and agriculture. In reality, however, the practical steps lagged behind officially proclaimed goals.

The Euromaidan (Revolution of Dignity), subsequent Russian attack on the territorial integrity of Ukraine, and Western sanctions against Moscow, created a new framework not only for Ukrainian foreign policy but also for international relations. For the first time in history, the country, which voluntarily rejected its nuclear arsenal, was attacked by a great power, even though its security was assured by all the great nuclear powers (the 1994 Budapest memorandum and relevant statements by France and China). Consequently, the Ukrainian elite and society as a whole now look with caution and even mistrust at the actions of great powers and their international obligations, especially regarding their position toward the Ukrainian-Russian conflict. To what extent will this influence China's image in Ukraine and Kyiv-Beijing relations? This article will attempt to provide answers to these questions.

First, we will briefly cover Kyiv's approaches to China before the 2014 events. Then we will move to international (including Chinese) reaction to Russia's annexation of Crimea and to the changes in the geopolitical orientations of Ukrainians which created a totally new framework both for Ukrainian society and Kyiv's foreign policy. We include data on the images of several countries in Ukrainian public opinion. The following section analyses how the crisis over

Ukraine influences the West-Russia-China triangle and how the PRC's position is viewed in Ukraine. The final section includes recommendations from Ukrainian Sinologists, according to whom, economic cooperation and the potential increase in Chinese investments in Ukraine may well become the key to deepening Beijing's interest in the strategic stabilization of Ukraine.

2   Before 2014: Building Background and Unrealized Plans

Before 2004, Kyiv was gradually moving towards Europe while trying at the same time to preserve a so called "multi-vector policy" between Russia and the West. This policy was not in contradiction of, and even created further possibilities for, the development of relations with China.

First, in the context of Ukraine's "multi-vector policy" China was seen by Ukrainian decision-makers as an additional pole to balance Russia and the West. Under Ukrainian President Leonid Kuchma (1994–2004), China's image in Ukraine seemed quite attractive.[1] Second, since the Gorbachov era, Chinese economic reforms were viewed as a model of opening a state-controlled economy to market mechanisms. Third, from an ideological point of view, given the nostalgia for Soviet era social benefits, Chinese "market socialism" was easy to be placed between socialism/state regulation and market/capitalism.

For China, Ukraine represented the second largest post-Soviet state. It was Ukraine whose relations with Russia to a great extent defined the configuration of the post-Soviet space, the future of the Commonwealth of Independent States (CIS) and the Customs Union which Russia wanted to create but which Ukraine resisted.[2]

However, after the 2004 Orange revolution, Kyiv-Beijing relations stagnated. China was suspicious as regards the "colour revolutions". On the Ukrainian side, "Orange" president Viktor Yushchenko (2005–2010) concentrated on European

---

1   Goncharuk A., Hobova E., Kiktenko V., Koval A., and Koshovy S. (2016). Foreign Policy Audit: Ukraine – China. Discussion Paper. Kyiv: Institute of World Policy, p. 13. http://neweurope.org.ua/wp-content/uploads/2017/10/Audyt-zovnishnoyi-polityky_Ukr_Kytaj _eng_inet.pdf; Mykal O. [Мыкал О.]. (2016). Japono-kytaiskaja dilemma Ukrainy [Японо-китайская дилемма Украини]. Novoje vremia [Новое время], 11 Oct. https://nv.ua/opinion/mykal/japono-kitajskaja-dilemma-ukrainy-241875.html.

2   Ukraine was a founding country of the CIS in December 1991 but it refused to sign the CIS statute.

and Euro-Atlantic vectors while becoming ineffective in domestic politics.[3] As a result, he neglected relations with China and Japan.[4]

The paradox is that the highest point in relations with China was reached under Ukrainian President Viktor Yanukovych (2010–2014), whose authoritarian style and refusal in autumn 2013 to sign a long-awaited Association Agreement with the EU, led to the Euromaidan – mass protests against his methods of ruling. Under Yanukovych, huge concessions to Russia were made,[5] and at the same time he somehow returned to the "multi-vector policy". His team used Kuchma-era arguments, trying to play on contradictions between the West and Russia and balancing their influences.[6]

Kyiv and Beijing exchanged official visits at the highest level: President Yanukovych visited China in 2010 and then Chinese President Hu Jintao visited Ukraine in 2011. Yanukovych made another visit to China in December 2013 (at the time of the Euromaidan protests in the centre of the Ukrainian capital). As a result of this visit, after fifteen years of negotiations, the Treaty on Friendship and Cooperation was finally signed (for ten years), and a strategic partnership was proclaimed. Also, both sides signed a memorandum on the construction of a new deep-sea terminal in Crimea and the reconstruction of Sevastopol sea-fishing terminal. China planned to invest $13 billion in Ukraine (while Russia's annexation of Crimea in 2014 undermined these plans, they could be renewed in the south of Ukraine which has an access to the Black Sea).[7]

The Yanukovych regime was ineffective and corrupt, which prevented the realization of these bilateral plans. As a result of the Euromaidan, in February 2014 the parliament restored the Constitution which limits the power of the president. Yanukovych proceeded to violate the agreement with the opposition and did not sign agreed constitutional changes. He finally left the country for Russia.[8]

---

3   Haran O. (2014). What Went Wrong with the Orange Revolution? Magisterium. Politychni Studii. [Магістеріум. Політичні студії.] 58, pp. 50–55; Lushnycky A., and Riabchuk M. (editors) (2009). Ukraine on Its Meandering Path Between East and West. Bern – Berlin – Bruxelles etc.: Peter Lang.

4   Mykal O. [Мыкал О.] (2016). Japono-kytaiskaja dilemma Ukrainy.

5   They included the adoption of non-bloc status and the lease of the military base in Sevastopol (Crimea) to Russia until 2042, with subsequent extension every five years.

6   Burkovsky P., and Haran O. (2011). Russian Expansion: A Challenge and Opportunity for the Emerging Authoritarian Regime in Ukraine. In: Schmemann A., and Welt C. (editors), New Balances: Russia, the EU, and the "Post-Soviet West". Policy Perspectives. v. 11. Washington: The George Washington University, pp. 21–26. http://www.ponarseurasia.org/memo/russian-expansion-challenge-and-opportunity-emerging-authoritarian-regime-ukraine.

7   Mykal O. (2016). Why China Is Interested in Ukraine. The Diplomat, 3 Oct. 2016. https://thediplomat.com/2016/03/why-china-is-interested-in-ukraine.

8   For analysis of the Euromaidan, see, for example, Stepanenko V., and Pylynskyi Ya. (editors) (2014). Ukraine after Euromaidan: Challenges and Hopes. Bern – Berlin – Bruxelles etc.: Peter Lang, pp. 73–83.

The reserved Chinese position on Euromaidan's victory reflected the traditional Beijing approach to regime changes. Nevertheless, China recognized early presidential elections in Ukraine in May 2014. At the same time, according to the views of some Ukrainian sinologists, the new government again repeated the mistakes of the Orange period by neglecting Asia, and specifically the Chinese direction of Ukrainian foreign policy.[9] To a certain extent, though, this was understandable, as the new Ukrainian authorities had to concentrate on other more pressing problems: economic stabilization, the Association Agreement and fighting Russian intervention.

3   Annexation of Crimea and International Reaction

In 2014, the crisis over Ukraine became the most serious European crisis since the end of the Cold War. According to the 1994 Budapest memorandum, Kyiv gave up its nuclear arsenal (the third largest in the world – larger than the British, French, and Chinese arsenals combined) in exchange for "security assurances" (but not "security guarantees") of territorial integrity from the US, UK, and Russia. France and China issued relevant statements. The parties agreed to respect Ukraine's borders; to abstain from the use or threat of force against Ukraine; to support Kyiv when an attempt was made to put pressure on it by economic coercion; and to bring any incident of aggression by a nuclear power before the UN Security Council.[10]

However, in March 2014, Russia annexed Crimea. Russian soldiers without insignia moved from the base in Sevastopol to other strategic points of Crimea.[11] Under armed occupation, a pseudo-referendum was held on 16 March 2014, in contradiction to all Ukrainian laws and international procedures. It was a clear violation of the 1994 Budapest memorandum and the 1997 Ukrainian-Russian treaty. It raised doubts about the credibility of "security assurances" provided by great powers, especially for those countries deciding whether or not to adhere to nuclear non-proliferation.

---

9   Goncharuk A. et al. (2016), p. 22.
10   UN General Assembly document A/49/765, UN Security Council document S/1994/1399, 19 December 1994, Memorandum on Security Assurances in connection with Ukraine's Accession to the Treaty on the Non-Proliferation of Nuclear Weapons.
11   Russian President Vladimir Putin denied it, but recognized it in a documentary which appeared on Russian TV a year later. See, Russia Today, 15 March 2015. http://russian.rt.com/article/79606 (in Russian).

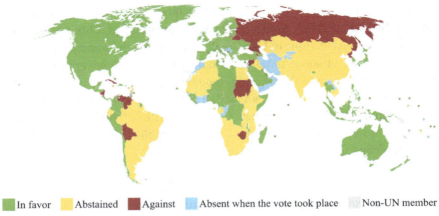

In favor   Abstained   Against   Absent when the vote took place   Non-UN member

FIGURE 3.1   Results of the UN General Assembly vote about the territorial integrity of Ukraine
(27 March 2014)
MAP FROM "UNITED NATIONS GENERAL ASSEMBLY RESOLUTION 68/262,"
HTTPS://EN.WIKIPEDIA.ORG/WIKI/UNITED_NATIONS_GENERAL_ASSEMBLY_
RESOLUTION_68/262.

It became the first case of an annexation in Europe (which was not the case of either Kosovo or Northern Cyprus) since the end of World War II. On 27 March 2014, the UN Assembly General resolution on the territorial integrity of Ukraine, which declared the change in Crimea's status illegal, was supported by 100 countries (including South Korea, Japan, the Philippines, Indonesia, Thailand, Malaysia, Singapore), with only 11 against (Russia, North Korea, Sudan, Syria, Bolivia, Cuba, Nicaragua, Zimbabwe, Venezuela, Armenia, and Belarus).

China's official position – repeated several times – was in favour of the territorial integrity of Ukraine.[12] But China, India, Vietnam, Pakistan and Afghanistan were among the 58 countries which abstained, and another 24 countries were absent.[13] Many Third World countries wrongly viewed the

---

12   See, for example: China Respects Ukraine's Sovereignty, Territorial Integrity: Premier. China Daily, 15 March 2015. http://www.chinadaily.com.cn/china/2015twosession/2015 -03/15/content_19815476.htm.

13   Qin Gang, a spokesman of China's Ministry of Foreign Affairs, clarified his country's position: "China always advocates respect for the sovereignty and territorial integrity of any country. China always sticks to this main course of foreign policy. The Chinese side believes that the Ukrainian crisis has a complicated historical background and is caused by modern realities. All this must be analyzed and taken into account when resolving the crisis." See: China Calls on All Stakeholders to Work towards a Political Settlement of the Crisis in Ukraine – The MFA of China. Xinhua, 17 March 2014. http://russian.people.com.cn/31521/ 8568055.html . Quoted from Goncharuk A.et al. (2016), p. 18.

annexation of Crimea in terms of the Cold War between enlarged NATO and Russia and were more afraid of 'Western domination' than their own problems with separatism. In some cases, such as the huge Russian pressure on Kazakhstan and other Central Asian countries, their decision not to vote 'against' may be interpreted as a sign of disagreement with Russia. The main consequence of China's abstention was the fact the resolution in favour of territorial integrity of Ukraine was not blocked.

Yet, for Russian President Vladimir Putin, international response to the occupation of Crimea looked weak[14] and he decided to repeat the 'Crimean scenario' in other Ukrainian southern and eastern regions. Russia tried to create civic unrest (the so called "Russian spring") and, when this failed, moved first irregular militia and then, in August 2014, regular armed forces into the Donbas. Serious Western economic (so called "sectoral") sanctions came only after Malaysian Airlines flight MH 17 was shot down by a Russian missile complex on 17 July 2014, and Russian regular troops entered the Donbas.

4 Changes in Ukrainian Public Opinion: A New Framework for Kyiv's Foreign Policy

Putin's view that Ukrainians and Russians are "one nation, one ethnos"[15] appeared to be a huge mistake and plans to either control all of Ukraine or at least to split it, failed. Contrary to certain stereotypes, the contemporary Ukrainian state proclaimed in 1991 is based not so much on ethnicity as on territorial, "inclusive" nationalism. Ukraine, compared to the Balkans, Caucasus,

---

14   In the absence of sanctions from the UN Security Council because of Russia's veto power, the key principle for introducing sanctions was the common approach from the US, other members of G7, and the EU. The first reaction was to cancel the G8 Summit in Sochi (Russia), freezing Russia's participation in G8, suspending EU talks with Russia on visa issues and on a new EU-Russia agreement. After the "referendum" in Crimea, Western countries introduced visa bans for individuals and froze the assets of individuals and legal entities involved in annexation. Then the ban came on imports from Crimea, investment in Crimea, the export of certain goods and technology concerning the transport, telecommunications and energy sectors. On 10 April 2014, the Parliamentary Assembly of the Council of Europe (PACE) suspended the voting rights of the Russian delegation and its representation in the institution's leading bodies. For more on this, see Haran O. (2015), 'Ukrainian-Russian Conflict and Its Implications for Northeast Asia', International Journal of Korean Unification Studies 24(3), pp.131–137. In spring 2019, using financial blackmail by stopping its payments to PACE, Russia successfully lobbied the restoration of its rights in PACE, without making any concessions regarding Crimea.

15   Russia Today, 19 June 2015. http://russian.rt.com/article/98387 (in Russian).

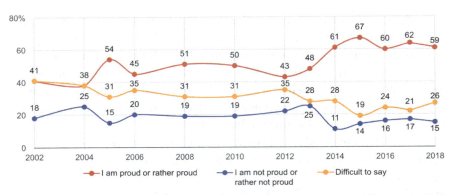

FIGURE 3.2   To what extent are you proud, or not proud, of being a citizen of Ukraine? (%)
SOURCE: ANNUAL POLLS "UKRAINIAN SOCIETY: THE MONITORING OF
THE SOCIAL CHANGES" CONDUCTED BY THE INSTITUTE OF SOCIOLOGY,
NATIONAL ACADEMY OF SCIENCES OF UKRAINE. SEE, HTTP://DIF.ORG.UA/
UPLOADS/PDF/2077223209599C1813B0FA85.06804039.PDF

and Russia, had avoided armed domestic conflicts until 2014. The paradox
is that, despite the war in the Donbas, Putin's aggression actually cemented
Ukraine's political identity (see figure 3.2).

Thus, the very term "Ukrainian crisis" is misleading. The domestic crisis
ended with the removal of Yanukovych, decisions by the Ukrainian parliament,
a return to the balanced 2004 constitutional reform, and early presidential and
parliamentary elections in 2014 recognised by international organizations as
free and fair.

The map below also clearly shows that it was not a "civil war", and by August
2014 pro-Russian fighters were on the verge of collapse.[16] They were saved only
by the invasion of regular Russian troops, which was part of Moscow's unde-
clared, "hybrid" war against Ukraine. However, even after that, the occupied
areas of the Donbas comprised only 3% of Ukrainian territory.

It is noteworthy that the language Beijing uses regarding the conflict contains
elements close to Moscow's language – in particular on "defending the rights
of Russians" or "the people of the Donbas". Explaining why Beijing abstained

---

16   The poll of the respectable Kyiv International Institute of Sociology in April 2014 con-
        firmed that separatism did not have support in the south and east of the country with the
        exception of the Donbas, but even there its supporters were in a minority. The same was
        true of Moscow's plans for the 'federalization' of Ukraine which was a tool to follow the
        Crimean 'example'. Even in the Donbas, polls confirmed that a majority favored decen-
        tralization, but not federalization. See, Zerkalo Nedeli [Зеркало недели], 19 April 2014,
        p. 6, http://gazeta.zn.ua/internal/yugo-vostok-vetv-dreva-nashego-_.html.

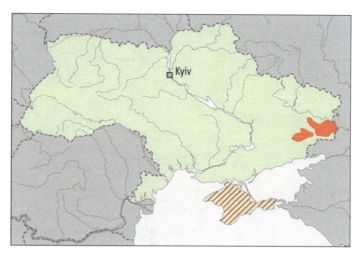

FIGURE 3.3 The area controlled by Russia's proxies by 24 August 2014 occupied territories in the Donbas in red. The territory of annexed Crimea is hatched.
SOURCE: HARAN (2015). P.135.

during the vote of the UN resolution on the territorial integrity of Ukraine, Chinese representatives pointed out that this resolution (which denounced the legality of the so-called referendum in Crimea) would "increase confrontation" and "only further complicate the situation"; the "Ukrainian crisis has complex historic background and is due to present realities".[17] On 2 February 2017, during the session of the UN Security Council called because of the escalation provoked by pro-Russian proxies, Chinese representatives demanded a ceasefire stressing that a long-term solution should take into account the "rights and hopes of all the regions and ethnic groups to find a balance among the interests of all the parties".[18] The Ukrainian side was therefore confused by the language Beijing used.

In Ukraine, Russia followed the same path as it had previously taken in Moldova and Georgia: war, separatism, economic destabilization, attempts to create social unrest leading, in Moscow's view, to regime change, and a blockade of the implementation of association agreements between these countries and the EU.

---

17   UN General Assembly Adopts Resolution Affirming Ukraine's Territorial Integrity. Xinhua. 28 March 2014. http://news.xinhuanet.com/english/world/2014-03/28/c_126325576.htm.
18   Quoted in: Institute of World Policy and TRUMAN Agency (2017), Foreign Policy Audit: Index of Relations, N 3 (January – March), p.19. https://truman.ua/sites/default/files/2018-02/Index%20of%20Relations%20%23%203.pdf.

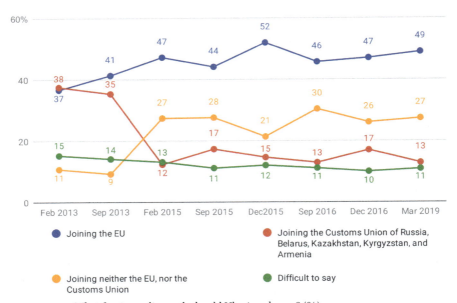

FIGURE 3.4   What foreign policy path should Ukraine choose? (%)
SOURCE: DATA COMPILED FROM THE POLLS CONDUCTED BY THE KYIV
INTERNATIONAL INSTITUTE OF SOCIOLOGY "WHICH INTEGRATION
DIRECTION SHOULD UKRAINE TAKE?"(HTTP://WWW.KIIS.COM.UA/
?LANG=UKR&CAT=REPORTS&ID=584&PAGE=6; HTTP://KIIS.COM.UA/
?LANG=UKR&CAT=REPORTS&ID=713&PAGE=1; HTTP://KIIS.COM.UA/
?LANG=UKR&CAT=REPORTS&ID=836&PAGE=6)

Contrary to Putin's plans, Russia's attack contributed to a dramatic shift in
the geopolitical orientations of Ukrainian society. Support for integration into
the Russia-led Customs Union totally collapsed (see figure 3.4).

Re-orientation towards joining NATO is even more striking. Previously in
Ukraine, supporters of NATO membership were always a minority but since a
potential referendum in 2015, Ukrainians would overwhelmingly say "yes" to
NATO (see figure 3.5). As the non-bloc status did not prevent Russian aggression, it was cancelled by the Ukrainian parliament in December 2014. In
early 2019, the strategic course to join the EU and NATO was enshrined in the
Constitution by the Ukrainian parliament.

Amid profound changes in favour of the EU and NATO, 85% of Ukrainians
view China mostly positively or at least neutrally (see table 3.1). This is a very
important finding which testifies to the good public atmosphere favourable to
the development of bilateral relations. It should be noted also that in Ukraine
there is no political force which is against relations with Beijing (with the
exception of the marginal far right forces).

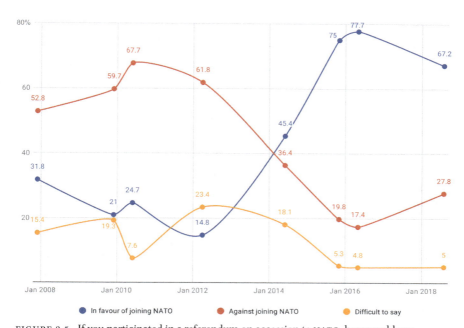

FIGURE 3.5   If you participated in a referendum on accession to NATO, how would you vote? (*%, among those who would take part in the referendum*) The changes during 2016–2018 can be explained by Ukrainian frustration with the inability of Western partners to provide a ceasefire in the Donbas and the activization of Russia's information attacks within Ukraine.

SOURCE: RESULTS OF THE NATIONWIDE POLLS CONDUCTED BY THE ILKO KUCHERIV DEMOCRATIC INITIATIVES FOUNDATION, KYIV (HTTP://DIF.ORG. UA/ARTICLE/REFERENDUM-SHCHODO-VSTUPU-DO-NATO-BUV-BI-VIGRANIY-PROTE-TSE-PITANNYA-DILIT-UKRAINU; HTTP://DIF.ORG.UA/ARTICLE/GROMADSKA-DUMKA-NASELENNYA-UKRAINI-PRO-NATO; HTTPS://DIF.ORG. UA/ARTICLE/SHCHO-UKRAINTSI-DUMAYUT-I-ZNAYUT-PRO-NATO243).

Beijing does not approve of NATO expansion to the east but it welcomed the signing of the EU-Ukraine Association Agreement as Ukraine may secure not only transport routes, but also an industrial base for Chinese producers to have easier access to European markets. Actually, given the currently limited EU financial resources, Brussels may also be interested in modernizing Ukraine through Chinese investments.[19]

This view, however, is challenged by some analysts who underline the geopolitical competition between the great powers. Steven Tsang, director of the China Institute at the School of Oriental and Asian Studies, University

---

19   Goncharuk A. et al. (2016), pp. 4–5.

TABLE 3.1   What is your attitude to …? (%)

	Very warm	Warm	Neutral	Cold	Very good	Difficult to say
1. Belarus	10.8	47.9	34.9	3.6	0.1	2.7
2. Georgia	5.4	40.4	45.7	4.2	0.6	3.7
3. European Union	8.1	43.3	40.1	3.8	1	3.8
4. Canada	10.4	40.2	41	3.3	0.9	4.2
5. China	1.9	24.8	58.5	8.4	0.9	5.5
6. Lithuania	6.3	38.4	45.4	3.9	1.2	4.7
7. Germany	8.2	40.6	42.7	3.2	1.2	4.1
8. The UN	3.5	31.2	49.1	6	1.5	8.8
9. Poland	8.4	44.8	39	3.9	0.6	3.2
10. Russia	2.6	19.1	27.3	24.4	23.4	3.3
11. The US	4.3	33.3	48.3	7.6	2.2	4.3
12. Japan	2.5	30.2	57.4	3.6	0.9	5.4

THE POLL WAS CONDUCTED BY THE ILKO KUCHERIV DEMOCRATIC INITIATIVES FOUNDA-
TION JOINTLY WITH THE KYIV INTERNATIONAL INSTITUTE OF SOCIOLOGY ON 23 OCTO-
BER – 5 NOVEMBER 2017.

of London, stresses that Beijing "does not want Ukraine back in Russia's orbit, but it does not want to see Ukraine in Western Europe's orbit either". Therefore, he continues, "Beijing is supportive of Russia's efforts to restrain Ukraine's relations with the West, though it also prefers Ukraine not to be so destabilized that it becomes bad for Chinese business".[20] According to Franklin Holcomb, from the Institute for the Study of War, Washington DC, there is both competition and convergence of interests between Moscow and Beijing regarding Ukraine. For Russia "China's ruthlessly pragmatic investment [in Ukraine] is preferable to similar Western initiatives which come tied with democratic values, which Moscow perceives as a strategic threat".[21] This way of geopolitical thinking reflects the complexities of the implications of

---

20   Quoted in: The Daily Signal, internet platform of the conservative The Heritage Foundation: Peterson N. (2017). As China Invests in Ukraine, Russia Stands to Gain. The Daily Signal, 8 Dec. http://dailysignal.com/2017/12/08/as-china-invests-in-ukraine-russia -stands-to-gain/.

21   Ibid.

the Ukrainian-Russian conflict for relations between the West-China-Russia, discussed below.

5   Consequences of the Ukraine Crisis for the West-China-Russia Triangle

Russian intervention in Ukraine led to huge geopolitical changes and concerns. It undermined the credibility of the great powers and created precedents which are dangerous for South Korea, Japan and other U.S. allies in Asia.[22] Washington was unable to establish clearly defined "red lines" regarding the war in Syria or the North Korean nuclear issue, and this became even more visible when the then U.S. President Barack Obama excluded military support for Ukraine from the very beginning of the conflict. The U.S. reaction to the annexation of Crimea, instead of creating a "red line", was seen by Russia as a "red carpet" for further actions in the Donbas.[23] Moreover, the annexation of Crimea was seen in North Korea as a chance to increase the margin of provocation in the peninsula. It increased tension in the Korean peninsula, making Pyongyang rely more on nuclear weapons.[24]

As an immediate result of the crisis, U.S. allies are seeking additional guarantees from Washington. Support of Asian allies for the U.S. position on Crimea may also help Washington's policy in Asia. Therefore, the role of allies in U.S. policy in the region has also increased. As Dmitri Trenin, director of the Carnegie Moscow Center, suggests, the crisis over Ukraine will strengthen, not Russian, but U.S. positions in relation to European and Asian allies, with "only one exception: China". One of his articles is tellingly entitled 'China's Victory in Ukraine'.[25] At the same time, Fyodor Lukyanov, Chairman of Russia's Council for Foreign and Defence Policy, goes much further in blackmailing the West in his political "fantasy" about the year 2025 in *Die Welt*: 'If the Russians and

---

22   This section is based on: Haran (2015). Ukrainian-Russian Conflict and Its Implications for Northeast Asia. International Journal of Korean Unification Studies 24 (3), pp.139–148. http://repo.kinu.or.kr/bitstream/2015.oak/2435/1/IJKUS_24-3.pdf.

23   Kotani T. (2014). Japan's 'Proactive Contribution to Peace' and the Annexation of Crimea. The National Bureau of Asian Research, 22 April. http://www.nbr.org/research/activity.aspx?id=422.

24   For more, see Haran (2015), pp. 151–152.

25   Trenin D. (2014). China's Victory in Ukraine. The Carnegie Moscow Center, 31 July. http://carnegie.ru/2014/07/31/china-s-victory-in-ukraine/hjht.

Chinese march together'.[26] We may ask ourselves: what was the real, rather than perceived, reaction of China to the conflict over Ukraine?

Neither the great Western powers nor China have fulfilled their obligations to denuclearized Ukraine under the Budapest memorandum, although Chinese commitments were much more limited and it was a unilateral and quite amorphous declaration that they submitted to the UN General Assembly in December 1994: China "fully understands the desire of Ukraine for security assurance … The Chinese Government has constantly opposed the practice of exerting political, economic or other pressure in international relations … China recognizes and respects the independence, sovereignty and territorial integrity of Ukraine".[27] China was the only permanent member of the UN Security Council which abstained during the vote of the UN General Assembly's resolution on the territorial integrity of Ukraine. However, one can treat this not as a Russian victory, but rather Russia's failure, as China's position did not block the resolution.

Beijing is wary of Western support for Chinese dissidents which, in perspective, could lead to regime change. Xinhua somehow followed the Russian argumentation of Western involvement in "regime change" in Ukraine in a commentary under the eloquent title 'The failure of the West in Ukraine'.[28] At the same time, China does not recognize Russia's reference to the "self-determination of Crimean people" because of debate over the proclamation of independence for Taiwan, the problems of Tibet and Xinjiang. Sticking to the principle of territorial integrity, Beijing had to freeze its economic projects in annexed Crimea.

What is much more important for Beijing in practical terms is the fact that it benefits considerably from Russia's isolation in the West and Russia's potential transformation into the "younger partner" of China. The official Chinese position is opposition to sanctions introduced by the West against Russia. In turn, Russia can blackmail the West by its *rapprochement* with China. This *rapprochement* started long before the Crimean crisis, but after the crisis it moved to another level. Trying to avoid sanctions and isolation, Russia moved closer to

---

26   Lukjanow F. (2015). Wenn Russen und Chinesen gemeinsam marschieren. Die Welt, 30 March. www.welt.de/debatte/kommentare/article138880727/Wenn-Russen-und -Chinesen-gemeinsam-marschieren.html. Quoted in: Umland A. (2015). Towards a Greater Asia? The Prospects of a Sino-Russian Entente. Eurozine. 22 June. http://www.eurozine .com/articles/2015-06-22-umland-en.html.

27   United Nations General Assembly, A/49/783, 14 December 1994. Statement of the Chinese Government on the Security Assurance to Ukraine Issued on 4 December 1994.

28   Xinhua.(2014). Kommentarij: Porazhenije Zapada v Ukraine [Комментарий: Поражение Запада в Украине], 7 March 2014. http://russian.people.com.cn/95181/8558922.html.

China, which Beijing uses to its own ends. But this *rapprochement* has natural limitations given the competition and contradictions between the two countries.[29] Opening Asian markets to Russia also has limitations due to the security concerns of U.S. allies and present Western sanctions. Events in Crimea, Russia's drift towards China and new opportunities for Beijing, increase the role of U.S. guarantees for its allies in Asia which strengthens the necessity of an alliance with Washington.

Chinese President Xi Jinping visited Moscow from 8–10 May 2015, and participated in the celebration of the 70th anniversary of Nazi Germany's defeat (most major Western leaders did not visit Moscow's military parade because of Russia's intervention in Ukraine). Chinese soldiers participated in this parade, as did Russian soldiers later in Beijing to celebrate the 70th anniversary of the defeat of Japan and the end of World War II. The Russia-China Joint Statement on Deepening Comprehensive Partnership and Strategic Interaction and Promoting Mutually Beneficial Cooperation, adopted during President Xi's visit, even mentioned the "legitimate interests of all regions and peoples (and here, this author wonders if the term "ethnic groups" has been wrongly translated in the Russian text of the document) of Ukraine".[30]

In December 2016, China voted against the UN resolution on human rights in annexed Crimea. However, as regards Ukrainian diplomacy, it is important to understand that this reflects China's traditional position which considers the international defence of human rights as interference in domestic affairs.

China can play its role in creating and maintaining a potential UN peacekeeping mission in the Donbas. It is true that among 21 Ukrainian non-governmental experts interviewed in September 2017,[31] none mentioned China among those countries whose participation they consider "the most beneficial for Ukraine". Most mentioned were the United Kingdom – 9, the USA – 7, Poland and the Baltics with 6 votes each. However, two experts mentioned China among the countries whose peacekeepers "would have been acceptable both for Russia and Ukraine", and in this category there was no clear leader (Germany obtained 6 votes and France 3). It is also clear that decisions on UN

29   Umland A. (2015).

30   President Rossii [Президент России]. 8 May 2015. http://www.kremlin.ru/supplement/ 4969.

31   "Peacekeeping mission in the Donbas: Is it desirable? Is it possible? On what terms?" The polling was conducted on 27–29 September 2017 by the Ilko Kucheriv Democratic Initiatives Foundation. http://dif.org.ua/article/mirotvorcha-misiya-na-donbasi-chi -bazhana-chi-mozhliva-za-yakikh-umov-opituvannya-ekspertiv.

peacekeeping missions can be taken only with the consent of the great powers, including Russia, who have a veto right in the UN Security Council.

6   How to Attract China: Economy above Politics – with Political Signals Required

Ukraine's interest in closer ties with China, a great nuclear power whose GDP (Purchasing Power Parity) is number 1 on the planet, is quite obvious, especially in the situation where there are both financial and politically conditioned limitations for aid from the West and a huge deterioration in economic relations with Russia.

In the context of the Chinese geopolitical Belt and Road Initiative, Ukraine is attractive for China because of the wide and comprehensive free trade area with the EU, proximity to the EU, and transit potential and possibility to bypass Russia (although competition with the transit route via Russia and Belarus is tough). In turn, Kyiv is considering joining the format of cooperation between China and Central-Eastern Europe known as "16+1" by transforming it into "17+1"[32] or at least obtaining the status of observer, like Belarus.[33]

Ukraine is one of the largest suppliers of modern weapons and military technology to China. According to SIPRI, in the period 2002–2016, Ukraine was the second largest exporter to China (16% of all military imports to the PRC) while Russia was the clear leader with 57%.[34] Using the problems in a Ukrainian economy weakened by war, Moscow is working hard to increase the role of Russia in this sector. During the years 2014–2018, Ukraine's share declined to 9%, while Russia's share increased to 70% and France moved up to second place, reaching 10%.[35] At the same time, a comparative advantage

32   Koshovy S. [Кошовий С.] (2017). Dosvid spivpratsi Kytaju i krain Tsentralnoi ta Skhidnoi Evropy u fromati «16+1» ta perspektyvy Ukrainy [Досвід співпраці Китаю і країн Центральної та Східної Європи у форматі «16+1» та перспективи України]. National Institute for Strategic Studies, June 2017, p. 17. http://old2.niss.gov.ua/content/articles/files/16plyus1-42a26.pdf.

33   Gerasymchuk S., Poita Yu. (2018). Ukraine-China after 2014: A New Chapter in the Relationship. Opportunities and Prospects, Obstacles and Risks. Kyiv: Friedrich Ebert Stiftung, p. 10. http://library.fes.de/pdf-files/bueros/ukraine/14703.pdf.

34   Blanchfield,K., Wezeman, P. D., and Wezeman, S. T. (2017). The State of Major Arms Transfers in 8 Graphics. SIPRI. www.sipri.org/commentary/blog/2017/state-major-arms-transfers-8-graphics.

35   Wezeman P.D., Fleurant A., Kuimova A., Tian N., Wezeman S.T. (2019). Trends in International Arms Transfers, 2018. SIPRI Fact Sheet, p. 6. https://www.sipri.org/sites/default/files/2019-03/fs_1903_at_2018.pdf.

for Ukraine is that Russian producers are under Western financial sanctions. There are ongoing projects of Ukrainian-Chinese cooperation in defence and the air and space industries. 2016 was marked by the signing of the Long-Term Ukrainian-Chinese Space Cooperation Program 2016–2020.[36]

Beijing's interest in Ukraine is also connected to the potential creation of so-called foreign food bases. As an example, in 2015, Ukraine overtook the U.S. as China's biggest corn supplier (although the dynamics are unstable as Beijing plans to decrease corn importation). The same year, China became the largest importer as regards Ukrainian agricultural products.[37]

However, there are concerns in Ukraine that Beijing may use Kyiv's current economic and political weaknesses to acquire Ukraine's lands, use the country as a mere agricultural and raw material base, and obtain secrets of Ukrainian industrial and military technologies.[38] China prefers to borrow technology and produce on its own. While providing loans, China brings its own engineering approaches, equipment, and workforce. Beijing has proposed the creation of a free-trade zone with Ukraine. However, in Kyiv there are concerns that in some spheres Ukrainian producers will not be able to compete with cheap Chinese goods.[39] Ukraine has a strong imbalance in trade with China, with a negative balance of $5.6 billion in 2019.[40]

Nevertheless, the change in atmosphere surrounding bilateral relations was signalled by the meeting of the two heads of state in Davos in January 2017. President Xi once again repeated that China "respects Ukrainian choice".[41] As a result, the PRC's Ambassador to Ukraine, Du Wei, on the 25th anniversary of diplomatic relations between the two countries, stressed: "The cold winter is over and now we welcome the lively spring".[42] In December 2017, Chinese Vice Premier Ma Kai visited Kyiv. During this visit, the long-awaited third session of the China-Ukraine Intergovernmental Commission took place. Ma Kai

---

36   For more on cooperation in these spheres, see Gerasymchuk S., Poita Yu. (2018), pp. 7–9.

37   Mykal O. (2016). Why China Is Interested in Ukraine.

38   Shpak Yu. Шпак Ю.]. (2017). Ukraina – Kitai: mezhu vorotami v Evropu i syrievoj koloniej Украина-Китай: между воротами в Европу и сырьевой колонией]. Golos.ua, 3 Feb. http://ru.golos.ua/ekonomika/ukrainakitay_mejdu_vorotami_v_evropu_i_syirevoy _koloniey_tablitsyi_5881

39   Ibid.

40   State Statistics Service of Ukraine. (2020). Ukraine's Foreign Trade in Goods, 2019. http:// www.ukrstat.gov.ua/

41   Quoted in: Institute of World Policy and TRUMAN Agency (2017). Foreign Policy Audit: Index of Relations, N 4 (April – June), p.18. https://truman.ua/sites/default/files/ 2018-02/Index%20of%20Relations%20%23%204.pdf

42   Ibid.

confirmed again that Beijing "considers Ukraine as one of the logistics and industrial hubs on the way to the European Union" and announced plans for $7 billion in joint projects between China and Ukraine.[43] In 2019, bilateral trade reached $12.8 billion, with China becoming Ukraine's second largest bilateral partner after Russia ($12 billion), though far less than the EU as a whole, with $45.7 billion.[44]

Ukrainian non-governmental experts formulated recommendations on how to increase the attractiveness of Ukraine for China.[45] Some of the views are summarized below.

While the Ukrainian cabinet depends on a majority in parliament, until the 2019 elections it did not have a lot of room for maneuver, and so the President has become a key figure for stability. Thus, it is the Ukrainian President who should take initiatives in bilateral relations on behalf of Ukraine. For Kyiv it is most important to have dialogue with Beijing at the highest level (Russia is much more successful). The new situation after the 2019 presidential and parliamentary elections, with a pro-presidential majority in parliament, opens new possibilities for bilateral contacts with China at the highest levels – presidents, prime ministers and ministers of foreign affairs.[46] Ukraine must demonstrate it has a clear strategy toward the Asian-Pacific region and China, and that it is not dependent on the U.S. position. However, improved relations between Ukraine and China would lead to complications in relations with Japan (and vice versa).[47] Therefore, it is important to disconnect this chain or at least to maintain a very delicate balance between these countries.

The Ukrainian side has a "lack of understanding of the way power functions in the Confucian world". In turn, Ukrainian experts stress that "the obstacle to the development of Ukraine-China partnership from the Chinese side is the unconscious perception of Ukraine as a part of the post-Soviet space to which Russia allegedly has some rights".[48]

---

43   Quoted in: Peterson N. (2017).
44   State Statistics Service of Ukraine. (2020).
45   Gerasymchuk S., Poita Yu. (2018), p. 11–12; Goncharuk A., Hobova E., Kiktenko V., Koval A., and Koshovy S. (2016). Foreign Policy Audit: Ukraine – China. Discussion Paper. Kyiv: Institute of World Policy, pp. 53–55; Korsunsky S. (2019). Relations Ukraine – China, Truman Index, N 10 (Jan.-March), pp. 19–20. https://truman.ua/sites/default/files/2019-05/TRUMAN%20Index%20%236%2810%29.pdf; Koshovy S. [Кошовий С.] (2017), pp. 16–19.
46   Korsunsky S. (2019), p. 20.
47   Mykal O. (2016). Japono-kytaiskaia dilemma Ukrainy.
48   Goncharuk A. et al. (2016), p.4.

Nevertheless, given China's pragmatism, economic cooperation is perhaps the main base for political cooperation. Kyiv should become an interesting economic partner, instead of simply positioning itself as a victim of Russian aggression. Growing Chinese investments in Ukraine, especially in the south and east,[49] are the best way to create Chinese support for Ukraine and its territorial integrity.[50]

7   Conclusion

Since the dissolution of the Soviet Union, the Ukrainian elite considers that Kyiv and Beijing have mutual interests and that Kyiv has multiple spheres to attract China. However, bilateral relations have had their ups and downs. The political problems coincided with the periods after two revolutions in Ukraine (2004 and 2014) when there were regime changes (traditionally viewed with caution by Beijing) and new post-revolutionary governments emphasised European and Euro-Atlantic integration.

Russia's annexation of Crimea and intervention in the Donbas, created the most serious post-Cold War crisis in Europe. It raised the issue of credibility of security assurances provided by the great powers as they were not able to secure the territorial integrity of Ukraine promised by the 1994 Budapest memorandum. This was a huge disappointment both for Ukrainian society and its decision-makers. Regarding the PRC, this feeling was reinforced by: growing Chinese cooperation with Russia as Beijing pragmatically benefitted from the weakening of the latter; China's abstention during the 2014 vote in the UN regarding the territorial integrity of Ukraine (though it is appreciated in Ukraine that Beijing did not block the resolution); and China's votes against the UN resolutions defending human rights in Russian occupied Crimea (though again, the expert community understands that this conforms to the traditional line of Beijing regarding human rights' resolutions).

Still, the image of China in Ukrainian public opinion is mostly positive, or at least neutral, which may serve as a good basis for the deepening of bilateral ties. The 2019 elections in Ukraine and formation of the presidential party's majority in parliament, created the background for an intensification of contacts with Beijing at the highest levels. According to the recommendations of Ukrainian experts, the key for China's interests is economic, that is, to attract

---

49   See the positive examples in: Gerasymchuk S., Poita Yu. (2018), p. 6.
50   Goncharuk A. et al. (2016), p.7.

Beijing's investment in Ukraine. However, the Chinese side has to overcome negative stereotypes about its economic expansion, especially regarding the leasing of Ukrainian lands and alleged transformation of Ukraine into a raw materials base for China. If economic ties between both countries intensify, and Beijing's economic interests in Ukraine become strategic ones, this, according to views in Kyiv, would be the best way to secure China's political support for Ukraine in the international arena.

Bibliography

Blanchfield, K., Wezeman, P. D., and Wezeman, S. T. (2017). The State of Major Arms Transfers in 8 Graphics. SIPRI. www.sipri.org/commentary/blog/2017/state-major-arms-transfers-8-graphics.

Burkovsky, P., and Haran, O. (2011). Russian Expansion: A Challenge and Opportunity for the Emerging Authoritarian Regime in Ukraine. In: A. Schmemann and C. Welt, (editors), New Balances: Russia, the EU, and the "Post-Soviet West". Policy Perspectives. Washington: The George Washington University, pp. 21–26. http://www.ponarseurasia.org/memo/russian-expansion-challenge-and-opportunity-emerging-authoritarian-regime-ukraine.

China Respects Ukraine's Sovereignty, Territorial Integrity: Premier. China Daily, 15 March 2015. http://www.chinadaily.com.cn/china/2015twosession/2015-03/15/content_19815476.htm.

Gerasymchuk, S., and Poita, Yu. (2018). Ukraine-China after 2014: A New Chapter in the Relationship. Opportunities and Prospects, Obstacles and Risks. Kyiv: Friedrich Ebert Stiftung. http://library.fes.de/pdf-files/bueros/ukraine/14703.pdf.

Goncharuk, A., Hobova, E., Kiktenko, V., Koval, A., and Koshovy, S. (2016). Foreign Policy Audit: Ukraine – China. Discussion Paper. Kyiv: Institute of World Policy. http://neweurope.org.ua/wp-content/uploads/2017/10/Audyt-zovnishnoyi-polityky_Ukr_Kytaj_eng_inet.pdf.

Haran, O., (2014). What Went Wrong with the Orange Revolution? Magisterium. Politychni Studii [Магістеріум. Політичні студії] 58, pp. 50–55.

Haran, O. (2015). Ukrainian-Russian Conflict and Its Implications for Northeast Asia. International Journal of Korean Unification Studies 24 (3), pp.125–158. http://repo.kinu.or.kr/bitstream/2015.oak/2435/1/IJKUS_24-3.pdf.

Institute of World Policy and TRUMAN Agency. (2017). Foreign Policy Audit: Index of Relations. N 4 (April–June), pp. 17–23. https://truman.ua/sites/default/files/2018-02/Index%20of%20Relations%20%23%204.pdf.

Institute of World Policy and TRUMAN Agency (2017). Foreign Policy Audit: Index of Relations. N 3 (January–March), pp. 18–23. https://truman.ua/sites/default/files/2018-02/Index%20of%20Relations%20%23%203.pdf.

Korsunsky, S. (2019). Relations Ukraine – China, Truman Index, N 10 (Jan.-March), pp. 19–25. https://truman.ua/sites/default/files/2019-05/TRUMAN%20Index%20%236%2810%29.pdf.

Koshovy, S. [Кошовий С.] (2017). Dosvid spivpratsi Kytaju i krain Tsentralnoi ta Skhidnoi Evropy u fromati «16+1» ta perspektyvy Ukrainy [Досвід співпраці Китаю і країн Центральної та Східної Європи у форматі «16+1» та перспективи України]. National Institute for Strategic Studies, June 2017. http://old2.niss.gov.ua/content/articles/files/16plyus1-42a26.pdf.

Kotani, T. (2014). Japan's 'Proactive Contribution to Peace' and the Annexation of Crimea. The National Bureau of Asian Research, 22 April. http://www.nbr.org/research/activity.aspx?id=422.

Laurenson, J. (2018). China Is on Track to Replace Russia as Ukraine's Biggest Trading Partner, The Kyiv Post, 6 Nov. https://www.kyivpost.com/business/china-is-on-track-to-replace-russia-as-ukraines-biggest-trading-partner.html.

Lukjanow, F. (2015). Wenn Russen und Chinesen gemeinsam marschieren. Die Welt, March 30. Quoted in: Umland, A. (2015). Towards a Greater Asia? The Prospects of a Sino-Russian Entente. Eurozine, 22 June.

Lushnycky, A., and Riabchuk, M. (editors) (2009). Ukraine on Its Meandering Path Between East and West. Bern – Berlin – Bruxelles etc.: Peter Lang.

Mykal, O. [Мыкал О.]. (2016). Japono-kytaiskaja dilemma Ukrainy [Японо-китайская дилемма Украины]. Novoje vremia [Новое время], 11 October. https://nv.ua/opinion/mykal/japono-kitajskaja-dilemma-ukrainy-241875.html.

Mykal, O. (2016). Why China Is Interested in Ukraine. The Diplomat, 3 October. https://thediplomat.com/2016/03/why-china-is-interested-in-ukraine.

Peterson, N. (2017). As China Invests in Ukraine, Russia Stands to Gain. The Daily Signal, 8 December. http://dailysignal.com/2017/12/08/as-china-invests-in-ukraine-russia-stands-to-gain/.

President Rossii [Президент России]. (2015). Совместное заявление Российской Федерации и Китайской Народной Республики об углублении всеобъемлющего партнерства и стратегического взаимодействия и о продвижении взаимовыгодного сотрудничества. Online: http://www.kremlin.ru/supplement/4969.

Russia Today (2015). 15 March. Online: http://russian.rt.com/article/79606 (in Russian).

Russia Today (2015). 19 June. Online: http://russian.rt.com/article/98387 (in Russian).

Shpak, Yu Шпак Ю] (2017). Ukraina – Kitai: mezdu vorotami v Evropu i syrievoj kolonijeУкраина-Китай: между воротами в Европу и сырьевой колонией]. Golos.ua, 3 Feb. http://ru.golos.ua/ekonomika/ukrainakitay_mejdu_vorotami_v_evropu_i_syirevoy_koloniey_tablitsyi_5881.

State Statistics Service of Ukraine (2019). Ukraine's Foreign Trade in Goods, 2018. http://www.ukrstat.gov.ua/.

Stepanenko, V., and Pylynskyi, Y. (editors) (2014). Ukraine after Euromaidan: Challenges and Hopes. Bern – Berlin – Bruxelles etc.: Peter Lang.

Trenin, D. (2014). China's Victory in Ukraine. The Carnegie Moscow Center, 31 July. http://carnegie.ru/2014/07/31/china-s-victory-in-ukraine/hjht.

United Nations General Assembly document A/49/765, UN Security Council document S/1994/1399. (1994). Memorandum on Security Assurances in connection with Ukraine's Accession to the Treaty on the Non-Proliferation of Nuclear Weapons.

United Nations General Assembly document A/49/783. (1994). Statement of the Chinese Government on the Security Assurance to Ukraine Issued on 4 December 1994.

Wezeman, P., Fleurant, A., Kuimova, A., Tian, N., and Wezeman, S. (2019). Trends in International Arms Transfers, 2018. SIPRI Fact Sheet. https://www.sipri.org/sites/default/files/2019-03/fs_1903_at_2018.pdf.

Xinhua. (2014) UN General Assembly Adopts Resolution Affirming Ukraine's Territorial Integrity. 28 March. http://news.xinhuanet.com/english/world/2014-03/28/c_126325576.htm.

Xinhua. (2014). Kitaj prizyvaet vse zaineresovannye storony prilagat usilia k politicheskomu uregulirovaniju krizisa v Ukraine – MID KNR [Китай призывает все заинтересованные стороны прилагать усилия к политическому урегулированию кризиса в Украине – МИД КНР]. 17 March. http://russian.people.com.cn/31521/8568055.html.

Xinhua. (2014). Kommentarij: Porazhenije Zapada v Ukraine [Комментарий: Поражение Запада в Украине]., 7 March. http://russian.people.com.cn/95181/8558922.html.

Zerkalo Nedeli [Зеркало недели]. (2014). 19 April, p. 6. http://gazeta.zn.ua/internal/yugo-vostok-vetv-dreva-nashego-_.html.

CHAPTER 4

Sino-Polish Relations

From Socialist Brothers to the Post-Cold War Period's Reconfigurations

Dominik Mierzejewski

1 Introduction

The question of historical memory in international relations has been widely discussed by the social constructivist school of thought. By introducing a discussion of the role of the interpretation of the past in the current course of events, this author attempts to answer the following questions:

- what is the purpose of historical memory in shaping contemporary international relations with special regards to the bilateral relations between Poland and China?
- how and who should define and select collective memory in the peculiar context of Sino-Polish relationships?
- and finally, what are the basic differences in conceptualization and the reading of historical memory between China and Poland?

History and historical memory play an important role in shaping both countries' current positions and stances. The Chinese have often repeated that "history can explain everything", while Poles, mainly the government of Law and Justice, have referred to the history of the Polish-Lithuanian Commonwealth and the democratic transitions as the leverage of their position in European affairs.[1] Through historical education, the Chinese government tries to assess the shortfall between being a victim and the acknowledgement of China's historical greatness – as with the Boxer Uprising, for example. The Chinese collapse in the 19th Century is perceived historically by the growing significance of global capitalism, especially after the 1825 and 1837 economic crises in the United Kingdom, and the weakness of the Qing government.[2] According to

---

1 Morawiecki, M. (2019), *Premier Mateusz Morawiecki podczas obchodów 450. rocznicy unii polsko – litewskiej* (Prime Minister Mateusz Morawiecki during the 450th anniversary of the Poland-Lithuania Commonwealth). https://www.gov.pl/web/premier/premier-mateusz-morawiecki-podczas-obchodow-450-rocznicy-unii-polsko--litewskiej (accessed 19 November 2020).

2 Spence, J. (1990), The Search for Modern China, New York, London, W.W. Norton & Company, pp. 143–157.

Chinese narratives in Chinese history coursebooks, China was exploited by the Western powers and became the victim of Japanese and Western imperialism.[3] This led to "one hundred years of humiliation" and ended with the final victory of the Communist Party of China in 1949. Apart from the close alliance with the Soviet Union, based on the "lying on one side" policy, this led to the conclusion that the West has slightly negative connotations in China and with the government in Beijing.[4]

In the case of Poland, the historical narrative shapes Polish understanding of contemporary relations, especially with Russia, Germany and the United States. The first two, due to the past, are perceived as threats and powers that hope to exploit Poland and encourage its partition, while Washington is seen in a very positive light. The two have become close partners because of: the memory of everyday struggles for freedom – Polish and American in the late 18th Century; Woodrow Wilson's declaration in 1917; the support for the Solidarity movement in the 1980s; and finally, a similar system of values of the "free world".

In this international context, bilateral relations between Poland and China, which are also rooted in history, have become a vivid and essential subject. Although relations with China belong to a different part of Polish history, the so-called "community of shared socialist values" should be perceived as an important element of the current course of events in bilateral and multilateral relations. This common-values platform, however, was not independently chosen by Poland, but rather imposed by the Soviet Union. After a few years of being in "one camp", Warsaw and Beijing realized that the so-called socialist values sponsored by Moscow could only serve Moscow's interests.[5] Opposition to so-called "social imperialism", coupled with the call for one's own model of socialism, built a stable platform for cooperation.

This article is divided into three major parts as it first discusses the theoretical explanations of collective, historical memory in the social sciences; then goes on to present the history of bilateral relations in the 1950s – from both Chinese and Polish perspectives; and finishes by comparing the current narrative presented by Polish Ministers of Foreign Affairs in special yearly information bulletins in the Polish Parliament concerning Polish foreign policy, and

3 *Zhongguo Jinxiandaishi Gangyao* (2010) (The guideline for Chinese contemporary and modern history, 2010 version), Beijing: Higher Education Press, pp. 138–139.

4 Shen, Zhihua ed. (2011), *Zhong-Su Guanxi Shigang 1917–1991* (History of Sino-Soviet Relations 1917–1991). Beijing: Social Sciences Academy Press, pp. 111–113.

5 Rowiński, J., ed. (2006), *Polski październik 1956 w polityce światowej* (Polish October 1956 in Global Politics), Warsaw: Polish Institute for International Affairs, pp. 71–108.

the Chinese Prime Minister's speeches delivered during the 16+1 meetings in Warsaw, Bucharest, Belgrade, Suzhou, Riga and Budapest respectively.

2   Discussing Collective Memory in International Relations

Discussion here focuses on the conceptualization of the collective memory of the past. From this perspective, collective memory is understood as a representation of the past shared by a group or community.[6] Collective memory is most contested at moments of uncertainty, locating groups of national identities, linked to identity challenges and complications. During periods of crisis and instability, groups shape collective memory to prevent and overcome problems (Ibid.: 195).[7] Taking this assumption into consideration, the 1950s represent a critical period of uncertainty for China and Poland. Both countries, located in the so-called socialist camp, shared the same fear of the future steps envisaged by the then Soviet Union.

From a different perspective, collective memory is a representation of the past shared by members of a group such as a generation or a nation-state. French sociologist Maurice Halbwachs identified individual and collective memories as tools through which social groups establish centrality in individuals' lives. He saw history as "a dead memory, a way of preserving pasts to which we no longer have an 'organic' experiential relation" and argued that "this understanding of the distinction negates the self-image of historiography as the more important or appropriate attitude towards the past".[8] As claimed by Olick and Robbins (2004), memory is a matter of how minds work together in society; how they operate is not merely mediated but rather structured by social arrangements.[9] They refer to social memory studies as a general rubric for an inquiry into the various ways people are shaped by the past, referring to "distinct sets of mnemonic practices in various social sites, rather than to collective memory as a thing". In fact, collective memory is not history itself but a collective phenomenon that is manifested in the actions and statements of individuals.[10] Following the above-mentioned statements, we need

---

6   Kansteiner, W. (2002), Finding Meaning in Memory: A Methodological Critique of Collective Memory Studies, History and Theory, no 41, pp. 179–197.

7   Ibid., p. 195.

8   Bosch T. E. (2016), *Memory Studies: A brief concept paper. Media, Conflict and Democratisation*, http://eprints.whiterose.ac.uk/117289/1/Bosch%202016_Memory%20Studies.pdf (accessed 12 March 2020).

9   Ibidem.

10   Kansteiner, W. (2002), op. cit., p. 180.

to acknowledge that collective memory is a socio-political construction, a version of the past, defined and negotiated through changing socio-political power circumstances and agendas.[11] As discussed by James Pennebaker (2013), collective memories are often " 'cohort memories', where members of a given cohort affected by a large-scale event will write the event's history and influence the collective memories for the future". Pennebaker (2013) also shows that "significant historical events form stronger collective memories, and present circumstances affect what events are remembered as significant".[12]

Deepening the discussion concerning historical narrative and memory, Jeffrey Olick outlines the existing terminological diversity. He specifies the different terms for different types of memories: official memory, vernacular memory, public memory, popular memory, local memory, family memory, historical memory or cultural memory.[13]

Apart from a definition given by Halbwachs, the concept of "collaborative remembering" was introduced by Mary Weldon (2001). For Wertsch, the latter "occurs when groups of individuals work together to recall information or events from the past and fundamentally organized by the 'textual resources' it employs, especially textual resources in the form of narratives, both spoken and written".[14] In this context, this account of collective memory grounded in these notions emphasizes the power of narrative to shape representations of the past. In this regard, this chapter follows Schwartz's assumption (1991) that "the past shapes our understanding of the present rather than the other way around". He contended that in most cases: "... we find the past to be neither precarious nor immutable, but a stable image upon which new elements are intermittently superimposed. The past, then, is a familiar rather than a foreign country; its people different, but not strangers to the present".[15] As Ben-Yehuda has observed, "collective memory and collective forgetting can be thought of as two ends of the same process – that of selecting historical facts and events".[16]

11   Neiger, M., Meyers, O., and Zandberg, E., eds. (2011), On Media Memory – Collective Memory in a New Media Age, London: Palgrave Macmillan.

12   Bosch, T. E. (2016), *Memory Studies: A brief concept paper. Media, Conflict and Democratization.* Accessed 12 March 2020. http://eprints.whiterose.ac.uk/117289/1/Bosch%202016_Memory%20Studies.pdf

13   Olick, J., and Robbins, J. (1998), Social Memory Studies: From "Collective Memory" to the Historical Sociology of Mnemonic Practices, Annual Review of Sociology, vol. 24, p. 112.

14   Wertsch, J. V. (2008), The Narrative Organization of Collective Memory, Ethos, Vol. 36, No. 1, pp. 120–135.

15   Schwartz, B. (1991), Social Change and Collective Memory: The Democratization of George Washington, American Sociological Review, Vol. 56, No. 2, pp. 221–236.

16   Walton, R. E. (2013), Collective Memory in Contemporary Poland and Pre-Independence (1918) Memorials. Review of European Studies no. 5, pp. 1–12 and Ben-Yehuda N. (1995),

The remarks mentioned above are rooted in a constructivist understanding of contemporary international relations. As pointed out by Wendt (1999), social constructivism emphasizes ideational and social non-material factors and how they interact with material elements, how they co-constitute each other. Although constructivists, (for example, Wendt, Onuf, or Kratochwil), give more weight to social factors, they still make room for material factors, and are sometimes mistaken for idealists. In this study, however, the author discusses only the role of historical narrative and interpretations in making bilateral relations between Poland and China.[17]

3   Recalling the Past: Sino-Polish Relations in the 1950s

As both sides have announced, Poland was the second country, after the Soviet Union, to recognize the People's Republic of China as an independent state in international relations.[18] Their friendship was catalysed by the fact of being in the same "socialist" camp and sharing similar socialist values. As we learn from the history of international politics, both sides, to a certain extent, were pushed towards that position by the two superpowers – the United States and the Soviet Union. After the Yalta conference, zones of influences in Europe were drawn up, and Moscow as one of the victors, was allowed to control Eastern and Southern Europe, while Washington formed alliances with Western Europe. In the context of China, during the home war in the late 1940s, Mao Zedong tried to establish relations with the United States and by so doing, balance Russia. Then, the Communist Party of China became a member of the socialist camp, and Mao Zedong proposed the "lying on one side" policy (*yibiandao*).

The role of China's diplomacy in the 'Polish October' is still under discussion. In current narratives there are two approaches: one represented by Jan Rowinski, Polish Sinologist, and diplomat Andrzej Werblan, advisor to Gomulka and Liu Yanshuan (China's former Ambassador to Poland), who support the more significant role of Chinese diplomacy and relations with the

---

Masada Myth: Collective Memory and Mythmaking in Israel, Wisconsin: Wisconsin Press, p. 302. Warfare: An Early 21st Century Foreign Traveler's Observations concerning Polish Battlefield.

17   Wendt, A. (1999), Social Theory of International Politics (Cambridge Studies in International Relations). Cambridge: Cambridge University Press.

18   Burdelski, M. (2011), 60 Years of Diplomatic Relations between Poland and the People's Republic of China – Historical Overview. Polish Political Science, no 9, pp. 211–237.

Soviet Union[19]; and the second represented by Shen Zhihua and Li Danhui (2006) who pointed to the smaller part played by China, and presented relations between Gomulka and Khrushchev as their "game".[20] The reason that Chinese scholars limit China's role to relations in the socialist camp is explained by China's foreign policy principles of non-interference and peaceful cooperation. Although the role of Chinese intervention is perceived as limited, it allowed China to go beyond Asian affairs to challenge Stalin's division of labour approach (China for Asia, Russia for Europe), and build its position within the international communist movement.[21]

Beyond the above debate, Sino-Polish relations had at least three dimensions: political, related to the political systems issues; strategic, related to the situation on the Korean Peninsula; and economic, related to maritime cooperation. Due to historical development, on the one hand, both countries were in the same political camp while on the other hand, both tried to be independent of Moscow. The Chinese called for "socialism with national characteristics" and hoped to be an equal partner among the socialist family of nations. Similar quandaries arose in Poland. As Polish history teaches, Poles have fought for their freedom and independence for the last 200 years.

The first official visit to Poland was paid by Vice-Chairman, Prime Minister and Minister of Foreign Affairs Zhou Enlai, in July 1954. Following the Chinese policymaker's visits, the Polish First Secretary, Bolesław Bierut, visited China in October 1954; Prime Minister Jozef Cyrankiewicz in April 1957; and the Minister of Defence in September and October 1957. What is worth mentioning is that all the Polish delegations had exceptional meetings and conversations with Chairman Mao Zedong.

In 1959, both sides signed an agreement of economic cooperation for 1959–1962, but due to the problems in China with the inefficiency of the Great Leap Forward and permanent political campaigns, as well as the pressure from the Soviet Union, this cooperation was not completed. Between 1954 and 1961, Chinese delegations were sent to Poland frequently: Poland was visited by Marshall Chen Yi (October 1954), Vice-Prime Minister, Marshall He Long (July and August 1955), first Vice-Chairman of the People's Republic of China,

---

19   Werblan, A. (1997), Rozmowa Władysława Gomułki z Zhou Enlaiem w 1957 r. (Conversation between Władysław Gomułka and Zhou Enlai in 1957), Dzieje Najnowsze, no 4, pp. 119–143.

20   Shen, Zhihua, Li, Danhui (2006), *Kryzys w Polsce 1956 roku i stosunki polsko-chińskie widziane z Pekinu* (1956 Crisis in Poland and Sino-Polish relations: view from Beijing), In eds. Jan Rowiński, Tytus Jaskułowski, *Polski Październik 1956 w polityce światowej*, Polish October 1956 in Global Politics]. Warsaw: Polish Institute for International Affairs, p. 73.

21   Shen, Zhihua ed. (2011), op.cit., pp. 111–113.

Marshall Zhu De (three times between 1956 and 1959), Prime Minister and Minister of Foreign Affairs Zhou Enlai (1954, 1957), Peng Dehuai (twice in May 1955, and April 1959), Ye Jianying (October 1957) and finally by Bo Yibo in May 1960. But, the most important meeting between leaders, according to Jan Rowinski (2009), former diplomat and scholar, was held in Beijing (September 1956) where the Chinese side offered 30 million USD of non-returnable loan. This was the symbol of support for the Polish way to communism.[22]

During the 8th Party Congress, Mao Zedong met Edward Ochab, then First Secretary of the Polish United Workers' Party, three times. Moreover, during the farewell meeting at the airport with the Vice-Chairman of the People's Republic of China, Zhu De met with E. Ochab. Not only was a secret message conveyed to the Chinese counterpart that the 'rehabilitation of Gomulka' was about to happen, but the Polish side also explained the reasons behind the workers' strikes and uprising in Poznan. What should be noted is that during the same period, similar problems were taking place in China. Having similar issues in Shanghai (August 1956), the Chinese paid more attention to the Polish lesson. Soon after protests started, the Chinese government used force to crack down on the movements. But after the information from Warsaw, especially that of how the forceful reaction of the government had inflamed anti-party sentiment in society, Chairman Mao Zedong admitted: "We learned a lot from the Polish side" (quoted after Rowiński, 2009).[23]

From this perspective, the Chinese side perceived the tensions in Poland as the natural way of evolution for the socialist system, while in Hungary, Beijing saw the real "counter-revolution" (Zhu Dandan, 2016).[24] In a conversation with Edward Ochab, Zhu De ensured the Polish side of Chinese support in the case of intervention by Moscow. The official Chinese statement was given to Kiryluk, the Polish Ambassador in Beijing. Mao Zedong stated: "The Soviet Union is ready to use military force in Poland and would break an elementary rule in international relations, this move is a sign of superpower chauvinism" and China declared it would use any measure against this move[25] (Werblan,

---

22   Rowiński, J. (2009), *ChRL a wydarzenia październikowe 1956 w Polsce. Czy Chińczycy uchronili nasz kraj przed interwencją radziecką?* (The People's Republic of China and Polish October 1956. Did the Chinese secure our country from Soviet intervention?) In ed. B. Góralczyk, Poland-China. Yesterday, Today, Tommorow, Toruń: Wyd. Adam Marszałek, p. 250.

23   Ibidem.

24   Zhu, Dandan (2016), China's Involvement in the Hungarian Revolution, October-November 1956 (November 2016), http://unipub.lib.uni-corvinus.hu/2591/1/COJOURN _Vol1_No3_06_Dandan_Zhu.pdf (accessed 14 May 2020).

25   Werblan, A. (1997), op.cit.

2006: 30–31). A similar view was expressed by Liu Shaoqi, who mentioned that small states were particularly afraid of the larger power's domination and imperial policy. Only by stopping such behaviour could the Soviet Union guarantee stability within the communist bloc (Rowinski, 2006). As stated by professor Gawlikowski (2017): "In fact, to a large extent, we owe the whole Polish October to China. Not only because they stopped the intervention and forced Moscow to recognize Gomułka, but also because if Ochab's talks in Beijing failed, if he did not get support, he would never dare to manoeuvre with Gomułka".[26]

The pressure from the Soviet Union pushed both sides towards further cooperation. As mentioned in the theoretical section above, the threat from Moscow, as well as historical experiences with Tsarist Russia, based on the feeling of inequality and domination, shaped mutual understanding and was the common denominator for cooperation. As observed by Huang Xiaodan and Sun Danyao (2016), Poland and China shared the same interests *vis à vis* the Soviet Union. Both sides demanded equality and reciprocity in relations with the 'older brother'.[27]

Apart from being in the same political camp, Poland was also a member of the Neutral Nations Supervisory Commission in the Korean Peninsula. The United Nations Command chose Switzerland and Sweden, while the Korean People's Army and Chinese People's Volunteers chose Czechoslovakia and Poland. Then in 1954, Poland became a member of the International Control Commission (ICC), which was an international force established that year that oversaw the implementation of the Geneva Accords which ended the First Indochina War, with the Partition of Vietnam. Both Commissions had the power to exercise inspections, observations and investigations, according to special regulations. According to Polish soldiers' memos, airgrams and other classified documents (Benken, 2014: 441–447),[28] North Korean and Chinese

---

26   Interview with professor Krzysztof Gawlikowski. (2017). *Chiński udział w polskim październiku* (China's participation in Polish October). *Tygodnik Przegląd*. https://www.tygodnikprzeglad.pl/chinski-udzial-polskim-pazdzierniku/ (accessed 14 May 2020).

27   Huang, Xiaodan, and Sun, Danyao (2016), *"Cankao Ziliao" zhong de Bo-Xiong Shijian, Zhonggong de Fanying* (The Reaction of the Central Committee for Crisis in Poland and Hungary in "References Materials"). http://zgdsw.net.cn/n1/2016/0426/c219022-28305527.html (accessed 14 May 2020).

28   Benken, P. (2014), *Problematyka stosunków między Misją Polską do Komisji Nadzorczej Państw Neutralnych a Sztabem Wojskowej Komisji Rozejmowej strony Koreańskiej Armii Ludowej/Chińskich Ochotników Ludowych w Kaesongu oraz wytyczne w tej sprawie* (Relations between the Polish mission in the Neutral Control Commission and its relations with the Korean People's Army and Chinese People's Volunteers in Kaesong Headquarters). Pamięć i Sprawiedliwość (Memory and Justice) vol. 13, no 1, pp. 441–447.

volunteers tried to impose their views and confront Sweden and Switzerland. Polish members of the NNSC observed that Czech delegates who had often changed their views were "discredited by continued acquiescence towards North Korean and Chinese partners" and had more freedom and were not severely controlled by the central government in Prague (Benken 2014: 445).[29]

The last important point in bilateral relations is economic cooperation, especially in the field of maritime industry. Due to the political conditions at the beginning of the 1950s, Western markets, as well as any economic interactions between China and the West, were blocked. By establishing Chipolbrok, the first ever joint venture in China (1951), Poland played a primary role in China's foreign trade. China was able to import goods, not only from the Eastern bloc, but also via the Polish channel which could import goods from the West. From Poland, China imported textiles, agricultural machines, electric machines, chemical products, pharmaceuticals, and railway track; from Czechoslovakia, machines and cars (Skoda); and from Hungary and the Soviet Union, cars, locomotives, textiles, glass, and bicycles. Chinese producers exported silk, tea, corn, wheat, cooking oils, tobacco, and other agricultural goods (Wrobel, 2017: 178–179).[30]

Furthermore, this cooperation had its practical military aspects, as revealed by Polish archives, since military equipment such as 80mm cannons from Czechoslovakia were shipped through Gdynia. As we know from the same Polish files, these shipments were inspected by Chinese military officers and then sent to China.

Moreover, as the Singapore media revealed in 1951, the Polish Merchant Navy broke the embargo imposed on China and shipped rubber produced in India to mainland China. As revealed in March 1953, the Polish government was interested in acquiring products embargoed to the wider Eastern bloc. This was possible by cooperation with the International Communist Movement in Western Europe.[31]

During the period 1953–1954, the Italian Communist Party, governed by Spartaco Vannoni and Norberto Dalessandri, managed a company in Switzerland named Terbita. Terbita, governed by Eugenio Reale, was dedicated to purchasing metals and non-ferrous metal, and these products were then smuggled to Poland. In this procedure, Polish SOE International Head Offices – Impexmetal and Transactor – served as individual agents or 'facilitators' for

---

29   Ibid., p. 445.
30   Wrobel, J. (2016), *Z dziejów polsko-chinskiego sojuszu morskiego 1950–1957* (Stories from the Sino-Polish Maritime Alliance), Lodz: Institute of National Remembrance, p. 178–179.
31   Ibidem.

the cooperation between China and socialist countries. Likewise, in Belgium, where Polish Metalexport cooperated with the Tracosa company sponsored by the Communist Party of Belgium and governed by Xavier Relecom, "was happy to make deals with Communist China". Moreover, Pachon and Cheminmetal companies opened by Guttmann – a businessman of Polish origin – sold aluminium and steel to China via a Polish channel.[32]

This maritime cooperation bypassed mainland China's maritime blockade. In June 1949, the National government of Chiang Kai-shek imposed a ban on foreign frigates. Ports like Tianjin, Ningbo and Shanghai were closed. After 1949, the Guomingdang government made free navigation difficult in the Cross-Strait from Guangzhou to Shanghai and to make navigation possible, Polish frigates, or Chinese frigates under the Polish flag, shipped goods and products to Shanghai.[33]

Apart from being in the same communist camp, Poland played a critical role in shaping Sino-American *rapprochement*. In 1955, the Sino-American ambassadorial talks began in Geneva (continued in Warsaw) and the Chinese side was represented by the Ambassador to Poland, Mr. Wang Binnan (later on by the succeeding Ambassador to Poland, Mr. Wang Guoquan) while the U.S. side was represented by the Ambassador to Czechoslovakia, Mr. Alexis Johnson. The talks were moved to Warsaw after the Second Taiwan Crisis (1958), when the American side appointed the chief negotiator – the then ambassador to Poland, John Beam (Garver, 1993: 297).[34]

4   Two Sides of the Same Coin: Approaching a Common Reading of
        History?

The period between the 1960s and 1980s was dominated by the fact that relations between Poland and China were the outcome of Sino-Soviet controversies, as well as Chinese domestic political campaign – for example, the Cultural Revolution or the Campaign against Bourgeois Liberalization. At the beginning of the 1990s, China recognized Poland's choice of society and declared a willingness for further cooperation. However, the Polish government rejected this proposal by saying that collaboration with the communist regime failed to fit Polish national interests. The Solidarity-based government accused China

---

32   Ibidem, p. 180–181.
33   Ibidem, p. 185.
34   Garver J. (1993), *Foreign Relations of the People's Republic of China*, Englewood Cliffs: Simon&Schuster Company, p. 297.

of being a cruel, red regime that violated human rights.[35] After the negative interpretation of post-Tiananmen China, the Polish government concentrated only on Poland's integration into NATO and the European Union. According to former President Aleksander Kwaśniewski, the pro-Western policy was necessary for the further development of Poland. In 1997, the Polish President paid the first official visit to China.[36]

After a decade of following Western concepts, joining NATO and the European Union, along with witnessing China's growing role in global affairs, the Polish government began to recognize the role of the Middle Kingdom in Europe. From at least 2008, Polish governments have discussed relations with China and the role of China in regional and global affairs. In 2008, then Polish Prime Minister Donald Tusk, was the first European leader to declare a boycott of the Olympic Games in China. The reason was, as stated by the then Prime Minister, human rights violations in Tibet. In 2008 also, in information delivered by Radosław Sikorski (2008), Minister of Foreign Affairs in the Polish parliament, China was perceived as a new, growing power with a non-democratic political system. Instead of seeking cooperation with China, the Minister of Foreign Affairs declared that Poland hoped to strengthen relations with Japan and India "tried-and-true democracies outside Europe".[37]

In 2011, dramatic changes occurred. Poland signed a strategic partnership with China, naming itself as a reliable partner in China's foreign policy. Only three years after boycotting the Olympic Games, the Polish government of the Civic Platform, along with the Polish People's Party, changed their approach. The reason for this *rapprochement*, not discussed in a very open manner, was the relations between Poland and Russia. In April 2010, the then Polish President Lech Kaczynski and his wife, former President Ryszard Kaczorowski, the entire general army command, the Chief of the Polish General Staff and other senior Polish military officers, along with the president of the National Bank of Poland, Poland's deputy foreign minister, and Polish government officials, all died in the plane catastrophe on Russian territory in Smolensk. This

---

35   Interview with professor Krzysztof Gawlikowski (2017), *Chiński udział w polskim październiku* (China's participation in Polish October), *Tygodnik Przegląd*, https://www.tygodnikprzeglad.pl/chinski-udzial-polska-pazdzierniku/ (accessed 14 May 2019).

36   Kwaśniewski, A. (2011), *Rozmowa z Aleksandrem Kwaśniewski* (Conversation with Aleksander Kwaśniewski), https://polskieradio24.pl/13/53/Artykul/502180,Rozmowa-z-Aleksandrem-Kwasniewskim (accessed 14 May 2020).

37   Sikorski, R. (2008), *Informacja ministra spraw zagranicznych o założeniach polskiej polityki zagranicznej w 2008 r.* (Address by the Minister of Foreign Affairs on the goals of Polish Foreign Policy in 2008). Accessed 12 May 2020. http://orka2.sejm.gov.pl/Debata6.nsf/main/20C4290E (accessed 20 May 2020).

tragedy provided the basis for further mistrust and suspicions concerning Russian intentions. In order to balance rather cold relations with the Russian Federation, Poland – mainly the President's office – turned to China.

Although the President's office was more open and positive, Minister of Foreign Affairs Sikorski presented a more dubious position. In 2011, when the agreement on a "strategic partnership" was signed in Beijing, Minister Sikorski (2012) perceived China more as a partner for the European Union as a whole rather than Poland in particular. In his speech, Sikorski did not mention political issues. As observed a year later, Europe failed to serve as a model, and China filled the vacuum after the sunset in Asia (Sikorski, 2012). In Polish discourse, from 2013 onwards, China has been presented as a strategic partner, but with some hesitation. For the Ministry of Foreign Affairs, the meaning of the strategic partnership was that Poland hoped "to share our experiences should China one day opt for a system of political pluralism" (Sikorski, 2012).[38]

For China, the meaning was the opposite: once we have a strategic partnership, please do not put sensitive issues on the bilateral agenda. It should be understood that the major problem was rooted in China's political difference and Poland's belief in the model of liberal democracy. The majority of Polish elites believed in Francoise Fukuyama's prediction of the end of history and the final victory of the Western model. In this context, China was placed opposite Japan "We will continue to pursue good cooperation with Japan, an outpost of democracy in the Pacific region", declared the Minister of Foreign Affairs.[39]

In 2014, in the address delivered by the Minister of Foreign Affairs, Radosław Sikorski, (2014), the perception changed, and China began to be perceived as an economic partner while Poland was the leader of the newly formed 16+1 format. The Polish government recognized the importance of local to local cooperation with the flagship project of a rail connection between Chengdu and Lodz.[40] In 2015, in the information on Polish foreign policy, China was mentioned seven times, and it was observed that "A multipolar and ideologically

---

38   Sikorski, R. (2011), *Expose ministra Sikorskiego na temat polityki zagranicznej RP w 2011 r.*
      (Address by the Minister of Foreign Affairs on the goals of Polish Foreign Policy in 2011),
      https://wyborcza.pl/1,76842,9261127,Expose_ministra_Sikorskiego_na_temat_polityki
      _zagranicznej.html (accessed 14 May 2020).

39   Sikorski, R. (2013), *Address by the Minister of Foreign Affairs on the goals of Polish Foreign
      Policy in 2013,* https://www.msz.gov.pl/en/news/address_by_the_minister_of_foreign
      _affairs_on_the_goals_of_polish_foreign_policy_in_2013 (accessed 14 May 2020).

40   Sikorski, R. (2014), *Address by the Minister of Foreign Affairs on the goals of Polish Foreign
      Policy in 2014,* https://www.msz.gov.pl/en/news/address_by_the_minister_of_foreign
      _affairs_on_the_goals_of_polish_foreign_policy_in_2014 (accessed 14 May 2020).

differentiated world is taking shape. The centre of its dynamics is pivoting towards the Pacific. China's role as a global power is growing. These changes bring new opportunities, but they can also be a source of rivalry and instability".[41] As the Minister pointed out, in this multipolar world, China and its relations with Central and Eastern Europe occupied a prominent place. Poland supports cooperation between regions.

To enhance cooperation with China's central and western regions, the Polish government decided to open a consulate general in Chengdu.[42] After the Law and Justice right-wing party won the election in autumn 2015, the general policy towards China was pursued, although the discourse was adjusted.[43] As Minister Jan Parys, head of the political cabinet in the Ministry of Foreign Affairs said, Poland took a more pragmatic stance towards China, mainly based on the non-interference principle. This assumption showed that China's political system was not perceived as an obstacle to further cooperation.[44]

Even though the economic dimensions of the cooperation became a priority, in 2017 the Minister of Foreign Affairs mentioned that "In an effort to strike a balance between different foreign policy components, Poland has taken a sharp turn in its non-European policy by opening more strongly to collaboration with countries in Asia, Africa, and the Middle East".[45] In this regard, China, and Asia as a whole, were placed as the balancing factor in shaping Polish foreign policy. The strategic partnership with the People's Republic of China has become a permanent part of Poland's foreign policy. The Polish MFA took advantage of the favourable atmosphere in Chinese-Polish relations brought about by high-level contacts in 2016. Further cooperation following the 16+1

---

41   Ibidem.

42   Schetyna, G. (2015), *Address by the Minister of Foreign Affairs on the goals of Polish Foreign Policy in 2015*, https://www.msz.gov.pl/en/ministry/polish_diplomacy_archive/former _ministers/remarks_mgs/address_by_the_minister_of_foreign_affairs_on_the_goals_of _polish_foreign_policy_in_2015 (accessed 14 May 2020).

43   Parys, J. (2015), *Polska zdekomunizowała Chiny* (Poland de-communized China). Accessed 20 May 2020. https://trybuna.info/polska/polska-zdekomunizowala-chiny/ and Day of Asia and Pacific in the Polish Parliament, November,2016, http://www.sejm.gov.pl/ sejm8.nsf/komunikat.xsp?documentId=4349210846C3FAC9C12580410046FFE4 (accessed 17 May 2020).

44   Ibidem.

45   Waszczykowski, W. (2017), *Address by the Minister of Foreign Affairs on the goals of Polish Foreign Policy in 2017*, https://www.msz.gov.pl/en/news/minister_witold_waszczykowski _on_priorities_of_polish_diplomacy (accessed 17 May 2020).

format, between Central European countries and China, including through the Secretariat for Maritime Affairs based in Poland, was welcomed.[46]

In Bucharest, the Chinese Prime Minister presented China's understanding of global issues. By repeating China's narrative on "small-big" countries – all should have equal opportunities for development – Li Keqiang tried to persuade partners from Central and Eastern Europe as to China's positive intentions. During the Belgrade Summit in 2014, the Chinese Prime Minister discussed the status of China and its Central European partners. As was remarked, both sides shared the similar condition of being classified as a developing world and emerging market economies. From this perspective, the great potential for cooperation was acknowledged. By working together in the same direction, both sides would be able to create exceptional cohesion and dynamism, which, in turn, would help us withstand downward pressure, facilitate growth and achieve industrial upgrading.[47] In the following years of the format's operation, the areas of cooperation were clarified. Starting in 2013, segments of economic and political cooperation were outlined. The latter includes the extension of the format with the collaboration of local authorities and that of young political leaders of the Communist Party of China, as well as selected parties of the Central and Eastern European region.[48]

However, in Suzhou in 2015, the Chinese side mainly concentrated on China's five-year plan and international cooperation in productivity. The international situation was placed in the context of the global economic system, financial markets and international cooperation in productivity. In the context of China's perception of the role of Poland and the whole of Central Europe, however, it should be noted that the region is perceived by Chinese authorities as the global South – the developing world.[49] On November 26, 2015, Chinese President Xi Jinping met with leaders of Central and Eastern

---

46   Waszczykowski, W. (2016), *Address by the Minister of Foreign Affairs on the goals of Polish Foreign Policy in 2016*, https://www.msz.gov.pl/resource/03ddaf74-39db-4db7-abf3 -c709842c4130:JCR (accessed 17 May 2020).

47   Li, Keqiang (2014), *Zai di san ci Zhongguo-Zhongdongou Guojia Lingdaoren Huiwushi de Jianghua* (Speech by H.E. Li Keqiang Premier of the State Council of The People's Republic of China, at the Third Summit of the Heads of Government of China and Central and Eastern European Countries), http://language.chinadaily.com.cn/news/2014-12/18/ content_19117369.htm (accessed 13 May 2020).

48   Mierzejewski D. Kowalski B. Ciborek p (2018) *Aktywność polityczna i gospodarcza Chińskiej Republiki Ludowej w regionie Europy Środkowej i Wschodniej* (China's political and economic actvities in Central and Eastern Europe), Lodz: University of Lodz Press.

49   Li, Keqiang (2015), *Zai di si ci Zhongguo-Zhongdongou Guojia Lingdaoren Huiwushi de Jianghua* [Speech by H.E. Li Keqiang Premier of the State Council of The People's Republic of China, at the Fourth Summit of the Heads of Government of China and Central and

European countries attending the fourth China-Central and Eastern European Leaders meeting. During the meeting, the Chinese President pointed out that the format of 16+1 had produced large, wide, and multi-level cooperation.

Moreover, the cooperation between China and Central and Eastern Europe opened up new channels for the development of relations between China and traditionally friendly countries. This friendship was rooted in post-socialist experiences. Due to the facts mentioned above, China perceives the cooperation between the two as the cooperation between global Souths. As Xi Jinping pointed out: "In the next step, China, together with the Central and Eastern European countries, should take the spirit of mutual benefits and win-win results, openness and inclusiveness and step up mutually beneficial cooperation in various fields".[50]

In Riga 2016, compared to Li Keqiang's speech in Suzhou, the perception of the future role of the format of 16+1 changed. Apart from the global trade and investment system (already mentioned), and the issue of productivity cooperation and cooperation in infrastructure and logistics, the Chinese Prime Minister placed Central Europe and China cooperation within the broader context of international society and cooperation: "the 16+1 platform cannot be separated from peace, stability and sustainable development, and at the same time has played a positive force for promoting world peace and development".[51] Moreover, as put forward by Li Keqiang, Central Europe, as part of a broader Europe, plays the role of pole in global affairs. Going even further, the 16+1 format was named as the creator and essential participant of the international system.[52] As the Minister of Foreign Affairs, Witold Waszczykowski, said, maritime cooperation brought both sides to more pragmatically oriented cooperation. Poland and China, however, have a different perception of building

---

Eastern European Countries], November 2015, http://www.mfa.gov.cn/chn//gxh/zlb/ldzyjh/t1318228.htm (accessed 12 May 2020).

50 Xi, Jinping (2015), *Xi Jinping meets collectively with the leaders of Central and Eastern European countries attending the 4th China-CEEC Leaders' Meeting*, https://www.fmprc.gov.cn/web/zyxw/t1318787.shtml (accessed 13 May 2020).

51 Li, Keqiang (2016), *Zai di wu ci Zhongguo-Zhongdongou Guojia Lingdaoren Huiwushi de Jianghua* [Speech by H.E. Li Keqiang Premier of the State Council of The People's Republic of China At the Fifth Summit of Heads of Government of China and Central and Eastern European Countries], November 2016. http://news.xinhuanet.com/politics/2016-11/06/c_1119859069.htm (accessed 17 May 2020).

52 Li, Keqiang (2017), *Zai di liu ci Zhongguo-Zhongdongou Guojia Lingdaoren Huiwushi de Jianghua* [Speech by H.E. Li Keqiang Premier of the State Council of The People's Republic of China, at the Sixth Summit of the Heads of Government of China and Central and Eastern European Countries], November 2017. http://news.xinhuanet.com/world/2017-11/28/c_1122022059.htm(accessed 17 May 2020).

South-South corridors in Europe. Poland and other countries in the region perceive South-South collaboration as an attempt at diversification of energy sources (e.g., through cooperation with the United States).[53] However, China sees the corridor as the way for exporting Chinese products to Western Europe via the Greek port of Piraeus. The arguments mentioned above pushed China and CEE countries to more pragmatic cooperation that was announced before the summit in Suzhou (2015). The Croatian Presidential Office has stressed that the China-Europe Land-Sea Express Line launched at the China+16 CEEC summit in Suzhou, corresponds significantly to the objectives of the Adriatic-Baltic-Black Sea Initiative. Developing a seaport corridor based on the Adriatic and Baltic ports is in line with the development of the Belt and Road Initiative and cooperation on industrial capacity[54] (President's Office, 2015). Following all these declarations in Riga, the topic of connectivity prevailed over that of trade. The main focus was on maritime issues. The Riga Declaration broadly presents the "Three Seas ABC" initiative announced at the Suzhou summit in 2015. It highlights the development of ports, including those in the hinterland, as well as logistic hubs, economic zones and transport corridors. The stress on maritime issues arises from the host country's interests, as maritime trade is crucial for Latvia. But it could also be that the thus far modest results of land transport under the 16+1 and Silk Road initiatives have led to a search for new areas of cooperation. The significance of maritime cooperation was confirmed by the decision to set up a secretariat for maritime issues in Poland, in 2017.[55]

In 2017 in Budapest, the official narrative presented by Li Keqiang went even further: stable cooperation within the 16+1 format brought stability to the "unstable international situation". By building cooperation into the Belt and Road Initiative, both sides could contribute to world stability and peace. By urging countries to follow international conventions or usual practices (惯例 *guan li*), China expressed its fear of the possibility of changing the rule of the game in the international economic order.[56] But on the other hand, at the 19th

---

53   Waszczykowski, W. (2016), *Address by the Minister of Foreign Affairs on the goals of Polish Foreign Policy in 2016*, https://www.msz.gov.pl/resource/03ddaf74-39db-4db7-abf3-c709842c4130:JCR (accessed 17 May 2020).

54   President's Office (2015) *Newsletter of the Office of the President of the Republic of Croatia.* https://www.predsjednik.hr/en/president-office/ (accessed 17 May 2020).

55   *The Riga Guidelines for Cooperation between China and Central and Eastern European Countries* (November 2016), http://english.gov.cn/news/international_exchanges/2016/11/06/content_281475484363051.htm (accessed 17 May 2020).

56   *The Budapest Guidelines for Cooperation between China and Central and Eastern European Countries* (November 2017), http://www.fmprc.gov.cn/mfa_eng/zxxx_662805/t1514534.shtml (accessed 17 May 2020).

Party Congress, the Chinese government called upon partners to build a "new type of international order" and be part of a "community of common destiny". During the next summit in Sofia, the capital of Bulgaria, the Chinese Prime Minister Li Keqiang (2018) tried to limit quandaries raised by the European Union and announced the platform as an open, inclusive and pan-European mechanism, without the intention of dividing the European Union. Similar to the summit in Budapest, the 16+1 platform was perceived as the mechanism for defending economic globalisation and free trade and opposing any kind of protectionism and unilateralism. The same arguments were repeated in Dubrovnik when Li Keqiang (2019) mentioned that 16+1 is a common proposal of 16 countries from Central and Eastern Europe and China. For the first time in the Chinese Prime Minister's speech, the post-socialist past echoed when he said that the 16+1 cooperation "helps to narrow the gap between the North and the South. China is willing to work with Central and Eastern European countries to promote economic globalization, jointly safeguard multilateralism, and promote the development of a global governance system in a more just and rational direction" (Li Keqiang, 2019).

5   Conclusion

As discussed, China has been placed at an important point in contemporary Polish history. Starting from the early 1950s, Poland and China shared a similar system of socialist values and political system. After the establishment of the "New China", Poland became an essential partner in opening up the People's Republic of China to the international trade system. Through the first joint venture – Chipolbrok shipping company – China had the opportunity to open itself to the outside world.

The second important characteristic was the 'common' approach toward the Soviet Union. Both sides voted against the uniformity of the socialist bloc, and this was particularly visible in 1956 and the Chinese impact on the Polish October Uprising in the city of Poznan. Then the split between China and the Soviet Union played a crucial role in shaping China-Poland relations. Polish foreign activities were *de-facto* subordinated to the *raison d'état* of the Soviet Union. Even during this period, Poland still enjoyed 'special status' and became the only single state that had a Consulate General in Shanghai during the Cultural Revolution.

In the 1980s, *détente* between Beijing and Moscow shaped the possibility for economic cooperation between China and the 'socialist camp'. After 1989, Chinese policymakers recognized the political choices taken by the newly established governments in Central European countries, while Polish elites, mainly based in the Solidarity Movement, criticized China for being a communist regime. The Civic Platform government enacted a shift in 2011. After boycotting the 2008 Olympic Games Opening ceremony and saying that China violated human rights in Tibet, Tusk's government decided to sign a strategic partnership with China. This approach has been continued by the current government of Law and Justice, and in 2016, the strategic partnership was upgraded to the comprehensive strategic partnership. However, it should be noted that for the domestic arena, the Law and Justice government is driven by its anti-communist sentiments, and this might play a role in future relations with China. But pragmatism is visible, and the government perceives Russia as the greatest threat to Polish security and therefore tries to use its ties with the big powers to counterbalance Moscow's aspirations.

As this study has argued, both sides have perceived each other through historical lenses and collective memory. From these perspectives, two narratives can be observed. The first is a pragmatic approach rooted in the history of the China-Poland-Russia triangular relations of the 1950s. The second is rooted in the post-socialist past of sharing a similar system of values.

The first, visible in both the Polish Minister for Foreign Affairs' assessments as well as the Chinese Prime Minister's speeches during the 16+1 meetings in Riga, Budapest and Dubrovnik, leads to the conclusion that both sides perceive each other as a significant player in the global power structure. This is a relatively new understanding of the roles of both parties in their respective foreign policies. The good relations with Central Europe, along with the intersection of Russian and American interests, might play a positive role in shaping China's arrival as a rising power. By balancing two major forces, the relations with Poland, and the broader Central Europe, might provide the basis for easing tensions between the powers.

As China's role and interests have been growing globally, the Chinese perspective of this initiative should be understood as building the economic corridor from South (Pireus) to North (Klaipeda, Gdansk), and playing an important role in accessing the European market. On the other hand, it might be used as leverage in power politics, especially in the China-Russia-United States triangle.

From the Polish point of view, the historical reading of the 1950s sounds similar. Special attention to maritime cooperation between three seas (the Adriatic, Black and Baltic Seas) was rooted in the Polish project of Intermarium. In the 1920s, the primary objective was to avoid the dominance of the big powers – Germany and Russia – in the Central Europe region. Due to fear of Soviet domination, and to prevent German and Russian expansionism and imperialism, this concept was supported by countries in Central Europe. From the pragmatic perspective of the use of China's presence in Europe, the government has emphasized the need for cooperation with China. This pragmatic perspective, driven by common experience and shared memory of relations with Russia, has played an important role in shaping a joint platform to balance actions. In this regard, the relations between Beijing and Moscow are perceived as critical and decisive in developing Poland's policy towards China.

The second reading of history – being part of the same socialist past – brought the understanding of South-South cooperation. The idea of equalizing Sino-CEE relations with developing-country mechanisms and their solidarity, apart from economic considerations, brings associations with Chinese history which constitute an important part of China's identity and its behaviour in the international arena. The former communist countries of the CEE, apart from those in the Austro-Hungarian Empire, were not involved in the process of 'carving up the melon', that is, the partition of China in the sphere of influence of relevant Western powers and Japan in the period between the Opium Wars and the Second World War. This might be further strengthened by the critical attitude towards Western values found in Chinese political circles which has begun to converge with the recent increasingly prominent trends in leading CEE countries. That is the direction of questioning the values of liberal democracy within the respective political establishments. As Chinese scholars have argued, "South-South cooperation (*nannan hezuo* 南南合作)" includes both traditional developing countries and less-developed countries and emerging markets (Interview, Chinese Academy of Social Science, 2016). Moreover, China also acknowledges that several Central and Eastern European countries are developed countries and therefore have one feature of "North-South cooperation." In sum, the purpose of the "new platform for South-South cooperation (*nannan hezuo xin pingtai* 南南合作新的平台)" is not to "belittle" Central and Eastern European countries. Moreover, as identified after seven years of the 16+1 platform, China is trying to utilize its concept of the division of labour. Placing all 16 countries in "one basket" allows China to identify the willingness and strengths of each participant. This approach is especially visible when it comes to different sectors of the economy: the Hungarian government decided to be an RMB (Chinese currency) internationalization hub, and logistic center; Poland took maritime cooperation as the leading sector; the Czech Republic went for automotive and high-tech; Romania leads in energy; Bulgaria in agriculture; and Albania in tourism (Mierzejewski, Kowalski, Ciborek, 2018). As mainly argued by Chinese scholars, each sector of the economy was voluntarily taken by a member state and there was no pressure from the Chinese side (Interview, 2018).

Some Central and Eastern European countries feel 'devalued' mainly because they are closely linked with international aid regardless of 'North-South cooperation' or 'South-South cooperation'. According to the traditional definition by the OECD, aid means "unilateral giving" and recipients are in a position of inequality and passivity. Obviously, 'South-South cooperation' and 'North-South cooperation' in this context, refer to the pragmatic cooperation of equality between countries in similar stages of development and are not unequal aid-aid relationships.

Two different interpretations of the common histories have become a major part of bilateral relations. The core puzzle is how both interpret current issues in international relations. The understanding of the international context, e.g., relations between powers, will test whether China and Poland will share a pragmatic way of seeing reality, or whether Beijing will follow the South-South narrative that will not necessarily help to shape win-win cooperation. From the perspective of China's strategy, Central and Eastern countries are placed on the same side as Beijing, that of the Developing World, and the Global South. On the other hand, when Sino-American controversies bring to the fore the history of Polish-American relations based on the common slogan "For yours and our freedom", the Revolutionary War, Woodrow Wilson's "Fourteen Points", and support for the "Solidarity Movement", then Poland may turn from its pragmatic medium power policy in order to side with one of the superpowers. In the context mentioned above, Poland should use the experience, historical narratives and memories of the time (1955–1970) when Warsaw was the place of Sino-American talks, and which led to the *rapprochement* of both adversaries.

Acknowledgment: This paper was prepared as part of research project no. 2019/33/B/HS5/01667 supported by the National Science Centre.

Bibliography

Benken, P. (2014), *Problematyka stosunków między Misją Polską do Komisji Nadzorczej Państw Neutralnych a Sztabem Wojskowej Komisji Rozejmowej strony Koreańskiej Armii Ludowej/Chińskich Ochotników Ludowych w Kaesongu oraz wytyczne w tej sprawie* (The relations between Polish mission in Neutral Control Commission and its relations with the Korean People's Army and Chinese People's Volunteers in Kaesong Headquarter). Pamięć i Sprawiedliwość (Memory and Justice) vol. 13, no 1, pp. 441–447.

Ben-Yehuda, N. (1995), *Masada Myth: Collective Memory and Mythmaking in Israel*, Wisconsin: Wisconsin Press.

Bosch, T. E. (2016), *Memory Studies: A brief concept paper. Media, Conflict and Democratisation.* http://eprints.whiterose.ac.uk/117289/1/Bosch%202016_Memory %20Studies.pdf (accessed 12 March 2020).

Burdelski, M. (2011), 60 Years of Diplomatic Relations between Poland and the People's Republic of China – Historical Overview. *Polish Political Science*, no 9, pp. 211–237.

Day of Asia and Pacific in the Polish Parliament, November 2016, http://www.sejm.gov .pl/sejm8.nsf/komunikat.xsp?documentId=4349210846C3FAC9C12580410046FFE4 (accessed 17 May 2020).

Garver J. (1993), *Foreign Relations of the People's Republic of China*, Englewood Cliffs: Simon&Schuster Company.

Huang, Xiaodan, and Sun, Danyao (2016). *"Cankao Ziliao" zhong de Bo-Xiong Shijian, Zhonggong de Fanying* (The Reaction of the Central Committee for Crisis in Poland and Hungary in "References Materials"). http://zgdsw.net.cn/n1/2016/0426/c219022 -28305527.html (accessed 14 May 2020).

Interview with professor Krzysztof Gawlikowski. (2017), Chiński udział w polskim październiku (China's participation in Polish October). *Tygodnik Przegląd.* https:// www.tygodnikprzeglad.pl/chinski-udzial-polskim-pazdzierniku/ (accessed 14 May 2020).

Kansteiner, W. (2002), Finding Meaning in Memory: A Methodological Critique of Collective Memory Studies. *History and Theory*, vol. 41, no, pp. 179–197.

Kwaśniewski A. (2011), *Rozmowa z Aleksandrem Kwaśniewski* (Conversation with Aleksander Kwaśniewski). https://polskieradio24.pl/13/53/Artykul/502180,Rozmowa -z-Aleksandrem-Kwasniewskim (accessed 14 May 2020).

Li, Keqiang (2014), *Zai di san ci Zhongguo-Zhongdongou Guojia Lingdaoren Huiwushi de Jianghua* (Speech by H.E. Li Keqiang Premier of the State Council of The People's Republic of China At the Third Summit of Heads of Government of China and Central and Eastern European Countries), http://language.chinadaily.com.cn/ news/2014-12/18/content_19117369.htm (accessed 13 May 2020).

Li, Keqiang (2015), *Zai di si ci Zhongguo-Zhongdongou Guojia Lingdaoren Huiwushi de Jianghua* (Speech by H.E. Li Keqiang Premier of the State Council of The People's Republic of China At the Fourth Summit of Heads of Government of China and Central and Eastern European Countries), November 2015, http://www.mfa.gov.cn/ chn//gxh/zlb/ldzyjh/t1318228.htm (accessed 12 May 2020).

Li, Keqiang (2016), *Zai di wu ci Zhongguo-Zhongdongou Guojia Lingdaoren Huiwushi de Jianghua* (Speech by H.E. Li Keqiang Premier of the State Council of The People's Republic of China At the Fifth Summit of Heads of Government of China and Central and Eastern European Countries), November 2016. http://news.xinhuanet.com/ politics/2016-11/06/c_1119859069.htm (accessed 17 May 2020).

Li, Keqiang (2017), *Zai di liu ci Zhongguo-Zhongdongou Guojia Lingdaoren Huiwushi de Jianghua* (Speech by H.E. Li Keqiang Premier of the State Council of The People's

Republic of China At the Sixth Summit of Heads of Government of China and Central and Eastern European Countries), November 2017. http://news.xinhuanet.com/world/2017-11/28/c_1122022059.htm (accessed 17 May 2020).

Mierzejewski D., Kowalski B., Ciborek. (2018), *Aktywność polityczna i gospodarcza Chińskiej Republiki Ludowej w regionie Europy Środkowej i Wschodniej* (China's political and economic actvities in Central and Eastern Europe), Lodz: University of Lodz Press.

Morawiecki, M.(2019), *Premier Mateusz Morawiecki podczas obchodów 450. rocznicy unii polsko – litewskiej* (Prime Minister Mateusz Morawiecki during the 450. Anniversary of Poland-Lithuania Commonwealth), https://www.gov.pl/web/premier/premier-mateusz-morawiecki-podczas-obchodow-450-rocznicy-unii-polsko--litewskiej (accessed 19 November 2020).

Neiger M., Meyers O., and Zandberg E., eds. (2011), *On Media Memory Collective Memory in a New Media Age*. London: Palgrave Macmillan.

Olick J., and Robbins J. (1998), Social Memory Studies: From "Collective Memory" to the Historical Sociology of Mnemonic Practices. *Annual Review of Sociology*, vol. 24, p. 112.

Parys J. (2015), *Polska zdekomunizowała Chiny* (Poland de-communized China), https://trybuna.info/polska/polska-zdekomunizowala-chiny/ (accessed 20 May 2020).

President's Office (2015), *Newsletter of the Office of the President of the Republic of Croatia*. https://www.predsjednik.hr/en/president-office/ (accessed 17 May 2020).

Rowiński, J. (2009), *ChRL a wydarzenia październikowe 1956 w Polsce. Czy Chińczycy uchronili nasz kraj przed interwencją radziecką?* (The People's Republic of China and Polish October 1956. Did the Chinese secure our country from the Soviet's intervention?) In ed. B. Góralczyk, Poland-China. Yesterday, today, tommorow, Toruń: Wyd. Adam Marszałek.

Rowiński, J., ed. (2006), *Polski październik 1956 w polityce światowej* (Polish October 1956 in the Global Politics). Warsaw: Polish Institute for International Affairs.

Schetyna, G. (2015), *Address by the Minister of Foreign Affairs on the goals of Polish Foreign Policy in 2015*, https://www.msz.gov.pl/en/ministry/polish_diplomacy_archive/former_ministers/remarks_mgs/address_by_the_minister_of_foreign_affairs_on_the_goals_of_polish_foreign_policy_in_2015 (accessed 14 May 2020).

Schwartz, B. (1991), Social Change and Collective Memory: The Democratization of George Washington, *American Sociological Review*, Vol. 56, No. 2, pp. 221–236.

Shen Zhihua, Li Danhui (2006), *Kryzys w Polsce 1956 roku i stosunki polsko-chińskie widziane z Pekinu* (1956 Crisis in Poland and Sino-Polish relations: view from Beijing), In eds. Jan Rowiński, Tytus Jaskułowski, Polski Październik 1956 w polityce światowej, (Polish October 1956 in the Global Politics). Warsaw: Polish Institute for International Affairs.

Shen, Zhihua ed. (2011), *Zhong-Su Guanxi Shigang 1917–1991* (History of Sino-Soviet Relations 1917–1991). Beijing: Social Sciences Academy Press.

Sikorski, R. (2008), *Informacja ministra spraw zagranicznych o założeniach polskiej polityki zagranicznej w 2008* r. (Address by the Minister of Foreign Affairs on the goals of Polish Foreign Policy in 2008), http://orka2.sejm.gov.pl/Debata6.nsf/main/20C4290E (accessed 20 May 2020).

Sikorski, R. (2011), *Expose ministra Sikorskiego na temat polityki zagranicznej RP w 2011 r.* (Address by the Minister of Foreign Affairs on the goals of Polish Foreign Policy in 2011), https://wyborcza.pl/1,76842,9261127,Expose_ministra_Sikorskiego_na_temat_polityki_zagranicznej.html (accessed 14 May 2020).

Sikorski, R. (2013), *Address by the Minister of Foreign Affairs on the goals of Polish Foreign Policy in 2013*, https://www.msz.gov.pl/en/news/address_by_the_minister_of_foreign_affairs_on_the_goals_of_polish_foreign_policy_in_2013 (accessed 14 May 2020).

Sikorski, R. (2014), *Address by the Minister of Foreign Affairs on the goals of Polish Foreign Policy in 2014*, https://www.msz.gov.pl/en/news/address_by_the_minister_of_foreign_affairs_on_the_goals_of_polish_foreign_policy_in_2014 (accessed 14 May 2020).

Spence, J. (1990), *The Search for Modern China*, New York, London, W.W. Norton & Company.

The Budapest Guidelines for Cooperation between China and Central and Eastern European Countries (November 2017), http://www.fmprc.gov.cn/mfa_eng/zxxx_662805/t1514534.shtml (accessed 17 May 2020).

The Riga Guidelines for Cooperation between China and Central and Eastern European Countries (November 2016), http://english.gov.cn/news/international_exchanges/2016/11/06/content_281475484363051.htm (accessed 17 May 2020).

Walton, R. E. (2013), Collective Memory in Contemporary Poland and Pre-Independence (1918) Warfare: An Early 21st Century Foreign Traveler's Observations concerning Polish Battlefield Memorials Review of European Studies. *Review of European Studies*, no 5, pp. 1–12.

Waszczykowski, W. (2016), *Address by the Minister of Foreign Affairs on the goals of Polish Foreign Policy in 2016*, https://www.msz.gov.pl/resource/03ddaf74-39db-4db7-abf3-c709842c4130:JCR (accessed 17 May 2020).

Waszczykowski, W. (2017), *Address by the Minister of Foreign Affairs on the goals of Polish Foreign Policy in 2017*, https://www.msz.gov.pl/en/news/minister_witold_waszczykowski_on_priorities_of_polish_diplomacy (accessed 17 May 2020).

Wendt, A. (1999), *Social Theory of International Politics* (Cambridge Studies in International Relations). Cambridge: Cambridge University Press.

Werblan, A. (1997), Rozmowa Władysława Gomułki z Zhou Enlaiem w 1957 r. (Conversation between Władysław Gomułka and Zhou Enlai in 1957), *Dzieje Najnowsze*, no 4, pp. 119–143.

Wertsch, J. V. (2008), The Narrative Organization of Collective Memory, *Ethos*, Vol. 36, No. 1, pp. 120–135.

Wrobel, J. (2016), *Z dziejów polsko-chińskiego sojuszu morskiego 1950–1957* (The stories of Sino-Polish Maritime Alliance), Lodz: Institute of National Remembrance.

Xi Jinping (2015), *Xi Jinping meets collectively with the leaders of Central and Eastern European countries attending the 4th China-CEEC Leaders' Meeting*, https://www.fmprc.gov.cn/web/zyxw/t1318787.shtml (accessed 13 May 2020).

Zhongguo Jinxiandaishi Gangyao (2010) (The guideline for Chinese contemporary and modern history, 2010 version), Beijing: Higher Education Press.

Zhu Dandan (2016), *China's Involvement in the Hungarian Revolution, October-November 1956* (November,2016),http://unipub.lib.unicorvinus.hu/2591/1/COJOURN_Vol1_No3_06_Dandan_Zhu.pdf (accessed 14 May 2020).

CHAPTER 5

German and Hungarian Views on the Belt and Road Initiative – A Power Game Balance in Central Europe?

Csaba Moldicz

1   Introduction

This article aims to give a brief, preliminary assessment of German and Hungarian views on the Belt and Road Initiative (BRI). The preliminary nature of the article derives from the fact that the BRI is still in the making, and it will be for years to come, thus its framing must constantly change as well. The author intends partly to analyse the media coverage of the BRI in both countries and partly to evaluate academic papers on the same subject. This evaluation is to be carried out by examining how events, information and commentaries related to the initiative are represented, and at the same time it will attempt to organize and classify arguments pro and contra, and interpret narratives arising from the views expressed.

Our focus is on German and Hungarian language materials published in these countries, and we do not seek to investigate other materials published in neighbouring countries (Switzerland, Austria, Romania, Serbia, etc.). One of the reasons for this is that different political environments change the focus of the discussions significantly, in particular in Hungarian communities living in countries like Serbia or Ukraine, which are not members of the European Union. Another reason is that traditionally, foreign policies have different focuses. For example, Romanian diplomacy has a strong US-orientation, while Serbian foreign policy is Russia-oriented. In other words, China's appreciation is here less positive than in Hungary since the cultural, political and economic backgrounds are different. Relevant differences in the Austrian and German interpretations of the BRI are traceable to dissimilar company structure; while German politicians are concerned about selling strategically important (high-tech) firms to Chinese, Austrian elites learned in the 1990s how much wealth can be generated by opening new markets. There is also the consideration of the Austrian experience of standing between the communist and capitalist blocs, which has resulted in Austrian firms having taken advantage of this 'bridge' position for many decades.

The other reason for choosing these two countries is that both have pursued a very different, if not opposite approach, as regards their China-policy. The author does not rely on comprehensive data collection in carrying out this evaluation, since as mentioned, the aim is to collect and classify typical arguments in the discourse.

2   Differing Geopolitical and Economic Interests in Germany and Hungary

Germany, being the most influential economic power in the EU, stands at the centre of regional supply chains and German firms dominate the Polish, Czech, Slovakian and Hungarian economies. (Piketty, 2018) A growing Chinese presence would diminish German influence in the region and German firms might also be threatened by Chinese firms looking to gain more market share in the EU. Chinese investment in Germany might also seek the acquisition of the cutting-edge technology of German firms. Until recently, Germany was one of the strongest advocates of cooperation with China, but the eurozone crisis provided a turning point. China's growing economic and geopolitical presence seems to threaten the unity of the zone, as well as the unity of the European Union, according to some critics. In particular, Greece and the Visegrad countries, where Chinese activity has been growing, are key countries for German foreign and economic policy. One must not forget that German firms relocated much of their production to Poland, the Czech Republic, Slovakia and Hungary. Therefore, we can argue that there is a triangle of interests, where Central Europe is the weakest link, and China and Germany are in competition to win over Central European countries.

Nevertheless, cooperation and competition are two sides of the same coin. The German coalition agreement strongly underlines the importance of cooperation with China. (Coalition Agreement, 2018: 153)

As the Chinese presence has grown on the European continent, Germany has found it increasingly more difficult to cooperate with China, although German politicians seem to be aware of the opportunities provided by developing cooperation with the latter. Since China might find cooperation difficult with Germany, one easy solution is to deepen ties with Hungary.

The Hungarian position has been very different[1] since the Hungarian government approved the so-called 'Eastern Opening Policy' in 2011. The underlying

---

1   When looking at the roots of 21st century bilateral relations, it is clear that these relations started to develop rapidly after the visit of the Hungarian Premier Minister, Péter Medgyessy

idea behind the concept of this policy is that, historically, the Hungarian economy was always reliant on capital and knowledge imported from Western Europe. That is the case even today.[2] The Great Recession (2008–2009) clearly revealed the vulnerability of the Hungarian economy since, as mentioned earlier, 79 percent of Hungarian exports targeted other EU-members (2017), and more than two thirds of exports are dealt with by multinational firms in Hungary.[3] Another channel of economic contagion was the reliance on Western European banks. The subsidiaries of these banks made up the majority of the Hungarian banking sector, and when they reduced and/or withdrew their credit in the first wave of the economic shock, they triggered a new wave of economic shock to the Hungarian economy. Thus, the 'Eastern Opening Policy', as a means to lessen the one-sided reliance on Western Europe, is an economic project of historic relevance to Hungary. It is not only a pet project of the present government, but the principal opportunity to make an economic breakthrough and go beyond middle-income country status.[4] Given the delineated background, it is no surprise that the concrete target indicator of the strategy is to double the exports of Hungarian small and medium enterprises. The strategy does not exclude, but neither does it focus upon, multinational enterprises. The main target countries of the strategy are China, Russia and India, where potential for trade growth is the highest.

---

in 2003. After this visit, every Hungarian Prime Minister has visited China, and the new Orban government after 2010 has continued this policy, aimed at strengthening relations with China. The most obvious example of these efforts was the launching of the so-called "Eastern Opening Policy" in 2011. The strategy was revised in 2012 by adopting a broader growth strategy (the Széll Kálmán plan). The strategy pointed out the importance of trade and investment diversification. The details of this policy were described by Becsey who explained that, besides the establishment of trading houses in emerging markets, and the promotion of Hungarian firms, in particular small and medium enterprises, initiatives in the education and tourism sectors are linked to the core "Eastern Opening Policy". (Becsey, 2014).

2   The first signs of the asymmetric reliance were visible after 1492 when trade routes shifted in Europe leading to growing Hungarian dependency on trade with the West. The one-sided reliance grew until WW2, when the formation of the socialist bloc in Eastern Europe cut these ties with Western Europe resulting in political dependency on the Soviet Union. Although the socialist era disrupted these links, they were swiftly rebuilt after 1990, again increasing the reliance on Western capital and technology in the Hungarian economy.

3   Based on the data of the Hungarian Central Statistical Office.

4   In economics, the middle-income country trap dilemma refers to difficulties of countries relying on cheap labor, which struggle to find new competitive advantages when incomes are already on the rise, and the difference in labor cost begins to disappear. It is clear that both China and Hungary face the same dilemma. However, China's maneuvering room is larger in resetting the course of the economy due to its large market and abundant capital.

3   German and Hungarian Views on the BRI

We will now attempt a more detailed classification of views on the Belt and Road Initiative and try to distinguish between geopolitical and economic arguments and considerations. This is not always an easy task but the endeavour may contribute to clarifying the real motivations behind the regional initiatives in Central Europe.

4   Geopolitical Reasoning

When it comes to the geopolitical explanations of the Belt and Road Initiative, German politicians and pundits are more concerned about the eventual geopolitical ramifications of the BRI than their Hungarian counterparts. There are many aspects which are absent from the Hungarian debate on the BRI (see later). For example, the question of how Indians and Russians view this initiative, is rarely debated. Similarly, none of the most vehement Hungarian opponents assume that the Chinese would intend to divide the EU by launching this initiative. We shall proceed to a brief overview of the typical arguments to be found in both the media and interviews made with politicians:

1.   The BRI was initiated because the new isolationism of the US provided a window of opportunity for the Chinese.
2.   The BRI is the answer to aggressive American foreign policy.
3.   The BRI is not supported by Russia and India.
4.   The BRI will not be successful if the Chinese do not solve problems in their 'backyard'.
5.   There is the Chinese will to divide Europe, possibly leading to the break-up of the eurozone and the EU itself.

Before turning to commonly held opinions, it is worth considering one rarely mentioned argument: that the BRI was initiated due to Chinese weakness in the Pacific Ocean region. This is underlined by a few analysts, who emphasize the shift in geopolitical power relations. They refer to political struggles in the South China Sea between the United States and China and add that China does not have the sufficient military power (navy) to counterbalance the United States in this region. Due to this fact and the traditionally non-confrontational approach of Chinese foreign policy, China turns to the Eurasian masses, where resistance is weaker. The Hungarian analyst, Eszterhai puts it this way:

> Since China would need a stronger navy in the traditionally US-domi-
> nated East-Southeast Asian sphere of influence to overshadow the United

States, it had to look for other options. The One Belt, One Road program serves this goal. The program ends the era of low intensity Chinese foreign policy, and it leads to an international activity, appropriate to China's new international status.[5]

ESZTERHAI, 2016a

However, China's economic and political rise needs a spatial dimension too. The phrase "All roads lead to Rome" was used when the Roman Empire was at its zenith because indeed, all roads did lead to Rome as a physical expression of Rome as the centre of an empire. No wonder then, that China's Belt and Road Initiative is so largely focused on improving transport between China and the rest of the world, since there is no trade without infrastructure.

If one adds the traditionally non-expansionist nature of Chinese foreign policy, the argument seems to be very logical, although unfortunately, it is rarely acknowledged by German analysts and politicians.

The opinion, that the new American isolationism provided a springboard for the Belt and Road Initiative can also be found in the corresponding literature. (again, see later) This interpretation relies more on political rather than economic reasoning. The question 'Why would China invest heavily in other countries?' is often explained by the United States withdrawing from the Trans-Pacific Partnership, and other signs of isolationism (Origo, 2017). It is often stated that China would use American withdrawal to gain more influence in the world economy and world politics through the launching of the BRI. (Hsiang, 2018) Nevertheless, the more realistic analysts emphasize the sequencing of events, pointing out that the Belt and Road Initiative started in 2013, while American elections took place later, in 2016. (Rabena, 2015) It was only after Trump's victory that a new approach to foreign policy was implemented. Whilst logic might suggest that aggressive American foreign policy came first, and was followed by the Chinese initiative, this was not the case.

It seems to be a fact that the new American president and his administration do not support American involvement in Asian economic integration. Moreover, the recent trade war also shows that bilateral trade and investment ties are also strained. However, the assertive American foreign policy moves, in the dispute over and with North Korea, shows that the US will not withdraw

---

5   The original text goes: Mivel hagyományosnak tekinthető kelet és délkelet-ázsiai érdekszférájában az USA fokozott jelenlétének a háttérbeszorításához erősebb flottára lenne szüksége, Kínának új lehetőségeket kellett keresnie. Ezt a célt hivatott az Egy Övezet, Egy Út program megvalósítani, amelyet egyben a korábbi alacsony intenzitású külpolitikájának végét, és Kína új hatalmi helyzetéhez méltó nemzetközi aktivitást jelent."

from the region but will shift the emphasis to military cooperation instead. That is why it is no coincidence that the Quadrilateral Security Dialogue, (QUAD, a navy cooperation platform between the US, India, Japan and Australia), shows signs of revival. The QUAD was proposed by Japanese Prime Minister Shinzo Abe in 2007, but the idea was dropped because China protested. Huang comments upon the first meeting which took place in Manila in November 2017:

> Economically, the strategy can be seen as an answer to China's Belt and Road Initiative, which seeks to establish a China-centric trade route from the Philippines to the Mediterranean Sea.
>
> HUANG, 2017

There is a lot of discussion over who made the first move and who simply responded to the other's aggressive policy. There are also analysts who highlight China's BRI project as part of a geopolitical game between the US and China. The Hungarian György states:

> When Hillary Clinton in 2011 announced America's Pacific Century, or the American Eastward Opening Policy, the Chinese didn't hesitate with the answer for long. In 2013, they started their Westward Opening Policy, the One Belt, One Road Initiative.
>
> GYÖRGY, 2017[6]

At this point, György referred to Hillary Clinton's article 'America's Pacific Century,' that signalled a definite change in American foreign policy in 2011, when she wrote "The future of politics will be decided in Asia, not Afghanistan or Iraq, and the United States will be right at the center of the action." (Clinton, 2011)

This sequencing is correct and is very likely the best explanation at this point. However, the problem is that the BRI cannot be explained only by geopolitical motives since, as is argued later, there are numerous economic ones as well. At the same time, it must be clear, that not only do we need explanations as to why the Chinese started the BRI, we must also look at the narrative of what the obstacles to a successful BRI are.

---

6   The original text: "Amikor Hillary Clinton 2011-ben meghirdette Amerika csendes vagy csendes-óceáni évszázadát (America's Pacific Century), vagyis az amerikai külpolitika „keleti nyitását", a kínaiak sem késlekedtek sokáig a stratégiai válasszal. 2013-ban nyilvánosságra hozták nyugati nyitásuk programját Egy övezet, egy út kezdeményezés néven (One Belt, One Road Initiative)."

That is a point where the Hungarian and German interpretations differ entirely. The reluctance of India, and the ambivalent position of Russia, is emphasized by the German Bessler, in addition to stressing the presumed evil and hidden intentions of the Chinese. Bessler underlines:

> As a result, the picture is ambivalent [referring to cooperation with India]. The same applies to Russia which is often featured as a supporter of the Chinese 'Silk Road' Initiative. However, Russia has its own free trade and investment initiative – the Eurasian Economic Union – with Belarus, Kazakhstan, Armenia, and Kirgizstan.
>
> BESSLER, 2015: 9[7]

On the one hand, this argument is accurate when assessing the reluctance of India and Russia, and is supported by the implications of the hegemon stability theory[8] – China as emerging hegemon can motivate other countries to participate in the Belt and Road Initiative, although it cannot force them to cooperate. The project must be built upon mutual benefit. On the other hand, it is less correct when overlooking the explicit non-interventionist policy of the Belt and Road Initiative.

Among the geopolitical arguments, it is rarely stressed that India did not join the initiative, which becomes increasingly less likely as tension between India and China grows. Not only old border disputes matter, but the Pakistan-China economic corridor will go through the disputed Kashmir region. In addition, traditionally strong allies of India (Nepal, Sri-Lanka) seem to have turned away from India during recent years. It is clear that problems or obstacles are rarely underlined in the Hungarian interpretations, which can be simply explained by an ignorance of international politics but is probably better explained by the very clear interest-based approach of Hungarian foreign policy which stands in sharp contrast to the more value-based approach of German foreign policy.

Similarly, the importance of a very friendly political environment is rarely reflected in Hungarian discussions. Erling (2017) highlights the importance of friendly-minded partners. He quotes the warning of the Shanghai historian, Shen Zhihua, who referred to North-Korea as a potential enemy, emphasizing that for as long as North-Korea poses a threat to the region, China cannot

---

7   The original text goes: "Das Bild, das sich daraus ergibt, ist ambivalent. Ähnliches gilt für Russland, das oft als Unterstützer der chinesischen „Seidenstraßen"-Initiative gilt. Allerdings verfolgt Russland zusammen mit Belarus, Kasachstan, Armenien und Kirgisistan eine eigene Freihandels- und Investitionsinitiative, die Eurasische Wirtschaftsunion."

8   More on the theory can be found in Schmidt, 2018.

further develop its Silk Road initiative. In this German view, China has the role of the benevolent hegemon whose peace-keeping efforts are necessary in the region. (Erling, 2017)

A day before the Belt and Road Forum in 2017, Ankenbrand (2017) in his FAZ article, analyzed the project and emphasized the tensions and differences in approach between the American and Chinese leaderships, in particular when it comes to global warming and globalization. He pointed out that the Chinese leadership wants to use Trump's hostile approach to free trade and the Paris climate agreement to position itself as the most important global power. (Ankenbrand, 2017) A very similar thought can be found in the N-TV article (2017), although the tone is much more positive.

In his article, Gaspers, from the Mercator Institute for China Studies, also gave an analysis of the Belt and Road Forum in Beijing on May 14, 2017. This short analysis was published in the German Journal of Economic Policy (Zeitschrift für Wirtschaftspolitik). Gaspers states:

> The New Silk Road is the symbol of an adjusted geopolitical strategy: Beijing makes with its generous credits the recipient countries dependent economically and it requires political support for financial aid from time to time.
>
> GASPERS, 2017[9]

This argument leads us to the problems of a rising hegemon power: whether or not the hegemon power interferes in the internal affairs of other countries will give rise to problems in both cases. But Chinese foreign policy and the BRI solve this dilemma by implementing the non-intervention principle. Therefore, this argument clearly does not consider the explicit non-intervention policy of the BRI.

To summarize Hungarian and German approaches and geopolitical explanations of the Belt and Road Initiative, it is very clear that Hungary sees more opportunities than threats in the BRI. Hungary's geopolitical interests are closely tied to its economic interests, which can also be said of Germany, but it is their assessment of the BRI's political importance which fundamentally differs. Germany's economic backyard is Central Europe where the growing Chinese presence is clearly not welcome.

---

9 The original text goes: "Die Neue Seidenstraße ist auch Ausdruck einer geänderten geopolitischen Strategie: Mit seinen großzügigen Krediten bringt Peking die Empfängerländer in wirtschaftliche Abhängigkeit – und verlangt mitunter politische Unterstützung im Gegenzug für Finanzspritzen."

5   Economic Arguments

In the analyses of German politicians, the importance of open markets is one of the often-recurring elements. Brigitte Zypries, Minister for Economic Affairs, underlined the importance of free trade and open markets in her May 2017 speech. She stressed that markets should be opened further in order to strengthen economic ties and boost growth. The EU, she argued, advocates open markets both among its members and among its non-European partners. She added "As close partners, we encourage China to implement reforms and open its market." (FAZ, 2017a)[10] In this paper, the author only discusses pro and con arguments related to the BRI and does not focus on the manner of presenting events in the media. In the quoted FAZ article, the support of the Russian and Turkish Premier Ministers does not make the best impression on German readers. This support is often emphasized in the article and the negative impression is clearly an effect the author of the article wanted to achieve.

The same speech was quoted by the German Newspaper *Die Welt*. (Erling, 2017) Zypries, the journalist Erling cited, stressed that in her opinion the Belt and Road Initiative must not be turned into one-way trade where Chinese products flood the Single Market of the EU, while access to the Chinese market is restricted.

N-TV[11] also quoted this speech in which the minister specifically underlined German carmakers' problems in the Chinese market where they are forced to set up companies with the Chinese. In the German view, this is a clear restriction on free trade. (N-TV, 2017)

The Single Market lies at the core of the European project and yet trade disputes are to be settled within the framework of the World Trade Organization. If there are problems with the Chinese treatment of European firms, the right place to discuss these questions is the WTO.

In the Hungarian understanding of the BRI, neither access to the Single Market nor the Chinese market is the crucial question, but access to Chinese capital is. In this aspect, Hungarian and Chinese relations are outstanding: between 2000 and 2018, Hungary attracted most of the Chinese FDI in the region – 2.4 billion Euro, while only 1.4 billion Euro was invested in Poland, which was second in the region. (Haneman – Huotari – Kratz, 2019: 10)[12]

---

10   The original text goes: "Als enge Partner ermutigen wir China, Reformen und Marktöffnung zu liefern."

11   N-TV is a private news channel and holds the largest market share in this market niche.

12   During the same period the following amounts were invested by Chinese firms in the form of FDI: Estonia 0.1, Latvia 0.1, Lithuania 0.1, Slovakia 0.1, Slovenia 0.3, Croatia 0.3, Bulgaria 0.4, Romania 0.9, Austria 1.0 and the Czech Republic 1.0 Euro billion.

Another aspect, often emphasized in both countries, is that, due to the over-capacity of Chinese capital and an abundance of the latter, there are clear incentives to go abroad. The Hungarian China expert, Gergely Salát, explains the BRI project in the light of economic pressures on China. He is quoted in an interview as saying:

> China has many goals. On the one hand China has abundant capital to invest and unused construction capacities along the Silk Road routes and investments by Chinese firms help absorb these capacities. On the other hand, China strives to build upon several import sources and markets, to minimize exposure.
>
> PATAKY, 2015[13]

The German Uebele, also discusses this aspect in his analysis published by the Institut der deutschen Wirtschaft Köln as guest commentary (Uebele, 2016). According to him, Beijing uses this strategy to reduce the overcapacity of its economy. This argument is well known, and it can also be found in development economics where there is a consensus among scholars that being land-locked is inimical to international trade. (Collier, 2017) This problem can be found in Western China, and of course in the landlocked countries of Central Asia (for example, in Kazakhstan, Mongolia, etc.). This argument refers to large distances and poor infrastructure which lead to excessive costs of transfer. The initiative aims to diminish these problems and clearly it would be easier to start in the neighbouring countries.

Another argument – very often found in both countries – is that access to raw materials and other resources motivated the Chinese to launch and implement the Belt and Road Initiative. (Origo, 2017) The Hungarian Eszterhai contends:

> The goal of the New Silk Road Project, easiest to identify, is to ensure import routes for raw materials. Due to the dynamic economic growth, China has been forced to import more and more raw materials from the 90s on.
>
> ESZTERHAI, 2016b: 118[14]

---

13   The original text: "Több célja is van. Egyrészt Kínának rengeteg a befektetni való tőkéje és kihasználatlan építőipari kapacitása, az útvonal mentén kínai cégek által végrehajtott rengeteg infrastrukturális beruházás segíthet ezeket lekötni. Másrészt Kína igyekszik mind importforrásaiban, mind piacaiban a lehető legtöbb lábon állni, hogy kevésbé legyen kiszolgáltatott."

14   The original text goes: "Az Új Selyemút projektum legkönnyebben azonosítható célja a nyersanyagok importútvonalainak biztosítása. A gazdaság dinamikus növekedésnek köszönhetően, az 1990-es évektől kezdve Kína egyre több nyersanyag importjára szorult."

Ensuring the flow of raw materials is one of the oldest motivations behind internationalization and is still very important even today. However, if the Chinese economic structural change is to be accelerated – creating services and a knowledge-based economy – this might be less important than the former presented above. In other words, these two motivations may seem contradictory.

The analysis of the 'Stiftung Asienhaus' describes China's efforts to boost world trade and economic growth, as an obvious attempt to secure raw materials and markets. The paper contains several short articles by different authors. For example, Sausmikat-Noesselt (2016) compiles different critical views of the Initiative which is seen as a way to absorb the over-capacities of the Chinese economy and to seek fossil energy sources. At the same time, the analysis emphasizes the clear Chinese need to shift to a new growth paradigm in which a services-based economy generating higher added value, brings about the major part of economic growth. (Sausmikat – Noesselt, 2016: 1)

The analysis of Bessler also refers to raw materials but he adds the importance of the economic development of Western China. He argues:

> OBOR means tools for the Chinese to develop backward regions of the country that lie along the planned routes. Ensuring raw materials as oil, gas, uranium, copper and gold are as essential elements as the creation/ extension of new trade routes and markets.[15]
>
> BESSLER, 2015: 2

Puls from the IW (German Economic Institute) goes further and points out that:

> OBOR is the international version of the Chinese infrastructure investment policy. The high costs are covered by China by no means out of altruism, but it promises sustainable growth impulses for its own economy. The welfare benefits of the last 20 years have been distributed in China very unequally.[16]
>
> PULS, 2016: 2–3

---

15   The original text goes: "Für China bedeutet OBOR zudem ein Mittel, eigene unterentwickelte Regionen zu fördern, die entlang der geplanten Korridore liegen. Die Sicherung von Ressourcen wie Öl, Gas, Uran, Kupfer und Gold ist ein weiteres zentrales Motiv. Ebenso wie der Auf- und Ausbau neuer Handelswege und Absatzmärkte."

16   The original text goes: "OBOR stellt eine internationale Weiterführung der chinesischen Infrastrukturinvestitionspolitik dar. Die hohen Kosten schultert China keineswegs aus Altruismus, sondern weil es sich nachhaltige Wachstumsimpulse für die eigene Wirtschaft verspricht. Die Wohlstandsgewinne der letzten 20 Jahre sind in China sehr ungleich verteilt."

The precondition of the Belt and Road Initiative is massive financial support from the Chinese side. Chinese credits lent to the projects will strengthen the role of the Chinese currency in financial transactions. Why? We can easily explain this by a historical analogy: before 1958, only the British pound was freely convertible in Europe, but the creation of the customs union forced the six participating countries to make their currencies freely convertible. Without that element, a customs union would not have made very much sense. In other words, the BRI needs a more liberal approach towards the RMB exchange rate; a strong, easily convertible renminbi will create more trade. There are very clear building blocks for this change.[17]

Although the internationalization of Chinese RMB is stressed in both countries, negative aspects are rarely mentioned in Hungarian literature while in the German approach, obstacles standing in the way of these efforts are underlined. For example, Bessler states:

> To date, the Yuan's role is inferior to the USD and EURO, even though it grew into the fourth most traded currency in the world. A 2.8 percentage share of currencies used worldwide is a weak fourth place.
>
> BESSLER, 2015: 7

In the already mentioned Asienhaus, Domianus and Weber paper, the role of the Asian Infrastructure and Investment Bank (AIIB), which is supposed to fund the BRI, is seen very positively. They, after referring to American criticism, make clear that the AIIB clearly cooperates with the World Bank and the Asian Development Bank. (Domianus – Weber, 2016: 2) They also focus on another problem. They maintain that the AIIB might be tempted not to pay too much attention to environmental and labour rights issues. According to the authors, the responsibility of the German government lies in the enforcement of these

---

17   (1) The Central Bank of Hungary (MNB) started its 5-year Renminbi Program in 2015. Under this framework, the Central Bank of Hungary signed a bilateral swap currency sap line agreement with the People's Bank of China. (MNB, 2016) (2) Not only Hungary, but more than 30 countries signed similar currency swap agreements with China between 2008 and 2015. (3) That policy is not new as it started with the creation of the Dim Sum bonds and offshore RMB market in 2007. (Li 2015) Dim sum bonds are traded in Hong Kong, nominated in RMB. (Mathur – De 2014) (4) In 2009, the Chinese launched the first pilot project scheme for RMB cross-border trade settlement. The scheme allowed selected companies in Shanghai, Guangzhou, Zhuhai, Shenzhen and Dongguan to invoice and settle trade transactions in RMB. (5) In early 2018, the Chinese allowed oil futures trading in the Shanghai International Energy Exchange. (Park, 2018)

rights. They argue, that would be a guarantee to ensure that the entire project would not be used for geopolitical ends.

The German Gasper also stresses the financial threats connected to the initiative by pointing out that Chinese foreign direct investment in the target countries of the initiative fell by 2 percent in 2016, and by 18 percent in the first quarter of 2017. Gasper also points out rumours that Chinese bureaucrats assume that 80 percent of credits to Pakistan, and 30 percent to Central Asian countries are not going to be repaid. (Gasper, 2017)

Understandably, these aspects are less focused on by Hungarian analysts and politicians. The Hungarian Matura puts a heavy emphasis on the need for financing in these countries. He states: "The crisis of the European Union and the resulting financial vacuum revealed potential opportunities in the CEE region." (Matura, 2017: 57)

The argument might be relevant in some of the Central and Eastern European countries but in recent years, EU funds have provided sufficient tools for infrastructure financing in Hungary and other Central European EU members. Although additional sources are always welcome, the term "financial vacuum" would have been more appropriate in the first months of the Global Financial Crisis when the financial vacuum led to credit withdrawals in Central and Eastern European banking systems.

When it comes to cooperation with China, being a member of the EU means competitive disadvantages compared to the Balkan countries like Serbia, Macedonia and Albania, where EU rules – in particular, EU procurement regulations – do not have to be followed. Matura describes this situation:

> Central European EU member states can apply for non-refundable financial support for infrastructure development, while the regulations of potential Chinese credit lines are not in accordance with EU procurement law. Therefore, Chinese loans are not attractive, while any attempts to pay off Chinese construction companies from European funds might likely provoke political turbulence. Both sides are looking for something different, which is a fundamental problem, with the exception of non-EU member states in the Balkans, where Chinese investment in infrastructure has been more successful.
>
> MATURA, 2017: 59

Matura is right in pointing out the different access opportunities for capital but this situation can quickly change with the adoption of the new EU budget. At this point, the German view underlines problems with the bilateral nature of the Chinese approach regarding investments.

Uebele discusses this aspect in his analysis, published by the Institut der deutschen Wirtschaft Köln as guest commentary:

> To a great extent, investment plans and other economic cooperation are being negotiated with the EU-members bilaterally. That improves the Chinese negotiating position and makes it more difficult to the EU to act in unison with the interests of the member states.[18]
>
> UEBELE, 2016

There is not a common investment policy with regards to foreign investments in the EU. In this case, only the common competition policy could be used as a reference point. In addition, the EU and China launched negotiations for an investment agreement in 2013 but until now the negotiations have not been concluded and thus China does not have much of a choice other than to negotiate with EU-members bilaterally. At this point, we must be aware of what the real German concerns involve.

6 A Game of Power Balance in Central Europe?

Generally, it can be stated, that the Belt and Road Initiative has been featured much more positively in Hungary than in Germany. If there are negative comments in Hungary, they are usually linked to criticism of Hungarian politicians and/or parties. The perception of both the 2017 16+1 summit in Budapest and the Belt and Road Initiative, was rather mixed in academic circles, which is understandable given that academic discussions evolve around the future world economic and political role of China rather than the project's direct possible economic effects. However, if we compare criticism of Russia, or Putin's visits to Budapest, the tone is milder, even among opposition partners since they are aware that China's room for maneuver is greater when it comes to investment in Central European countries and China does not pose any serious geopolitical threat to Hungary – in contrast to Russia.

It must be added that there is one element rarely emphasized by Hungarian politicians and experts and that is that China offers an alternative model of development policy to the developing countries of Asia, Africa, South America,

---

18   The original text: "Zu einem großen Teil werden Investitionsvorhaben oder andere wirtschaftliche Kooperationen mit den Einzelstaaten Europas bilateral verhandelt. Das verbessert die chinesische Verhandlungsposition und erschwert es der EU, mit einer Stimme zu sprechen."

as well as Central and Eastern European countries. If there is something one can miss from the branding of this initiative, it is to emphasize that the different Chinese initiatives can put the whole Central European region at the centre of the world economy by offering the region a once in a lifetime chance to catch up.

As for Germany, the ambivalent view must be interpreted more in a European context than in a bilateral context. On the one hand, Germany is concerned about access to the Chinese market and it will ensure that economic cooperation does not turn into one-way trade. On the other hand, there are two aspects which make their view of the BRI very different from the Hungarian one. There are German firms with cutting-edge technology, firms with relevant global market share, whose acquisition could pose strategic disadvantages to German industry. That is something Hungary does not have, since Hungarian industry is dominated by German firms. And this leads us to the other difference: Germany does not seem to have a real interest in seeing China establish a rising presence in Central Europe. Thus, the logical conclusion to be drawn from this geopolitical and economic balance of power game is that it is in Germany's interest to keep China out of Central Europe, while Hungary may conclude it would be beneficial to seek a greater diversification of its economic ties.

Bibliography

Ankenbrand, V. H. (2017). Der Welthandel soll über Chinas Seidenstraße rollen. FrankfurterAllgemeine Zeitung, May 13.

Balogun, M. J. (2011) Hegemony and Sovereign Equality: The Interest Contiguity Theory in International Relations, Springer Group.

Becsey, Z. (2014). A keleti nyitás súlya a magyar külgazdaságban. Polgári Szemle.

Bessler, P. (2015). China's Neue Seidene Straße. EU-Asia Economic Governance Forum.

Catley, R., and Mosler, D. (2007) The American Challenge: The World Resists US Liberalism, Ashgate Publishing.

Clinton, H. (2011). America's Pacific Century. Foreign Policy.

Coalition Agreement. (2018). Available form: https://www.cdu.de/system/tdf/media/dokumente/koalitionsvertrag_2018.pdf?file=1&type=field_collection_item&id=12643.

Collier, P. (2017). The Bottom Billion. Why the Poorest Countries are Failing and What can Be Done About It. Oxford University Press.

Domianus, A., and Weber, P. (2016). Lean, Clean and Green. China's neue Investitionsbank. In: Alte Seidenstraße in neuem Gewand. Chinas Globalisierungsoffensive. Stiftung Asienhaus.

Erling, V.J. (2017). China startet sein Billionen-Projekt für die „Menschheit". Welt, May 14.

EU riskiert Eklat in China (2017). Frankfurter Allgemeine Zeitung.

Gaspers, J. (2017). China: Seidenstraße: Licht und Schatten. Zeitschrift für Wirtshaftspolitik, 97(6), pp. 382.

Hanemann, T., Huotari, M., and Kratz, A. (2019). Chinese FDI in Europe: 2018 trends and impact of new screening policies. A report by Rhodium Group (RHG) and the Mercator Institute for China Studies (MERICS).

Hsiang, A. C. (2018). As America Withdraws From Latin America, China Steps in. The Diplomat. January 4, 2018.

Huang, C. (2017). US, Japan, India, Australia ... Is Quad the First Step to An Asian NATO? South China Morning Post, November 25.

László, G. (2017). Új selyemút, régi célok. Világgazdaság, May 21.

Li, C. (2015). Banking on China through Currency Swap Agreements. Federal Reserve Bank of San Francisco.

Magyar Nemzeti Bank (2016). The bilateral currency swap line agreement between the People's Bank of China and the Central Bank of Hungary has been renewed.

Marthur, I., and De, S. (2014). The Dim Sum Bond Market in Hong Kong. England: Emerald Group Publishing Limited.

Matura, T. (2017). Chinese Investments in the EU and Central and Eastern Europe. In: author G, (editor), China's Attraction: The Case of Central Europe, Oriental Business and Innovation Center, Budapest Business School, University of Applied Sciences.

Miért építik az új selyemutat? (2017). Origo.

Nye, J. S. (2011) The Future of Power, Perseus Books Group.

Park, S. (2018). How China Will Shake Up the Oil Futures Market. Bloomberg Businessweek.

Pataky, I. (2015). Elmaradtak a nagy kínai beruházások. Magyar Nemzet, June 6.

Peking beklagt "viel Gegenwind" (2017). N-TV. Available form: https://www.n-tv.de/politik/Peking-beklagt-viel-Gegenwind-article19841541.html.

Piketty, T. (2018). 2018, the Year of Europe. Le Blog de Thomas Piketty. Available form: https://www.lemonde.fr/blog/piketty/2018/01/16/2018-the-year-of-europe/.

Puls, T. (2016). One Belt One Road – Chinas neue Seidenstraße. Institut der deutschen Wirtschaft Köln.

Rabena, A. J. (2015) China's Counter-Pivot Response. International Policy Digest. May 11, 2015.

Saumikat, N., and Noesselt, N. (2016). Alte Seidenstraße in neuem Gewand. Chinas Globalisierungsoffensive. Stiftung Asienhaus.

Schmidt, Brian (2018). Hegemony: A conceptual and theoretical analysis. Dialogue of Civilizations Research Institute. August 15, 2018.

Sobel, A.C. (2012). Birth of Hegemony: Crisis, Financial Revolution, and Emerging Global Networks, University of Chicago Press.

Uebele, M. (2016). Was China mit der Neuen Seidenstraße wirklich will. Institut der deutschen Wirtschaft Köln.

Viktor, E. (2016a). Az Egy Övezet, Egy Út geopolitikai jelentősége a történelmi távlatban. Pageo Geopolitikai Intézet.

Viktor, E. (2016b). Az Új Selyemút terv. Eszmélet, pp. 116–131.

Zhang, B. (2012). Chinese Perceptions of the US: an exploration of China's foreign policy motivations, Lexicon Books.

CHAPTER 6

Transnational Organized Crime and Foreign Direct Investment in Spain

What Could the Government-Supported Chinese FDI Learn from the Russian Precedent?

Rubén Ruiz-Ramas

The impact of transnational organised crime (TOC) on foreign direct investments (FDI) cannot be examined exclusively by public opinion surveys, even when focused on significant social groups such as entrepreneurs or high-ranking officials. Of course, foreign companies are concerned about their state's local perception before establishing or investing in a country, and they adapt their communication and advertising strategies to what they observe in market and opinion studies. However, much of the critical information which influences major investments by multinational companies is not collected in surveys, as the most relevant decision-makers count on alternative access to privileged non-public information, and operate under specific communication management strategies. They include governments and state agencies, as a significant part of foreign direct investments affects national strategic sectors such as energy, infrastructures, and banking systems, among others. In addition, when a foreign investor tries to enter industries which are strategic for national security, the communication management within governmental and state agencies assumes the momentum of a crisis. Suspicion of connections or collusion between the foreign investor and criminal activities, as well as an opaque foreign policy strategy, can only raise the alarm level.

China's FDI investments in the European Union (EU) are not suspected of being associated with TOC. However, in spite of their direct economic benefits, Chinese FDI investments in the EU remain controversial. This is mostly due to operations in which state-owned companies penetrate strategic sectors and high-tech industries. As a consequence, some EU member states have proposed to reinforce FDI screening mechanisms. For its part, Spain is a country which combines a positive attitude to Chinese FDI within its authorities and business elites, with a more cautious general opinion as regards Chinese investments, and a recent past of a Government blocking FDI operations on behalf of national security. After introducing all these factors, this article will analyse the challenges that the TOC generates for China-Spain relations, with a focus on Chinese FDI in Spain, as well as the perception of the Chinese community in Spain.

1   Chinese FDI in the EU: Sources of Concern and Screening Mechanisms

Over the last decade, Chinese FDI in the EU has developed, reaching a peak of EUR 35 billion in 2016, compared with 1.6 billion in 2010. The global recession marked a historic shift, when the declining amount of EU direct investment in China was surpassed by Chinese FDI in the EU (Seaman et al. 2017: 9). The sudden surge in Chinese FDI in 2013 coincided with the economic reforms adopted at the Third Plenum of the Chinese Communist Party (CCP) following Xi Jinping's arrival to the Presidency, and the presentation of the Belt and Road (BRI) connectivity imitative. This project covers Europe, Eurasia, Africa, the Middle East and South Asia. New funding tools accompany it, such as the Silk Road Fund and the Asian Infrastructure Investment Bank (AIIB). In 2017, the Chinese leadership approved a package of regulatory reforms on outbound capital flows in order to reduce leverage in the financial sector. The decision provoked the first decrease in four years, with a drop in Chinese FDI in the EU to EUR 30 billion. However, that was a minor percentage compared with the 29% decline in China's global outbound investment in 2017. The EU remains a priority destination for Chinese investors, whilst the big three within the EU – the United Kingdom, France and Germany – continue to be on the podium of Chinese investment receivers, accounting for 75% of China's total EU investment. To put this into perspective, we need to bear in mind that China's construction projects within the BRI in Central and Eastern Europe do not count as a direct investment.[1]

The reasons why Chinese investors approach the EU, range from seeking cutting-edge technology assets and know-how, to accessing the EU market and other third markets, through EU companies, as well as achieving a better and more constant integration into global value chains. It is not a secret that the growing Chinese economic presence in the EU has raised concerns not only about its final impact in the European socio-economic landscape, but also regarding the political leverage that China can amass thanks to its economic power. There are three primary sources of concern in the EU. First, the

---

1 Hanemann, T., and Huotari, M. (2018). Chinese FDI in Europe in 2017. Rapid recovery after initial slowdown. New York-Berlin: Rhodium Group (RHG) and the Mercator Institute for China Studies (MERICS).

imbalance between acquisitions (94% of total investment in 2017) and green-field projects. Second, the high percentage of sovereign and state-owned entities (68% in 2017) – in comparison to private companies – handling Chinese investment in Europe. Third, the interest of Chinese investors in strategic sector companies which are perceived as relevant to national security and which involve the IT and high-tech sectors including defence inputs, energy, transport infrastructure and finance. For instance, in 2017 the main Chinese FDI operations in the EU were: CIC's EUR 12.3 billion acquisition of Logicor; CIC's purchase of a block of shares in the UK national grid's gas distribution business; China Jianyin Investment and Wise Road Capital's acquisition of NXP Semiconductors' Standard Products business for EUR 2.4 billion; HNA's investment in Glencore's petroleum products unit; State Grid's buying of a stake in ADMIE; and COSCO's purchase of a 51% stake in Noatum port in Spain. Moreover, other Chinese companies, already established in Europe, gained more weight with new purchases of stakes, such as the Geely Group in the Volvo Group and Saxo Bank, and Legend Holdings' acquisition of 90% in Banque Internationale in Luxembourg (BIL). Also, non-FDI investment in companies, that is, venture capital and portfolio investment stakes of less than 10%, saw relevant developments in 2017 increase Chinese companies' portfolios in Daimler or Deutsche Bank.[2]

The worries about the strategic impact of China's investments have spurred the debate regarding the efficiency of the mechanisms for screening FDI in the EU. These screening tools operate in many countries both inside and outside the EU. This is the case of nearly half of EU member states, including Germany, France, the UK, Italy and Spain, but also of the United States (US), Australia, Japan, and China. Indeed, in comparison to the EU, China's legislation to protect national and economic security from FDI is more restricted.[3] Also, the US has been faster in tightening controls, following alarming reports of the Committee on Foreign Investment in the United States (CFIUS) about the perceived impact of Chinese FDI.[4] In the EU, countries like France, Germany

---

2   Seaman, J., Huotari, M., and Otero-Iglesias, M. (2017). Introduction: Sizing Up Chinese Investments in Europe. In: J. Seaman, M. Huotari, and M. Otero-Iglesias, (editors), Chinese Investment in Europe. A Country-Level Approach. Madrid-Paris-Berlin: European Think-tank Network on China, pp. 9–18; Hanemann, T., and Huotari, M. (2018).

3   Li, Y., and Bian, C. (2016). A new dimension of foreign investment law in China – evolution and impacts of the national security review system. Asia Pacific Law Review 24 (2), pp. 149–175.

4   Moran, T. H. (2017). CFIUS and National Security: Challenges for the United States, Opportunities for the European Union. Washington D.C.: Peterson Institute for International Economics; U.S.-China Economic and Security Review Commission (2017). 2017 Report

and even Hungary implemented new national legislation after earlier Chinese FDI experiences. Over the course of 2016, several Chinese FDI proposals in strategic sectors – such as Hinckley Point C and Eandis – were delayed, and some ultimately withdrawn subsequent to scrutiny at EU member-state level, such as Philips Lumileds, Osram and Aixtron.[5] In this context, there is a movement to coordinate the EU member states' screening mechanisms with EU competition rules. In parallel, there are voices calling to establish a new FDI screening mechanism at EU level.[6] The letter to the European Commission in February 2017 by Ministers of the Economy from Germany, France and Italy, showing growing concerns on the issue, may represent a turning point. Meanwhile, in September 2017, the Commission proposed establishing a common European framework for screening FDI.[7]

Nevertheless, the increasing regulations are not associated with intentional action to reduce the volume of Chinese FDI in the EU. The overall opinion in the European establishment is that Chinese FDI is mainly based on commercial interests. However, the current situation reflects a problem of reciprocity with states like China in which there are sectors open to Chinese FDI in the EU, while EU companies find it more difficult to invest in China. The proposed mechanisms are focused on protecting strategic assets critical to EU security, and up to this point, cannot be considered a previous phase of a further protectionist trade economy. Moreover, whereas it is manifest that the discussions about improving the screening mechanisms are a consequence of the growing Chinese FDI, EU spokespersons avoid making direct accusations against

---

to Congress of the U.S.-China Economic and Security Review Commission, One Hundred Fifteenth Congress First Session. Washington D.C.: U.S.-China Economic and Security Review Commission; Koch-Weser, I., and Ditz, G. (2017). Chinese Investment in the United States: Recent Trends in Real Estate, Industry, and Investment Promotion. Washington DC: U.S.-China Economic and Security Review Commission Washington DC.

5   Grieger, G. (2017). Foreign direct investment screening. A debate in light of China-EU FDI flows. Brussels: European Parliament.

6   Hanemann, T., and Rosen, D.H. (2012). China invests in Europe – patterns, impacts and policy implications. New York: Rhodium Group; Nicolas, F. (2014). China's Direct Investment in the European Union: Challenges and Policy Responses. China Economic Journal 7, pp.103–125; Škoba, L. (2014). Chinese investment in the EU. European Parliament Research Service, May 23; Meunier, S. (2014). Divide and conquer? China and the cacophony of foreign investment rules in the EU. Journal of European Public Policy 21 (7), pp. 996–1016; Zhang, H., and Van den Bulcke, D. (2014). China's direct investment in the European Union: a new regulatory challenge? Asia Europe Journal 12, pp. 159–177, Grieger, (2017); Seaman et al. (2017); Hanemann and Huotari, (2018).

7   European Commission. (2017). State of the Union 2017: Trade Package: European Commission: Proposes Framework for Screening of Foreign Direct Investments. Brussels: European Commission.

Chinese companies, as is the case in the US. Having said that, the media, along with political analysts and even a few political leaders, increasingly refer to the expansion of Chinese companies with negative and alarming narratives such as "assault", "conquest", "invasion" or "looting". An example is the tone used by the French finance minister Bruno Le Maire, when on a state visit to China in January 2018, who said: "France welcomes long-term investments from China, but only after screening deals to ensure French assets are not looted".[8]

2   Chinese FDI in Spain: Meagre Investment despite the Positive
          Attitude

After the bursting of the housing bubble and the economic crisis in 2008, the Spanish government sought the financial support of Chinese investors, who answered positively by buying up bonds at the staggering rate of 5.4%. In 2011 alone, China purchased EUR 7 billion in Spanish debt. Besides, both the José Luis Zapatero and Mariano Rajoy governments approved regulations to attract another kind of foreign investment – the so-called Golden Visa – which offered residence permits to foreigners who buy homes worth more than EUR 500,000. The official figures for this program say that one-third of Golden Visas went to 702 Chinese investors who altogether spent EUR 409 million. Notwithstanding this financial assistance, as Mario Esteban explains in his article in this same book, Spain is a late and modest destination for Chinese FDI. For China, Spain is only the ninth target country for its direct investment, and for Spain, China ranks tenth amongst its foreign direct investors. Moreover, at least until 2016, there have not been significant acquisitions of companies belonging to strategic sectors. However, according to Esteban and Otero-Iglesias[9] (2017: 142), there was interest in doing so from different Chinese companies: "State Grid did attempt to buy the electric company Red Eléctrica de España, Fosun was after the public insurance firm CESCE, specialised in corporate risk, and the China Investment Corporation showed an interest in Repsol (energy), Canal de Isabel II (water), and the above-mentioned Red Eléctrica". Eventually, China entered Spain's strategically important energy market by acquiring third companies in

---

8   Sourbes, C. (2018). France ponders difficult decisions over Chinese FDI. FDI Intelligence, April 12.

9   Esteban, M. and Otero-Iglesias, M. (2017). Chinese Investment in Spain: Open for Business, but not at any Price, pp. 141–151. In: Seaman J., Huotari M., and Otero-Iglesias, M. (editor) (2017). Chinese Investment in Europe. A Country-Level Approach. Madrid-Paris-Berlin: European Think-tank Network on China.

transnational operations whose developments, apparently, show an economic rather than political interest.[10]

It was in 2016 that Chinese firms finally bought companies within sectors that can be perceived as strategic. This was the case with the acquisitions of Aritex by Aviation Industry Corporation of China (AVIC); engineering Eptisa by the JSTIC group; and when COSCO Shipping Ports acquired 51 percent of shares in Noatum, the biggest Spanish port terminal manager. These operations show that the Spanish government is far from the level of concern of Germany, France and Italy – countries which asked the European Commission to improve screening mechanisms at the EU level. On the one hand, it was ICEX, the main Spanish foreign trade and investment agency, which organised trade missions for Spanish aerospace companies to approach the Commercial Aircraft Corporation of China. That is, ICEX facilitated the acquisition of Aritex by AVIC.[11] On the other hand, Noatum is the company that manages the ports of Valencia, Barcelona, Bilbao and Santander, as well as the dry ports of Madrid and Zaragoza.[12] The Port of Valencia is the main facilitator of foreign trade in Spain, and the first port in the Mediterranean Sea in billing terms. But investigations into Port of Valencia activities have revealed some of the major cases of customs fraud associated with Chinese-led organised crime groups (OCGs). As President Mariano Rajoy supported the operation personally when he visited China in 2017 for the presentation of the Belt and Road Initiative, this means that the Spanish government does not see any reason not to trust COSCO.

Therefore, Spain is an odd case within the central EU economies since there has not been an in-depth debate on the impact of Chinese FDI, and the perception of political and economic elites remains positive without relevant actors warning about potential risks to national security. Up to the present,

---

10   According to Esteban and Otero-Iglesias (2017:142–143), "by buying Energias de Portugal (EDP) in 2011, the Chinese state-owned company China Three Gorges became the main shareholder of EDP Spain and invested the sizable sum of EUR 600 million in EDP Spain from 2012 to 2016. Moreover, Gingko Tree Investment acquired for EUR 714 million a 35 percent share of Madrileña Red de Gas in 2015, which was sold to an international consortium formed by Gingko Tree, the Dutch pension fund PGGM, and the French electricity group EDF. In June 2017, however, EDP sold its gas distribution business in Spain to an international consortium for EUR 2.6 billion, which essentially means that China Three Gorges now only operates a Spanish electricity distribution business through a company called EDP HC Energia. Hence, the presence of Chinese actors in the Spanish energy market is still rather small".

11   Esteban and Otero-Iglesias (2017), pp. 145.

12   In the Port of Barcelona, the Chinese state company Hutchison Ports, has owned BEST (Barcelona Europe South Terminal) since 2006, the only terminal in the Mediterranean with 11 cranes capable of handling the largest ships in operation.

no Chinese company has been restrained – much less withdrawn – in its FDI activity in Spain. The screening mechanisms have remained silent. No association between Chinese foreign direct investors and OCGs has been established. Spanish businesses find the association with Chinese partners to cover their financial needs and to gain access to the very attractive Chinese consumer market. Both the government and public works companies, one of the few sectors in which Spain is a global leader, recognise great opportunities to take part in the public-private consortiums that will develop BRI projects (high-speed trains, roads and highways, ports, telecommunication infrastructures, energy pipelines, etc.).

The Elcano Royal Institute Barometer corroborates this welcoming attitude of elites to Chinese FDI. However, as Mario Esteban again details in his chapter, there is a gap between attitudes among the political and economic elites and society at large, as regards Chinese investment in Spain. In particular, it is noteworthy that 24% of Spaniards declare that they wish less investment from China, in comparison to 21% who would like to see Chinese investments expanded. The survey shows the generally positive attitude of Spaniards to other countries' foreign investment, with China being the only country in which the negative sentiment overcomes the positive. Such tough response is difficult to explain, precisely when Spain is a country in which Chinese FDI has not been discussed widely, and the public is not familiar either with FDI operations or the BRI program. On the contrary, Spaniards are familiar on a daily basis with another kind of Chinese investment which applies to small and medium businesses owned by Chinese migrants and their descendants – most of them in direct contact with the public. From this perspective, the question: "From which countries would you like Spain to receive more or less investments?"[13] many Spaniards would understand they had to answer according to their wish to see more restaurants, bars, shops, service and retail companies owned by Chinese, rather than notable FDI investments, or at least, not only FDI investments. Regardless of how accurate this assumption is, the point is that, whereas elites still observe the growing Chinese economic activity in Spain as an opportunity, society at large perceives it more as a threat. This perception, apart from providing a breeding ground for potential social risks, is an element that can affect, in combination with other factors, the perspective on Chinese FDI investments, and push for a re-evaluation of their impact on national security.

---

13   Question 37 in the Barometer of the Elcano Royal Institute, November 2015.

3   The Perception of the Chinese Community's Economic Activity in
     Spain: The 'Chinese Mafia' as both a Matrix of Stereotypes and as
     a System

Before describing the current representation of the Chinese in Spain, Beltran[14] quotes the seminal Dawson study[15] on how contradictions are pervasive in the representations of the Chinese in the West: "Thus China has at one time or another been thought to be rich and poor, advanced and backward, wise and stupid, beautiful and ugly, strong and weak, honest and deceitful – there is no end to the list of contradictory qualities which have been attributed to her". Beltran, and other authors who agree on the current validity of Dawson's conclusions today in the West,[16] conclude that the representations of China are contradictory because those who represent her are categorically different. In other words, the divergent interests, perceptions, information, fears and ambitions of those who receive, create or expand the representations, contribute to their polarization.

    According to Beltran,[17] in Spain the representations of the Chinese are within a continuum, full of nuances, which eventually present two poles in moral terms. The set of stereotyped representations on the moral extreme incorporate a strong work ethic; the values of effort and respect for authority; interest in avoiding conflict; and academic success. Besides, recently within the business community and administration, there is a growing representation of China and the Chinese as big money, involving big spending tourists, investors and the new 'El Dorado', that is, the Chinese market. At the other extreme, many of the stereotyped representations revolve around the informal economy – some directly illegal, such as organised crime; money laundering; informal credit leading to extortion; human trafficking; prostitution; and labour exploitation. All of these, plus others like tax and rules avoidance, fraud, forgery and seeing the Chinese as a 'secretive community', feed what can be called the 'Chinese Mafia' matrix of stereotypes. Although there is no statistical test, the contradiction in the representations corresponds to our understanding

14   Beltrán, J. (2016). China en España: un tropo polivalente. In: Beltrán, Haro, F., and Sáiz, A. (eds). Representaciones de China en las Américas y la Península Ibérica. Barcelona: Edicions Bellaterra., pp. 101–124.

15   Dawson, R. (1967). The Chinese Chamaleon. An Analysis of European Conceptions of Chinese Civilisation. New York: Oxford University Press, pp. 13.

16   Yangwen, Z. (2017). The Chinese Chameleon Revisited: From the Jesuits to Zhang Yimou. Cambridge: Cambridge Scholars Publishing, pp. 3–17; Van Dijk, T. A. (2003). Racismo y discurso de las élites. Barcelona: Gedisa.

17   Beltrán, J. (2016), pp. 116.

of the ambivalent results of the Royal Institute Elcano surveys on the views on Chinese investment in Spain. The gap between elites and society at large (small and medium business owners too) is fed by the different interests and the perception of the opportunities and risks affecting them. In this sense, the self-perception of each individual will impact on how he or she produces, promotes and disseminates facts and narratives about the Chinese, as well as how receptive he or she is when facing a given stereotype about them.

One of the essences of stereotyping an ethnicity is the homogenization of all the individuals as members of a given corpus of beliefs and characteristics. When applied to economic activity, the 'Chinese Mafia' not only works as a matrix of stereotypes, but also as a system endowed with obscure norms and actors which pervades the whole Chinese community. Whereas the centripetal attraction of the 'Chinese Mafia' matrix of stereotypes captures many daily based economic behaviours – such as carrying significantly large amounts of cash; the 'Chinese Mafia', considered as a system, helps to provide an explanation based on speculation for behaviours and processes that do not match local codes and standards.

One example of this is the attempt to elucidate the successful growth of Chinese businesses during the crisis in Spain – in particular, their financial mechanisms in a period in which the banks almost blocked the credit concession. Academic scholars who have researched the business practices of the Chinese community in Spain for decades, focus their explanation for this phenomenon mostly on family loans. Families save money collectively and then lend it to other family members to open new businesses.[18] However, many journalists, both in the media or in books, choose to give insufficient weight to this kind of explanation and connect the phenomenon with pervasive, ill-defined and organised crime. The book, *El imperio invisible. El éxito empresarial chino y sus vínculos con la criminalidad económica en España y Europa* ["The

---

18   Beltrán and Sáiz, (2009). *Empresariado asiático en España.* Barcelona: CIDOB; Beltrán, J., and Sáiz, A. (2013a). De la invisibilidad a la espectacularidad. Cuarenta años de inmigración china España. In Rios, X. (ed.), *Las relaciones hispano-chinas. Historia y futuro.* Madrid: Los Libros de la Catarata, pp. 114–131; Beltrán, J., and Sáiz, A. (2013b). Del restaurante chino al bar autóctono. Evolución del empresariado de origen chino en España y su compleja relación con la etnicidad. In: Barros Nock, M. and Valenzuela, H., Retos y estrategias del empresariado étnico. Estudios de caso de empresarios latinos en los Estados Unidos y empresarios inmigrantes en España, México DF: Centro de Investigaciones y Estudios Superiores en Antropología Social (CIESAS); Beltrán, J., and Sáiz, A. (2015). A contracorriente. Trabajadores y empresarios chinos en España ante la crisis económica (2007–2013). *Migraciones. Revista del Instituto Universitario de Estudios sobre Migraciones,* nº 37, pp. 125–147.

Invisible Empire. Chinese business success and its links with economic criminality in Spain and Europe"[19]], is a piece of research journalism endowed with rich empirical work on transnational organised crime undertaken by people of Chinese origin. However, the authors tend to fall into generalisations and depict Chinese economic activity as dependent on organised crime. In the book, and in some other journalistic pieces, the approach to the financing of Chinese businesses contributes to the stereotyping of the Chinese community as a systemic 'Chinese Mafia'. In a press article, Cardenal and Araújo[20] ask themselves "Would so many Chinese retailer businesses have proliferated if, in the middle of the current banking illiquidity, they hadn't had the finance which comes from smuggling, fiscal fraud and other illicit activities committed by their countrymen?". In their answer, they first make it clear that they lack an "empirical and irrefutable reply", but go on to say: "we can conclude [...] that part of the explanation [is] that the initial investment of the new businesses comes from people that amassed their fortunes illegally. And incidentally, the same can be true of cash purchases [...] of real estate assets".

Undoubtedly, several studies of the representation of the Chinese in the Spanish media expose the over-representation of criminal activity and the informal economy, both in the press[21] and on TV.[22] A dynamic equally present in the portrayal of the Chinese in popular cultural items in the cinema ('The Yellow Fountain', 1999, by Miguel Santesmases; 'Biutiful', 2010, by Alejandro González Iñárritu; 'The Pelayos', 2012, by Eduard Cortés; 'Schimbare', 2014, by Álex Sampayo); in TV series ('Sin Identidad', 2014, by Joan Noguera; 'Félix' (2018) by Cesc Gay and inspired by the real Spanish police's 'Operation Emperor', 'Vis a Vis' – in its 3rd season in 2018, by Jesús Colmenar); or in literature ('Un tros de cel' 2012, by Isabel-Clara Simó; 'Sociedad negra', 2013, by Andreu Martín). Although some of the events depicted may be based on fact,

---

19   Cardenal, J.P., and Araújo, H. (2013). El imperio invisible. El éxito empresarial chino y sus vínculos con la criminalidad económica en España y Europa. Madrid: Crítica.

20   Cardenal, J. P., and Araújo, H. (2014). El Imperio Invisible. La falta de transparencia y de fuentes fiables envuelven el entramado empresarial chino en Europa, un búnker por el que desfilan miles millones y del que sabemos muy poco. Ethic, September 1.

21   Merino Sancho, J. M. (2008). La Inmigración **China** En España: ¿Qué Imagen?, Observatorio de la Economía y la Sociedad China 6, pp. 1–18 ; Zhou Hang (2013), *La imagen de China en la prensa española Una visión desde los diarios: El País, ABC, El Periódico y La Vanguardia,* Master Thesis, Universitat Autònoma de Barcelona.; Hughes, K. L. (2014), Racismo y xenofobia: representaciones de la comunidad asiática en la prensa española, Dickinson College Honors Theses, Paper 142; Beltrán, J. (2016).

22   Rodríguez Wangüemert, C. Rodríguez Breijo, V., and Pestano Rodríguez, J. M. (2017). China tras la mirada de la televisión española. Estudios sobre el Mensaje Periodístico 23 (2), pp. 969–985.

the over-representation of informal and illicit economic activities gives the audience a distorted image of the Chinese in daily life. Taken collectively, we can see that in the media and popular culture representations of the Chinese, almost no social group of this community is unconnected to either the informal economy or directly to economic crime activities. Because of its international success, with two nominations to the Academy Awards, 'Biutiful' provided one of the most influential portraits of how Chinese migrants live in Spain. However, as Begin[23] suggests: "Biutiful, perhaps unwittingly, also reifies stereotyping as well as neoliberal fears of immigration, in particular as it relates to Chinese migrants and their business practices, ultimately creating an image of the immigrant Chinese entrepreneur as a global villain whose moral turpitude plays a large role in the current cycle of labour exploitation".

Aside from this over-representation, the specific media treatment of the transnationally organised crime cases in Spain involving people of Chinese origin contributes to the stereotyping of that community in at least two other ways. On the one hand, by using the term 'Chinese Mafia', all the responsibility is attributed to only one ethnicity, whilst in different transnational criminal organisations the membership is multi-ethnic. There is even one extreme example in the so-called 'Operation Toys': the leader of the plot was a Spanish fiscal agent but the case was introduced as "Chinese mafia".[24] On the other hand, the exploitation of the iconic concept of 'Chinese Mafia' for any case of economic crime, fraud, and for common crimes involving the participation of people of Chinese origin, provides a wider social and political dimension to those events that is far from being accurate. The label of 'Chinese Mafia' is applied to criminal cases that can barely be considered as organised crime, such as small groups of youngsters manipulating slot machines, or individual entrepreneurs accused of tax avoidance and failing to comply with the law. Indeed, most of the OCGs investigated in Spain in which Chinese people participate, lack a 'mafia-type' structure (which requires deep social and political penetration) but they are nevertheless constantly coined in the media as 'Chinese Mafia'. Having said that, the media treatment of organised crime, related in one way or another to the Chinese community in Spain, has avoided establishing an association between criminal activity and the Chinese state or government. In this sense, the media emulated the

23   Begin, P. (2015). Empathy and sinophobia: depicting Chinese migration in *Biutiful* (Iñárritu, 2010), Transnational Cinemas, 6:1, pp. 2.
24   Recuero, M. (2018). La Audiencia Nacional imputa a CaixaBank por ayudar a blanquear dinero a la mafia china. El Mundo, April 19; Economía Digital. (2018). Tras la sombra de Gao Ping: así actúa la mafia china en España. Economía Digital, April 19.

authorities in striving not to see repercussions on bilateral relations between Spain and China. Neither the media nor the Spanish authorities allude to the investigations when they approach issues concerning bilateral relations between Spain and China.

4   Reactions to the Stereotyping of Chinese Economic Activity in Spain

Allegedly, the recurring stereotyping of the Chinese community has led to the general acceptation that Spanish society associates the Chinese with a set of phenomena related to the informal economy, that matches the 'Chinese Mafia' matrix of stereotypes. Indeed, there are studies based upon the spread of "urban legends" linked to the Chinese, questioning not only how factual they are, but also if their propagation is likewise a myth. A well-known example of a journalist's book on the urban legends of the Chinese community's business activity is Villarino,[25] which takes its name from one of these legends: "Where do the Chinese go when they die?". In any case, regardless of whether or not the indigenous population interiorized the exaggerated stereotypes and prejudices concerning the economic activity of the Chinese, direct conflict between both communities has been the exception. The most worrying case occurred in 2004 in one of the Spanish hubs of the shoe industry – the town of Elche – where several hundred Spaniards protested against Chinese-owned shoe firms. The campaigners complained about the unfair competition exerted by Chinese businesses, blaming them for undercutting the prosperity of their legitimate companies.[26] Apart from this event, other collectively organised actions referred to business associations pressuring local administrations to limit the opening of new shops owned by Chinese in the district of Lavapies in Madrid and downtown Barcelona.[27] Nevertheless, educational work undertaken by both governmental institutions and civil society associations active in the field of immigration, is also noteworthy. They have launched anti-rumour

---

25   Villarino, Á. (2012). ¿A dónde van los chinos cuándo mueren? Vida y negocios de la comunidad china en España. Madrid: Debate.

26   Cachón, L. (2006). Intereses contrapuestos y racismo: El incendio de los almacenes chinos en Elche (septiembre de 2004). Circunstancia 10, pp. 1–19.

27   Nadali, D. B. (2007). Migración, comercio mayorista chino y etnicidad. Revista CIDOB D'AfersInternacionals 78, pp. 77–95; Merino Sancho (2008).

campaigns in Catalonia, Andalusia and Madrid, to counteract the spread of stereotypes that may one day lead to justify xenophobic attitudes.[28]

Over the last decade, a number of Chinese organisations distributed across the Spanish territory, have also reacted to the several crises that have affected the reputation of the Chinese in Spain. More specifically, the most relevant of these crises by far, according to this community, was triggered in October 2012 by the most critical police operation ever launched in Spain in relation to the TOC: 'Operation Emperor'. This operation, carried out by the National Police and the Service of Customs Surveillance, with the support of the Police Intervention Unit, led to the detention of 83 people in a warrant arrest list of 108, with 58 Chinese and 17 Spaniards among them. The leader of the OCG is a well-known Chinese businessman established in Spain since the end of the 80s, Gao Ping. He was accused of running a scheme involved in economic crimes such as massive money laundering (allegedly EUR 300 million a year), tax evasion, the illegal import of goods and smuggling, as well as being responsible for labour crimes, extortion and prostitution. Although the warrant list includes petitions to seven other countries, the epicentre of the plot was the industrial park of 'Cobo Calleja' in Fuenlabrada, Madrid – the *biggest* Chinese industrial and trade *area* in *Europe*.

A few weeks after the launching of the police raids, which were followed by detentions, the representatives of the Chinese business and community associations in Spain said that 'Operation Emperor' had changed the attitude of many Spaniards towards the Chinese. They complained first about the media treatment of the police operation which, according to them, led to a wave of hostilities against their community, and a fall in their associate sales. Julia Zhang, head of *Ni Hao*, an association that represents Chinese businesses in Spain, told El País: "They are calling us Mafiosi, and there are cases of customers in stores refusing to pay the full amount for goods, claiming that shopkeepers do not pay their taxes".[29] Ye Yulan, the head of the Association of Chinese in Spain (ACHE) and Xu Songhua, the president of EFCO, the European Federation of Chinese Organizations, expressed similar worries in various media appearances. As the story also made headlines in China, the representatives speculated that the coverage had a negative impact on foreign direct investment and tourism in Spain, although further figures did not confirm this. In this context,

---

28   Nieto, G. (2007). La inmigración china en España. Madrid: Los libros de la Catarata; Beltrán (2016); Rosati, S. (2017). 'Chiñol': el dilema de ser chino y nacer en España. El País, December 29.

29   Vidales, R. (2012). Has Operation Emperor led to 'Chinaphobia' in Spain? El País, December 17.

Chinese associations decided to cancel the 2013 Chinese New Year celebrations in Madrid, because of "social persecution after Operation Emperor".[30] In addition to the Chinese organisations, a few mixed lobbies, founded in the last decade and a half, promoted action to protect the image of the Chinese in Spain. Among them were: the Spain-China Foundation Council, the Hispanic-Chinese Chamber of Commerce, and China Club Spain.

Although Spain's immigration office replied that it was unaware of these hostilities as no major conflicts or complaints were registered, the Chinese government sent a delegation to Spain to show its concern to the Spanish authorities and asked to distinguish between the activities of criminals from those of the rest of the Chinese community. After listening to the Chinese community representatives, Yang Guangyu, the delegate in charge of the mission to Spain, criticised the conduct of the police during the raids and the media coverage of the event, before declaring the need for "proof that there is no Sinophobia in Spain".[31] And as Begin[32] (2015: 5) comments, it is evident that "the need to prove that something does not exist is driven by a suspicion or mounting evidence that something does, in fact, exist". Notwithstanding, there was no escalation in bilateral relations on this issue. This was the first signal ever of the potential risk that transnational organised crime might involve not only Chinese economic activity in Spain, but also bilateral relations.

5   Briefing the Russian/Post-Soviet and Chinese TOC, and Rising Spanish Concerns

This section, far from providing an in-depth analysis of the TOC in Spain, aims only to outline the main characteristics of the Russian/Post-Soviet and Chinese OCGs operating in Spain, as well as to introduce the Spanish police and legal reaction against this challenge. Tables 6.1 and 6.2 present a selection of ten police operations against the TOC, which, as a whole, well capture their activity in Spain. In this sense, the selection does not aim to choose the most significant in terms of people arrested, condemned, or goods confiscated. We prefer to include some of the first operations or to display cases affecting various types of crimes if they were representative of these OCGs in a given

---

30   Medialdea, S. (2013). Suspendido el Año Nuevo Chino en Madrid. La comunidad china lo justifica por la crisis y la «persecución social tras la Operación Emperador». El País, February 2.

31   EFE. (2012). Un delegado enviado por China: «Necesito pruebas de que en España no existechinofobia».EFE Agency Press, November 27.

32   Begin (2015), pp. 2.

phase of their activity in Spain. Since the middle of the nineties, following the disintegration of the USSR, the Russian/Post-Soviet OCG s were present in Spain in money laundering activities using real estate, hotels and gaming. Initially, these OCG s moved to Spain to 'rest', buying properties to escape from the gang wars in their countries. After a period of adaptation, some of these OCG s began to commit illegal acts such as extortion, human trafficking, prostitution and illegal firearms trafficking. However, for years the largest Russian, Ukrainian or Georgian OCG s' proceeds were generated mostly from illicit markets in their home countries, and they came to Spain to invest in the legitimate economy through money laundering operations with the frequent assistance of local financial, construction and legal professionals.

As can be seen in Table 6.2, the Chinese OCG s' presence in Spain is particularly meaningful in wholesale and retail trade fraud, the smuggling of imported goods, counterfeiting, human trafficking, labour exploitation, prostitution, loan sharking, extortion, and coupled with all of these, money laundering. Indeed, the direction of the money laundered is an essential contrast to Russian/Post-Soviet OCG s activity in Spain. Chinese-led OCG s illegally transfer to China proceeds generated in Spain by both criminal activities and certain legal businesses. A fundamental difference when comparing the Russian/Post-Soviet and Chinese OCG s as a whole is that the former are criminal networks previously active in their home countries – some of them very well connected to members of the political and economic elite. Consequently, in cases like Operations 'Red Marble', 'Troika' and 'Wasp', police investigations reach relevant elite members and even some so-called 'oligarchs'. For instance, in the trial of the case 'Troika', which is ongoing at the moment of writing this article, there is a Russian Duma MP in the dock, Vladislav Reznik. Contrary to this, Chinese OCG s active in Spain, originated there within the migrant community and had no previous connections with Chinese political and economic elites.

Apart from money laundering, which has been present during the whole trajectory of Chinese OCG s in Spain, their first illegal activities were associated with labour and the sexual exploitation of nationals, as well as human trafficking towards the end of the twentieth century. Step by step, during the first half of the new century, the scope of criminal actions included counterfeiting, fiscal fraud, smuggling, loan sharking and extortion. 'Operation Long' (2007/2011), 'Operation Wei' (2009/2013) and 'Operation Emperor' (2012/present time) constituted a turning point as they, according to police investigation reports, uncovered large networks involved in several criminal activities. Moreover, these networks, not considered by police experts as composing a 'mafia structure', enjoyed both local political connections and a recognised influence within the Chinese community. From these years onwards, the

TABLE 6.1   Operations against Russian/Post-Soviet OCG s in Spain

Police Operation Name	Period	Type of crime	Number arrested	Main nationalities involved
'Cobalt'	1999/ 2001	Money laundering	7	Russian
'White Whale'	2004/ 2005	Money laundering, tax avoidance and forgery	56	Spanish, Russian, Ukrainian, Chilean, Finish, British, Swedish, Turkish, Algerian, Iranian and French
'Red Marble'	2004/ 2009	Money laundering	13	Ukrainian and Spanish
'Wasp'	2003/ 2013	Money laundering and criminal conspiracy	27	Georgian, Russian and Spanish
'Clotilde'	2012/ 2013	Money laundering	4	Russian
'Majestic'	2012/ 2017	Money laundering, fraud, bribery	9	Russian, Ukrainian and Spanish
'Java'	2010/ 2015	Money laundering, drug trafficking, extortion and criminal conspiracy	20	Georgian
'Troika'	2008/ present time	Money laundering, forgery and criminal conspiracy	26	Russian

TABLE 6.1   Operations against Russian/Post-Soviet OCGs in Spain (*cont.*)

Police Operation Name	Period	Type of crime	Number arrested	Main nationalities involved
'Usury'	2014/ 2018	Money laundering	8	Russian, Ukrainian and Spanish
'Naples'	2016/ 2017	Money laundering, robbery	23	Georgian

SOURCE: AUTHOR'S ELABORATION

criminal activities of the Chinese-led OCGs, without abandoning the above-mentioned, extended to drug production and trafficking.

The Spanish security forces, and increasingly, the Spanish authorities, are aware of the multiple factors of vulnerability to TOC. The literature analyses elements from several perspectives. The rapid increase in immigrant arrivals, as well as the homogenous and self-enclosed nature of immigrant communities, have been related to favourable scenarios for TOC development.[33] This is important in understanding how risks concerning the Chinese community are perceived in Spain. Within the EU, Spain has had the most substantial increase in immigrant population, with a total increase of 317% between 2001 and 2012, while the Chinese community grew 538% in the same period. Regarding the 'closeness' of the Chinese in Spain, it is one of the most widespread, and probably least controversial, stereotypes of the community. Besides, many testimonies from Spanish security force members confirm that they perceive this feature as one that most complicates investigations of Chinese-led OCGs. According to them, it is difficult to find witnesses and complainants within the community, whilst OCGs are hard to penetrate as they commonly do not integrate members of a different nationality.

---

33   Garoupa, N. (2007). 'Optimal Law Enforcement and Criminal Organization', 63 Journal of Economic Behavior and Organization, pp. 461–474; Alonso-Borrego, C., Garoupa, N., and Vázquez, P. (2012). Does Immigration Cause Crime? Evidence from Spain. American Law and Economics Review 14 (1), pp. 171.

TABLE 6.2   Operations against Mainland Chinese/Taiwanese OCGs in Spain

Police Operation Name	Period	Type of crime	Number arrested	Main nationalities involved
'Katana'	2005	Counterfeiting and fiscal fraud	69	Chinese
'Long'	2007/ 2011	Money laundering, smuggling, illicit flight of capital, fiscal fraud	34	Chinese
'Wei'	2009/ 2013	Labour exploitation, human-trafficking, and fraud	77	Chinese
'Emperor'	2012/ present time	Money laundering, fiscal fraud, smuggling and extortion	80	Chinese and Spanish
'Heijin'	2012/ 2014	Money laundering, loan sharking and extortion	31	Chinese
'Snake'	2015	Money laundering, fraud, and smuggling	32	Chinese
'Shadow'	2016/ present time	Money laundering, fiscal fraud, smuggling	30	Chinese
'Hokkien'	2017/ present time	Counterfeiting, drug trafficking, and prostitution	25	Chinese

TABLE 6.2   Operations against Mainland Chinese/Taiwanese OCGs in Spain (cont.)

Police Operation Name	Period	Type of crime	Number arrested	Main nationalities involved
'Shooping'	2016/ 2017	Money laundering, fiscal fraud, and criminal association	104	Chinese
'Wall'	2016/ 2018	Fraud	288	Taiwanese and Mainland Chinese

SOURCE: AUTHOR'S ELABORATION

In economic terms, related to the structure of the economy, there are two significant elements. One is the weight of the tourist industry, which is linked to a high demand for illegal products like drugs, and services such as a large prostitution market. Another element is real-estate, which attracts money laundering schemes in a country with an off-shore economy equivalent to 20% of economic production.[34] All these components, in combination with Spanish geography, partly explain why Spain is the southwest gateway for drug traffickers entering Europe, as well as having a coastline that attracts smugglers and money-launderers. The other group of economic factors has to do with the rhythms and dynamics of the economy. Since the middle of the nineties, accelerated economic development has favoured the introduction of organised crime resources in legitimate businesses in Spain, especially in the tourist industry and real-estate sector. However, the sharp economic downturn since 2008 and the further severe increase in unemployment, similarly created an appropriate setting for OCGs' performance. The crisis pushed many of the self-employed and businessmen into the shadow economy, whilst a certain administrative tolerance eased some of the management challenges that OCGs face.[35]

---

34   Cinco Días El País. (2013). La economía sumergida en España supone el 20% del PIB. Cinco Días El País, July 13.

35   Gounev, P., and Bezlov, T. (2009). Study to examine the links between organised crime and corruption. Sofia: Center for the Study of Democracy, pp. 19; Gómez-Cespedes, A. (2012).

Some of the factors mentioned above elucidate the principal vulnerability of Spain to corruption. Indeed, the same coastal tourist regions and cities share incidences of both corruption and organised crime (Andalusia, Valencia, Murcia and Catalonia). Madrid, as a vast residential area and urban import hub, is also significant for the analysis of both phenomena. In this manner, the institutional weakness to corruption means further vulnerability for the country when faced with organised crime and implies one of the most critical risk elements when thinking of organised crime as a threat to national security. Specific institutional weaknesses affecting both corruption and TOC were identified several years ago[36] and remain much the same.[37] Among them, the slowness of the judicial system, a favourable criminal law regarding economic crime, and the lack of enough resources to implement the necessary transnational investigations in a period when national security focused on ETA and Islamic terrorism, should be highlighted. With these shortcomings unresolved, both corruption and TOC figures remain at worrying levels. While a recent study by this same author shows that 465 prosecutions related to corruption cases were opened between 2005 and 2015,[38] the Ministry of Interior data identifies around 600 organised groups each year (active plus dismantled), of which 80% or more are transnational. Institutional weakness to corruption and the presence of TOC produce a dangerous combination that generates serious concern within the security and legal systems.

Hence, despite the fact that resources in the fight against the TOC are not optimal, several signs of progress have accompanied a rising awareness of the threat. First, the increasing consciousness of the problem is present in the last three documents of Strategy of National Security (2011, 2013, and 2017), where organized crime is mentioned among the main threats along with conflicts, terrorism, the proliferation of weapons of mass destruction, cyberthreats, and

---

Spain: A Criminal Hub, in Gounev, P., Ruggiero, V. Corruption and Organized Crime in Europe. Illegal partnerships. London: Routledge, pp. 175–188; Fernández, D. (2012). Las mafias eligen España por su ubicación, el turismo y el ladrillo. Revista Policía y Criminalidad 18, pp. 14–16; Sansó, D., and Giménez-Salinas, A. (2014). Crimen organizado. In: L. De la Corte Ibañez and J.M. Blanco Navarro, (editors), Seguridad nacional, amenazas y respuestas, Madrid: Editorial LID, pp. 141–143; Savona, E.U., and Riccardi, M., (editors) (2015). From illegal markets to legitimate businesses: the portfolio of organised crime in Europe. Trento: Transcrime – Università degli Studi di Trento.

36   Sands, J. (2007). Organized Crime and Illicit Activities in Spain: Causes and Facilitating Factors. Mediterranean Politics, 12(2), 211–232; Trapero, J. L. (2013). Una valoración de las jornadas sobre crimen organizado. Revista Catalana de Seguretat Pública 26, pp. 45–51.

37   Ruiz-Ramas, R. (2018). Accountability after the crisis in Spain, London: City University of London, pp. 1–36. Available in: https://accountabilityaftereconomiccrisis.com/outputs/

38   Ruiz-Ramas, R. (2018), pp. 14–21.

threats to critical infrastructures.[39] In practical terms, the growing cooperation among the different Spanish security forces and the General Attorney Office, with the particular role of the 'Special Attorney Office Against Corruption and Organized Crime', represent an advance. Combined with this is the creation of different specialised operative units and strategies on organised crime.[40] A few of these focus on OCGs from specific regions such as Eastern Europe or Asia. A unit, within the Judicial Police Unit of Violent and Specialized Criminality, is explicitly working on OCGs from China and India.

Spain is increasing attention, expertise and means to face organised crime, but when tackling TOC, international cooperation and mutual trust between the authorities of different countries are pivotal elements for success. For instance, bilateral cooperation between Spain and the Russian Federation regarding TOC has been ambivalent, alternating episodes of fruitful recipro-cal assistance with severe disagreements and negative experiences that pre-vent the satisfying conclusion of significant operations. Several hindrances to judicial requirements, along with poor communication flows between security forces, have damaged the Spanish authorities' trust in their Russian partners. Notwithstanding these difficulties, Spain and Russia have remained active channels of cooperation, as recent encouraging examples show. Probably the most representative case is 'Operation Mosaic', in which the Russian Federal Service of Control of Narcotics (SFCN) invited the Spanish Unit of Drugs and Organized Crime (UDYCO) to cooperate with the Chinese

---

39   Consejo de Seguridad Nacional. (2017). Estrategia de Seguridad Nacional 2017. Madrid: Gobierno de España; Departamento de Seguridad Nacional del Gobierno de España. (2016). Informe Anual de Seguridad Nacional 2016. Madrid: Gobierno de España.

40   Firstly, in October 2014, the Intelligence Center for Counter-Terrorism and Organized Crime (CITCO), an intelligence agency responsible for the prevention of domestic ter-rorism and organized crime organizations by managing and analyzing all the internal information of the security and intelligence agencies, was established. The center belongs to the structure of the Ministry of Interior and is the result of the union of the National Anti-Terrorism Coordination Center (CNCA) and the Intelligence Center against Organized Crime (CICO) founded in 2010. Secondly, within the National Police Corps, GRECO (Groups of Special Response to the Organized Crime) was founded. Thirdly, in the sphere of the Civil Guards, the Plan of Action Against Organized Crime (PACCO) which provides support to the Operative Central Unit (UCO) in charge of the central-ization of all the information on organized crime collected by Civil Guards units, was activated. In the fight against fiscal and financial crimes, the creation of the Central Unit of Economic and Fiscal Crime, has excelled, along with the Money Laundering Brigade within the Unit of Economic and Financial Crime (UDEF). Other units of recent origin are the Unit of Undercover Agents, the Brigade of Technological Research and the Teams of Technological Research (EDITE), and the Groups of Support in Information Technology (GATI).

police authorities. This is the first anti-drug operation in which the three states have worked together and it concluded with the arrest of the network leader, a Russian citizen, and the identification of 10,000 drug dealers from 47 countries.[41]

Since 2013, coinciding with 'Operation Emperor', Spain and China have expanded their bilateral cooperation in combating organised crime. That year, a delegation from the Chinese Ministry of Public Security visited Spain to promote reciprocal assistance and the exchange of information. They met with the General Police Station of the Judicial Police, OCN-INTERPOL among other agencies. After that encounter, cooperation improved in fields such as human trafficking, prostitution and drug trafficking.[42] Other areas for potential cooperation associated with economic crime, such as money laundering, counterfeiting and fiscal fraud, still need further development.

A successful, but controversial case of bilateral cooperation between Spain and China, is 'Operation Wall' launched in December 2016. The INTERPOL service of the Spanish National Police Corps collaborated with the Chinese Police Services in the detection and arrest of 269 Taiwanese Chinese accused of taking part in a massive phone fraud of people in Mainland China, from different houses located in Spain. Police cooperation, with the presence of Chinese officials in Spain and a celebration dinner after concluding the operation, ran smoothly. The controversial side of the case lies, on the one hand, in the opposing views of the Spanish and Chinese attorneys regarding the evidence against the arrested, and on the other hand, the country to where the accused had to be extradited, as they were claimed by both the P.R.C. and Taiwan. Eventually, Spain's National Audience court decided on December 2017 to extradite 214 of those arrested to the P.R.C., through a court order with clear nods to the alleged similarities between Taiwan and Catalonia.[43]

---

41   EFE. (2016). Rusia ha abierto la puerta a la cooperación antidroga entre España y China. EFE Agency Press, March 13.

42   EFE. (2013). España y China impulsan su cooperación policial contra el crimen organizado. EFE Agency Press, September 24; Policía Nacional. (2014). Incautada una tonelada de Glicidato de PMK con la que se podrían haber fabricado siete millones de pastillas de éxtasis, June 21.

43   Ballesteros, R. (2017). La Fiscalía dice ahora que no hay delito en la macrorredada de la Policía contra 280 chinos. El Confidencial, May 10; Marraco, M. (2017). La Audiencia entrega a China a 121 taiwaneses porque la independencia "no puede ser unilateral". El Mundo, December 15.

6   The Lukoil and Gazprom Precedents

At the end of 2008, the Spanish media began to cover the projects of the Russian Energy sector in expanding to the Spanish market. The media treatment initially addressed the issue as merely commercial operations and pointed first to the world's biggest natural gas producer and Russia's third-largest oil producer, Gazprom, a company majority-owned by the Russian State, though technically private. In November, Gazprom's interest in buying 20% of Repsol, the main Spanish oil sector company, was made public. During that month, it was confirmed that it was Lukoil and not Gazprom, which was the Russian company involved in a multilateral, commercial and political agreement, to acquire between 20% and 30% of Repsol shares. Lukoil is the second largest Russian company after Gazprom, and one of the biggest global producers of crude oil. Lukoil was planning to buy 20% of the construction company Sacyr-Vallehermoso, and another 10% of La Caixa, the second largest savings bank at that time. As the consultations intensified and the likelihood of having Lukoil as the biggest stake owner in Repsol, documentation and reports on the connections between key Russian and Georgian OCGs and the Lukoil leadership reached the offices of the Government and the main Ministries. Immediately, the media released some of the names involved and their links with the Russian company.[44] The key actors were two Georgian-born Russian citizens, considered as *vory v zakone* ('thieves in law'), the formal status of a professional criminal who enjoys an elite position within the organised crime environment. Both have been involved in the money laundering 'Operation Wasp', launched by the Spanish police forces in 2003. According to the information of Spanish intelligence, the most important of them at that time, Zakhar Kalashov, was a key Lukoil shareowner and an influential advisor. The other, Tariel Oniani, had acted as a Lukoil agent in Spain. Kalashov was in a Spanish jail in 2008 and Oniani would enter one in 2011, after being extradited by Russia.[45]

From the economic point of view, the stake sale was a profitable transaction, and Sacyr-Vallerhermoso lobbied the Government to obtain its approval. The socialist Government of José Luis Rodriguez Zapatero was divided, with Miguel Sebastian, Minister of Industry, assessing the introduction of Lukoil to Repsol as a severe national security threat, and Pedro Solbes, the Minister of Economy, remaining silent. Mariano Rajoy, who in 2008 was the leader of the main opposition party and later Prime Minister, shared Sebastian's critical

---

44   Público. (2008). Capo, preso y accionista de Lukoil. Público, November 20.
45   López-Muñoz, J. (2017). La Mafia Rusa. Génesis, desarrollo y asentamiento en España. Madrid: Dykinson, S.L, pp. 200–211.

stand. However, according to several sources, the then King and Head of State, Juan Carlos I, supported Lukoil's ambitions actively, even through direct phone calls to Rodriguez Zapatero.[46] At the same time, the principal Spanish intelligence agency, the National Intelligence Centre (CNI), prepared different reports which strongly advised against the transaction on the basis of available information. At the same time, (Lukoil was not a state company) Russian foreign policy on uses of hydrocarbons was an issue of growing concern in the EU because of its energy security. Eventually, the Ministries of Industry, Interior and Defence joined forces and Zapatero decided not to support the operation. Two years later, in April 2010, during a Nuclear Security Summit in Washington DC, the Russian President Dmitry Medvedev officially met Rodriguez Zapatero and openly suggested the possibility of Gazprom and other Russian oil companies working together with Spanish energy companies. Zapatero directly avoided the issue and opted to focus on cooperation in fighting terrorism.[47]

7   Concluding Remarks

In the EU at present, Chinese companies engaged in FDI investments are not associated with OCGs, and Spain is not an exception on that point. As has been shown above, growing concerns within the EU regarding China's FDI impact in national security are connected to factors such as the volume of state-owned firms and their access to strategic sectors and critical technologies. Nevertheless, Spain is not an exception either when the sources of contemporary stereotyping of the Chinese community in Europe point towards a 'Chinese Mafia', both as a matrix of stereotypes and as systemic functioning. Despite the campaigns oriented to deactivate rumours, the extension of the derogatory narratives about the Chinese community's economic activities, at least partly, may explain the poor support within Spanish society at large for receiving more investment from China. To be conclusive in this aspect, it would require more survey data about the perception of the Chinese community's economic activity, as well as its association with informal practices, the illegal economy, and finally, organised crime.

---

46   El Confidencial. (2008). Zarzuela reconoce la participación del Rey Juan Carlos en la 'Operación Lukoil'. El Confidencial, November 25; Escolar, I., and Kovaliov, A. (2008). El rey llamó a Zapatero seis veces para apoyar a Lukoil. Público, November 26.

47   Morcillo, C., and Muñoz, P. (2010). Palabra de Vor. Las mafias rusas en España. Madrid: Espasa Forum, pp. 50.

Chinese authorities have stated privately to their Spanish counterparts how worrying the stereotyping of the Chinese in Spanish media is for them. On several occasions, the Chinese embassy in Spain has issued a press release to evince its concern about what it considered as unfair, and sometimes humiliating, representations of the Chinese in TV series and shows (Begin, 2015: 5). In one of the few episodes of peak tension, after 'Operation Emperor', a Chinese ministerial-level delegation travelled to Madrid. Once there, the delegation supported the Chinese community in what they perceived as a growing atmosphere of Sinophobia. Nevertheless, as the Chinese authorities understand that the TOC cases damage their country's image as well as their business interests abroad, the delegation spokesman also warned of the potential impact of 'Operation Emperor' on bilateral relations.

A more recent example of this is related to a joint investigation by the Civil Guard and the Anti-Corruption Attorney's Office which opened in 2016 and is still active. The investigation is a follow-up to the previous 'Operation Shadow' and affects the Industrial and Commercial Bank of China's (ICBC) Madrid branch and the ICBC's European headquarters in Luxembourg. The Civil Guard arrested five ICBC executives of the Madrid branch, including its director who was accused of providing support to Chinese-led OCGs in an alleged crime of money laundering of at least EUR 225 million. China's Ambassador to Spain, Lu Fan, gave a sharp warning about the potential consequences of the case for Sino-Spanish relations at an investment conference in March 2017: "This has undermined the confidence of Chinese business people and investment here and also that of the Chinese government. A prompt solution would help this confidence to return and for the cooperation between both countries to return to normality".[48]

Spain has remained one of the best allies of China within the EU, easing pressure on some EU consensuses concerning China, such as the arms embargo and vetoing of China's status as a market economy. Moreover, as the Spanish authorities did with the communication management of 'Operation Emperor', attempts have been made to prevent the case harming both the image of Chinese investors and the projection of Spain as a destination for Chinese investments. However, in a country with a strong perception of vulnerability, faced with corruption and TOC, the police and legal system have run their course in working to neutralise threats to national security, such as money laundering. The same happened with investigations brought before the

---

48   Bermick, A., and Lague, D. (2017). How China's biggest bank became ensnared in a sprawling money laundering probe. Reuters, July 31; Shanghai Daily. (2017). Spain looks into ICBC's European unit for alleged money laundering. Shanghai Daily, September 13.

justice system of Spanish and other foreign politicians and business people. China too, is not alien to anti-corruption campaigns. Chinese and Spanish authorities, like Spanish and Chinese communities, have a long way to go together. No doubt they will follow this path because there are enough reasons to build mutual trust free of stereotypes and prejudices, both within the spheres of international relations and society as a whole.

Bibliography

Alonso-Borrego, C., Garoupa, N., and Vázquez, P. (2012). Does Immigration Cause Crime? Evidence from Spain. American Law and Economics Review 14 (1), pp. 165–191.

Ballesteros, R. (2017). La Fiscalía dice ahora que no hay delito en la macrorredada de la Policía contra 280 chinos. El Confidencial, May 10.

Begin, P. (2015). Empathy and sinophobia: depicting Chinese migration in *Biutiful* (Iñárritu, 2010), Transnational Cinemas, 6:1, pp. 1–16.

Beltrán, J. (2016) China en España: un tropo polivalente. In: Beltrán, Haro, F., and Sáiz, A. (eds). Representaciones de China en las Américas y la Península Ibérica. Barcelona: Edicions Bellaterra, pp 101–124.

Beltrán, J., and Sáiz, A. (2009). *Empresariado asiático en España*. Barcelona: CIDOB.

Beltrán, J., and Sáiz, A. (2013a). De la invisibilidad a la espectacularidad. Cuarenta años de inmigración china España. In Rios, X. (ed.), *Las relaciones hispano-chinas. Historia y futuro*. Madrid: Los Libros de la Catarata, pp. 114–131.

Beltrán, J., and Sáiz, A. (2013b). Del restaurante chino al bar autóctono. Evolución del empresariado de origen chino en España y su compleja relación con la etnicidad. In: Barros Nock, M. and Valenzuela, H., Retos y estrategias del empresariado étnico. Estudios de caso de empresarios latinos en los Estados Unidos y empresarios inmigrantes en España, México DF: Centro de Investigaciones y Estudios Superiores en Antropología Social (CIESAS).

Beltrán, J., and Sáiz, A. (2015). A contracorriente. Trabajadores y empresarios chinos en España ante la crisis económica (2007–2013). *Migraciones. Revista del Instituto Universitario de Estudios sobre Migraciones*, n° 37, pp. 125–147.

Bermick, A., and Lague, D. (2017). How China's biggest bank became ensnared in a sprawling money laundering probe. Reuters, July 31.

Cachón, L. (2006). Intereses contrapuestos y racismo: El incendio de los almacenes chinos en Elche (septiembre de 2004). Circunstancia 10, pp. 1–19.

Cardenal, J.P., and Araújo, H. (2013). El imperio invisible. El éxito empresarial chino y sus vínculos con la criminalidad económica en España y Europa. Madrid: Crítica.

Cardenal, J. P., and Araújo, H. (2014). El Imperio Invisible. La falta de transparencia y de fuentes fiables envuelven el entramado empresarial chino en Europa, un búnker por el que desfilan miles millones y del que sabemos muy poco. Ethic, September 1.

Cinco Días El País. (2013). La economía sumergida en España supone el 20% del PIB. Cinco Días El País, July 13.

Consejo de Seguridad Nacional. (2017). Estrategia de Seguridad Nacional 2017. Madrid: Gobierno de España.

Dawson, R. (1967). The Chinese Chamaleon. An Analysis of European Conceptions of Chinese Civilisation. New York: Oxford University Press.

Departamento de Seguridad Nacional del Gobierno de España. (2016). Informe Anual de Seguridad Nacional 2016. Madrid: Gobierno de España.

Díez, P. M. (2013). La cara oculta del éxito empresarial chino. ABC, December 29.

Economía Digital. (2018). Tras la sombra de Gao Ping: así actúa la mafia china en España. Economía Digital, April 19.

EFE. (2012). Un delegado enviado por China: «Necesito pruebas de que en España no existechinofobia». EFE Agency Press, November 27.

EFE. (2013). España y China impulsan su cooperación policial contra el crimen organizado. EFE Agency Press, September 24.

EFE. (2016). Rusia ha abierto la puerta a la cooperación antidroga entre España y China. EFE Agency Press, March 13.

El Confidencial. (2008). Zarzuela reconoce la participación del Rey Juan Carlos en la 'Operación Lukoil'. El Confidencial, November 25.

Escolar, I., and Kovaliov, A. (2008). El rey llamó a Zapatero seis veces para apoyar a Lukoil. Público, November 26.

Esteban, M. and Otero-Iglesias, M. (2017). Chinese Investment in Spain: Open for Business, but not at any Price, pp. 141–151. In: Seaman J., Huotari M., and Otero-Iglesias, M. (editor) (2017). Chinese Investment in Europe. A Country-Level Approach. Madrid-Paris-Berlin: European Think-tank Network on China.

European Commission. (2017). State of the Union 2017: Trade Package: European Commission: Proposes Framework for Screening of Foreign Direct Investments. Brussels: European Commission.

Fernández, D. (2012). Las mafias eligen España por su ubicación, el turismo y el ladrillo. Revista Policía y Criminalidad 18, pp. 14–16.

Garoupa, N. (2007). Optimal Law Enforcement and Criminal Organization, 63 Journal of Economic Behavior and Organization, pp. 461–474.

Gobierno de España. (2011). Estrategia Española de Seguridad. Una responsabilidad de todos. Madrid: Gobierno de España.

Gómez-Cespedes, A. (2012). Spain: A Criminal Hub, in Gounev, P., Ruggiero, V. Corruption and Organized Crime in Europe. Illegal partnerships. London: Routledge, pp. 175–188.

Gounev, P., and Bezlov, T. (2009). Study to examine the links between organised crime and corruption. Sofia: Center for the Study of Democracy.

Grieger, G. (2017). Foreign direct investment screening. A debate in light of China-EU FDI flows. Brussels: European Parliament.

Hanemann, T., and Rosen, D.H. (2012). China invests in Europe – patterns, impacts and policy implications. New York: Rhodium Group.

Hanemann, T., and Huotari, M. (2017). Record Flows and Growing Imbalances, Chinese Investment in Europe in 2016. Merics Papers on China 3, pp. 1–12.

Hanemann, T., and Huotari, M. (2018). Chinese FDI in Europe in 2017. Rapid recovery after initial slowdown. New York-Berlin: Rhodium Group (RHG) and the Mercator Institute for China Studies (MERICS).

Hang, Z. (2013). La imagen de China en la prensa española. Una visión desde los diarios: El País, ABC, El Periódico y La Vanguardia. Barcelona: Universitat Autònoma de Barcelona.

Hughes, K. L. (2014). Racismo y xenofobia: representaciones de la comunidad asiática en la prensa española. Dickinson College Honors Theses, Paper 142.

Koch-Weser, I., and Ditz, G. (2017). Chinese Investment in the United States: Recent Trends in Real Estate, Industry, and Investment Promotion. Washington DC: U.S.-China Economic and Security Review Commission Washington DC.

Li, Y., and Bian, C. (2016). A new dimension of foreign investment law in China – evolution and impacts of the national security review system. Asia Pacific Law Review 24 (2), pp. 149–175. DOI: 10.1080/10192557.2016.1243212.

López-Muñoz, J. (2017). La Mafia Rusa. Génesis, desarrollo y asentamiento en España. Madrid: Dykinson, S.L.

Marraco, M. (2017). La Audiencia entrega a China a 121 taiwaneses porque la independencia "no puede ser unilateral". El Mundo, December 15.

Medialdea, S. (2013). Suspendido el Año Nuevo Chino en Madrid. La comunidad china lo justifica por la crisis y la «persecución social tras la Operación Emperador». El País, February 2.

Merino Sancho, J. M. (2008). La Inmigración China En España: ¿Qué Imagen?, Observatorio de la Economía y la Sociedad China 6, pp. 1–18.

Meunier, S. (2014). Divide and conquer? China and the cacophony of foreign investment rules in the EU. Journal of European Public Policy 21 (7), pp. 996–1016.

Moran, T. H. (2017). CFIUS and National Security: Challenges for the United States, Opportunities for the European Union. Washington D.C.: Peterson Institute for International Economics.

Morcillo, C., and Muñoz, P. (2010). Palabra de Vor. Las mafias rusas en España. Madrid: Espasa Forum.

Nadali, D. B. (2007). Migración, comercio mayorista chino y etnicidad. Revista CIDOB D'AfersInternacionals 78, pp. 77–95.

Nicolas, F. (2014). China's Direct Investment in the European Union: Challenges and Policy Responses. China Economic Journal 7, pp.103–125.

Nieto, G. (2007). La inmigración china en España. Madrid: Los libros de la Catarata.

Policía Nacional. (2014). Incautada una tonelada de Glicidato de PMK con la que se podrían haber fabricado siete millones de pastillas de éxtasis. June 21.

Público. (2008). Capo, preso y accionista de Lukoil. Público, November 20. http://especiales.publico.es/hemeroteca/176264/capo-preso-y-accionista-de-lukoil.

Rodríguez Wangüemert, C. Rodríguez Breijo, V., and Pestano Rodríguez, J. M. (2017). China tras la mirada de la televisión española. Estudios sobre el Mensaje Periodístico 23 (2), pp. 969–985.

Rosati, S. (2017). 'Chiñol': el dilema de ser chino y nacer en España. El País, December 29.

Ruiz-Ramas, Rubén. (2018). Accountability after the Crisis. Spain. London: City University of London.

Sands, J. (2007). Organized Crime and Illicit Activities in Spain: Causes and Facilitating Factors. Mediterranean Politics, 12(2), 211232.

Sansó, D., and Giménez-Salinas, A. (2014). Crimen organizado. In: L. De la Corte Ibañez and J.M. Blanco Navarro, (editors), Seguridad nacional, amenazas y respuestas, Madrid: Editorial LID, pp.133–149.

Savona, E.U., and Riccardi, M., (editors) (2015). From illegal markets to legitimate businesses: the portfolio of organised crime in Europe. Trento: Transcrime – Università degli Studi di Trento.

Seaman J., Huotari M., and Otero-Iglesias, M. (editor) (2017). Chinese Investment in Europe. A Country-Level Approach. Madrid-Paris-Berlin: European Think-tank Network on China.

Seaman, J., Huotari, M., and Otero-Iglesias, M. (2017). Introduction: Sizing Up Chinese Investments in Europe. In: J. Seaman, M. Huotari, and M. Otero-Iglesias, (editors), Chinese Investment in Europe. A Country-Level Approach. Madrid-Paris-Berlin: European Think-tank Network on China, pp. 9–18.

Shanghai Daily. (2017). Spain looks into ICBC's European unit for alleged money laundering. Shanghai Daily, September 13.

Škoba, L. (2014). Chinese investment in the EU. European Parliament Research Service, May 23.

Sourbes, C. (2018). France ponders difficult decisions over Chinese FDI. FDI Intelligence, April 12.

Recuero, M. (2018). La Audiencia Nacional imputa a CaixaBank por ayudar a blanquear dinero a la mafia china. El Mundo, April 19.

Ruiz-Ramas, R. (2018). Accountability after the crisis in Spain, London: City University of London, pp. 1–36. Available in: https://accountabilityaftereconomiccrisis.com/outputs/.

Trapero, J. L. (2013). Una valoración de las jornadas sobre crimen organizado. Revista Catalana de Seguretat Pública 26, pp. 45–51.

U.S.-China Economic and Security Review Commission (2017). 2017 Report to Congress of the U.S.-China Economic and Security Review Commission, One Hundred Fifteenth Congress First Session. Washington D.C.: U.S.-China Economic and Security Review Commission.

Van Dijk, T. A. (2003). Racismo y discurso de las élites. Barcelona: Gedisa.

Vidales, R. (2012). Has Operation Emperor led to 'Chinaphobia' in Spain? El País, December 17.

Villarino, Á. (2012). ¿A dónde van los chinos cuándo mueren? Vida y negocios de la comunidad china en España. Madrid: Debate.

Villoria Mendieta, M., Gimeno Feliú, J.M., and Tejedor Bielsa, J. (2016). La corrupción en España. Ámbitos, causas y remedios jurídicos. Barcelona: Atelier Libros Jurídicos.

Yangwen, Z. (2017). The Chinese Chameleon Revisited: From the Jesuits to Zhang Yimou. Cambridge: Cambridge Scholars Publishing.

Zhang, H., and Van den Bulcke, D. (2014). China's direct investment in the European Union: a new regulatory challenge? Asia Europe Journal 12, pp. 159–177.

Zhou Hang (2013), La imagen de China en la prensa española Una visión desde los diarios: El País, ABC, El Periódico y La Vanguardia, Master Thesis, Universitat Autònoma de Barcelona.

CHAPTER 7

Know Better, Like Better

An Appraisal of the Effect of the Belt and Road Initiative on Chinese Brand Image in France

Youssef Elhaoussine

1   Introduction

The objective of the Belt and Road Initiative (hereinafter referred to as BRI) is to further develop an understanding of China globally through several interconnected spheres: economic, political, cultural and technological. From a marketing point of view, the question arises: how could such an initiative help Chinese brands to develop? Chinese brands have suffered in the past from negative evaluation due to their association with the *Made in China* label. Many brands which have suffered from these same symptoms have developed a long and arduous plan to create their own singular brand identity, far from the negative collective stereotype associated with their country of origin. In the case of Chinese brands, the aim is to accomplish the same end result, only faster. So how could the BRI help in this context? The latter is supposed to create a better understanding of China abroad. It is therefore more than an economic corridor. It transfers a mass of information about China and creates multiple ties between populations. In other words, it increases the self-reference criterion of consumers outside China. Such integration will allow foreign populations, such as Europeans, to have a better understanding of China. And this better understanding could in turn benefit Chinese brands. However, since the BRI is relatively new, and since it will take time to observe its effects, the purpose of this article is to synthetize the BRI information transfer and to assess its effect on Chinese brand evaluation at three levels: tangible, service and affective. From the conclusion of this study, Chinese authorities in charge of international initiatives and brands would be able to better understand their interdependence and develop a coherent strategy along the BRI corridor.

1.1   *Brands as Information Carriers*

Brands act as powerful information transmitters. They represent a set of information that is transmitted to consumers.[1] In other words, this information is a cognitive shortcut that allows consumers to understand the product benefits faster and consistently. Marketing executives manage these in order to obtain an edge over competitors. Such information packages are observable through advertising campaigns within the several media channels available to consumers. In the current modern era, exposure to such information has increased. This endeavour, to be perceived as different and superior to the competition, pushes brands to associate themselves with more and more diverse values. Brands have moved from advertising their quality – tangible value – to advertising a lifestyle – affective value.[2] On the other hand, consumers comprehend brands through an information package and use this understanding within their decision-making process.[3] Their cognitive and affective ability will allow them to translate that information into product benefits or values and determine what is the best offer to satisfy their large array of needs. It is also important to note that consumers perceive the newness of a value only over a period of time and that after a while a new value is perceived as acquired and loses its competitive advantage. In order to better understand the trend of brand development, it is important to understand how brand values, and the information they carry, are categorized.

Brand information evolved around two dimensions[4]: tangible values and intangible values. Tangible values are often related to the physical characteristics of the product (i.e. quality, design, features, and packaging). Intangible values are represented by the non-physical benefits that a product can offer to the consumer. This dimension can be divided into two parts: service intangible and affective intangible. Service intangible values are all the non-physical benefits that support the experience of tangible values. For example, delivery is important to gain access to the physical goods. A warranty is critical to

---

1 Vicenti and Fortat, V. (2017). Les nouvelles routes de la soie, Taoïsme économique ou nouvel imperialisme, Institut des Relations Internationales et Stratégiques. Asia Focus 45; Cai, P. (2017). Understanding China's Belt and Road Initiative. LOWY Institute for International Policy.

2 Poels, K., and Dewitte, S. (2006). How to Capture the Heart? Reviewing 20 Years of Emotion Measurement in Advertising. Journal of Advertising Research 46 (1), pp. 18–37.

3 Keller, K. L., and Lehmann, D. R. (2006). Brands and Branding: Research Findings and Future Priorities. Marketing Science 25 (6), pp. 740–759.

4 Padgett, D., and Allen, D. (1997). Communicating Experiences: A Narrative Approach to Creating Service Brand Image. Journal of advertising 26 (4), pp. 49–62; Martineau, P. (1958). The Personality of the Retail Store. Harvard Business Review 36 (1), pp. 47–55.

guarantee continuous quality or the durability of tangible values. Affective intangible values on the other hand, are more abstract. They add a more aspirational dimension to the brands. For example, a brand can be perceived as 'cool' or 'geek'. In recent years, the concept of brand personality has been introduced.[5] This theory has proposed that in order to foster a positive consumer evaluation, a brand should develop a personality that matches the customer's aspiration. Following those dimensions, brands will be represented by the sum of the values they carry. However, although the brand marketing team crafts certain values, others are just associated due to uncontrollable external factors. In this article, the country of origin effect is an example. Because of its extraneous and macro-level nature, it is very difficult for brand managers to implement actions to monitor it.[6] Only macro-level initiatives, such as the BRI, could help in that direction by shaping the country's image, and consequently, the brand's evaluation.

1.2   *Brands as Representatives of a Country*

Brands can be associated with their country of origin (COO),[7] and vice versa. It is difficult to assess which will influence the other first – countries or brands? On one hand, the COO can represent a value that can be carried by the brand information package and processed by consumers during their decision-making process. It can be linked with product tangible (quality) or intangible values (affective).[8] Such values can have different valance. For *Made in Germany* products, the COO element is considered as positive. For *Made in China* products, the evaluation can be perceived negatively. Therefore, what could create or affect such direction in valance? Many researchers have called upon interesting elements to answer this question.[9] In the context of this article, it is argued that the past and present geopolitical situations of a country

---

5   Aaker, J. L. (1997). Dimensions of Brand Personality, in the Journal of Marketing Research, pp. 347–356.

6   Verlegh, P. W., Steenkamp, J. B. E., and Meulenberg, M. T. (2005). Country-of-Origin Effects in Consumer Processing of Advertising Claims. International Journal of Research in Marketing 22 (2), pp. 127–139.

7   Hong, S. T., and WyerJr, R. S. (1989). Effects of Country-of-Origin and Product-Attribute Information on Product Evaluation: An Information Processing Perspective. Journal of Consumer Research 16(2), pp. 175–187.

8   Chen, C. Y., Mathur, P., and Maheswaran, D. (2014). The Effects of Country-Related Affect on Product Evaluations. Journal of Consumer Research 41(4), pp. 1033–1046.

9   Samiee, S., Leonidou, L. C., Aykol, B., Stöttinger, B., and Christodoulides, P. (2016). Fifty Years of Empirical Research on Country-of-Origin Effects on Consumer Behavior: A Meta-Analysis. In Rediscovering the Essentiality of Marketing, Cham: Springer, pp. 505–510.

can influence the evolution of its domestic brands. In addition, any substantial diplomatic initiative could be considered to have an impact on brand perception. On the other hand, many examples have shown that people experience a country through its network of international brands. This has been the case for the USA with cheeseburgers, soft drinks, sports goods, and mobile phones; and for France with its wine, cheese, cosmetics and luxuries. Compared to public relations initiatives controlled by governments and which are non-profit oriented, brand developments are more dynamic. The more the brand is successful, the more it can develop internationally across markets and in return, the more it can carry its COO element. In the case of Chinese brands, their development reveals certain specificities that differentiate them from others.

1.3   *A Historical Perspective on the Development of Chinese Brands*
Chinese brands entered the global marketplace through a political initiative. In the 1980's, Chairman Deng Xiao Ping encouraged the development of the Chinese manufacturing industry, domestically and internationally. Under such a dynamic, foreign buyers began to access a cheaper labour force which in turn led to cheaper products. In this context, the concept of brand identity was not important. Only the production output cost and the product price were relevant, leaving Chinese products without brand identities. In order to build a relevant brand identity, a brand needs to cover the brand dimensions mentioned earlier. Most importantly, it needs to differentiate itself from other competing options. Here it may be observed that Chinese manufacturers and their 'embryo' brands acted as a collective group under the same banner: China. They did not focus on being different from each other but rather on being price-different from international competitors. This attitude could be explained through the Chinese cultural or political aspect related to collectivism.[10] In Chinese culture, collectivism is a positive value. And under the communist political system, all business ventures have had to follow a similar development. In other words, Chinese brand identity was not a priority. Once the Chinese government pushed factories toward a price advantage strategy, everyone followed.

This direction of course helped the Chinese economy to develop rapidly, with all the accompanying benefits. It is also this development that put Chinese brands in today's global market. However, Chinese brands are now facing a major challenge to develop a singular brand identity, the *Made in China*

---

10   Spencer-Rodgers, J., Peng, K., Wang, L., and Hou, Y. (2004). Dialectical Self-esteem and East-West Differences in Psychological Well-being. Personality and Social Psychology Bulletin 30 (11), pp. 1416–1432.

identity, which is associated with a negative stereotype.[11] Global consumers see the price advantage of Chinese products but as they use them, they grasp a better understanding of the values associated with low pricing. They are confronted with lower tangible values such as poorer quality, poorer design, fewer features, and lower performance. It is unfortunately this negative evaluation that mostly characterizes the *Made in China* identity.[12] Thus, such an identity follows modern Chinese brands that want to develop their own singular positive brand identity. This behaviour is well observed between people of different origin. When one person meets another person from a different social background for the first time, it is the characteristics of this background that will feed the primo evaluation process. The first impression that *Made in China* products conveyed to the world still affects Chinese brands, and will continue to do so. Furthermore, such stereotypes are hard to eradicate. Therefore, the question is: how to break free of this negative collective evaluation? For people, it is through better cultural exchange and mutual understanding that they move beyond the first impression and the stereotypes. For brands, this process could also be useful. And any political initiative that promotes a better exchange of information between countries will benefit brands.

1.4   *The Global Emergence of Singular Chinese Brands*

Chinese brands are currently developing their own specific brands with their own identity. Many examples can be observed in the global market place: Huawei, Lenovo, Haier, BYD, etc ... However, as mentioned earlier, they still suffer from their collective identity, in the same way as an immigrant suffers from his or her collective identity when he or she enters a new country. Italian or Irish immigrants suffered many stereotypes when they arrived in the US in the 19th or 20th century. Only time and positive reinforcement helped those immigrants to be perceived for what they are as persons rather than as members of a community. However, for Chinese brands, time is of the essence.

Along with the BRI, Chinese President Xi Jinping launched a brand initiative called *Made in China 2025*,[13] leaving less than 7 years for the *Made in China*

---

11   Maheswaran, D. (1994). Country of Origin as a Stereotype: Effects of Consumer Expertise and Attribute Strength on Product Evaluations. Journal of Consumer Research *21* (2), pp. 354–365.

12   Klein, J. G., Ettenson, R., and Morris, M. D. (1998). The Animosity Model of Foreign Product Purchase: An Empirical Test in the People's Republic of China. The Journal of Marketing, pp. 89–100.

13   Wang, Y. Made in China 2025 Plan Unveiled to Boost Manufacturing. Xinhua News, May 15, 2015.

image to be perceived for what it is (positive), rather than what it was (negative). This called upon Chinese manufacturers to develop the high-end and pioneer industrial technology – especially in high tech industries. But can this shift be fully achieved in less than 7 years? The *Made in China* initiative will surely improve the tangible values of Chinese products but the stereotype will likely remain. To support this argument, it is possible to refer to similar situations in the past, where brands suffered from negative COO and decided to undertake a new strategy to overcome this. A brief overview of Japanese and Korean brand development could show that it takes time and hard work to overcome successfully the shift from a negative collective identity to a positive (or actual) singular identity.

1.5   *Shift from Collective to Singular Identity*

In the 70s, Japanese and Korean brands were considered as cheaper alternatives to American brands. It took a long and tenacious process to shift from a negative collective image to a singular positive image. Toyota is a good example and the brand is today one of the leading global car manufacturers.[14] Not only are its cars sold in most countries all over the world, they are also perceived positively. Such progress is quite extraordinary considering that the brand recovered from a negative image associated with Japanese COO. For example, although the models sold in the US during the 70's and 80's were more affordable and equally reliable as American brands, consumers still perceived the Japanese cars negatively. Of course, such a necessary shift in brand image came at a very high price, and over a relatively long period of time.

The Japanese car manufacturer had to innovate, not only in terms of technology, but also in management practices. Toyota executives introduced the '*Kaizen*' corporate philosophy, which is a derivative of *Lean Management* and *Total Quality Management* practices. Such practices focused on reducing waste in order to improve quality and produce value for consumers. Its other aspect is to identify and solve problems before they become a major issue. In addition to '*Kaizen*', Toyota evolved under the '*jojo*' concept, which means 'gradually' and 'steadily' in Japanese. The brand image of Toyota followed this development trend. Toyota's primary goals at the beginning of their international development were to produce cars that were both reliable and affordable (a focus on tangible values). Today, consumer perception of Toyota has totally

---

14   Stewart, T., and Raman, A. (2007). Lessons from Toyota's Long Drive. Harvard Business Review (July–August), pp.74–83.

changed – which is the same for other Japanese brands too. By changing their singular identity, they affected their collective identity.

1.6   BRI to Help Speed up the Shifting Process

Changing a tangible image is costly, time consuming and risky. If Chinese brands adopt the same pattern as Japanese and Korean brands, they would require (in addition to time) adapting their management, spending a lot of resources, and taking considerable risks. This delicate shift is already in place within many major Chinese brands sold globally. But it is not yet generalized to the whole pool of brands under the *Made in China* banner. Some brands may not have the resources or are not willing to take such a risk to invest individually. Following the Chinese collectivist approach, collective initiatives could therefore help Chinese brands in this domain. This is now the case with the BRI.[15] Collective initiatives can affect the COO effect and in return, the COO effect can affect brand evaluation. In the case of the COO effect, brand knowledge is composed, among other things, of the information that the consumer has aggregated about the focal country,[16] in this case, China. The information package sent along with those collective initiatives could help change the perception of China and in return offset the negative stereotype. In other words, collective information will help to form an opinion and affect how consumers perceive a brand.

1.7   Research Question

In this chapter, the purpose is to assess if a collective information package about China (in this instance, the BRI) could affect the evaluation of Chinese brands. It is hypothesized that in order to reduce a negative stereotype embedded in a collective brand group, a transfer of positive information on behalf of the collective group needs to be performed. In the Chinese brand context, the BRI is believed to be a process that allows the collective group (under the Chinese banner) to transfer positive information across borders. The more a consumer is aware of the Chinese environment, the better is the evaluation of Chinese brands. In this case, many analysts consider the BRI as the demonstration of Chinese soft power in international relations.[17] Such an international

15   Courmont B., and Setti A. (2017). Belgrade – Pekin: Quand la Chine se positionne au coeur de l'Europe, Institut des Relations Internationales et Stratégiques. Asia Focus 18.

16   Keller, K. L. (2003). Brand Synthesis: The Multidimensionality of Brand Knowledge. Journal of Consumer Research 29 (4), pp. 595–600.

17   Courmont B., and Setti A. (2017). Belgrade – Pekin: Quand la Chine se positionne au coeur de l'Europe, Institut des Relations Internationales et Stratégiques. Asia Focus 18.

initiative covers various domains: cultural, economic, political, technological, and social. However, to observe the results of the BRI would take time. It is therefore necessary to develop a synthetic setting in order to assess the effect of how a better understanding of China could help boost the evaluation of Chinese brands.

2   Methodology

2.1   *Research Design*

A comparative study between westerners living in their own country (Domestic Westerners or DW) and westerners living in China (WLC) will be carried out in order to assess the effect of the BRI on Chinese brand evaluation. Compared to DW, WLC have developed a better understanding of China. This understanding covers different dimensions: cultural, economic, political and social, technological, and demographic. Since the BRI favours a better knowledge and understanding of China, the WLC condition will therefore represent the synthetic effect of the BRI over time (high condition). And the DW condition will represent the current effect of BRI, which is assumed to be minimal since the initiative was officially started and announced in 2017 (low condition). To control for external effect, DW and WLC from the same country have been chosen. An online survey was consequently sent to French nationals living in China (WLC) and French nationals living in France (DW). They were asked to answer questions that would define their level of understanding of China (independent variable). They are then evaluated on their general impression of Chinese brands within three levels of product dimensions (dependent variable). The interaction between those two variables will allow us to assess and predict the effect of the BRI on Chinese brand evaluation. In order to better control for extraneous effect and to allocate participants the right condition, control variables such as their opinion of China and their experience of living in China will be measured.

3   Measurements

3.1   *Independent Variable*

Participants will be evaluated on their understanding of China in order to confirm their condition attribution. To reduce bias and extraneous effect, a comparison will be drawn between French participants in France and those in China. The understanding of China will be measured according to the PEST model (Political, Economic, Social and Technological). This framework is used in strategic management to assess the understanding of an environment before making decisions. All four dimensions will be measured on a 5-point rating scale expressing their familiarity with China's environment. The questions are framed as follows:

– "How would you express your level of understanding and knowledge of the political environment in China?" (Political dimension)
– "How would you express your level of understanding and knowledge of the economic and business situation in China?" (Economic dimension)
– "How would you express your level of understanding and knowledge of Chinese culture and Chinese society?" (Social dimension)
– "How would you express your level of knowledge about Chinese technology?" (Technological dimension)

3.2   *Dependent Variables*

Brand evaluation will be carried out using the knowledge of Chinese brands in general. No specific brands have been used in order to avoid bias from the focal brand image as well as from the brand product category. Brand evaluation will be measured through the three product levels of value dimension: tangible, service and affective. This process allows a more general response and an opportunity to observe which value level is more affected by BRI.

Tangible values will be measured on a 5-point rating scale. Participants are asked to give their general impression on how they assess the physical characteristic of a Chinese product such as quality, features, design, etc. *Made in China* stereotypes are often developed from this brand value dimension since the stereotype is usually related to products with low quality and design copied from others.

Service values will be measured based on the trust related to the service provided by the brand. A service is an abstract construct that cannot be measured physically. Therefore, in order to measure it, it is relevant to use another construct – trust will be used here. In the service industry, customers build an expectation prior to the consumption of the service. They then build a certain level of trust related to the probability the service will keep its promises. Therefore, trust will be measured on a 5-point rating scale asking how participants would trust the service provided by a Chinese product company, such as delivery, warranty, and after-sales service.

Affective intangible values are in Business to Consumer markets often related to aspirational values. Consumers in that situation use the affective values of the product to reinforce their self-concept. Therefore, affective values could be measured by assessing how close consumers feel to the brand affective values. As an example, we can say that the brand Jeep uses affective values such as adventure, thrills and independence. Some people can see themselves reflected in those values.

3.3   Control Variables

Confirmation questions will be asked in order to discriminate or eliminate participants. In addition, socio-economic status such as age, gender, geographic location and time spent in China, will be taken into account. Similarly, a control variable will be set up to assess the number of years spent in China. Participants may be in France but they may have spent time in China and therefore have become more familiarized with the Chinese environment.

3.4   Method of Analysis

To test the main hypotheses of this research, independent-samples T-test and Mann-Whitney U test will be used. They both aim to compare the means between two unrelated groups on the same dependent variable. Such tests will allow us to understand whether there is a significant difference between the two cohorts (DW and WLC). First, in order to confirm the pertinence of the independent variable, a separate comparison test will be performed as a manipulation check to observe the difference in knowledge based on different locations. The cohort of French people in France should have a lower understanding of the Chinese political, economic, cultural and technological environment than the cohort of French people in China. Then, a comparison on product evaluation will be made. The dependent variable would be the product evaluation for tangible, service and affective values evaluated on a 5-point rating scale. The independent variable would be the location (in France or in China).

3.5   Assumptions about the Independent T-test and Mann-Whitney U Test

Parametric (Independent T-test) and non-parametric (Mann-Whitney U) tests will be used to assess the difference between the two groups on product evaluation, as well as in the manipulation check. The reason for using both types of test is that the dependent variable in both cases (knowledge of China and product evaluation) was measured on a rating scale using statements that could open the results to criticism based on the equivalence of interval between the

different levels. Such criticism is of course legitimate but in social science studies, the practice of using rating scales, such as the Likert scale – alone or as a
sum – as continuous measurement, is common.[18] If both tests converge then
the results will have more credibility.

Assumptions about an Independent T-test must be verified before analysis.
The dependent variable in both T-tests (knowledge of China and product evaluation) are measured on a rating scale that is considered as continuous. The
independent variable consists of two categorical groups represented by geographical difference. There were no interactions between the two conditions
to guarantee the independence of observations, which means that there is no
relationship between the observations in each group or between the groups
themselves. In addition, a scatter plot in SPSS shows that there were no significant outliers to remove. And, from observation, as well as using the Shapiro-
Wilk test for normality, dependent variables were mostly normally distributed.
An independent T-test only requires approximately normal data because it is
quite robust as regards violations of normality. In addition, the sample differences in terms of frequency and variance are small. Finally, homogeneity of
variances has been checked with the Levene test. Therefore, all independent
sample T-tests can be performed in the following studies.

In order to confirm the results of the T-test, a non-parametric test – the
Mann-Whitney U test – will be conducted on the dependent variable by
both conditions in the independent variables. The Mann-Whitney U test is a
nonparametric equivalent to the independent T-test and it is an appropriate
analysis to compare differences that come from the same population when
the dependent variable is ordinal or continuous. The Mann-Whitney U test
compares the number of times a score from one sample is ranked higher than
a score from another sample. The scores from both samples will be ranked
together; rank 1 is used for the lowest score, rank 2 for the next lowest score,
and so on. When scores have the same value, a tie is determined. The scores
are ranked and those ranks are added together and then divided by the number of scores. Each of the tied scores is then assigned the same ranking. Once
the data is ranked, calculations are carried out on the ranks. The assumptions
include random samples from populations. Both samples have independent
observations, and the measure of the two samples has at least an ordinal scale
of measurement.

---

18   Jamleson, S. (2004). Likert Scales: How to (Ab) use Them. Medical Education 38(12),
      pp. 1217–1218; Allen, I. E., and Seaman, C. A. (2007). Likert Scales and Data Analyses, in
      Quality Progress 40(7), pp. 64.

3.6   *Test for Effect Size*

The T-test and Mann-Whitney U test are used to assess whether the mean difference between two groups is significant. However, it does not provide a reliable measure to assess the intensity of this difference. Of course, it is possible to compare the values of the mean and provide a basic evaluation. However, the effect size can be calculated. Effect size is a statistical concept that measures the strength of the relationship between two variables. The greater the effect size, the greater the difference between the two groups will be. For an independent T-test, a Cohen's effect size value, d, is used. Cohen's d is known as the difference of two population means and it is divided by the standard deviation from the data, providing levels of 0.2, 0.5 and 0.8 for small, medium and large magnitudes respectively. When performing nonparametric group tests, Field (2005) suggests an effect size analogous to Cohen's d for parametric group testing. It can be calculated by dividing the absolute (positive) standardized test statistic z by the square root of the number of pairs, and provide levels of 0.1, 0.3 and 0.5 for small, medium and large magnitudes respectively.

3.7   *Regression Analysis*

Linear regressions are relevant analytical tools to analyze the relationship between variables. The tool is used to predict the value of a given variable based on the value of one variable. However, linear regressions require us to respect several assumptions. Here, the variables are ordinals but could be to some extent considered intervals. This issue has been mentioned earlier and was the reason why parametric and non-parametric tests were considered. In the present study, regressions will still be considered, not to test the hypothesis, but rather to observe the effect on the control variable: opinion of China. Two regressions are proposed to test the effect of knowledge about China on opinion toward China and the effect of opinion toward China on product evaluation. An opinion is developed through the acquisition of information from the focal object, in this case, China. Therefore, the direction of the relationship between those variables can be assessed in this way. In addition, from the COO field of research, it was shown that an opinion toward a country affects its product evaluation.

Despite the limitations set out above, there are two reasons to still perform a regression: first, opinion about China was measured using a rating scale with a simpler statement of evaluations than the other rating questions in the questionnaire. Therefore, the intervals are more likely to be considered equal. To support this argument, many researchers have considered the Likert scale to provide continuous variable.[19] Secondly, the variables in the hypotheses can be represented as a sum of the several dimensions of knowledge of China and product evaluation. Such a computation could allow us to make ordinal measures more as an interval suitable for linear regression since this offers a better representation of intensity.

4   Data analysis

4.1   *Pre-Test: Manipulation Check on Country Understanding and Knowledge*

A total number N=235 of questionnaires were received from French participants in France (Ndw=105), in China (Nwlc=120) and other countries (Nother=10). In order to keep the consistency of this research, the 10 responses from participants neither in France nor in China were excluded, leaving a sample of N=225. No missing data were identified due to the short and convenient design of the questionnaire.

To assess the manipulation, an independent-sample T-test and Mann-Whitney U test were carried out in order to compare the level of knowledge means between the two groups (France and China). All assumptions for the test have been respected. The T-test and the Mann-Whitney test revealed the differences between the two groups for the four dimensions of knowledge about China (political, economic, cultural, technological) and for the sum of those four dimensions. The sum is a variable representing the addition of all dimension scores into one score. Both tests converge toward the same results and succeed in showing a significant difference between the two groups with a medium to large effect size.[20]

The two conditions, determined by their geographical locations, show a significant difference in knowledge of China, with the cohort in China having a higher level of knowledge. This conclusion is of course logical and straightforward. But it was essential to double-check this logic before the next analysis. A person can learn about a country not only by living in this country. It is also interesting to note that the level of cultural knowledge about China shows the greatest difference between the two cohorts. Therefore, special attention will be afforded this variable in the next analysis.

---

19   Allen, I. E., and Seaman, C. A. (2007). Likert Scales and Data Analyses, in Quality Progress 40(7), pp. 64.

20   Cohen, J. (1988). Statistical Power Analysis for the Behavioral Sciences. 2nd ed. Hillsdale, NJ: Erlbaum; Field, A. (2005). Discovering Statistics Using SPSS. 2nd ed. London: Sage.

TABLE 7.1   Independent T-Test summary of results for the manipulation check

	Mean WLC	SD	Mean DW	SD	t	df	sig	Cohen's d
Political	3.08	0.84	2.48	0.91	5.13	223	0.00	0.69
Economic	3.25	0.84	2.54	0.86	6.24	223	0.00	0.79
Cultural	3.36	0.81	2.54	0.89	7.21	223	0.00	0.91
Technological	3.21	0.81	2.44	0.89	6.81	223	0.00	0.85
SUM PEST	12.89	2.56	10	3.13	7.63	223	0.00	1.01

TABLE 7.2   Mann-Whitney U test summary of results for the manipulation check

	Median WLC	Median DW	U	Z	Sig	Effect Size r
Political	3	2	3956.00	-5.089	0.00	0.34
Economic	3	2	3542.00	-5.950	0.00	0.40
Cultural	3	2	8732.50	-6.762	0.00	0.45
Technological	3	2	9032.50	-6.138	0.00	0.41
SUM PEST	13	9	8430.50	-7.083	0.00	0.47

4.2   *Main Study: Product Evaluation*

Similar to the pre-test, to assess the difference on product evaluation, an independent-sample T-test and Mann-Whitney U test will be carried out in order to compare the evaluation between the two groups (WLC and DW). All assumptions for the tests have been respected. Both the T-test and the Mann-Whitney test reveal differences between the two groups for the three dimensions of product evaluation (tangible, service, affect) and for the sum of those three dimensions. Both tests converge towards the same results and succeed in demonstrating a significant difference between the two groups with a small to medium effect size.[21]

---

21   Cohen, J. (1988). Statistical Power Analysis for the Behavioral Sciences. 2nd ed. Hillsdale, NJ: Erlbaum; Field, A. (2005). Discovering Statistics Using SPSS. 2nd ed. London: Sage.

TABLE 7.3   Independent T-Test summary of results for the evaluation comparison

	Mean WLC	SD	Mean DW	SD	t	df	sig	Cohen's d
Tangible	2.62	0.74	2.40	0.73	2.21	223	0.28	0.3
Service	3.43	1.15	2.71	1.06	4.79	223	0.00	0.65
Affect*	2.88	0.76	2.40	0.82	4.49	214	0.00	0.61
SUM VALUE	8.85	2.07	7.51	2.06	4.83	223	0.00	0.65

*EQUAL VARIANCE NOT ASSUMED BY LEVENE TEST

TABLE 7.4   Mann-Whitney U test summary of results for the evaluation comparison

	Median WLC	Median DW	U	Z	Sig	Effect Size r
Tangible	3	2	5213	-2.45	0.14	0.16
Service	4	3	4110	-4.71	0.00	0.31
Affect	3	3	4480	-4.09	0.00	0.27
SUM VALUE	9	8	4048	-4.67	0.00	0.31

For each dimension, the difference in evaluation is present. However, for the affect dimension in the independent T-test, the equality of variance was not assumed. The results were therefore collected with a different degree of freedom and were still significant. The Mann-Whitney test helped to confirm the difference on the affect dimension. From a general perspective, the results show a small/medium effect for the tangible dimension and a medium effect size for the other dimensions as well as the sum of values.

4.3   *Analysis with Exclusion of Participants*

The first set of data with N=225 considered all participants based on their location at the moment the questionnaire was administered. However, the control variable asking the participants in France how many years they had spent in China, revealed that 24 participants had lived in China in the past. Such an

TABLE 7.5   Independent T-Test summary of results for the manipulation check after exclusion

	Mean WLC	SD	Mean DW	SD	t	df	sig	Cohen's d
Political	3.11	0.84	2.28	0.76	6.99	192	0.00	1.04
Economic	3.28	0.84	2.37	0.72	7.94	192	0.00	1.16
Cultural	3.36	0.80	2.28	0.69	9.76	192	0.00	1.44
Technological	3.24	0.81	2.22	0.76	8.81	192	0.00	1.30
SUM PEST	12.99	2.53	9.16	2.48	10.47	192	0.00	1.52

TABLE 7.6   Mann-Whitney U test summary of results for the manipulation check after exclusion

	Median WLC	Median DW	U	Z	Sig	Effect Size r
Political	3	2	2282	-6.30	0.00	0.45
Economic	3	2	1999	-7.03	0.00	0.50
Cultural	3	2	1563	-8.24	0.00	0.59
Technological	3	2	1844	-7.47	0.00	0.54
SUM PEST	13	9	1304	-8.52	0.00	0.61

indication can represent a bias in the above results. It is not possible to know when they lived in China and if their return to France has affected their level of knowledge of China and therefore their evaluation of Chinese products. In addition, from a symmetrical point of view, 9 participants living in China for less than one year have also been excluded. It could be assumed that their short stay at the time of the questionnaire did not allow them enough time to have gathered sufficient relevant knowledge of their experience in China. Both exclusions left a sample of N=194 (with Nwlc=113 and Ndw=81). Therefore, a new set of analysis, similar to the above, will be performed to guarantee the results stated previously. Below is the replication of the analysis.

The results after exclusions show stronger differences and effect sizes, and confirm the first set of results, in that French participants in China build a better knowledge of China and have a better evaluation of Chinese products.

TABLE 7.7   Independent T-Test summary of results for the evaluation comparison after exclusion

	Mean WLC	SD	Mean DW	SD	t	df	sig	Cohen's d
Tangible	2.61	0.74	2.32	0.70	2.75	192	0.06	0.40
Service	3.41	1.16	2.60	1.03	4.96	192	0.00	0.74
Affect*	2.88	0.77	2.32	0.80	4.87	167	0.00	0.71
SUM VALUE	8.82	2.09	7.25	1.97	5.31	192	0.00	0.77

TABLE 7.8   Mann-Whitney U test summary of results for the evaluation comparison after exclusion

	Median WLC	Median DW	U	Z	Sig	Effect Size r
Tangible	3	2	3518	-3.02	0.03	0.22
Service	4	2	2806	-4.80	0.00	0.34
Affect	3	3	3043	-4.36	0.00	0.31
SUM VALUE	9	7	2630	-5.10	0.00	0.37

4.4   *Regression Results*

For the regression analysis, the full set of data was considered, as the analysis does not require the geographical variable to play a role. Here, the effect of opinion of China is the focal point. As mentioned earlier, both variables are considered to be continuous and other assumptions for a linear regression have been met. Therefore, the analysis can be carried out to show positive results.

Two linear regressions were run to understand the effect of knowledge of China on opinion, and the effect of opinion of China on product evaluation. To assess linearity, a scatterplot with superimposed regression line, was plotted. Visual inspection of these plots indicated a suitable linear relationship between the variables. There was homoscedasticity and normality of the residuals. And no outliers were identified. The prediction equations and interpretations were:

(1)   Opinion=2.26+ 0.11*Knowledge

Knowledge of China statistically, significantly predicted opinion toward China, $F_{(1, 223)}=42.20$, $p< .05$, accounting for 15.9% of the variation in knowledge of China with adjusted $R2=15.5\%$, a medium size effect according to Cohen (1988).

(2)   Product evaluation=3.28 + 1.40 *Opinion

Opinion toward China statistically, significantly predicted product evaluation, $F_{(1, 223)}=105.25$, $p< .05$, accounting for 32.1% of the variation in product evaluation with adjusted $R2=31.8\%$, a large size effect according to Cohen (1988).

5   Conclusions and Limitations of the Analysis

The comparison of the means using both parametric and non-parametric tests showed that the level of knowledge of China is greater for French participants living in China than those living in France, with a greater effect size for knowledge about culture. These results confirmed the difference between the two groups and allowed us to move forward in analyzing the difference in product evaluation between the two groups. In this regard, participants living in China showed a more positive evaluation of Chinese products in all dimensions with lower evaluation on product tangible values. In addition, linear regressions showed that a better knowledge of China would favour a positive opinion towards China and also that a better opinion of China would favour a better product evaluation. A mediation analysis was attempted to link the two linear regressions into one mediation model with knowledge of China as predictor, opinion as mediator and product evaluation as outcome. However, the results did not show a significant effect. This could be due to the fact that the measurement of the variables was not purely continuous. This issue was addressed and represented a limitation that needs to be considered when interpreting the results.

6   Further Discussion and Possible Outcomes

Before discussing the results, it is important to elucidate the context of the research. Firstly, this study has relied upon the straightforward postulate that providing information about a focal element would help to better understand it and allow a better evaluation, especially if the information is perceived positively. However, the actual purpose here was more to focus on a specific message carrier (the BRI) and the specific focal element (Brand Evaluation). The BRI is a tremendous geopolitical move by China. It is therefore important to study it from different perspectives in order to characterize it and project its effect in different circumstances. This research has attempted to discover if the BRI is a factor that can influence the foreign consumer decision process through product evaluations. The growth of the Chinese economy depends to some extent on the success of Chinese brands abroad. The more foreign consumers who positively evaluate Chinese brands, the greater the chance they will buy them.

Secondly, the study was conducted on two French cohorts in order to control extraneous effect. The French cohort living in China represents westerners living in China (WLC) and the French cohort living in France represents westerners living in their home country – or domestic westerners, (DW). So, we may ask if it is possible to extend the results of the study to all western countries. It is rational to acknowledge that all western countries have certain differences. However, it is equally rational to allow that they also have certain similarities. Nevertheless, this is still a limitation and the question of whether or not we extend the findings will depend on which side the reader comes down. In any event, people living in so-called western countries will feel that they have more similarities with each other than with the Chinese, for example.

From the analysis of the results, several points may be discussed as regards the research hypothesis of the study: first, the role of BRI in the acquisition of knowledge of China and the importance of the acquired information in developing a positive opinion toward China; second, the effect of knowledge of China to increase product evaluation; third, the importance of the Belt and Road Initiative for Chinese brands suffering from the negative stereotype related to their collective Chinese identity.

Knowledge of China can be acquired from different situations and sources. In this article, the acquisition is represented by the experience of living in China, meaning that a westerner living in China will obviously acquire more information about China. The BRI is also a source of information about China for westerners. In certain aspects it could replace the experience of living in China by carrying an engineered information package that could be accessible to the populations outside China. Such a package could include more information on Chinese culture as well as information on other dimensions. The Belt and Road Initiative should also be oriented toward the objective of developing a more favourable opinion of China by carrying the appropriate information package mentioned above. A better opinion of China would in turn develop a better evaluation of Chinese products and consequently, generate more sales. This is obviously good for the Chinese economy and for its people. In addition, a better economic performance could boost the BRI and create a positive cycle. This needs to be coordinated and monitored through a large-scale global public relations campaign about China. This coordinated effort could help to rebalance the negative effect of *Made in China* brands by replacing or enhancing the existing information package in the western consumer's mind.

Bibliography

Aaker, J. L. (1997). Dimensions of brand personality in the Journal of Marketing Research, pp.347–356.

Allen, I. E., and Seaman, C. A. (2007). Likert scales and data analyses in Quality Progress 40(7), pp. 64.

Cai, P. (2017). Understanding China's Belt and Road Initiative. LOWY Institute for International Policy.

Chen, C. Y., Mathur, P., and Maheswaran, D. (2014). The Effects of Country-Related Affect on Product Evaluations. Journal of Consumer Research 41(4), pp. 1033–1046.

Cohen, J. (1988). Statistical Power Analysis for the Behavioral Sciences. 2nd ed. Hillsdale, NJ: Erlbaum.

Courmont B., and Setti A. (2017). Belgrade – Pekin: *Quand la Chine se positionne au coeur de l'Europe, Institut des Relations Internationales et Stratégiques. Asia Focus* 18.

Field, A. (2005). Discovering Statistics Using SPSS. 2nd ed. London: Sage.

Hong, S. T., and WyerJr, R. S. (1989). Effects of Country-of-Origin and Product-Attribute Information on Product Evaluation: An Information Processing Perspective. Journal of Consumer Research 16(2), pp. 175–187.

Jamleson, S. (2004). Likert Scales: How to (Ab) use Them. Medical education 38(12), pp. 1217–1218.

Keller, K. L. (2003). Brand Synthesis: The Multidimensionality of Brand Knowledge. Journal of consumer research 29 (4), pp. 595–600.

Keller, K. L., and Lehmann, D. R. (2006). Brands and Branding: Research Findings and Future Priorities. Marketing Science 25 (6), pp. 740–759.

Klein, J. G., Ettenson, R., and Morris, M. D. (1998). The Animosity Model of Foreign Product Purchase: An Empirical Test in the People's Republic of China. The Journal of Marketing, pp. 89–100.

Maheswaran, D. (1994). Country of Origin as a Stereotype: Effects of Consumer Expertise and Attribute Strength on Product Evaluations. Journal of Consumer Research *21* (2), pp. 354–365.

Martineau, P. (1958). The Personality of the Retail Store. Harvard Business Review 36 (1), pp. 47–55.

Padgett, D., and Allen, D. (1997). Communicating Experiences: A Narrative Approach to Creating Service Brand Image. Journal of Advertising 26 (4), pp. 49–62.

Poels, K., and Dewitte, S. (2006). How to Capture the Heart? Reviewing 20 Years of Emotion Measurement in Advertising. Journal of Advertising Research 46 (1), pp. 18–37.

Samiee, S., Leonidou, L. C., Aykol, B., Stöttinger, B., and Christodoulides, P. (2016). Fifty Years of Empirical Research on Country-of-Origin Effects on Consumer Behavior: A Meta-Analysis. In Rediscovering the Essentiality of Marketing, Cham: Springer, pp. 505–510.

Spencer-Rodgers, J., Peng, K., Wang, L., and Hou, Y. (2004). Dialectical Self-esteem and East-West Differences in Psychological Well-being. Personality and Social Psychology Bulletin 30 (11), pp. 1416–1432.

Stewart, T., and Raman, A. (2007). Lessons from Toyota's Long Drive. Harvard Business Review (July–August), pp.74–83.

Verlegh, P. W., Steenkamp, J. B. E., and Meulenberg, M. T. (2005). Country-of-Origin Effects in Consumer Processing of Advertising Claims. International Journal of Research in Marketing 22 (2), pp. 127–139.

Vicenti, C., and Fortat, V. (2017). *Les nouvelles routes de la soie, Taoïsme économique ou nouvel imperialism, Institut des Relations Internationales et Stratégiques. Asia Focus* 45.

Wang, Y. Made in China 2025 plan unveiled to boost manufacturing. Xinhua News, May 15, 2015.

CHAPTER 8

China's Image in the Czech Republic

Media Reflection of Elite Policies

Ivana Karásková

1 Introduction

China has become an increasingly important topic of the political, media and broader public discourse in the Czech Republic. The trend can be traced back to the election of Miloš Zeman as Czech president in the first direct election of the head of state in 2013. However, even before that Czech political discourse, which had been firmly rooted in the normative underpinning of Czech foreign policy and was a legacy of Václav Havel's founding contribution to post-communist statehood, expressions and metaphors that opened the way for a more welcoming attitude towards China, had begun to penetrate public and political discourse.

Tectonic shifts in international politics and the global order have undeniably contributed to such developments. As many have noted,[1] over the past ten years, the People's Republic of China has become an international power to be reckoned with. After a series of predecessors who had mostly adhered to Deng Xiaoping's foreign policy principle which advocated "keep low profile", Xi Jinping has gradually become much more explicit in demonstrating and wielding China's power. Some of the initiatives, like the 16+1, may have been founded before Xi took power, but others, most importantly the Belt and Road Initiative and the Asia Infrastructure Investment Bank, were fully of his making. Generally speaking, the PRC's more assertive stance in international politics under Xi raised Beijing's profile across various regions, including Central Europe and the Czech Republic in particular.

---

1 For example: David Shambaugh, China Goes Global: The Partial Power (London, UK: Oxford University Press, 2013); Jennifer Rudolph and Michael Szonyi (editors), China Questions: Critical Insights into a Rising Power (Boston, US: Harvard University Press, 2018); Robert S. Ross and Zhu Feng (editors), China's Ascent: Power, Security and the Future of International Politics (Ithaca, US: Cornell University Press, 2008); Donovan C. Chau and Thomas M. Kane (editors), China and International Security: History, Strategy and 21st-Century Politics (Santa Barbara, US: Praeger, 2014).

This article, however, argues that the aforementioned Chinese activities have, in themselves, contributed relatively sparsely to the country's increased media presence in the Czech Republic. They have certainly provided an overall context, but the shifts which this article records and reflects, where mostly produced by various Czech politicians and business leaders with an interest in promoting stronger Czech-China economic and/or political relations. Interestingly, while the intensity of focus on China has translated into an increase in media attention, the positive presentation of the partnership with Beijing has not been mirrored by the prevailing media sentiment (with an exception of cases where media ownership was transferred into Chinese hands). While this finding documents a degree of resilience among mainstream Czech media, it also contains a more problematic element: the fact that China's image in Czech Republic discourse is not in fact formed by Beijing's policies and activities, but rather by political and ideological preferences of Czech making. In short, China's image may, in the extreme, have relatively little in common with the country itself.

The article begins with a brief overview of the formative moments in Czech-China relations and the Czech Republic's China policy. It then presents the conceptual framework and research design of media analysis, undertaken with the aim of empirically and in detail, documenting the development of China's image in the Czech Republic since 2010. A reflection of the results of the analysis is then presented and final conclusions reached.

2   Rising China, Media Discourse and Its Academic Reflection

The Czech Republic started its independent existence in international politics under the strong influence of its first president Václav Havel's ideal of normative underpinning in foreign policy, based on a critical reflection of the experience with the totalitarian ideologies of the 20th century. From this perspective, China was long regarded as a problematic actor, and economic relations prior to, and shortly after, the Velvet Revolution in 1989 were limited as a result of the ideological drift between the Soviet Union and the People's Republic of China.[2] While open hostility to China was rare, Havel continued in his meetings with the Dalai Lama and political and economic ignorance of China. As a result, after accessing the European Union in 2004, the Czech Republic represented

---

2   "Léta 2004–2006, krátké jaro česko-čínských vztahů", PSSI, accessed March 21, 2018, http://www.pssi.cz/download/docs/503_leta-2004-2006-kratke-jaro-cesko-cinskych-vztahu.pdf.

the most critical voice in the Union on economic and political relations with the People's Republic of China,[3] despite some Czech companies' or politicians' favourable view of opportunities provided by the Chinese market.[4]

However, the global financial crisis in 2008–2009 and the rise of business opportunities in China, changed this situation. Gradually, the idea of the alleged negative impact of human rights promotion on economic interactions, took hold. Even before the election of Miloš Zeman as the Czech president in 2013, China began to be promoted as a potential economic partner by the then ruling Civic Democratic Party (*Občanská demokratická strana, ODS*). With the election of Zeman, China became portrayed not only as a business opportunity, but even as a normative model.[5] Hynek Kmoníček, former director of Zeman's foreign policy office and current ambassador in Washington, explained Zeman's favorable position on China as a calculated strategy used for promoting Czech economic interests. He argued that, unlike big states whose representatives are invited to China due to their country's importance, the Czech Republic needs to have a "particularity, something where it is able and willing to go the extra mile to ensure reciprocity".[6]

The media research and mapping of Zeman's proclamations on China reveal that his positive view of China was not directed exclusively at a Chinese audience. Using the discourse of economic profitability, Zeman and a part of the Czech political and economic elite began promoting opportunities for Czech businessmen in China and Chinese investment in the Czech Republic – a move which followed similar foreign policy U-turns exhibited by other EU member states. As a component of the whole process, these protagonists have undeniably, openly but (as will be demonstrated below) not fully successfully, strived for a categorical improvement of Beijing's image in Czech public discourse.

---

3   John Fox and Francois Godement, A Power Audit of EU-China Relations (London, UK: European Council on Foreign Relations, April 2009), http://www.ecfr.eu/page/-/ECFR12_-_A_POWER_AUDIT_OF_EU-CHINA_RELATIONS.pdf.

4   For a detailed analysis of the evolution of political parties' stances in the Czech Parliament, see Ivana Karásková, Alžběta Bajerová, and Tamás Matura. Images of China in Czech and Hungarian Parliaments. (Prague, Czech Republic: Association for International Affairs, policy paper 02, March 2019).

5   See Zeman's opinion given on CCTV during his visit to Beijing in October 2014 that China could help teach the Czech Republic to "stabilize the society".

6   "Kmoníček: Státy EU nám chtěly zabránit získat čínské investice, Čína předefinovala slovo komunista," interview by Martin Veselovský, DVTV, April 1, 2016, https://video.aktualne.cz/dvtv/kmonicek-cina-zcela-predefinovala-obsah-slova-komunista-komu/r~157b2d04f76911e5a652002590604f2e/ Tao Xie and Benjamin I. Page. 2013. "What Affects China's National Image? A cross-national study of public opinion". Journal of Contemporary China 22(83), pp. 850–867.

Academic reflection on China's external image in other countries is, in general, not completely rare – especially in China itself. As Tao Xie and Benjamin I. Page argue "national image has become arguably the fastest-growing research field in Chinese academia".[7] Numerous studies by Chinese scholars indicate that foreign media tend to be highly selective in their coverage of China. As Wang Qiu, a member of China's legislature and head of state-owned broadcaster China National Radio, noted "sixty percent of all mainstream Western media reports smear China.[8] To some Chinese scholars, the coverage of China by foreign – particularly Western – media is so biased and distorted that it amounts to a concerted effort to 'demonize' China. (Tao Xie and Benjamin I. Page 2013: 855). According to Stone and Xiao, the "rise of anti-China coverage led to a claim that Western media anointed China a new enemy in place of the USSR".[9] The authors also state that China received significantly more coverage than any other country in the world in the post-Cold War era.[10]

Even beyond the confines of Chinese academia, the image of China in other countries has not been ignored. Articles have been published that focus on China's image in a specific political domain[11] or indeed on a specific country[12] but often limited to single-media outlet case studies or over a short period of time. Alongside literature focusing on China's influence in the world[13] these

---

7   As cited in Bethany Allen-Ebrahimian. 2016. "How China won the war against Western media". Foreign Policy, 4 March 2016). http://foreignpolicy.com/2016/03/04/china-won-war-western-media-censorship-propaganda-communist-party/.

8   Gerald C. Stone and Zhiwen Xiao. 2007. "Anointing a new enemy: The rise of anti-China coverage after the USSR's demise". The International Communication Gazette 69 (1), pp. 91–108.

9   Ibid.

10   See Sanna Kopra. 2012. "A Responsible Developing Country: China's National Image Building and International Negotiations on Climate". Quarterly Journal of Chinese Studies 1 (3), pp. 121–137. Gang (Kevin) Han and Xiuli Wang. 2015. "From Product-Country Image to National Image: "Made In China" and Integrated Valence Framing Effects". International Journal of Strategic Communication 9: 62–77.

11   See Felix Heiduk. 2014. "Conflicting Images? Germany and the Rise of China". German Politics 23 (1–2), pp. 118–133.

12   See Evelyn Goh, ed., Rising China's Influence in Developing World (London, UK: Oxford University Press, 2016); Jacques deLisle and Avery Goldstein (editors), China's Global Engagement: Cooperation, Competition and Influence in the 21st Century (Washington, US: Brookings Institution Press, 2017); Joseph S. Nye Jr., "How Sharp Power Threatens Soft Power: The Right and Wrong Ways to Respond to Authoritarian Influence", Foreign Affairs, 24 January 2018. Accessed at https://www.foreignaffairs.com/articles/china/2018-01-24/how-sharp-power-threatens-soft-power.

13   For data for each media outlet and its readership across the period see Media Projekt database: http://www.unievydavatelu.cz/cs/unie_vydavatelu/medialni_data/vyzkum_ctenosti.

studies represent a logical response to a more assertive and frequent presence of China not only in the international space but also in various states that compose it. Nevertheless, the analyses that have been conducted are largely limited to single-case studies or small-number media content analysis. Even more importantly, no such academic studies exist for the Czech Republic or, for that matter, the region of Central and Eastern Europe as a whole. While the following analysis is thus not novel in the sense of breaking new thematic ground, it represents a first effort at a structured, in-depth analysis of China's media image in one of the Central and Eastern European countries. Through its methodology, explained below, it also attempts to present a more rigorous and systematic approach to the issue.

3   Assessing China's Image: Research Design and Methodology

In order to understand the transformation of Czech discourse on China, this author executed an analysis of Czech media, mapping the period of 2010 till mid-2017, thus including the time prior, during and after the official Czech foreign policy turn towards China in 2012/2013. The analysis covered newspapers, weeklies with political and/or economic focus, radio and TV stations and news servers. Altogether, 42 of the most followed Czech media outlets were selected for the analysis.

In the case of newspapers, the inclusion to the dataset was based on the number of readers, not the number of prints, as the number of readers (which is usually higher than the number of prints itself) better reflects the spread of the agenda among the audience. The newspapers also included their supplements. To ensure that the composition of the set remained constant throughout the whole period, the popularity of the media was checked every quarter of the year, i.e. from 2010 (Q1-Q4) to 2017 (Q1 or Q1 and Q2), using data from Media Projekt,[14] an online, quarterly-published list of the most read printed media, based on interviews with a randomly selected pool of respondents. The six most widely read newspapers in the period from 2010 to 2017 were *Blesk*, *MF Dnes*, *Právo*, *Aha!*, *Lidové noviny* and *Hospodářské noviny*. Additionally, the author included *Haló noviny* to the set as a control variable. Though the number of its readers is relatively marginal (the smallest of all Czech national newspapers), *Haló noviny* is linked to the Communist Party of Bohemia and Moravia

---

14   Association of TV organizations, http://www.ato.cz.

(*Komunistická strana Čech a Moravy* – ksčm) and as such was expected to view the issue from a specific angle.

Weekly magazines with an economic and/or political focus represented the second source of media outlets subjected to the analysis. The magazines were selected using the same criteria (i.e. popularity among the readers) as the national newspapers. Special attention was paid to the magazines *Týden* and *Instinkt* (regardless of their popularity among readers), which were co-owned by Empresa Media, a publishing house that was partially owned by the cefc China Energy Company Limited from September 2015 to February 2017. In the Czech Republic, the composition of the set of most widely read weekly magazines changed significantly within the studied period. Some of the magazines perished, some lost their popularity among readers and some were newly established. The dataset thus included eleven magazines altogether (*Ekonom, Euro, Eurozpravodaj, Nový Profit/Profit, Forbes, Týden, Respekt, Reflex, TýdeníkKvěty, Téma*).

The third source of media output was daily news and debates broadcast by TV stations with a nation-wide reach. The outlets were selected based on their annual share, using publicly available data published by the Association of TV Organizations.[15] Three major TV groups were selected, and from those the relevant channels (excluding channels focusing on for example, art and sport) were analyzed. More concretely, they included the three most viewed news channels of Česká Televize (čT), a public service broadcaster, (*ČT1, ČT2, ČT24*), Nova Group (cme Media – *TV Nova*) and Prima Group (*TV Prima*). Special attention was given to *TV Barrandov*. Though its share is relatively modest, the television is also part of the Empresa Media group that was partially owned by the cefc China Energy Company Limited from September 2015 to February 2017. *TV Barrandov* has enjoyed a rather peculiar relation with one of the key China agenda setters, president Miloš Zeman, who grants exclusive interviews to the television on a weekly basis. Additionally, a popular investigative online TV *DVTV,* a project run from 2014 that frequently covers China-related topics, was included as a control variable.

Given the fact that a significant proportion of the Czech population (63 % in the first quarter of 2017) listens to a radio broadcast on a daily basis,[16] radio broadcasting stations with nation-wide reach were also included in the media content analysis, focusing on national radio, a public service broadcaster, and

15   "Poslechovost rádií: Impuls stále vede, nejvíc rostl ČRo Plus". Mediahub. 3 May 2017.
       https://mediahub.cz/media/954224-poslechovost.

16   We mean, those media that did not fulfill the criteria for being the most followed, i.e.
       Hlídací pes, DVTV, TV Barrandov, Týden and communist daily Haló noviny.

private radios that cover news, have their own interview program(s) and the largest share. To determine the share of listeners, the author used data from Radio Projekt, a quarterly-published list of most listened to radio broadcasts conceived from interviews with a randomly selected pool of respondents. Apart from the channels of the national public broadcaster Český rozhlas (*Radiožurnál, Český rozhlas 6, Rádio Česko, Plus, Dvojka*), the analysis covered the three most listened-to private radio stations – *Rádio Impuls, Evropa 2, Frekvence 1.*

Online versions of printed media and information gathered on servers providing news and their own reports, constituted the final source for media content analysis. Ten sources were selected based on their popularity among netizens, as measured by NetMonitor, a project that counts a number of unique accesses to various websites and links the data to the socio-demographic characteristics of their visitors. Analysis of online news servers covered www.novinky.cz, www.idnes.cz, www.aktualne.cz (without the content provided by DVTV, which was covered in the nation-wide TV broadcasting section), www.tn.cz, www.blesk.cz, www.denik.cz, www.lidovky.cz, www.ihned.cz and www.eurozpravy.cz. Special attention was given to the online news server www.parlamentnilisty.cz, one of the 'alternative' outlets which tends to publish controversial content (allegedly without any censorship).

In the next phase, the pre-selected media outlets were searched for China-related agenda using Newton Media Search, a database of all major Czech media, covering their output, including TV and radio transcripts, since 1996. To further limit the scope and increase the relevance of output, additional filters (combination of the words politic(s) and economic(s) – in Czech, a search string "čín* AND politi* OR economi*" with asterisks enabling a search of words with the same stem) were applied. As Newton Media Search did not allow easy filtering in sub-sources (e.g. sections in prints), an additional check of the search outcomes and elimination of irrelevant results had to be performed manually.

A text which provided an answer to the question "How is China depicted in media?" or "How does the author reflect on China?" was considered relevant no matter how many times China was mentioned. On the other hand, irrelevant – and thus rejected – texts were those that, while containing the searched for phrase, did not focus on China (i.e. constituting the search tool's error) or did not provide any clue to the question of how China is depicted in the media or how the author reflects on China (e.g. articles which listed China among other countries while not providing any subjective view of the country, such as "the company started its business in Brazil, Russia and China (...)". A text which did not deal primarily with China, yet where the author still used China as an example to illustrate his/her opinion (e.g. an article dealing with an authoritative regime in Africa where, in one sentence, the author diverts his/her attention and then continues: "there is an abuse of human rights among prisoners, similar to the situation in China") was considered relevant. Also, texts that covered different sections other than news and commentaries, yet still reflected generally on China or provided a view of China by the author or media outlet (i.e. "Chinese athletes won because the state supplied them with the doping") were considered relevant to China's image created by the given media outlet.

The application of the search string resulted in establishing a dataset of 1,257 texts dealing with China and politics and/or economics. The media output was then subjected to a multi-stage analysis. The research focused on both quantitative and qualitative aspects of the transformation of the discourse. It presupposed there was a rise in the amount of China-related output as the topic became increasingly prioritized in the political debate in the region. Accordingly, the research started with the presumption that the tone and form of discussing and reporting about China has undergone a shift toward increasingly positive coverage. The aforementioned aspects motivated the subsequent research questions: *How did the China-related media discourse evolve during the period? Does the increase in the number of articles correspond to events in bilateral relations* (e.g. the visit of the president to the other country)? *Can the increase in articles be attributed to another, identifiable issue?*

Secondly, key prevailing topics were identified and their frequency, distribution across media output as well as relation *vis-a-vis* each other (e.g. human rights vs. economic diplomacy), were measured, providing a detailed knowledge of the discourse. Themes were not artificially selected by the author at the beginning of coding, but emerged during the coding process, essentially rising from the discourse. This approach prevented the author from influencing the analysis of the discourse by focusing on 'favoured' topics while missing other themes. The themes provided an instrument for 'measuring' the depth of the discourse and details that are considered common knowledge by agenda setters. For example, some agenda setters mentioned only 'human rights' in connection with China while others went into detail by talking specifically about real or perceived human rights abuses such as child labour, the treatment of homosexuals in China, the situation in Chinese prisons, etc. As many as 94 themes were recorded, some of them counted exactly as expressed (e.g. 'dalailamism', 'authoritarian regime'), others representing a larger group of words that together constituted a logical category (e.g. Chinese domestic problems, world politics, etc.) The themes were subsequently reassessed through the perspective of more general 'discursive clouds', i.e. proposed and gradually sedimented links between key topics (or parts thereof) that establish habitual images with a power to shape the public discourse (e.g. 'dalailamism' as a negative image of a human rights 'ideology' which supposedly prevents more intensive development of Czech-China economic relations). An important part of this analytical stage included an identification of the process of 'contamination' of the discourse by the discursive clouds. The key question corresponding to this point of the analysis asked *what the agenda setters consider important in relation to China.*

Thirdly, the author measured the 'sentiment' (neutral, negative or positive attitudes *vis-a-vis* China) of the opinions presented in the set of key themes, including possible variations between different media outlets. It needs to be underlined that the author did not pay attention to the objectivity of articles or correctness of the facts mentioned in them. Each text received only one sentiment value. The article was considered positive or negative, if the overall tone of the article was such. It must have been clearly perceived that the author of the text or the media outlet had a stance regarding China (e.g. "our president collaborates with a totalitarian regime that oppresses its own citizens"). The text was not considered positive or negative if the positive or negative opinion was attributed to another source (e.g. "as actor XY claims, China is an authoritative regime"), or if the article provided both negative and positive views or explanations of China's behavior (e.g. "US is concerned with Chinese hackers" in one paragraph, "Chinese state however replied by proving that the alleged hacking attack was not done from China" in another paragraph). Such texts were coded as neutral. Key research questions included: *How is China depicted in the text? Is the view of China in a specific media outlet generally neutral, positive or negative? Did it change throughout the studied period?*

Finally, the author recorded phrases used within the discourse. A phrase was understood as a group of words with a special idiomatic meaning. A phrase simplifies a broader argument or serves as a catchy label to promote an idea in a discourse (e.g. Czechia is a "guberniya of China", etc.). Key questions the author asked were: *Who provides phrases to the discourse and how does the phrase circulate? How powerful are the phrases (or the 'phrase setters') within the discourse?*

4   Whose Discourse? What China?

The analysis revealed that between 2000 and mid-2017 the number of texts on China in Czech media outlets rose steadily with the intensification of Czech-Chinese bilateral relations. However, a closer look at the topics and major focus of the texts revealed that the rise of media output reporting on China

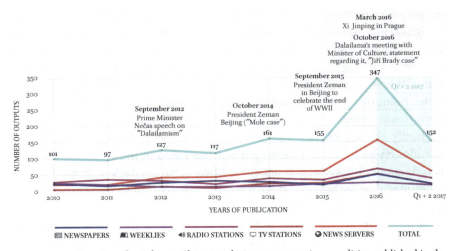

FIGURE 8.1   Quantity of articles on China in relation to economics or politics published in the
Czech Republic across the period
CHINFLUENCE, WWW.CHINFLUENCE.EU, ACCESSED FEBRUARY 1, 2018.

(almost 250%) resulted almost entirely from the embedding of Chinese topics in Czech domestic politics. The expansion of coverage correlates with
years that brought about changes in Czech foreign policy towards China. This
is clearly evident in reactions to the statements and activities of President
Miloš Zeman. This trend culminated in 2016 in response to the official visit
by Chinese President Xi Jinping to the Czech Republic; the Prague stay of the
Dalai Lama and his meeting with the Minister of Culture, Daniel Herman;
and the subsequent proclamation on Czech adherence to the One China
Policy signed by four of the highest ranking representatives of the Czech
Republic.

The increasing attention afforded to China-related political and economic
topics has been confirmed across a range of different media sources. The
majority of the articles in the dataset originated in news servers, followed by
radio stations and newspapers. Czech weeklies and TV stations included in the
analysis reported on China the least.

While the overall amount underlines the intensification of Czech-China
relations, a closer look is needed to evaluate the impact this shift made on
the perception of the PRC and its policies. Interestingly, the overall sentiment
of the combined political-economic reporting and commentary on China
has been clearly polarized across the analyzed period. The image of China in
the Czech media over the researched period was mostly neutral or negative,
with only 14% of the analyzed media output inclined to view China positively.

FIGURE 8.2 Number of articles on China in relation to economics or politics in all analyzed Czech media
CHINFLUENCE, WWW.CHINFLUENCE.EU, ACCESSED FEBRUARY 1, 2018.

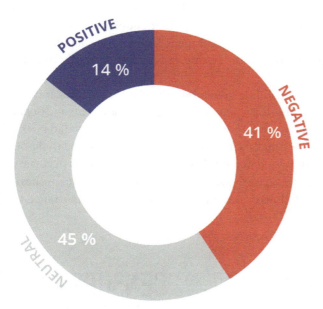

FIGURE 8.3 Image of China in all analyzed Czech media
CHINFLUENCE, WWW.CHINFLUENCE.EU, ACCESSED FEBRUARY 1, 2018.

When focusing on the media outlets without control variables[17] the position becomes stronger still, with just 10% of positive accounts and close to 50% negative occurrences. In hardline leftist media *Haló noviny* or in media with a Chinese (co)owner, the image of China was distinctly more positive. In the

---

17   See e.g. Ivana Karásková, Alžběta Bajerová, Tamás Matura. Images of China in Czech and Hungarian Parliaments (Prague, Czech Republic: Association for International Affairs, policy paper 02, March 2019).

cases of *Týden* and *TV Barrandov*, it is evident that ownership by the Chinese company CEFC led to an exclusively positive coverage of China.

However, the overall polarity of the analyzed output did not evolve significantly over the researched period (2010 till mid-2017). Despite public proclamations on future Chinese investment by Chinese representatives and Czech political elites, the image of China in the Czech media remained significantly negative. What is even more interesting, Czech media outlets generally started to exhibit a tendency to portray China as a direct opposite to the values and preferences of the Czech Republic. This process of the 'othering' of China gradually infiltrated even output that, ostensibly, did not contain any link to the country (e.g. articles on alleged 'censorship' on the Czech internet).

Regarding the prevalence of the topics, Czech media paid most attention to Chinese economic and political relations with other countries and organizations (United States, Russian Federation, European Union, India, Japan, etc.) – a logical reflection of journalists on the position China has gradually risen to, as shown in Figure 8.4.

However, human rights, including general information on abuses and the violation of minority rights, the death penalty, detention of dissidents and organ harvesting, were the second most important category of topics covered by the Czech media, proving that journalists did not subscribe to the alleged trade-off between human rights issues and economic benefits, advocated as necessary by a part of the Czech political and economic elites. Communism, authoritarianism and censorship followed in frequency, revealing the importance of

FIGURE 8.4   Representation of topics in articles on China in relation to economics or politics in all analyzed Czech media (2010–6/2017)

CHINFLUENCE, WWW.CHINFLUENCE.EU, ACCESSED FEBRUARY 1, 2018.

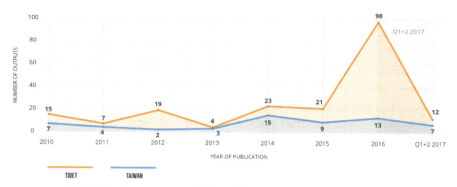

FIGURE 8.5   Number of appearances of Tibet and Taiwan issues in articles on China in
relation to economics or politics in all analyzed Czech media (2010–2017)
CHINFLUENCE, WWW.CHINFLUENCE.EU, ACCESSED FEBRUARY 1, 2018.

the issue to Czech journalists and Czech society in general, which has still not
digested its own Communist past.

While the prevalence of the above-mentioned categories remained constant in the studied period, notions of Tibet, though high in frequency, fluctu-
ated through time, culminating in 2016 when the Chinese president Xi Jinping
and Dalai Lama both visited Prague (see Figure 8.5). Interestingly, the issue
of strategic position and economic and political relations with Taiwan were –
in comparison to the Tibet issue – largely marginalized, though Taiwan and
the Czech Republic share a similar history of transition from an authoritarian
regime to democracy and Taiwan is one of the three most important Asian
investors in the Czech Republic.

Despite a joint push by the political and economic elites[18] to portray China
as a business opportunity, Czech media paid less attention to Chinese investment in the Czech Republic and to China's influence in the country than to
bilateral cultural exchanges.

Throughout the researched period, the media showed a sceptical position
towards both China and the promotion of closer Czech-Chinese relations.
When analyzing journalists as agenda-setters in matters of political and economic affairs concerning China, the picture is clearer still: only 6% of analyzed occurrences were positive, 64% were neutral and 30% negative. In other

18   Miloš Gregor and Petra Vejvodová. Analýza manipulativních technik na vybraných
      českých serverech (Analysis of manipulative techniques on selected Czech news serv-
      ers) (Brno: Masaryk University, 2016). https://www.academia.edu/26046763/Výzkumná_
      zpráva_Analýza_manipulativn%C3%ADch_technik_na_vybraných_českých_serverech.

words, open promotion of China by Czech journalists was rare, and this finding holds throughout the researched period.

The attitude of the journalists towards China was found not to be influenced by the nature of ownership of the media where they worked (whether public or private). In both cases, the proportion of positive attitude toward China was similarly low (6% of journalists working in public media and 7% of journalists from privately owned media) and the share of the negative attitude was also very similar (China was covered negatively by 28% of journalists working in public media and by 31% of those working in media outlets owned privately). The average sentiment with both groups was around -0.26 (with +1 representing positive attitude and -1 standing for absolute negative). Therefore, it can be concluded that regardless of who owns the media outlet, journalists form a key social group which perceives politics regarding China primarily from a normative perspective and which is (for now) resilient to the strong pro-China narrative of political and economic agenda-setters. This is with the exception of those journalists publishing in *Parlamentní listy*, an 'alternative' online media outlet, during the reviewed period. From the analysis, it follows that 21% of journalists in *Parlamentní listy* published positive texts on China, whilst only 5% of them published negative comments. The average sentiment of journalists publishing texts about China in *Parlamentní listy* was +0.19. The difference between mainstream and alternative media (*Parlamentní listy*) in their coverage of China can result from the allegedly pro-Russian (generally anti-West) leaning of the alternative media outlet though more detailed and systematic academic research on the issue still needs to be carried out.

Finally, from the key words, it can be demonstrated that the Czech debate on China is highly politicized and stereotyped. The media often did not inform the Czech audience about China as such, i.e. its domestic politics or social issues. In all these topics, the Czech public is relegated to a minimum of first-hand, detailed information. News is mostly imported from foreign news agencies or English-speaking media sources. Even the outlets which have their own correspondents in China (i.e. Czech Television and Czech Radio) may be relegated to foreign language sources as access to other sources in China is limited by the Chinese state authorities and further complicated by language barriers between journalists and their local sources.

5 Conclusion

The analysis established a firm empirical base for claims concerning China's image in the Czech media discourse, claims which are habitually – and typically, forcefully – presented but often lack substantiated evidence to support them. The scope of analyzed media output is exceptional, not only in the Czech Republic but, judging by the available comparison of wider academic reflection on the issue, also in the wider international context. It opens a way to possible replication in other countries (and in other states), potentially leading to interesting comparative results.

The analytical findings reveal that the image of China in the Czech media is constructed through political, ideological or more broadly normative lenses that are largely parochial and unrelated to China as an international actor. Interestingly, the push of a segment of the Czech political and economic elite to elevate the PRC to the position of a new strategic partner (and, essentially, to normalize the Chinese political regime), has met resistance on the part of mainstream media. Paradoxically, the incessant promotion of better relations with Beijing by the Czech president Miloš Zeman, his political allies and related business circles, has led to a novel situation in which China has started to be constructed as the normative 'Other' for Czech society. At least from this perspective, the effort to improve the quality and expand the scope of Czech-China relations has not been successful – and leads to the tentative but inescapable conclusion that a more measured and nuanced approach might have secured the goal more safely and sustainably.

Note: An earlier and shorter version of this chapter was published in Karásková et. al. Central Europe for Sale: The Politics of China's Influence (Prague, Czech Republic: Association for International Affairs (AMO), Policy Paper 03/2018). The research on China's image in Central European media and Czech politicians' views on China was made possible thanks to the grant of the National Endowment for Democracy, implemented by the Association for International Affairs (AMO). The research does not reflect the views of either NED or AMO, and the views expressed here are those of the author.

Bibliography

Allen-Ebrahimian, B. (2016). How China won the war against Western media. Foreign Policy, March 4.

Association of TV organizations. www.ato.cz.

Chau, D. C., and Kane, T. M. (editors) (2014). China and International Security: History, Strategy and 21st-Century Politics. Santa Barbara, US: Praeger.

DVTV (2016). Kmoníček: Státy EU nám chtěly zabránit získat čínské investice, Čína předefinovala slovo komunista [Kmoníček: EU states wanted to cut us from Chinese investment, China redefined the word Communist], interview by Martin Veselovský, April 1, 2016, https://video.aktualne.cz/dvtv/kmonicek-cina-zcela-predefinovala -obsah-slova-komunista-komu/r~157b2d04f76911e5a652002590604f2e/.

Fox, J., and Godement, F. (2009). A Power Audit of EU-China Relations. London, UK: European Council on Foreign Relations.

Goh, E., ed. (2016). Rising China's Influence in Developing World. London, UK: Oxford University Press.

Gregor, M., and Vejvodová, P. (2016). Analýza manipulativních technik na vybraných českých serverech [Analysis of manipulative techniques on selected Czech news servers]. Brno: Masaryk University. https://www.academia.edu/26046763/ Výzkumná_zpráva_Analýza_manipulativn%C3%ADch_technik_na_vybraných _českých_serverech.

Han, G., and Wang, X. (2015). From Product-Country Image to National Image: "Made in China" and Integrated Valence Framing Effects. International Journal of Strategic Communication 9, pp. 62–77.

Heiduk, F. (2014). Conflicting Images? Germany and the Rise of China. German Politics 23 (1–2), pp. 118–133.

Karásková, I. et al. (2018). Central Europe for Sale: The Politics of China's Influence. Prague, Czech Republic: Association for International Affairs (AMO).

Karásková I., Bajerová A., and Matura, T. (2019). Images of China in Czech and Hungarian Parliaments. Prague, Czech Republic: Association for International Affairs (AMO).

Kopra, S. (2012). A Responsible Developing Country: China's National Image Building and International Negotiations on Climate. Quarterly Journal of Chinese Studies 1 (3), pp. 121–137.

Lisle, J., and Goldstein, A. (editors) (2017). China's Global Engagement: Cooperation, Competition and Influence in the 21st Century. Washington, US: Brookings Institution Press.

Mediahub (2017). Poslechovost rádií: Impuls stále vede, nejvíc rostl ČRo Plus.

Media Projekt. http://www.unievydavatelu.cz/cs/unie_vydavatelu/medialni_data/ vyzkum_ctenosti.

Nye Jr, J. S. (2018). How Sharp Power Threatens Soft Power: The Right and Wrong Ways to Respond to Authoritarian Influence. Foreign Affairs, January 24.

PSSI [Prague Security Studies Institute] (2018). Léta 2004–2006, krátké jaro česko-čínských vztahů. Accessed March 21, 2018.

Ross, R. S., and Feng, Z. (editors) (2008). China's Ascent: Power, Security and the Future of International Politics. Ithaca, US: Cornell University Press.

Rudolph, J., and Szonyi, M. (editors) (2018). China Questions: Critical Insights into a Rising Power. Boston, US: Harvard University Press.

Shambaugh, D. (2013). China Goes Global: The Partial Power. London, UK: Oxford University Press.

Stone, G. C., and Xiao, Z. (2007). Anointing a new enemy: The rise of anti-China coverage after the USSR's demise. The International Communication Gazette 69 (1), pp. 91–108.

Xie, T., and Benjamin, I. (2013). What Affects China's National Image? A cross-national study of public opinion. Journal of Contemporary China 22 (83), pp. 850–867.

CHAPTER 9

China's Image in Belgian Media

Between Fascination and Fear

Erik Vlaeminck

1   Introduction

Since China's economic reform in the late seventies, the world has witnessed the re-emergence and rise of the country in the international arena. In current times of global transformation and digitalization, image building and reputation management have become priorities in a country's foreign policy in order to manage its image. Similar to other growing global actors such as Russia and Iran, China, which has suffered long-term racialization and stereotyping, has invested in turning perceptions of it by engaging in the multidimensional field of strategic communication and soft power.

This process originated in the first decade of the 21st century and goes back specifically to 2007, when Hu Jintao, at the 17th National Congress of the Communist Party, proposed to enhance culture as part of China's soft power.[1] He conceptualized its purpose in two ways which involved promoting "national cohesion and creativity in order to meet the spiritual demands of modern life and to strengthen China's competitiveness within the international arena."[2] Since then, aimed at domestic and international audiences,[3] investments and efforts in the complex field of soft power have been made to improve China's image abroad. Successful soft power initiatives include the setting up of Confucius and cultural institutes and centres all around the world, the Shanghai World Expo (2010) and the 2008 Olympic games in Beijing. It is not a coincidence that these efforts have been intensified since the launching of the Belt and Road Initiative in 2013.

However, the question arises whether these efforts are well accommodated within the rest of the world, particularly in the West where many stereotypes involving China originated. One way to answer this question is to analyse China's image in Western media. Mainstream media are situated within

---

1   In Chinese scholarly circles, the thinking about soft power began much earlier.
2   Barr, 2012: 82.
3   Barr, 2012: 83.

ideological norms of society, connected to corporate and governmental entities, and therefore are highly influential in shaping public opinion.[4] In order to understand public perception of China, analysis of its media representation is therefore inevitable.

In this study, China's image is analysed within the context of the Belgian media landscape. Chinese-Belgian relations go back far and are characterized by 'ups' and 'downs,' as expressed in their current relations where diplomatic crises alternate with the sealing of high-profile deals within, but not limited to, the economic sphere. This raises questions regarding the public perception of China. For instance, what is China's image as represented in the Belgian media? Do Walloon and Flemish media publish different content, from a different perspective or in a different way? Primarily relying on context analysis, this study examines China's image in prominent Belgian newspapers on both sides of the linguistic divide.

Drawing on the results, and against the background of a socio-cultural informed context, the results suggest that despite the efforts to promote a positive image, the Belgian newspapers under analysis have largely, but not entirely, a neutral coverage of China. The national image however, can best be summarized by the words "fascination and fear," referring to the binary way in which China tends to be portrayed in the selected newspapers during the given time frame. Whereas "fascination" largely points to the astonishment which accompanies China's fast paced development – primarily in the economic and financial spheres – "fear" denotes the expression of anxiety, suspicion and in some cases even rejection, as expressed in the selected Belgian newspapers.

This study aims not only to contribute to the academic field of Chinese image studies, but also to the promotion of mutual understanding in Chinese-Belgian bilateral relations in order to, at the same time, impact on an operational level. The article is structured as follows: the first part sketches out a theoretical background regarding national image; the second covers the literary review on framing and the social construction of media and news reports; and the third part presents and discusses the results of the content analysis and proposes some concluding thoughts for discussion.

---

4 Xiang, 2013:256.

2   Deconstructing China's National Image in Belgian Newspapers

The 21st century is characterized by a set of global transformations which
have impacts on all aspects of life, ranging from communication and health,
to security and sustainable development. Living in the so-called information
age – characterized by the almost uncontrollable flow of information – the
struggle for perception and image-building seems to be more important than
ever. This is not surprising because images of public figures, cities, regions and
countries influence a range of other processes in society.

   In relation to countries, national images have influence on many aspects
within international politics ranging from the economy to foreign policy and
cultural relations, and therefore, their importance should not be underesti-
mated.[5] Few definitions of national image exist. Yu Huang and Christine Chi
Mei Leung have conceptualised it as a "generalized and abstract profile of a
nation or its people."[6] Zengjun Peng understood it as a "product of a complex
historical process involving the interplay of many factors, such as the political
and social realities of a particular country, diplomatic relations, and changes in
the international political and economic spheres as well as symbolic representations in the mass media and popular culture."[7] Michael Kunczik understands
a national image as the "cognitive perception that a person holds of a given
country, what a person believes to be true about a nation and its people."[8]
This study builds upon these definitions and understands national image as a
historically-rooted, socially constructed, cognitive perception of a country and
its people which, through a range of channels – among which mass media – is
established, maintained and/or challenged.

   National images which are very often based on historical stereotypes of
a country,[9] tend to categorize countries and nations as ally, enemy, dependent, barbarian, or imperialist, which has in turn consequences for potential
(international) relations, ranging from cooperation and conflict to exploitation, invasion, or sabotage.[10] Rather than seeing such images as a reflection
of reality, it is important to understand them as social constructions created
by specific actors. The media is one such actor that shapes a country's reputation abroad. According to Paddy Scannell and David Cardiff, media make "the

---

5   Wang, 2006.
6   Huang & Chi Mei Leung, 2005: 304.
7   Peng, 2004: 53.
8   Kunczik, 1997: 46.
9   Li, 2012: 173.
10   Alexander, Levin and Henry, 2005.

nation real and tangible through a whole range of images and symbols, events and ceremonies."[11] It is therefore not surprising that negative media content of a given foreign country influences public perception of that nation and eventually leads to negative perception of that nation.[12]

In this paper, we attempt to examine the national image of China as presented in contemporary Belgian media. The media in Belgium is characterized by the linguistic divide in the country. Most newspapers are printed monolingually in Dutch or in French. There is one major German newspaper – *Grenz Echo,* and newspapers in many other languages are printed in Belgium, which is understandable given the presence of many international institutions and supranational organizations in the country. The major Belgian news agency is Belga. In terms of readership, among the major Dutch-language daily newspapers are *De Standaard, De Tijd* and *De Morgen,* branded as quality newspapers. To this we can add other Flemish newspapers such as *De Gazet van Antwerpen, Het Laatste Nieuws* and *Het Nieuwsblad* which are arguably more directed towards sensation. In terms of readership, among the major French-language daily newspapers are *Le Soir, L'Echo* and *La Libre Belgique,* generally known as quality newspapers as well as the more sensational and popular (in terms of readership) *La Dernièrre Heure* which is widely distributed throughout the country. Research has shown that there is a general decline in the sale of newspapers in the country and that only the sale of quality newspapers increases, mainly because of the existence of digital versions.[13] This is particularly true for Flemish-language newspapers; in Wallonia, digital newspapers have not been able to stop the decline of the sale of newspapers in paper version.[14]

Many studies of China's national image as constructed in the mainstream media, have already been conducted. China has been represented in many ways ranging from a third world country[15] to a threat to the world.[16] Wang differentiated various images, namely: "a peace-loving country, victim of foreign aggression, socialist country, bastion of revolution, anti-hegemonic force, developing country, major power, international co-operator, and autonomous

---

11   Scannel & Cardiff, 1991: 277.
12   Wanta, Golan and Lee, 2004:364; Zhang &William Meadow III, 2012.
13   Vlaamse Regulator voor de Media. Analyse of basis van populariteitscijfers. URL: http:// www.vlaamseregulatormedia.be/nl/3-informatie-over-mediaconcentratie/31-informatie-over-mediaconcentratie-mediavorm/313-geschreven-6 (Accessed: 27 November 2017).
14   Verkoopcijfers kranten lopen verder terug. Deredactie.be. URL: http://deredactie.be/cm/vrtnieuws/cultuur%2Ben%2Bmedia/media/1.2827660 (Accessed: 27 November 2017).
15   Todaro, 1989.
16   Xiang, 2013: 255, 268.

actor."[17] Foreign media analyses of China's national image show a complex and heterogeneous picture that – often depending on the socio-cultural and political context wherein it emerges – ranges from a balanced and even positive image[18] to a rather negative and/or one-dimensional image that primarily focusses on ideological frames and politics.[19] In contrast to traditional media, research has demonstrated that social media present "a more diverse and multi-faceted picture of China"[20] that focusses more on Chinese social and economic issues as well as China's cultural and technological aspects.

3   Framing and Reality Construction through the Media

> It is social actors who use the conceptual system of their culture and the linguistic and other representation systems to construct meaning, to make the world meaningful and to communicate about that world meaningfully to others.[21]

The role of the media (internet, radio, written press, television, social media) in the information age is more important than ever. Often referred to as the 4th power, the media creates and breaks images and reputations and shapes our understanding of reality. Maxwell McCombs writes that the mediated view of the world shapes our knowledge and priorities.[22] This makes media a powerful instrument within political processes, often used by governments and other actors to influence and persuade. Paraphrasing Douglas Kellner, Debao Xiang writes that the media tend to report "within ideological, political and cultural contexts, producing representative images that individuals use to picture the world mentally and construct their conception of 'us and them'."[23] Similarly, Linda Jean Kenix argues that the mainstream media are "situated completely within ... the ideological norms of society, enjoy a widespread scale of influence, rely on professionalized reporters and are heavily connected with other corporate and governmental entities."[24]

---

17   Wang, 2003: 52.
18   Wekesa, 2013; Annune and Yan, 2018.
19   Xiang, 2013; Tonchev, 2018; Syed, 2010.
20   Xiang, 2013: 267.
21   Hall, 1997: 25.
22   McCombs, 2004.
23   Xiang, 2013: 253.
24   Kenix, 2011: 3.

Therefore, it is important to understand that news is a socially constructed product, and not a reflection of an objective reality. Scholarship tends to explain the way in which media influences public perceptions in terms of framing and framing devices. Frame, as a noun, implies "a set of lenses through which information is selected." As a verb, it refers to "a process of creating [...] frames."[25] Pippa Norris in her study of network news in the pre- and post-cold war periods, conceptualized news frames as cognitive schemata used to "simplify, prioritize and structure the narrative flow of events."[26] Jinbong Choi's research on the image of North Korea in American newspapers showed that media framing stands central in the meaning making activity in the production of media products.[27] Similarly, Robert Entman argues it is inevitably linked to the process of producing news, defining problems, diagnosing causes, making moral judgments and suggesting remedies.[28] He explains framing as "selecting and highlighting some facets of events or issues, and making connections among them so as to promote a particular interpretation, evaluation and/or solution."[29] This is demonstrated in various studies dealing with the national imagery of (non-Western) countries ranging from Russia to North Korea and China, which have demonstrated that, through framing, media outlets effectively manage to create (political) meaning.[30]

4 Research Questions and Methodological Framework[31]

Following the above theory and review, this study will now analyse the national image of China between 2013 and 2017, as 2013 marks the launch of the Belt and Road Initiative. The following research questions are proposed:

RQ I. How is China represented in the selected newspapers over the given period?

RQ II. Is there a difference between French-language and Flemish-language newspapers?

RQ III. What are the factors and framing strategies affecting the representation of China?

---

25 Kaufman, Eliot and Shmueli: 2017 in Li, 2012: 174.
26 Norris, 1995: 2.
27 Choi, 2010.
28 Entman, 1993: 52.
29 Entman, 2003: 417.
30 Choi, 2010; Repina et al., 2018; Peng, 2004.
31 In the design of its methodology, this article was inspired by Chen, 2012.

The method of content analysis has been chosen to analyse the media content as it offers "the advantage of being unobtrusive and efficient".[32] Following Kerlinger, this study approaches content analysis as "a method of studying and analyzing communication in a *systematic, objective,* and *quantitative* manner for the purpose of measuring variables."[33] The electronic versions of two highly esteemed Belgian newspapers – *De Standaard* on the Flemish-language side and *La Libre Belgique* on the French-language side – have been selected for this study. *De Standaard*, the biggest quality newspaper in Flanders[34] is a center-leaning newspaper with a big (digital) readership (a combined digital and analog daily readership of 671,700).[35] *La Libre Belgique* is a former Catholic oriented newspaper and represents one of the biggest newspapers in the French-language press. In Belgium, each newspaper is seen as the equivalent of the other.

Through the selection of the word "China" (respectively "China" in Flemish and "Chine" in French) the electronic version of the newspapers was examined[36] over three years: 2013, 2015 and 2017. The decision to compare these years was primarily motivated by the fact that they cover the period since the launch of the Belt and Road Initiative and include news on events and issues of both global and national importance. Two variables were examined in this study: themes and favorability. The six themes were: Politics, Economy, Military and Foreign Affairs, Sino-Belgian relations, Society and Sports, Culture and Technology. Following Chen, we understand favorability as "the overall tone manifested in the individual stories"[37] which we assessed as positive (1), negative (-1) or neutral (0). While positive reports dealt with stories reflecting national unity, economic stability or general progress, negative stories particularly reflected ongoing conflicts, economic decline or explicitly expressed critique; with respect to neutral stories, the focus was on reports which contained only factual information and stories with a limited evaluative character.

---

32   Chen, 2012: 66.

33   Keller, 2000, cited in Dominick and Wimmer, 2010: 156–157.

34   CIM Perstudie 2018: de analyse van mediahuis. 18.09.2018. URL: https://www.mediaspecs
      .be/cim-persstudie-2018-de-analyse-van-mediahuis/ (accessed 2019).

35   De Standaard groter dan De Morgen en De Tijd samen. 12.10.2017. URL:http://www
      .standaard.be/cnt/dmf20171012_03127386(accessed: 2017).

36   Digital articles with only video or photo material were not included. "Articles" include
      relevant news coverage as well as opinion pieces.

37   Chen, 2012: 7.

5   Results: Numbers, Themes and Favourability[38]

Table 9.1 sums up the total number of news reports as well as the favorability rating as represented in the electronic version of two Belgian newspapers over three specified years: 2013, 2015 and 2017. A total of 2,117 news
articles related to China were collected. The Flemish-language newspaper *De
Standaard* had 1,503 news stories devoted to China which constituted 70% of
all analysed news reports. The coverage of stories on China in *De Standaard*
decreased significantly over the period under examination. Starting in 2013, it
decreased significantly by 2015, to drop further in 2017. *La Libre Belgique* had a
total of 614 news stories devoted to China which constituted 30% of the coverage and which was characterised by a fluctuation in its distribution over time.

   With regard to the manifested favorability of the whole sampled population
over time, 61.1 % (n=1293/2117) was neutral in tone, 10.7 % (n: 227/2117) was positive and 28.2% (n: 597/2117) was negative. Although the average favorability of
the examined news reports was negative (M: -0.175), Table 9.1 shows that across
the years the reporting steadily takes on a more positive tone. In 2013, the average tone (M: -0.201) was less favorable towards China than in 2015 (M: -0.170)
and 2017 (M: -0.144) respectively. Of particular interest is the increase in positive tone in 2017, compared to the relatively higher favorability rate in 2015.The
reason for such an increase in positive tone may be because of issues related
to China's global repositioning in a rapidly changing world and specific issues
related to the election of Donald Trump as President of the United States. The
coverage of China in *La Libre Belgique* was more negative (-0.225), compared to
De Standaard (-0.154). This difference is due to the editorial style and framing,
as well as events within the Sino-Belgian context.

   Table 9.2 indicates that the news reports concerning Chinese society
encompassed the bulk of the whole sampled population (25.6%, n=541).
However, they have been decreasing over the years. A large majority of the
news articles are concerned with scandals or public outrages, accidents and
disasters, peculiarities of Chinese society and its people, and climate issues
(for instance, pollution). Following in terms of number, were stories dealing
with economic issues namely: finance, macro-economics and investments
(23.4%, n=496). Here we can notice a significant drop in coverage by 2017, after
an upswing in 2015. The third largest share was constituted by news reports
on Chinese politics (18%, n=381), fluctuating over the years and characterized
by a steady increase by 2017. The focus of these stories most often concerned

---

38   The model for the tables was inspired by Chen, 2012.

TABLE 9.1   Total sampled population and corresponding favorability means

	2013			2015			2017			Total		
	N	%	Mean	N	%	Mean	N	%	Mean	N	%	Mean
De Standaard	605	40.3	-0.183	495	32.9	-0.162	403	26.8	-0.102	150	70	-0.154
La Libre	230	37.5	-0.248	188	30.6	-0.191	196	31.9	-0.230	614	30	-0.225
Total	835	39.4	-0.201	683	32.3	-0.170	599	28.3	-0.144	2117	100	-0.175

internal Chinese politics, reforms and restrictions. Issues on military and foreign affairs, made up 15.1 % (n: 319) of all the stories. Their coverage significantly decreased by 2015, but increased again by 2017. The focus of the stories was on China's position in the world, the modernization of the army and specific issues and 'hot topics' such as the South China Sea or Sino-American relations in the age of American President Donald Trump. Next came stories covering Sino-Belgian relations (9.6 %, n: 204); then Chinese sports, arts and technology (8.3%, n: 176) dealing with scientific innovations, the film industry and football. Whereas the coverage over the years on the topics of culture, science and sport steadily increased; the coverage of Belgian-Chinese issues was reduced over the years under examination.

With respect to the average tone of the coverage, Figure 9.1 demonstrates that coverage related to Politics constituted the most negative theme (M: -0.499), particularly in relation to the organisation of the political system, dissidents, ideology and (social) restrictions. Similarly depicted in negative terms were the topics related to Military and Foreign Affairs (M: -0.282) particularly concerning accusations of hacking and espionage, China's increasing presence in world affairs and the developments within the sphere of the military. Stories with a negative tone appeared also with respect to Chinese society, particularly in relation to pollution. The themes with rather balanced and/or outspokenly positive stories were respectively: Culture, Sport and Technology (M: 0.068); Economy (M: -0.073) and Sino-Belgian relations (M: -0.049), most often in relation to developments and innovations in the broader cultural sphere, global and regional investments and specific, most often regionally bound, Sino-Belgian issues. The topic of Politics appeared to be most negative both in *La Libre Belgique* (M: -0.485) and *De Standaard* (M: -0.506). *La Libre Belgique* was most favourable towards Sino-Belgian relations (M: 0.014), while the *De Standaard* covered more negatively on these issues (M: -0.082). *De Standaard* was most favourable towards the topic of Sport-Culture and Technology (+0.111), while the *La Libre Belgique* appeared to be more critical (M: -0.073) in relation to the latter topic.

6 Between Fascination and Fear: A Discussion and Analysis of China's National Image

In its examination of the coverage of China in two major Belgian newspapers, this study took into account the total numbers of stories, the recurring themes as well as the variation in favorability, over time since the launching of China's

TABLE 9.2 Overview of Themes Over Time

Themes	2013		2015		2017		Total	
	N	%	N	%	N	%	N	%
Politics	171	20.5	96	14.1	114	19	381	18
Economy	181	21.7	222	32.5	93	15.5	496	23.4
Military/For. Affairs	121	14.5	74	10.8	124	20.7	319	15.1
Society	244	29.2	173	25.3	124	20.7	541	25.6
Sino-Belgian relations	69	8.3	68	10	67	11.2	204	9.6
Culture/science/sports	49	5.8	50	7.3	77	12.9	176	8.3
Total	835	100	683	100	599	100	2117	10

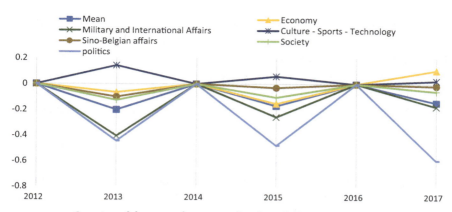

FIGURE 9.1   Overview of themes and corresponding favorability means

Belt and Road Initiative in 2013. The results showcase some peculiar findings that deserve more attention.

First of all, there is a difference in coverage of news stories on China in the Flemish-language and French-language Belgian newspapers under analysis. The Flemish-language newspaper accounted for the vast majority of the covered stories. Besides the frequency of coverage, another remarkable difference is found in the coverage of Sino-Belgium relations and issues related to Culture/Society and Technology. Whereas *La Libre Belgique* devoted more attention to the former, *De Standaard* covered more issues related to the latter. However, a comparison between the different newspapers also shows some remarkable similarities. First, as regards both newspapers, a general neutral tone is attributed to the coverage over the years. Second, the most popular topics are issues concerning Chinese society, economy and issues related to military and foreign affairs. Third, similarly in both newspapers, there is a fluctuation in coverage and favorability, and ultimately, on approaching 2017, a steady decline in number and slightly more positive tone. Although less visible in *La Libre Belgique*, the significant drop in general coverage in 2017 compared to 2015 may be explained by a range of important events during that year such as: the Chinese stock market crash; the Shenzhen landslide; the reforms with respect to the one-child policy; major technological developments; the explosions in Tianjin; several events within the context of Sino-Belgian relations such as royal missions and major Chinese investments; and finally, the rising tension in the South China Sea area.

Regardless of the decline in general coverage in 2017, a significant increase occurred concerning the coverage of Chinese politics and military and foreign affairs, at the expense of stories covering the economy and society. As regards the topic of politics, this can be explained by the Hong Kong elections, the illness and passing of human rights activist and dissident Liu Xiaobo, and the re-election of Xi Jinping as General Secretary of the Central Committee of the Communist Party of China. Military and foreign affairs, the election of Donald Trump as President of the United States and the renegotiation of Sino-American relations, together with the North Korean crisis and the increase in defence budget, were widely covered.

The general image that is created of China in both newspapers examined is twofold. On the one hand, a rising and ambitious world power that is characterized by its high productivity and integration into world politics, and on the other, an alien and closed society presenting a potential danger to the rest of the world. Consequently, the attitude as presented in the two Belgian newspapers towards China can best be described as 'between fear and fascination.'

In terms of (national) economy, the coverage often focussed on variations and trends therefore to be framed in extremes. On the one hand, China is framed as a major economic player with high ambitions and potential, arising from its booming companies such as the Chinese multinational conglomerate holding company Alibaba, and investments in many sectors, along with green energy. On the other hand, however, China's economic growth is often represented as irresponsible, leading to financial disaster and not always in favour of other actors (as appears from the solar panel issue or the Chinese presence in Africa). As an actor in military and foreign affairs, China is viewed as a rising alternative power. This is certainly true in the current age of American President Donald Trump. In this context, China is seen as a potential peace negotiator in the North Korean crisis; a propagator of a responsible climate policy; and a growing soft power player. However, at the same time it is perceived as an enemy power associated with a growing army, hacking and espionage, and hybrid warfare, particularly in the context of the South China Sea issue. In addition, its ties with countries such as Russia and North Korea are negatively looked upon.

Similarly characterized by conflicting stances is the view of Chinese politics: on the one hand, China represents a country dominated by ideology, inter-ethnic tensions, growing restrictions and an all-powerful leader. On the other, it is a country heavily investing in its integration into world politics by reforming and investing in, for instance, clean and renewable energy. With respect to Chinese society, the newspapers presented an image of a traditional and sometimes stereotypically depicted oriental society characterised by 'alien' habits and plagued by (natural) disasters, scandals and accidents. Remarkable is the constant 'wow-factor' in relation to Chinese society whether it is related to the many billionaires in the country or specific achievements in sports, inventions or actions.

Positive reports have been given on several topics, such as scientific innovation – for example, the launching of the world's largest radio telescope – or the first screening of a Chinese LGBT film, *Seeking McCartney* (2015). In addition, reforms in Chinese society regarding the battle against corruption, the one-child policy and prison camps, are featured. Similarly, China's active stance on the propagation of a responsible climate policy within the context of the Treaty of Paris, and national measures to diminish pollution, have been well received.

Opposed to these positive reports, a rather negative stance was taken in relation to topics such as China's attitude towards regions like Tibet and Xinjiang and towards dissidents such as Liu Xiaobo (1955–2017) and Ai Wei Wei (*1957). China's share in the stock market crash of 2015 was predominantly seen as negative to the global economy and the re-election of Xi Jinping was often framed as undemocratic. Finally, negative reports occurred in relation to investments or economic presence which was anticipated as being disadvantageous to Belgium or Europe, as expressed by the (Flemish) reception of the Belt and Road Initiative.

In relation to Belgium, China's national image in the newspapers is similarly characterized by a 'fascination and fear attitude' with, on the one hand, a positive and often astonished stance in relation to Chinese investments – particularly in Wallonia – and intercultural dialogue; on the other hand, a negative impression, often accompanied by fear, is frequently expressed – for instance, with respect to the transfer of the Belgian football player Axel Witsel (*1989) to Tianjin Quanjian in 2017, or the distribution of cheap solar panels on the European market in 2013.

7   Concluding Thoughts

Regardless of the obvious framing at the basis of the electronic versions of the Belgian newspapers examined in this article, we can conclude that the Belgian coverage of China is largely neutral and reflects a fair level of journalistic practice. As the average favorability has been steadily increasing as we move towards 2017, this could suggest that China's soft power efforts since the launching of the Belt and Road Initiative have indeed been successful. Respectively, Sino-Belgian relations and issues on Sport, Culture and Technology were most favourable; and China's international image has been rising, as is expressed from the increasing coverage of the topic.

Following a socio-constructionist view on news, the question arises of how such an image of China has come into being? Three factors can be distinguished at this stage. First and foremost, China's image has been created by a combination of verbal and non-verbal techniques used to convey a message in the most effective ways. In terms of linguistic and narrative tools, it is of interest to point to the means of playing upon emotions by the accentuation of negative and ideological information, the use of draconian words, metaphors, comparisons and citations – the discursive creation of an 'us vs them' scenario. Second, the type and commercial inclination of the chosen newspapers can be examined as a factor to understand some of the results. For instance, the focus on society, and not on economy. Important events on a global and national scale influenced the coverage. Third, regional (rather than linguistic) factors seem also to have played a role in the construction of China's image, as expressed in the differences in newspapers regarding frequency and favorability, particularly with respect to the theme of Sino-Belgian relations.

By answering the principal research question, this study has achieved its objective. However, the study has also inevitable limitations that can be further explored in future studies. First and foremost, only two (digital) Belgian newspapers were analysed over a limited time space. This inevitably narrows the study by inhibiting it in terms of identifying other possible trends in China's media representation within this time period. Second, only digital newspapers were analyzed whilst a comprehensive picture of China's image would require a similar analysis of other media, and certainly social media. Third, in order to better interpret the results, it would be advisable to complement content analysis studies with textual analysis.

Bibliography

Alexander, M. G., Levin, S., and Henry, P.J. (2005). Image Theory, Social Identity, and Social Dominance: Structural Characteristics and Individual Motives Underlying International Image. Political Psychology 26 (1), pp. 27–45.

Annune, Uchenna Kingsley and Yan, Lifeng (2018). China in Foreign Media: Assessing China's Image in Online Editions of Nigeria's Leading Newspapers in 2017. European Scientific Journal 14 (35), pp. 165–188.

Barr, M. (2012). Nation Branding as Nation Building: China's Image Campaign. East Asia 29 (81), pp. 81–94.

Chen, W. (2012). The Image of China in Hong Kong Media: Content Analysis of the Coverage in Three Hong Kong Newspapers. China Media Research 8 (3), pp. 65–71.

Choi, J. (2010). The Representation of North Korean National Image in National Newspapers in the United States. Public Relations Review 36, pp. 392–394.

Dominick, R., and Wimmer, R. (1991). Mass Media Research: an Introduction. Belmont, Calif: Wadsworth Publishing.

Entman, R. (1993). Framing: Toward a Clarification of a Fractured Paradigm. Journal of Communication 434, pp. 51–8.

Entman, R. (2004). Cascading Activation: Contesting the White House's Frame After 9/11. Political Communication 20 (4), pp. 415–432.

Hall, S. (1997). Representation: Cultural Representations and Signifying Practices. SAGE, Open University Press.

Huang, Y., and Leung, C.C.M. (2005). Western-Led Press Coverage of Mainland China and Vietnam during the SARS Crisis: Reassessing the Concept of 'Media Representation of the Other'. Asian Journal of Communication 15 (3), pp. 302–318.

Kaufman, S., Eliot, M., and Shmueli, D. (2017). Frames, Framing and Reframing. Beyond Intractability.

Kellner, D. (1995). Media Culture. Cultural Studies, Identity, and Politics between the Modern and the Postmodern. London and New York: Routledge.

Kenix, K.L. (2011). Alternative and Mainstream Media: The Converging Spectrum. London: Bloomsbury Academic.

Kunczik, M. (1997). Images of Nations and International Public Relations. Lawrence Erlbaum: Mahweh, N. J.

Li, X. (2012). Images of China: A Comparative Framing Analysis of Australian Current Affairs Programming. Intercultural Communication Studies XXI (1), pp. 173–188.

McCombs, M. (2004). Setting the Agenda: Mass Media and Public Opinion. Cambridge, England: Polity Press.

Norris, P. (1995). The Restless Searchlight. Network News Framing of the Post-cold War. Political Communication 2, pp. 357–370.

Peng, Z. (2004). Representation of China: An Across Time Analysis of Coverage in the New York Times and Los Angeles Times. Asian Journal of Communication 14 (1), pp. 53–67.

Scannell, P., and Cardiff, D. (1991). A Social History of British Broadcasting 1, 1922–1939. London: Arnold, pp. 319–325.

Syed, N.A. (2010). The Effects of Beijing 2008 on China's Image in the United States: A Study of Media and Polls. The International Journal of the History of Sport 27 (16–18), pp. 2863–2892.

Todaro, M.P. (1989). Economic Development in the Third World. New York: Longman.

Tonchev, P. Ed. (2018). China's Image in Greece 2008–2018. Athens: Institute of International Economic Relations.

Wang, H. (2003). National Image Building and Chinese Foreign Policy. China: An International Journal 1 (1), pp. 46–72.

Wang, J. (2006). Managing National Reputation and International Relations in the Global era: Public Diplomacy Revisited. Public Relations Review 32 (2), pp. 91–96.

Wanta, W; Golan, G., and Lee, C. (2004). Agenda Setting and International News: Media Influence on Public Perceptions of Foreign Nations. Journalism & Mass Communication Quarterly 81 (2), pp. 364–377.

Wekesa, B. (2013) The Media Framing of China's Image in East Africa: An Exploratory Study. African East-Asian Affairs. The China Monitor 1, pp. 15–41.

Xiang, D. (2013). China's Image on Internet English language Social Media. The Journal of International Communication 19 (12), pp. 252–271.

CHAPTER 10

Exploring Public Perceptions of, and Interactions with, the Chinese in Hungary

Irina Golubeva

1   Introduction: The Context of the Study

In November 2017, the world's attention was centred on Hungary, when the 16+1 summit was held in its capital, Budapest. The visit of the Prime Minister of China was viewed as a promising sign that the cooperation between China and the sixteen Central and Eastern European (CEE) countries, including Hungary, would be strengthened. The media came up with numerous articles and posts analysing the perspectives of CEE – Chinese relations. To the present, collaboration in various fields has been discussed and several agreements have been signed between Chinese and Hungarian partners. However, for the future success of these projects and possible cooperation within the "Belt and Road Initiative", the atmosphere of trust and mutual understanding should be developed.

Intercultural communication can be enhanced, one can learn about other people's culture, behaviour, communicative styles, etc., but for this the possible problematic areas in communication between given cultures should be "diagnosed".

The author of this paper worked for ten years in Hungary as the coordinator of international student admissions and later as the Head of International Office, and during these years she observed that each group of international students brings new "cultural issues" that should be considered in the educational process. Today, the admission statistics show that the number of Chinese students is one of the most rapidly growing in Hungary. Hungarian higher education institutions, following global tendencies, view educational exchange as one of the main instruments of internationalization.[1] But, in spite of the fact that Chinese are one of the largest groups of international students studying in Hungary (https://vs.hu/mega/kulfoldi-diakok-magyarorszagon), still

---

1   Golubeva, I. (2017) Intercultural Communication for International Mobility. In: D.K. Deardorff, and L. A. Arasarathnam-Smith, eds., *Intercultural Competence in International Higher Education*, New York: Routledge, Taylor and Francis, pp. 186–191.

there is little empirical research concerning communication in the Chinese-Hungarian context. This is the main reason why this study was initiated.

The author makes an attempt to explore Hungarians' perceptions of Chinese, and whether the growing number of Chinese students is perceived positively by the broader public in Hungary, the country which lately has been stigmatised for its xenophobic atmosphere.[2]

Readers will attain insight into the data collected from 386 Hungarian respondents regarding their interactions and willingness to communicate with Chinese. Although the data were gained from a small-scale survey and the results of the analysis cannot be generalised, the study fills the gap that now exists in intercultural research in a Chinese-Hungarian context, and the author hopes that it will provide some thought-provoking information to those who are planning collaboration within the "Belt and Road Initiative".

2   Theoretical Underpinnings

Intercultural communication, in general, and intercultural communication in professional settings, in particular, depends quite a lot on the perceptions of each other and the willingness to communicate. If one has only superficial knowledge of another cultural/ethnic/etc. group, it often leads to quite stereotypical perceptions of that group,[3] which impedes effective and appropriate communication. Stereotypes, both negative and positive, may become obstacles for successful intercultural communication.[4] The first step to improve intercultural communication and mutual understanding in the Chinese-Hungarian context is to diagnose what perceptions Hungarians and Chinese hold about each other, and what kinds of interactions are taking place between the two groups in Hungary.

The majority of studies concerning Chinese students were conducted in countries which are considered as the main destinations for Chinese students

2   European Commission against Racism and Intolerance. (2015) *ECRI Report on Hungary.* Strasbourg: Council of Europe; Kounalakis, E. (2015) Hungary's Xenophobic Response. *New York Times.* September 7; World Policy (2015) *Hungary's Blame Game About Xenophobia.* Available from: http://www.worldpolicy.org/blog/2015/08/20/hungarys-blame-game-about-xenophobia.

3   Golubeva, I. (2003) Interkulturális kompetencia – túl a sztereotípiákon. In: E. Kiss, ed., *Interdiszciplináris pedagógia és a tudás társadalma. II. Kiss Árpád Emlékkonferencia előadásai 2001,* Debrecen: Debreceni Egyetem Neveléstudományi Tanszék, pp. 209–218.

4   Golubeva, 2003, op. cit.

willing to study abroad, namely the USA,[5] UK,[6] Australia,[7] and New Zealand.[8] Fewer studies refer to Chinese students in a European context.[9]

5   Heng, T.T. (2017) Voices of Chinese international students in USA colleges: 'I want to tell them that ...', *Studies in Higher Education* 42(5), pp. 833–850; Ruble, R. A., and Zhang, Y. B. (2013) Stereotypes of Chinese international students held by Americans. *International Journal of Intercultural Relations* 37, pp. 202–211; Yan, K., and Berliner, D. C. (2009) Chinese international students' academic stressors in the United States. *College Student Journal* 43(4), pp. 939–960.

6   Gu, Q., and Maley, A. (2008) Changing places: A study of Chinese students in the UK. *Language and Intercultural Communication* 8(4), pp. 224–245; Gu, Q. (2011) An emotional journey of change: The case of Chinese students in UK higher education. In L. Jin, and M. Cortazzi, eds., *Researching Chinese learners – Skills, perceptions and intercultural adaptations*, Basingstoke, Hampshire: Palgrave Macmillan, pp. 212–232; Lihong, W., and Byram, M. (2011) "But when You Are Doing Your Exams It Is the Same as in China" – Chinese Students Adjusting to Western Approaches to Teaching and Learning. *Cambridge Journal of Education* 41(4), pp. 407–424; Zhou, Y., and Todman, J. (2008) Chinese postgraduate students in the UK: A two-way reciprocal adaptation. *Journal of International and Intercultural Communication* 1(3), pp. 221–243.

7   Hiu, L. (2001) Chinese cultural schema of education: implications for communication between Chinese students and Australian educators. *Issues in Educational Research* 15(1), pp. 17–36; Pan, J.Y. (2015) Predictors of post-migration growth for Chinese international students in Australia. *International Journal of Intercultural Relations* 47, pp. 69–77; Yang, M. (2007) Why mainland China's students study in Australian higher education. In: I. Morley, ed., *The Value of Knowledge: At the Interface*. Papers presented at the 1st Global Conference on the Value of Knowledge, February, Sydney, Australia; Yao, L. (2004) The Chinese overseas students: an overview of the flows change. *Paper presented at the Australian National University 12th Biennial Conference of the Australian Population Association*, September, Canberra.

8   Campbell, J., and Li, M. (2008) Asian students' voices: An empirical study of Asian students' learning experiences at a New Zealand university. *Journal of Studies in International Education* 12(4), pp. 375–396; Holmes, P. (2004) Negotiating differences in learning and intercultural communication: Ethnic Chinese students in a New Zealand university. *Business Communication Quarterly* 67(3), pp. 294–307; Holmes, P. (2005). Teachers' perceptions of and Interactions with international students: A qualitative analysis. *Interactions with International Students: Report Prepared for Education New Zealand*, pp. 86–120; Holmes, P. (2007). Ethnic Chinese students' communication with cultural others in a New Zealand university. *Communication Education* 54(4), pp. 289–311; Zhang, J., and Goodson, P. (2011). Acculturation and psychosocial adjustment of Chinese international students: Examining mediation and moderation effects. *International Journal of Intercultural Relations* 35, pp. 139–162; Zhang, Z., and Brunton, M. (2007) Differences in living and learning: Chinese international students in New Zealand. *Journal of Studies in International Education* 11(2), pp. 124–140.

9   See among others Gareis, E. (2012). Intercultural friendship: Effects of home and host region. *Journal of International and Intercultural Communication* 5, pp. 309–328; Hong, T.M., Pieke, F.N., Steehouder, L., and van Veldhuizen, J.L. (2017) *Dutch higher education and Chinese students in the Netherlands: External Research report*. Leiden: Leiden Asia Centre.

The papers on Chinese students mainly deal with their acculturation and adjustment,[10] stereotypes about them,[11] their academic performance,[12] and interaction with them.[13] The analysis of literature shows that Chinese students together with other Asian students typically are perceived in a stereotyped way, which often obstructs appropriate and deep intercultural encounter.[14]

As in the case of stereotypes about any other cultural group, stereotypes about Chinese can be positive, neutral, or negative, focusing on various characteristics. For example, according to Ruble and Zhang,[15] US-Americans see Chinese as loud, rude, annoying, ambitious, mathematical, obedient, serious, traditional, cold, etc. And, although a lot of these perceived traits are positive, these stereotypes may lead the locals to feel less likely to communicate with Chinese (and other Asians). As they explain,[16] even positive characteristics related to hard-working, self-discipline or intelligence can influence the creation of not only positive attitudes like admiration, but also negative ones as, for example, fear.

As one of the major barriers to communication with Chinese students, researchers mention language knowledge, especially listening comprehension and oral communication which cause major problems.[17] This is confirmed by Chinese students themselves: the majority of whom feel that Americans speak too fast and that it is impossible for them to follow.[18] According to Ruble and Zhang's[19] observation, the lack of good language knowledge is perceived negatively by representatives of the host culture. This is due to the fact that they tend to associate it with a lack of assimilation or unfamiliarity with the host culture. Such negative perception may explain an unwillingness to communicate with Chinese.

Another problem mentioned by Yan and Berliner[20] is so-called sociocultural stress such as culture shock and social isolation. Usually, cultural shock is

---

10   Zhang, Goodson, op. cit.

11   Ruble, Zhang, op. cit.

12   Yan, Berliner, op. cit.

13   Gareis, op. cit.; Hiu, op. cit.; Holmes, 2004, op. cit.; Holmes, 2005, op. cit..

14   Operio, D., and Fiske, S.T. (2003) Stereotypes: Content, structures processes and context.
      In: R. Brown, and S. Gaertner, eds., *Blackwell handbook of social psychology: Intergroup
      processes*, Blackwell, Malden, MA, pp. 22–44.

15   Ruble, Zhang, op. cit.

16   Ruble, Zhang, op. cit.

17   Yan, Berliner, op. cit.

18   Yan, Berliner, op. cit.

19   Ruble, Zhang, op. cit.

20   Yan, Berliner, op. cit.

caused by a significant sociocultural distance. In the specific case of Chinese-Hungarian communication, due to differences between the two cultures, such distance can be expected to be rather significant (compare the two cultures according to (1) Hall's[21] high- vs low-context classification, and (2) directness vs indirectness of communication styles).[22]

However, the good news is that it is possible to improve the situation regarding intergroup contact and communication across cultural boundaries. In their study, Imamura and Zhang,[23] guided by Allport's[24] contact hypothesis and intergroup contact theory,[25] succeeded in identifying ways to improve intergroup relations. They referred to Pettigrew,[26] who stated that contact conditions should offer the participants the opportunity to become friends because people are more likely to communicate with individuals from the same culture. The unfamiliarity with each other's cultural norms will serve as a constant obstacle to developing meaningful relationships among the two groups.[27] When people from one cultural/ethnic/etc. group feel themselves as very different or "other" than people from another group, the willingness to communicate decreases.

At the beginning of the 20th century, Emory S. Bogardus[28] offered a social distance scale to empirically measure people's willingness to interact with representatives of other ethnic groups. His idea was based on the assumption that there is no social distance between two groups if they would accept each other as close relatives, e.g. spouses. Bogardus[29] developed a seven-point social

21   Hall, E. T. (1976) *Beyond culture*. New York: Doubleday.

22   Spencer-Oatey, H. (2008) Face, (im)politeness and rapport. In H. Spencer-Oatey (ed.) *Culturally Speaking: Culture, Communication and Politeness Theory*, 2 edn, pp. 11–47. London: Continuum; Comfort, J., and Franklin, P. (2008) *The Mindful International Manager: Competences for Working Effectively Across Cultures*. York: York Associates.

23   Imamura, M., and Zhang, Y. B. (2014) Functions of the common ingroup identity model and acculturation strategies in intercultural communication: American host nationals' communication with Chinese international students. *International Journal of Intercultural Relations* 43, pp. 227–238.

24   Allport, G. W. (1954) *The nature of prejudice*. Reading, MA: Addison-Wesley.

25   Brown, R., and Hewstone, M. (2005). An integrative theory of intergroup contact. *Advances in Experimental Social Psychology* 37, pp. 255–343; Pettigrew, T. F. (1998) Intergroup contact theory. *Annual Review of Psychology* 49, pp. 65–85.

26   Pettigrew, op. cit.

27   Imamura, Zhang, op. cit.; referring to Kassing, J. W. (1997) Development of the intercultural willingness to communicate scale. *Communication Research Reports* 14, pp. 399–403. Nesdale, D., and Mak, A. S. (2003). Ethnic identification, self-esteem and immigrant psychological health. *International Journal of Intercultural Relations* 27, pp. 23–40.

28   Bogardus, E. S. (1933) A social distance scale. *Sociology and Social Research* 17, pp. 265–271.

29   Bogardus, op. cit.

distance scale, ranging from positive attitude of "accepting as close relative" (score 1.00) and "accepting as personal friend" (score 2.00) to negative ones, i.e. accepting only "as a visitor to my country" (score 6.00) and rejecting "entry into my country" (score 7.00). The author is aware of the facts that Bogardus' idea[30] can be criticized as oversimplified and that a lot has changed in societies over the past decades. But, asking people to provide answers to similar questions (e.g. *'Would you marry someone who is …?'*, etc.) can certainly help to diagnose the tendency and show the level of sociocultural distance. In other words, it can help to shed light on the affective side of communication between the members of two different cultural groups.

3   Research Questions, Methodology, and Population

3.1   *Research Questions*
The following research questions (RQ) were posed in the survey demonstrated in this paper:
RQ1: What are the perceptions of Chinese held by Hungarians?
RQ2: What sort of interaction between Chinese and Hungarians is taking place?
RQ3: Is the growing number of Chinese international students perceived positively in Hungary?

3.2   *Research Methodology*
A *Survey questionnaire* was chosen to collect quantitative data on the issue under discussion because this instrument is the most often used to obtain a general picture of a research phenomenon,[31] it allows us to approach large number of respondents at the same time, and it is relatively easy to administer.[32]

Both closed- and open-ended questions were included in the surveys. For some questions a multiple-choice list was offered, for others a four- or a five-point Likert scales, or just 'yes'/'no' answers.

---

30   Bogardus, op. cit.
31   Yang, L. H. (2016) Resources through which Chinese students learn about Western society and culture. *Journal of Research in International Education* 15(1), pp. 67 –78; referring to Cohen L., Manion L., and Morrison, K. (2007). *Research Methods in Education.* London; New York: Routledge; De Vaus, D. (2002) *Surveys in Social Research.* London: Routledge, p. 94; McMillan, J. H., and Schumacher, S. (1997) *Research in Education: A Conceptual Introduction.* New York: Longman; Wilson, N., and McClean, S. (1994) *Questionnaire Design: A Practical Introduction.* Newtown Abbey: University of Ulster Press.
32   Yang, 2016, op. cit. referring to Basit, T. N. (2010) *Conducting Research in Educational Contexts.* London: Continuum International Publishing Group.

The *Survey on Public Opinion about Chinese in general and on Chinese international students studying in Hungary* had three blocks to obtain data on:

1.   demographic *Survey on Public Opinion* characteristics of respondents (age, gender, higher education degree, occupation, place of living, etc.);
2.   their general opinion about and interaction with Chinese people;
3.   their opinion about Chinese international students.

The study examined perceptions, interactions and opinions about Chinese people in general and Chinese international students studying in Hungary. To have insight into the (perceived) sociocultural distance between Hungarians and Chinese, the idea of Bogardus[33] (as referred to in Liu, Volcic & Gallois)[34] – who developed a scale that measured the social distance between people from different (cultural) groups – was borrowed, and the questions like *'Would you have Chinese people as regular friends or as speaking acquaintances?'* and *'Would you marry someone who is Chinese?'* were inserted in the questionnaire.

The data were collected in November 2017 over a ten-day period through an online survey (google forms), making it clear that it is subject to the Google privacy policy. The respondents were explicitly informed about research ethics policy when the author obtained their participation consent, assuring them of anonymity, confidentiality, the right to withdraw at any time of their choosing.

The author surveyed the convenience sample. The link was sent to her students enrolled in *Intercultural Communication* and *Intercultural Studies* courses and they were asked to gather the responses. The statistical analysis was performed with SPSS Version 23.0 statistic software package, following Takács.[35]

3.3   *Research Population*

The *Survey on Public Opinion about Chinese in general and on Chinese international students studying in Hungary* was answered by 386 adult (18+) respondents: 48.4% male, 51.6% female; age distribution as in Figure 1.

Respondents by occupation were distributed in such categories as: students (214 Rs); people working in various workplaces and positions (to name but a few: doctor, teacher, waiter, policeman, hairdresser, shop-assistant, cook, turner, miner, businessman, IT-expert, librarian, social worker, cashier, cleaner,

33   Bogardus, op. cit.
34   Liu, S., Volcic, Z., and Gallois, C. (2015) *Introducing Intercultural Communication: Global Cultures and Contexts*. London: SAGE.
35   Takács, Sz. (2012) Érzékenységvizsgálatok a statisztikai eljárásokban [Sensitivity analysis in a statistical process] *Alkalmazott Matematikai Lapok* 29, pp. 67–100.

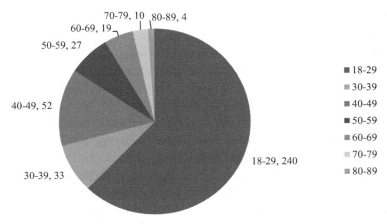

FIGURE 10.1 Age of respondents

secretary, city council officer, etc.) (124 Rs); retired (32 Rs), and unemployed (12 Rs).

The majority of the respondents had as their highest degree secondary or vocational school diploma (66.4%); Bachelor's diploma (17.6%); Master's diploma (8.8%); have finished primary school (6.2%), or completed PhD training (1.0%).

4   Findings and Discussion

4.1   *Perceptions of Chinese Held by Hungarians*
The analysis of the answers shows that Hungarian respondents' perceptions of Chinese are quite stereotypical. After comparing the results with those reported in the literature on the issue under discussion, the author discovered that stereotypes held by Hungarians are quite similar to those held by US-Americans (see above in the section on *Theoretical underpinnings*). Ruble and Zhang,[36] while studying stereotypes of Chinese international students held by Americans, found out that the most-widespread stereotypes are influenced by (portrayed in) the media. Most probably, the situation is the same in Hungary, because when asked *'Where have you met or seen Chinese people?'*, Hungarian respondents' most frequent answer was "in TV and films" (68.13%, 263 Rs, see Table 10.1).

---

36   Ruble, Zhang, op. cit.

Hungarian respondents mentioned the following characteristics of Chinese people: (1) as being positive: intelligent (23.78%); hard-working (22.75%); kind, nice, lovely people (20.22%); friendly (12.64%); polite, well-educated, good manners (8.43%); respectful (7.3%); mathematical (2.8%); (2) as being neutral: reserved, distance-keeping, introverted (7.02%); shy (4.49%); and (3) as being negative: talkative, loud (12.08%); annoying (2.8%); pushy (1.12%); narrow-minded (0.56%); nerdy (0.56%); sly (0.28%), etc. If we compare these answers to the stereotypes on Asian Americans reported in Ho and Jackson,[37] who conducted a study involving nearly 900 non-Asian American university students, we will see quite a significant overlap (1) of positive characteristics: ambitious, hard-working, intelligent, mathematical, family-oriented, obedient, self-disciplined, serious, and traditional, etc.; (2) neutral characteristics: quiet, and reserved, etc.; and (3) negative characteristics: cold, deceitful, narrow-minded, nerdy, pushy, selfish, and sly, etc.

Quite a high number of Hungarian respondents listed such traits as short height (20.79%), facial features and hair/eyes/skin colouring (21.63%). Some Hungarian respondents associate Chinese people with Chinese food (14.77%), martial arts and Jackie Chan (3.37%), Chinese medicine (1.39%), and The Great Wall (1.12%), or, even have erroneous associations, with some typical artifacts of Japanese culture (sushi, anime, naruto, etc.).

When expressing their overall opinion about Chinese people, some Hungarian (14.77%) respondents used words like:
– *strange*, e.g. habits, traditions, language, culture, people, eyes, food;
– *different*, e.g. culture, education, world-view;
– *interesting*, e.g. lifestyle, people, culture, cuisine;
– *special*, e.g. language, culture, food;
– *unique*, e.g. traditions, language, way of thinking, etc.
The above-mentioned examples show that these respondents view Chinese as being different, i.e. 'other' than them. And, only 1.81% of respondents perceive Chinese as similar to them.

After completing the content analysis of the features/personality traits/ characteristics which the respondents listed when expressing their opinions about Chinese people, the author could define the following most salient categories in which the answers can be classified, namely:
1.   attitudes/capability to work (e.g. hard-working, disciplined, decent workers, diligent, fast, skilful, precise, punctual, bossy, lazy, etc.);

---

37   Ho, C., and Jackson, J. W. (2001) Attitudes toward Asian Americans: Theory and measurement. *Journal of Applied Social Psychology* 31(8), pp. 1553–1581.

2.   behaviour & communication (e.g. annoying, loud, friendly/unfriendly, distance keeping, unsocial, etc.);

3.   intelligence (e.g. intelligent, smart, mathematical, oafish, silly, bad at learning foreign languages, etc.);

4.   personality traits (e.g. reserved, persistent, respectful, shy, sly, stubborn, etc.);

5.   trade & commerce (e.g. "are good traders", "sell poor quality products", "make fake, cheap things", greedy, etc.);

6.   ethnic features (e.g. short, dark hair, almond-shaped eyes, etc.);

7.   associated with food;

8.   associated with a large and overpopulated country, artefacts of Chinese culture, the Great Wall;

9.   associated with martial arts;

10. associated with technology;

11. erroneous associations with things from other Asian cultures (karate, sushi, etc.);

12. refusing to provide an opinion by saying: "Can't really say anything about them. I don't have any close Chinese person", "I don't know any of them", "I don't know them well enough to form an opinion", etc.

Out of these twelve categories Hungarian respondents more frequently mentioned Chinese people behaviour and their way to communicate (297 Rs); attitude/capability to work (119 Rs); personality traits (132 Rs); ethnic features (119 Rs); intelligence (103 Rs); and less often associated Chinese people with a large, overpopulated country and its culture (71 Rs); food (57 Rs); trade/commerce (44 Rs); technology (19 Rs); and, martial arts (13 Rs).

Meanwhile, 88.1% of Hungarian respondents reported that they have little or no experience of interacting with Chinese people and 66.8% of Hungarian respondents confessed that it is difficult for them to distinguish between Chinese people and other Asians. 6.74% (26Rs) refused to answer the question *'What is your overall opinion of Chinese?'*, saying that they do not want to write anything since they have very little knowledge and experience with regard to Chinese people.

The following findings strengthen the concern that most probably, Hungarians hold so-called second-hand stereotypes about Chinese, which are imposed by the media and most probably by US-American films[38]:

---

38   Hungarian films typically do not have Chinese characters, so when respondents said "films", these are most probably films produced in the USA that are typically shown on Hungarian TV.

- 43.5% of respondents reported that they have NO interaction with Chinese, and 44.6% – have LITTLE interaction with Chinese. Only 8% of respondents interact with Chinese several times a week, and 3.9% every day.
- 97.2% do not speak the Chinese language, and 27.2% do not speak English, which considerably limits the opportunity to communicate with Chinese people in Hungary.
- Only 15.5% have Chinese colleagues or classmates.
- Only 14.8% have friends or relatives among Chinese.

The Pearson Chi-Square test (khi2(1)=4,305, SIG=0,038) showed that there is a relationship between the positive perception of Chinese personality traits and giving a positive answer to the question *'Would you marry someone who is Chinese?'*, which sounds very logical. On the contrary, among those who gave a negative answer to the same question the proportion of respondents who associated Chinese with ethnic features such as eye-shape or short height was significantly higher, which is quite thought-provoking.

Also, the Pearson Chi-Square test (khi2(1)=4,591, SIG=0,032) showed that there is a relationship between perceiving positively "behaviour & communication" of Chinese and the fact that Hungarians have experience of "meaningful" interaction with Chinese (e.g. work or study together, or are friends/acquaintances/relatives). Among those who do not have such experience, only 60 Rs (out of 192) mention words which positively assess behaviour of Chinese people, and among those who have such experience the number grew to 81 (out of 194). Similar results were observed in case of associating positive personality traits to Chinese: the Pearson Chi-Sqare test (khi2(1)=6,441, SIG=0,011) showed that those who have regular and "meaningful" interactions with Chinese significantly more often hold positive perceptions of Chinese personality traits 59 Rs (out of 194 Rs), in comparison to those who do not have such contact – 37 Rs (out of 192 Rs). Interestingly, in cases when the interaction is of everyday character or frequent, the number of Hungarians perceiving negatively Chinese people's attitudes/capability to work, is significantly higher than in the case of those who have little or no experience of Chinese: the Pearson Chi-Square test (khi2(1)=10,344, SIG=0,016) showed that negative perception is held by

- 3 out of 43 who have an everyday or frequent interaction with Chinese,
- 5 out 335 who have little or no contact with Chinese.

The behaviour and communication of Chinese people are perceived in a significantly more positive way by those who have everyday contact with them. According to the results of the Pearson Chi-Square test (khi2(1)=10,529, SIG=0,015), 6 Rs out of 15 have a positive perception of the way in which

Chinese behave and communicate in comparison to 47 Rs out of 168 of those who have no interaction with Chinese.

To the overall question '*How do you feel about Chinese people?*', 29.8% gave a positive answer, 61.4% were neutral, and 8.8% negative.

4.2   *Interactions between Hungarians and Chinese in Hungary*
Quite a large proportion of Hungarian respondents (88.1%) reported that they have little or no experience with Chinese people. When analysing the answers to the '*How much experience do you have of Chinese people?*' question, the author discovered that less than 10% (34 out of 386) of respondents have "meaningful" interaction or close contact with Chinese every day or at least several times a week. The rest have either little or no interaction with Chinese people, or contacts which are typically limited to shopping in Chinese stores or eating in Chinese fast food restaurants, or to observing Chinese people without interacting with them. Based on the Pearson Chi-Square test ($khi2(3)=27,041$, $SIG=0,000$), there is a significant relationship between the two variables – "having experience of Chinese people" and "interacting in a meaningful way", which confirms the validity of answers to open-ended questions.

To the question '*Where have you met or seen Chinese people?*', as mentioned above, the most frequent answer was "on TV and films" (68.13%, 263 Rs), followed by "in Chinese shops" (67.88%, 262 Rs), "in the town where I live" (55.44%, 214 Rs); "in Chinese restaurants" (53.37%, 206 Rs), "as tourists in Hungary" (51.55%, 199 Rs), etc. (see Table 10.1).

As can be observed from the data (see Table 10.1), the contact between the two cultural groups is quite limited; therefore, it is not surprising that the (perceived) sociocultural distance seems to be quite significant between Hungarians and Chinese. Only 60.6% (234 Rs) mentioned that they would like to have friends or speaking acquaintances among Chinese people, and only 22.5% (87 Rs) said they would marry someone who is Chinese (see Bogardus[39] about social distance).

Those who have experience of frequent and "meaningful" interactions with Chinese people are considerably more likely to give a positive answer to the question '*Would you have Chinese people as regular friends or as speaking acquaintances?*' (see Table 10.2).

A similar tendency can be observed in the case of responses to the question '*Would you marry someone who is Chinese?*' (see Table 10.3).

---

39   Bogardus, op. cit.

TABLE 10.1 The most typical situations/places where Hungarian respondents meet or see Chinese

Situations/places where Hungarian respondents meet or see Chinese people	N of respondents (out of 386)	% of respondents
see in TV and films	263	68.13%
meet in Chinese shops	262	67.88%
see in the town where the respondent lives	214	55.44%
meet in Chinese restaurants	206	53.37%
see as tourists in Hungary	199	51.55%
meet at the university	164	42.49%
see while travelling abroad	143	37.05%
meet at respondents' workplace	64	16.38%
meet in China	12	3.11%
Other	2	0.52%

TABLE 10.2 Relationship between having regular meaningful interactions with Chinese people and openness to having Chinese people as regular friends or as speaking acquaintances (Pearson Chi-Square test: khi2(3)=10,287; SIG=0,001)

			Would you have Chinese people as regular friends or as speaking acquaintances?		Total
			NO	YES	
Do you have regular meaningful contact with Chinese people?	NO	Count	91	101	192
		Expected Count	75,6	116,4	192,0
		Standardized Residual	1,8	-1,4	
	YES	Count	61	133	194
		Expected Count	76,4	117,6	194,0
		Standardized Residual	-1,8	1,4	
Total		Count	152	234	386
		Expected Count	152,0	234,0	386,0

TABLE 10.3 Relationship between having regular meaningful interactions with Chinese people and openness to marry someone who is Chinese (Pearson Chi-Square test: khi2(3)=5,106, SIG=0,024)

			Would you marry someone who is Chinese?		Total
			NO	YES	
Do you have regular meaningful contact with Chinese people?	NO	Count	158	34	192
		Expected Count	148,7	43,3	192,0
		Standardized Residual	,8	-1,4	
	YES	Count	141	53	194
		Expected Count	150,3	43,7	194,0
		Standardized Residual	-,8	1,4	
Total		Count	152	299	87
		Expected Count	152,0	299,0	87,0

According to the data collected from the respondents, a clear tendency can be observed that those who have more experience of communicating with Chinese people are more open to having them as both friends or spouses (see Tables 10.4 and 10.5).

The idea of Bogardus[40] about measuring social distance, as mentioned earlier, can be criticized. However, the analysis of the answers to *'Would you marry someone who is Chinese?'* and *'Would you have Chinese people as regular friends or as speaking acquaintances?'*, helps to diagnose at least the perceived socio-cultural distance among Hungarians and Chinese. And, we can see, that such (perceived) distance exists.

4.3 Hungarians' Opinion about the Growing Number of Chinese International Students in Hungary

Altogether, 69.2% of respondents answered that they have met Chinese international students in their towns. 83.7% stated that their opinion about Chinese

---

40 Bogardus, op. cit.

TABLE 10.4 Relationship between experience of communicating with Chinese and openness to having a Chinese friend or acquaintance (Pearson Chi-Square test: khi2(3)=21,594, SIG=0,000)

		Would you have Chinese people as regular friends or as speaking acquaintances?		Total
		NO	YES	
How much experience do you have with Chinese people?	I have no interaction with Chinese			
	Count	86	82	168
	Expected Count	66,2	101,8	168,0
	Standardized Residual	2,4	-2,0	
	I have little interaction with Chinese			
	Count	58	114	172
	Expected Count	67,7	104,3	172,0
	Standardized Residual	-1,2	1,0	
	I interact with Chinese at least several times a week			
	Count	6	25	31
	Expected Count	12,2	18,8	31,0
	Standardized Residual	-1,8	1,4	
	I interact with Chinese every day			
	Count	2	13	15
	Expected Count	5,9	9,1	15,0
	Standardized Residual	-1,6	1,3	
Total				
	Count	152	234	386
	Expected Count	152,0	234,0	386,0

TABLE 10.5   Relationship between experience of communicating with Chinese and openness to marrying someone who is Chinese (Pearson Chi-Square test: khi2(3)=13,078, SIG=0,000)

			Would you marry someone who is Chinese?		Total
			NO	YES	
How much experience do you have with Chinese people?	I have no interaction with Chinese	Count	142	26	168
		Expected Count	130,1	37,9	168,0
		Standardized Residual	1,0	-1,9	
	I have little interaction with Chinese	Count	129	43	172
		Expected Count	133,2	38,8	172,0
		Standardized Residual	-,4	,7	
	I interact with Chinese at least several times a week	Count	18	13	31
		Expected Count	24,0	7,0	31,0
		Standardized Residual	-1,2	2,3	
	I interact with Chinese every day	Count	10	5	15
		Expected Count	11,6	3,4	15,0
		Standardized Residual	-,5	,9	
Total		Count	299	87	386
		Expected Count	299,0	87,0	386,0

international students is the same as about Chinese people in general; 15.0% thought more positively about students, and 1.3% – more negatively. And, the comparison of the answers to the following two questions *'Is an increase in Chinese immigrants good for Hungary?'* and *'Is an increase in Chinese international students good for Hungary?'* also confirmed that the attitude of the wider Hungarian public towards Chinese international students is more positive than towards Chinese immigrants in general (see Figure 2). To the question *'Is an increase in Chinese immigrants good for Hungary?',* 9.3% answered "yes", 21.0% – "probably yes", 42.2% – "don't know/uncertain", 15.5% – "probably no", and 11.9% – "no", and to the question *'Is an increase in Chinese international students good for Hungary?',* 12.2% answered "yes", 35.8% – "probably yes", 40.2% – "don't know/uncertain", 5.7% – "probably no", and 6.2% – "no" (see Figure 10.2).

The analysis of Hungarians' perceptions of, and interactions with, Chinese and their opinion about the increasing number of Chinese international students in Hungary, showed that there is a relationship between having "meaningful" and frequent interactions with Chinese and having positive perceptions of them. Even more, those Hungarian respondents who have frequent contact seem to be more open and more willing to have Chinese as friends or relatives. Of course, this small-scale survey does not provide a basis for making any further conclusions, but the results of the analysis helped to diagnose that there is little interaction between Hungarians and Chinese and the perceptions of Hungarians of Chinese people are quite stereotyped.

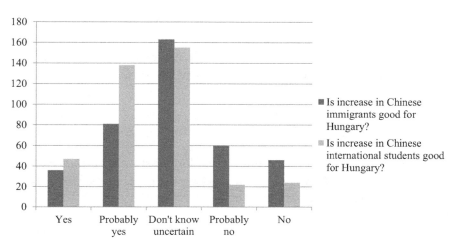

FIGURE 10.2 Comparison of Hungarian respondents' attitudes towards Chinese immigrants and Chinese international students

The author views the development of educational exchange as an instrument to enhance intercultural communication in the Chinese-Hungarian context and improve Hungarians' perceptions of Chinese people in general.

5   Conclusion: Further Research Plans

The study reported in this chapter has certain limitations. First of all, it is a small-scale study, therefore the data collected during this survey cannot and should not (!) be generalised as "the Hungarians' opinion about the Chinese". Another limitation is the method itself used for collecting the data, because surveys always contain a certain degree of mistake: survey respondents may try to provide a "better picture" about themselves or simply tick any random answer if they get tired of a lengthy questionnaire. To increase the validity, the author included in her survey open-ended questions as well.

Although the author managed to find answers to the research questions, and this study sheds light on Hungarians' perceptions of, and interaction with, Chinese people and their opinion about the growing number of Chinese international students in Hungary, new questions arise, and further research into the subject is needed.

The study was conducted to identify some possible problematic areas of Chinese-Hungarian communication. In the context of strengthening cooperation between China and Central and Eastern European countries, the topic itself deserves a closer investigation to fill a gap in intercultural research. However, answering the above-mentioned research questions is not the final goal of the author's work on this topic. The next step will be to identify the critical areas of Chinese-Hungarian communication in a higher education context,[41] and explore the potential of educational exchange in improving the perceptions of Chinese held by Hungarians, and vice versa.

Acknowledgements

I would like to express my gratitude to my former students of *Intercultural Communication* and *Intercultural Studies* classes at the University of Miskolc (Hungary) who helped to gather the data.

---

41   Golubeva, I. Exploring the motivations and intercultural experiences of Chinese international students who study in Hungary. (in progress).

Bibliography

Allport, G. W. (1954) *The nature of prejudice*. Reading, MA: Addison-Wesley.

Basit, T. N. (2010) *Conducting Research in Educational Contexts*. London: Continuum International Publishing Group.

Bogardus, E. S. (1933) A social distance scale. *Sociology and Social Research* 17, pp. 265–271.

Brown, R., and Hewstone, M. (2005) An integrative theory of intergroup contact. *Advances in Experimental Social Psychology* 37, pp. 255–343.

Campbell, J., and Li, M. (2008) Asian students' voices: An empirical study of Asian students' learning experiences at a New Zealand university. *Journal of Studies in International Education* 12(4), pp. 375–396.

Cohen, L., Manion, L., and Morrison, K. (2007) *Research Methods in Education*. London; New York: Routledge.

Comfort, J., and Franklin, P. (2008) *The Mindful International Manager: Competences for Working Effectively Across Cultures*. York: York Associates.

De Vaus, D. (2002) *Surveys in Social Research*. London: Routledge.

European Commission against Racism and Intolerance (2015) *ECRI Report on Hungary*. Strasbourg: Council of Europe.

Gareis, E. (2012) Intercultural friendship: Effects of home and host region. *Journal of International and Intercultural Communication* 5, pp. 309–328.

Golubeva, I. (2003) Interkulturális kompetencia – túl a sztereotípiákon. In: E. Kiss, ed., *Interdiszciplináris pedagógia és a tudás társadalma. II. Kiss Árpád Emlékkonferencia előadásai 2001*, Debrecen: Debreceni Egyetem Neveléstudományi Tanszék, pp. 209–218.

Golubeva, I. (2017) Intercultural Communication for International Mobility. In: D.K. Deardorff, and L. A. Arasarathnam-Smith, eds., *Intercultural Competence in International Higher Education*, New York: Routledge, Taylor and Francis, pp. 186–191.

Golubeva, I. Exploring the motivations and intercultural experiences of Chinese international students who study in Hungary. (in progress).

Gu, Q. (2011). An emotional journey of change: The case of Chinese students in UK higher education. In L. Jin, and M. Cortazzi, eds., *Researching Chinese learners – Skills, perceptions and intercultural adaptations*, Basingstoke, Hampshire: Palgrave Macmillan, pp. 212–232.

Gu, Q., and Maley, A. (2008) Changing places: A study of Chinese students in the UK. *Language and Intercultural Communication* 8(4), pp. 224–245.

Hall, E. T. (1976) *Beyond culture*. New York: Doubleday.

Heng, T.T. (2017) Voices of Chinese international students in USA colleges: 'I want to tell them that …', *Studies in Higher Education* 42(5), pp. 833–850.

Hiu, L. (2001) Chinese cultural schema of education: implications for communication between Chinese students and Australian educators. Issues in Educational Research 15(1), 17–36.

Ho, C., and Jackson, J. W. (2001) Attitudes toward Asian Americans: Theory and measurement. *Journal of Applied Social Psychology* 31(8), pp. 1553–1581.

Holmes, P. (2004) Negotiating differences in learning and intercultural communication: Ethnic Chinese students in a New Zealand university. *Business Communication Quarterly* 67(3), pp. 294–307.

Holmes, P. (2005) Teachers' perceptions of and Interactions with international students: A qualitative analysis. *Interactions with International Students: Report Prepared for Education New Zealand*, pp. 86–120.

Holmes, P. (2007) Ethnic Chinese students' communication with cultural others in a New Zealand university. *Communication Education* 54(4), pp. 289–311.

Hong, T.M., Pieke, F.N., Steehouder, L., and van Veldhuizen, J.L. (2017) *Dutch higher education and Chinese students in the Netherlands: External Research report.* Leiden: Leiden Asia Centre.

Kassing, J. W. (1997) Development of the intercultural willingness to communicate scale. *Communication Research Reports* 14, pp. 399–403.

Kounalakis, E. (2015) Hungary's Xenophobic Response. *New York Times.* September 7.

Imamura, M., and Zhang, Y. B. (2014) Functions of the common ingroup identity model and acculturation strategies in intercultural communication: American host nationals' communication with Chinese international students. *International Journal of Intercultural Relations* 43, pp. 227–238.

Lihong, W., and Byram, M. (2011) "But when You Are Doing Your Exams It Is the Same as in China" – Chinese Students Adjusting to Western Approaches to Teaching and Learning. *Cambridge Journal of Education* 41(4), pp. 407–424.

Liu, S., Volcic, Z., and Gallois, C. (2015) *Introducing Intercultural Communication: Global Cultures and Contexts.* London: SAGE.

McMillan, J. H., and Schumacher, S. (1997) *Research in Education: A Conceptual Introduction.* New York: Longman.

Nesdale, D., and Mak, A. S. (2003) Ethnic identification, self-esteem and immigrant psychological health. *International Journal of Intercultural Relations* 27, pp. 23–40.

Operio, D., and Fiske, S.T. (2003) Stereotypes: Content, structures processes and context. In: R. Brown, and S. Gaertner, eds., *Blackwell handbook of social psychology: Intergroup processes*, Blackwell, Malden, MA, pp. 22–44.

Pan, J.Y. (2015) Predictors of post-migration growth for Chinese international students in Australia. *International Journal of Intercultural Relations* 47, pp. 69–77.

Pettigrew, T. F. (1998) Intergroup contact theory. *Annual Review of Psychology* 49, pp. 65–85.

Ruble, R. A., and Zhang, Y. B. (2013) Stereotypes of Chinese international students held by Americans. *International Journal of Intercultural Relations* 37, pp. 202–211.

Spencer-Oatey, H. (2008) Face, (im)politeness and rapport. In H. Spencer-Oatey (ed.) *Culturally Speaking: Culture, Communication and Politeness Theory*, 2 edn, pp. 11–47. London: Continuum.

Takács, Sz. (2012) Érzékenységvizsgálatok a statisztikai eljárásokban [Sensitivity analysis in a statistical process] *Alkalmazott Matematikai Lapok* 29, pp. 67–100.

Wilson, N., and McClean, S. (1994) *Questionnaire Design: A Practical Introduction.* Newtown Abbey: University of Ulster Press.

World Policy. (2015) *Hungary's Blame Game About Xenophobia.* Available from: http://www.worldpolicy.org/blog/2015/08/20/hungarys-blame-game-about-xenophobia.

Yan, K., and Berliner, D. C. (2009) Chinese international students' academic stressors in the United States. *College Student Journal* 43(4), pp. 939–960.

Yang, L. H. (2016) Resources through which Chinese students learn about Western society and culture. *Journal of Research in International Education* 15(1), pp. 67–78.

Yang, M. (2007) Why mainland China's students study in Australian higher education. In: I. Morley, ed., *The Value of Knowledge: At the Interface.* Papers presented at the 1st Global Conference on the Value of Knowledge, February, Sydney, Australia.

Yao, L. (2004) The Chinese overseas students: an overview of the flows change. Paper presented at the Australian National University 12th Biennial Conference of the Australian Population Association, September, Canberra.

Zhang, J., and Goodson, P. (2011) Acculturation and psychosocial adjustment of Chinese international students: Examining mediation and moderation effects. *International Journal of Intercultural Relations* 35, pp. 139–162.

Zhang, Z., and Brunton, M. (2007) Differences in living and learning: Chinese international students in New Zealand. *Journal of Studies in International Education* 11(2), pp. 124–140.

Zhou, Y., and Todman, J. (2008) Chinese postgraduate students in the UK: A two-way reciprocal adaptation. *Journal of International and Intercultural Communication* 1(3), pp. 221–243.

CHAPTER 11

China – A View from Romania beyond Perceptions and Stereotypes

Mariana Nicolae

1 Introduction

China has been a rising force in today's world for some time now which, to many people, is no longer news. However, the way people and various entities tend to react to this fact is another discussion depending on various issues among which, level of education and personal or group interests, are just some.

In exploring the popular stereotypes and/or clichés about China, we may be surprised by the paradox that surrounds perceptions of a country that is presumably marching towards world hegemony or leadership. This fast pace of progress is taking place despite and against cheap or counterfeited Chinese products; of the existence of a still significant, even if generally unacknowledged layer of poor, almost-illiterate and obedient workers; of the already abandoned (in 2015) one-child-policy; of a communist country which is still very much looking inward in spite of its discourses of openness and internationalization; and which is blocking Western social media and continues to be suspicious of its international visitors.

In an attempt to discuss China's paradoxical presence in today's world, a Chinese student who lived and studied both in China and the US tries to articulate why China is so 'uncool' even though it has all the ingredients to be a much appreciated and even loved country. Gao[1] explains that China's music, films and fashion are relatively unpopular internationally, at least in comparison with those of the US. And he says that "being cool" is an important aspect of what Joseph Nye[2] called "soft power" through which Nye explained the popularity and, therefore, support of large parts of the world's population for the US policies and positions during the Cold War, compared to the Soviet Union. Gao considers that this soft power deficiency is a valid and important question to ask as China is now in a situation in which its political model is

---

1 Gao, G. (2017). Why China is so ... uncool.
2 Nye Jr., J. S. (2005). Soft Power: The Means to Success In World Politics.

not appreciated in Europe or the US while its economic model, of command and control, is admired by most of the developing world. And he concludes, that one way to become cool, and consequently to increase its soft power, is for China to allow its people to be creative without the fear of censorship or the obligation to conform to government agendas. Gao underlines that "China needs to rethink some of its soft power strategies and political values, and in the process rebrand itself – if not for its image abroad, then for its own people at home". His main argument for this is that the world's most numerous middle class and population of billionaires live in China and, thus, Chinese consumers should be the world's new trendsetters. And he concludes that, in spite of these quantitative advantages, current Chinese tastes in entertainment and fashion generally come from outside the country.

Things are never as simple as Gao attempts to explain in his article (see my Bibliography) – especially in relation to China and its position in today's world. And the world today will itself further undergo tremendous and, some scholars[3] fear even fatal transformations if humans do not find the strength to shift direction. We are therefore looking at a very complex picture made even more complicated by the incredible fabric of powerful group and individual interests. It is the strong belief of the author of this study that part of the problem is the level of education or rather the degrees of knowledge that most people acquire from various sources which have become less and less reliable nowadays in the age of "fake news" or "post-truth". This study then, attempts to explore, from a Romanian perspective, the evolution of current popular perceptions on China and to offer some explanations for the way those perceptions have evolved.

2   A Brief Overview of the Relations between China and Romania

Modern day relations between Romania and China have their regular ups and downs depending on the position of the observer, but they are characterized by continuity and resilience. Besides the legendary author Milescu Spătarul[4] – certainly the most popular source of reference for Romanians – the first documented official contacts between Romania and Imperial China took place in

---

3   Harari, Y. N. (2014); Rees, M. (2003).
4   https://www.historia.ro/sectiune/portret/articol/spatarul-milescu-erudit-de-meserie-diplomat-de-cariera. Milescu Spătarul (1636–1708), a Moldavian scholar and diplomat. Between 1675–1678 he travelled to China as the ambassador of the Russian Empire to Beijing.

the period of King Charles I, and Emperor Guang Xu, through an exchange of state letters.[5]

In 2004, Xu Jiang,[6] China's then ambassador to Romania, gave a speech at one of the Romanian universities to mark the 55 years of uninterrupted relations between Romania and China and briefly reviewed those relations by acknowledging their special characteristics. Starting from the fact that Romania had been the third country in the world to recognize the People's Republic of China on October 5, 1949, Xu Jiang went on to argue that the relations between the two countries could be considered a model in international relations, which is a line of argumentation that is constantly used to describe Romanian-Chinese relations. The first argument he introduces is the continuation of these relations in spite of the tremendous changes that the world, and particularly central and eastern Europe, have gone through. He refers to the 1960s, when relations with the Soviet Union were tense and Romania was among the very few countries in the region to stand by China; then to the 1970s with the Cultural Revolution; and the 1980s when, in spite of the huge changes after the fall of the Berlin Wall, Romania continued its relations with China, even if at a much lower level. He points out, as a second argument, the instances of economic aid, caring and human understanding between the two countries and the help given in moments of sadness and suffering such as the Romanian exports of equipment and technology, including oil and trucks, to China which contributed to her economic development.

During July 2017, this author had a very revealing discussion from this point of view with the former director of the Confucius Institute in Sibiu, Romania. The director underlined Romania's level of economic development in the 1970s and pointed out the huge pace of development China had gone through while Romania had been dramatically altering her social, political and, mainly, economic situation. As in many other cases, this is a story that we often hear about Romanian exports to China or to former Soviet Union republics which are markets Romania lost for various reasons. This story is part of a common narrative and part of the public memory of people in the respective regions as well as in Romania, though to a lesser degree. At present, however, the reverse is happening and Romania is importing massively from China.

Continuing his line of argument, Xu Jiang remembers the 1995 earthquake in Yunnan to which the then Romanian government, in spite of its own enormous financial problems, contributed substantial material aid. The same happened

---

5   Tomozei, D. (2016), p. 40.
6   Xu, J. (2004).

in 2008 after the devastating earthquake in Wenchuan about which ambassador Liu Zengwen gives powerful and moving hands on information.[7] In 2004, the Romanian Prime Minister at that time, offered to go to China to express support during the SARS outbreak while many other heads of state and government avoided visiting China during the same period. Romania has always supported China's quest for reunification whilst China helped Romania in 1968 when Romania's independence was under threat, or after the 1970 floods. High level visits, as well as grassroots exchanges, have continued between China and Romania though, for various reasons, they have been rather neglected by mainstream media or, if covered, they have been assigned an ideological criticism – particularly as regards political contacts. By 2005, over 200 treaties and agreements had been signed between the two countries.

And yet the level of Chinese investments in Romania has fallen. From a preferred economic partner, Romania has become an insensitive, and therefore, an uninteresting one. In terms of FDIs, the level of investment grew in Romania from 2003 to 2015, as shown in Table 11.1 but compared to the rest of the region, the actual levels are amongst the lowest.

A former Romanian ambassador to Beijing, Doru Costea, underlined in an interview[8] that one of the main challenges for most Romanian diplomats stationed in China is to accept the complexity and diversity of the present Chinese society. Speaking, or rather not speaking, Mandarin might be a challenge, but not as important as the stereotypes, clichés and prejudices which might raise barriers and "Great Walls" in communication and lead to a tendency to simplify reality which would be detrimental to working together. And Chinese reality is seen by Costea as the result of many processes and century-long evolutions in a space comparable to that of the whole European continent.

One of the relatively few books about China published in the last decade in Romania is Tomozei's "The State in the 21st Century. The Chinese Model" (see my Bibliography for Romanian title). The author is very much aware of the challenging ideas that he communicates to a Romanian public who, to a large extent, are assailed by a mass media relaying mainstream Western topics and ideas, mainly in black and white terms (democracy vs. communism, allies vs. enemies), without offering an alternative view at the same time. He gives the example of Mao Zedong, an exceptional public speaker, poet and scholar of China's imperial history and culture, and a political leader who is too simplistically depicted abroad (mainly as a cruel dictator). Tomozei is convinced by

---

7   Liu, Z., (2009).
8   Daradan, B., (2015).

TABLE 11.1   China's outward FDI stock in Central and Eastern European countries (unit: 10000 USD)

Country	2003	2004	2005	2006	2007	2008	2009	2010	2011	2012	2013
Albania	--	--	50	51	51	51	435	443	443	443	703
Bosnia and Herzegovina	146	401	351	351	351	351	592	598	601	607	613
Macedonia	--	--	20	20	20	20	20	20	20	26	209
Serbia	--	--	--	--	200	200	268	484	505	647	1854
Montenegro	--	--	--	--	32	32	32	32	32	32	32
Croatia	--	--	75	75	784	784	810	813	818	863	831
Bulgaria	60	146	299	474	474	474	231	1860	7256	12674	14985
Poland	272	287	1239	8718	9893	10993	10030	14031	20126	20811	25704
Czech Republic	33	111	138	1467	1964	3243	4934	52333	668	20245	20468
Estonia	--	--	126	126	126	126	750	750	750	350	350
Latvia	161	161	161	231	57	57	54	54	54	54	54
Lithuania	--	--	393	393	393	393	393	393	393	697	1248
Romania	2975	3110	3943	6563	7288	8566	9334	12495	12583	16109	14513
Slovakia	10	10	10	10	510	510	936	982	2578	8601	8277
Slovenia	--	--	12	140	140	140	500	500	500	500	500
Hungary	543	542	281	5365	7817	8875	9741	46570	47535	50741	53235

SOURCE: MINISTRY OF COMMERCE OF THE PEOPLE'S REPUBLIC OF CHINA, NATIONAL BUREAU OF STATISTICS OF CHINA, 2013 STATISTICAL BULLETIN OF CHINA'S OUTWARD FDI (APUD HTTP://COUNCILFOREUROPEANSTUDIES.ORG/CRITCOM/161-FRAMEWORK-AND-ECONOMIC-RELATIONS-BETWEEN-CHINA-AND-CEEC/).

China's present and long-term success which have become the Chinese Dream. He explains that part of this success is objectively analysing social, cultural, political phenomena and errors, both national and international, and trying to look for opportunities, to build, evolve and adapt everything to the Chinese model and specificity. The important point being that China does not apply anything without analysis, modelling and adaptation to its own culture and history.

An interesting article[9] appeared in the Italian journal of geopolitics, *Limes*, aimed at analysing the Three Seas Initiative – the Baltic, Adriatic and Black Sea – or the Trimarium, from the perspective of its synergies with China's Belt and Road Initiative and the 16+1 cooperation between China and Central and Eastern European countries. It is one of the relatively few articles covering the subject from a Romanian perspective, though the author of this chapter is aware of the existence of an increasing interest in the subject and therefore of the possibility for more research and concrete developments such as the academic contacts that have led to the publication of the present book.

3   Perceptions of China by Romanian Students of International Business

The author of this article conducted a simple, general survey on a sample of convenience made up of 121 students of international business and applied modern languages in the Faculty of International Business and Economics in the Bucharest University of Economic Studies, in order to identify how they perceive China and what they actually know about the country and its culture. The survey was given in Romanian to Romanian students and in English to international students (15 students). It was applied face-to-face, on paper, and the students were instructed not to attempt to find their answers on the internet or to discuss among themselves. This is an important point and explains in part the lack of answers to certain questions. The English version of the questionnaire is presented in Annex 1.

The author is very much aware of the limitations of this brief study both in terms of content and of the size and selection of the sample. However, considering that the respondents are students of one of the most prestigious business universities in Romania, it is relatively safe to assume that, beyond obvious

---

9   Mureşan, L., Georgescu, A., (2017).

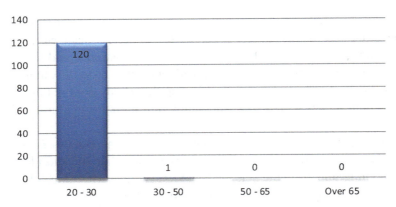

FIGURE 11.1 Respondents by age

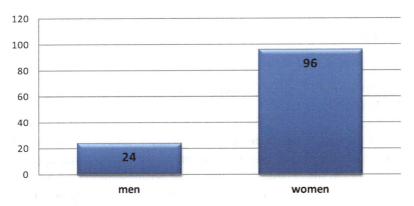

FIGURE 11.2 Respondents by gender

individual differences, a majority of educated young people in Romania might have similar perceptions of the subject.

From a demographic point of view, the respondents were 97 women and 24 men between 20 and 30 years old, 106 in Bachelor study programmes and 15 in Master programmes. Out of the total, 1 is an employer, 1 a freelancer, 30 are employed and 115 consider themselves as simply students. The characteristics of the respondents can be visualised in the figures below.

I will briefly comment upon the results of the answers given to this survey. In terms of popular knowledge of China, and answering questions 1 and 2 where they were asked to write the first five things/ideas/concepts that they thought of when referring to China and to give examples of Chinese fields/products/services that they were very familiar with, the answers are in Table 11.2.

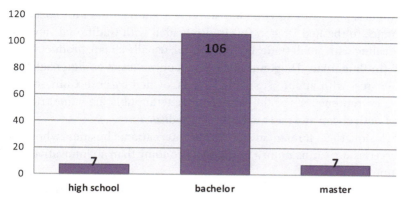

FIGURE 11.3 Respondents by level of education

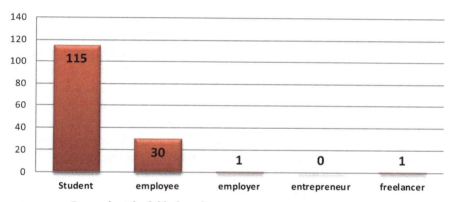

FIGURE 11.4 Respondents by field of employment

Quite expectedly, most of the things evoked by the reference to China in the mind of Romanian students are related to technology (52), but only 6 answers to innovation and creativity, though they usually go together. In my view, this is linked, in general, to the widespread stereotypes in Romania, often reinforced by tabloids, social media and TV, about a traditional Chinese society, strongly controlled ideologically (15 respondents chose communism/ideology as trigger words), poor and uneducated people manufacturing only traditional or fake products in dire conditions. That this is the case is shown by the 29 references to textiles/garments, the 27 references to various types of Chinese food and 12 references to Traditional Chinese medicine. There are very few references to innovative and creative Chinese industries or companies, which is curious given that the respondents are students of international business and economics: 2 for Ali Express; 1 for New Silk Road Belt and 1 for Foxconn. The reference to the Red Dragon (12) is also loaded with traditional views of a China dealing with small trade and traditional, usually cheap, products. Red Dragon[10] (in Romanian "Dragonul Roșu") is a controversial commercial centre in Bucharest with about 5,500 small shops, owned by both Chinese and Romanian entrepreneurs. For the Romanian general public its name triggers notions of both cheap and bad quality merchandise.

In conclusion, then, Romanian students of international business who took this survey consider China more a traditional economy than an innovative and creative one.

From the 121 respondents only 81 answered the questions referring to Chinese personalities and/or celebrities, giving examples of well-known people from various fields in politics, business and cinema, etc. This means that only about 67% of the respondents remembered or knew the names of a few Chinese personalities. However, only 6 mentioned Confucius, with one even saying "the famous philosopher", and 2 mentioned Sun Tzu. The rest of the answers are given in Table 11.3. Romanian students of international business know more film actors (Jackie Chan, Bruce Lee, Jet Li) – 50 occurrences, than political leaders (Mao Zedong, Xi Jinping, Hu Jintao) – only 23 occurrences, or historical or cultural figures (such as Confucius or Sun Tzu), with only 8 occurrences. It is important to bear in mind that the respondents were not allowed to access the internet during this survey. As an educator, the author of the present chapter cannot help briefly noting here the way popular culture and the internet influence the types of knowledge of our students and their mechanisms of transfer from one area to another.

In answer to question 5, about the existence or not of typical Chinese values, 96 respondents said they thought Chinese values existed, while 18 said they did not think there were specific Chinese values. However, when asked to give examples of Chinese values, only 55 answers were given and they mostly describe a traditional society with respect for family and traditions, with a strong work discipline and ethic as well as a strong respect for hierarchy and authority.

The values mentioned by the respondents are presented in Table 11.4. Even if some of the concepts may not usually be described as 'values' (such as feng-shui or financial equality), they are still presented in Table 11.4 as indicated by the respondents, although some allowances have to be made for their translation into English.

---

10   https://www.dragonulrosu.ro/

In terms of material culture, explored through question 6 which refers to the use of any Chinese products, the overall majority of the respondents answered that they use or have used a Chinese product. Only seven respondents say they have never used one. Most of the products used are phones/technology, clothing/textiles, cosmetics, toys, stationery, household goods and food or food ingredients such as spices.

None of the respondents have visited China so far, but 92 expressed their wish to do so as compared with 24 who do not intend to visit in the future. As regards their availability to do business with Chinese business people, 65 answered they would like to, 20 were against the idea, while 8 answered maybe and the rest (28) did not answer this question.

As a general description of China, almost half of the respondents 58 (47.9%) consider it to be a communist state; 28 think of it as a developing country; 45 (37.1 %) consider it a developed country; 23 say it has a market economy; 20 say it has a centralized economy; while 29 consider China's economy to be mixed.

TABLE 11.2   Most popular Chinese things/topics that Romanian students know about

Chinese things/ideas/concepts	Number of occurrences
Huawei/phones/technology	52
Textiles/garments	29
Chinese food/rice/sushi/Shanghai chicken/tea	27
Population/cheap labour force/export	18
Communism/ideologies	15
Red Dragon	12
Traditional Chinese Balm/medicine	12
Great Wall	9
Fake handbags/brands	8
Innovation/creativity	6
Jackie Chan	3
Pollution	3
Ali Express, Alibaba	2
Beautiful women	2
New Silk Road Belt	1
Foxconn	1

As regards the type of society China is, 11 respondents describe it as a civilization; 8 as a nation state; and 6 as a pluralist society.

Such a diversity of views reflects several things, one being that it is clearly difficult to label China at present. For students of international business this also reflects, to a certain extent, the general state of knowledge on China in one of the best Romanian business universities. It may also reflect a lack of individual understanding of the respective concepts or personal disinterest in the topic.

Only 30 respondents answered the question about the Confucius Institute: 21 said it was the cultural institute of China with the mission to promote Chinese language and culture; 6 people did not know what it was, but had heard of it; 1 said it was a research centre; 1 a non-profit institute; and 1 a university. The fact remains that out of the sample surveyed only approximately 17.3 % knew about the Confucius Institute. At the same time, although 86 respondents considered Chinese a useful language to learn in the future, only 34 said they knew several words, such as greetings or 'thank you' in Chinese. And yet, for

TABLE 11.3   Romanian students and their most well-known personalities/celebrities in China

Name of personalities	Number of occurrences
Jackie Chan	35
Mao Zedong	13
Bruce Lee	12
Xi Jinping	9
Confucius	6
Jack Ma/CEO Alibaba	5
Jet Li	3
Sun Tzu	2
Li Na	2
Yao Ming	2
Dalai Lama	1
Lucy Liu	1
Cixi	1
Wu Zetian	1
Hu Jintao	1
Patrick Chan	1
Ding Junhui	1

those interested in Chinese language and culture, the Department of Modern Languages and Business Communication of the Faculty of International Business and Economics in the university offers Chinese courses taught by a native instructor.

The following statements have been used in order to identify whether students of international business have a genuine interest in finding out more about China beyond the general discourse offered in the mainstream Romanian media and whether their economics and business education underlines specific knowledge not readily available to the general public or offers a framework for discussion about business and economic realities as studied in their specialized disciplines such as History of World Economy, International Finance, Economic Geography of the World, etc.[11] The statements have been designed based on both media reports or articles and specialized literature on the subject and were answered as shown in Table 11.5.

TABLE 11.4   Specific Chinese values as perceived by Romanian business students

Values	Number of occurrences
Respect for tradition/elderly	8
Family	8
Discipline, seriousness and self-control	6
Honesty and correctness	6
Respect for culture	5
Food	5
Feng-shui	3
Punctuality and politeness	3
Hierarchy and respect for authority	2
Collectivism	1
Common sense	1
Financial equality	1
Meditation	1
Modesty	1
Patience	1
Patriotism	1
Perseverance	1
Taoism/Buddhism	1

---

11   http://planinvatamant.ase.ro/SelectiePlan.aspx?pp=16

On the one hand, the answers show that there is a genuine interest at personal level in one of the most dynamic economies in the world, backed by the alluring temptation of low prices and the constantly increasing and improving quality-price ratio of most goods, particularly technological, as seen from the answers in Tables 11.2 and 11.3. On the other hand, students in business have a pragmatic attitude. Even if the answers to question 7 of the survey ('Choose 2 of the following phrases that best describe your opinion about China') reflect a large diversity of views on China, from almost half of the respondents (47.9%) who considered China a communist state, which in present day Romania is viewed almost as anathema, and 37.1 % who considered it a developed country. The position of the respondents is that from practical and business points of view, ideology should not matter. The responses to Q 14.1 – see Questionnaire in Annex – ('China has been and is a danger to Europe/Romania and, therefore, it is best to keep economic relations with it to a minimum') are clear: 92 disagree and 16 are indifferent to the statement which means an almost unanimous answer in favour of business relations with China. This is reinforced by the answers to Q 14.3 ('In the relations with China ideology is, obviously, an influencing factor, but it should not influence Romania's economic pragmatism.') to which 67 respondents agree and 41 are indifferent, leaving only 8 to disagree. Also, Q 14.8 about Chinese individuals replicating at individual level the "arrogance" of China's power and communism and being themselves, as some media clichés show, "arrogant, aggressive, taking advantage of any kind of situation" was answered by disagreement by 81 respondents. Only 13 agreed with the statement and 21 were indifferent, which is in line with the answers to Q 14.3. This attitude of individual pragmatism of Romanian students exists among the respondents to this survey in spite of a strong ideological discourse in Romania against communism and anything connected with it, induced and maintained by a massively pro-western media.[12]

Such a diversity of views may reflect, in the author's opinion, several things, but again, one is clearly the difficulty of labelling China at present. For students of international business this also reflects, to a certain extent, the general interest in, and state of knowledge of, China, in those attending one of the best business universities in Romania. It may also reflect a lack of individual understanding of the respective concepts or simply personal disinterest in the topic.

As already stated, the limitations of this small-scale survey of Romanian business and economics students are obvious in terms of size and, therefore,

---

12   Fota, (2017).

possibility of generalization. However, from a qualitative point of view, this sample may be relevant in comparative terms for the discussions of China in groups with similar demographics across Romania. Why? Because the Bucharest University of Economic Studies is one of the most prestigious, and certainly largest, business and economic universities in Romania, with advanced research interests. According to the 2018 QS World University Rankings, the university has the best employer reputation in Romania, which means that its graduates are considered so well-prepared that 81.35% of them found employment within 3 months upon finishing their studies in 2017. Also, at regional level, ASE is one of the top 2.6% universities in Eastern Europe according to the same QS World University Rankings 2018, maintaining its position among the top 301–350 universities in the field of Economics and Econometrics. The data is available on the university website[13] and raises the following question: if the interest and knowledge concerning China of the university's students are so superficial and circumstantial, what happens with the larger public in the same age and education category as the surveyed respondents?

4   Conclusions

This study has looked at how the rise of China in today's world is perceived in Romania by a selected group of people, namely, students of international business and economics attending one of the most important universities in the country. We have explored certain issues from a very complex picture of the world today with its complicated fabric of powerful group and individual interests. The study has attempted to explore, from a Romanian perspective, the evolution of current popular perceptions of China and to offer some explanations for the way those perceptions have progressed by looking at the evolution of the relations between China and Romania.

There is still an important capital of goodwill and empathy at various levels in China towards Romania that could be capitalized upon even more for the mutual benefit of the peoples of both countries.

More official and significant political support, as well as administrative encouragement to further develop business relations with China, are needed far beyond the lip service Romanian government authorities pay to these relations.

---

13   https:/ www.ase.ro/index_en.asp

TABLE 11.5   Respondents' answers requiring more in-depth knowledge on China

Statement	Total disagreement/ disagreement	Total agreement/ agreement	Indifferent
China has been and is a danger to Europe/Romania and, therefore, it is best to keep economic relations with it to a minimum.	35 + 57=92	10	16
China's imperial or communist ideology has been and continues to be influenced by the desire for domination – it therefore poses a threat to Europe/Romania or any other state in the world.	16 + 51=67	19	30
In the relations with China ideology is, obviously, an influencing factor, but it should not influence Romania's economic pragmatism.	1 + 7=8	7 + 60=67	41
China is a huge consumer market with relatively low quality standards. Romania needs to take advantage of that fact and businesspeople need to focus on this area.	8 + 22=30	11 + 49=60	26
The Romanian state does not encourage economic relations with China, but Romanian businesspeople know their economic priorities and invest in the relationship with the Chinese.	4 + 12=16	4 + 47=51	47
China is the symbol of communism, but the Chinese, as individuals, are generally very hardworking people, respectful, good employees and colleagues.	2 + 5=7	27 + 57=84	24

TABLE 11.5   Respondents' answers requiring more in-depth knowledge on China (*cont.*)

Statement	Total disagreement/ disagreement	Total agreement/ agreement	Indifferent
China is aware of its imperial heritage and its present statute, and acts as any great power – widening its sphere of influence, without any sentimentality towards its partners or opponents.	2 + 11=13	9 + 55=64	38
China is the symbol of arrogant power and of communism, and the Chinese, as individuals, are generally a miniature image of China – arrogant, aggressive, taking advantage of any kind of situation.	27 + 54=81	1 + 12=13	21
China has managed to bring more people out of poverty than any other country in the world.	24 + 4=28	3 + 23=26	60
China is the second largest country in the world generating foreign direct investments (FDI) and the first beneficiary country of this type of investment (FDI).	0 + 7=7	10 + 58=68	38

The level of individual appeal of Chinese culture and civilization is increasing in Romania as part of the efforts of Chinese agencies, including the Confucius Institute, and of some Romanian entrepreneurial individuals and institutions. However, it is important that cultural and academic contacts continue to be strengthened in order to educate the stakeholders in such a process, from students and academics to the general public, the media and relevant decision makers.

Bibliography

Buzatu, I. (2009). Istoria Chinei şi a civilizaţiei chineze (album). România şi China [History of China and Chinese Civilization (album). Romania and China]. Bucharest: URANUS Publishing House.

Buzatu, I. (2009). Viaţa şi gândirea lui Confucius [The Life and Thinking of Confucius]. Bucharest: Meteor Publishing.

Câmpeanu, V., and Pencea, S. (2012). CHINA -Un elefant care nu mai poate fi ignorant [An Elephant Which can no Longer be Ignored]. Bucharest: Universitară Publishing House.

China (2012). Beijing: Foreign Language Press.

Christensen, T. J. (2016). China ca o provocare: cum pot fi modelate alegerile unei puteri în ascensiune [The China Challenge: Shaping the Choices of a Rising Power]. Romania:comunicare.ro.

Daradan, B. (2015). INTERVIU – DORU COSTEA, ambasadorul României în Republica Populară Chineză [Interview – Doru Costea, Romania's ambassador in the People's Republic of China].

Eno, R. (2015). The Analects of Confucius. An Online Teaching Translation.

Ferguson, N. (2011). Civilization: The West and the Rest. London: Penguin Books.

Fota, I. (2017). Restauraţia anti-occidentală. Marea bătălie pentru viitorul României [The Anti-Western Restauration. The Great Battle for Romania's Future].

Frankopan, P. (2016). The Silk Roads: a New History of the World. London: Bloomsbury Publishing.

Gao, G. (2017). Why China is so ... uncool. Foreign Policy (March, 8).

Harari, Y. N. (2014). Sapiens: A Brief History of Humankind. New York: Penguin, Random House.

Jacques, M. (2012). When China Rules the World: The End of the Western World and the Birth of a New Global Order. 2nd ed. London: Penguin Books.

Liu, Z. (2009). Reflecţii la 60 de ani de relaţii sino-române [Reflections on 60 years of Sino-Romanian Relations], http://www.chinaembassy.org.ro/rom/xw/t622125.htm.

Mureşan, L., and Georgescu, A. (2017). A Romanian Perspective on the Three Seas Initiative. *Limes*, la rivista italiana di geopolitica, pp. 231–239.

My Thirty Years in China, 1978–2008 True Life Stories of a Changing China (2008). West Sussex: ACA Publishing Limited.

Nye Jr., J. S. (2005). Soft Power: The Means To Success In World Politics. New York: Public Affairs.

Rees, M. (2003). Our Final Century: Will Civilisation Survive the Twenty-First Century? UK: Arrow Books.

Seligman, D. S. (1999). Chinese Business Ettiquette: A Guide to Protocol, Manners, and Culture in the People's Republic of China. US: Warner Business Books.

The Analects (2015). Beijing: Foreign Language Teaching and Research Press.

Tomozei, D. (2012). Descoperind China-Beijing.

Tomozei, D. (2016). Statul în secolul XXI – Modelul chinez [The State in the 21st century. The Chinese Model]. Romania: Corint Books.

Wasserstrom, J. N. (2010). China in the 21st Century: What Everyone Needs to Know. Oxford: Oxford University Press.

Xu J. (2004). 55 de ani de relaţii româno-chineze constante [55 Years of Constant Romanian-Chinese Relations], http://www.scipio.ro/documents/173004/188173/04.+Xu+Jiang%2C+55+de+ani+de+relatii+romano-chineze+constante.

Xu W. (2015). Cartea Cântecelor [The Book of Songs].

Annex

Questionnaire

The following questionnaire is part of a research project on how China is perceived in Romania. In this context, we are conducting a study on the values and attitudes that Romanians have towards the Chinese and China/People's Republic of China. We invite you to participate in this study by writing down your answers or ticking the boxes corresponding to your chosen answer.

We ensure the anonymity of your personal information and the confidentiality of the provided answers, which are necessary exclusively for the statistical processing of the information submitted.

Thank you for your availability.

A. Personal Information
Age

20–30   30–50   50–65   Over 65

Gender

male   female

Education

High-school   Post-secondary Bachelor Master Ph.D. Postdoctoral
              education   Studies

Field of activity

Student Employee Employer/ Entrepreneur Freelancer other
                   owner   Retired   (specify)

Environment in which you live/work

Romania: urban   rural   **Other country:** urban   rural

B.

1. Write the first 5 things/ideas/concepts that you think about when refer-
    ring to China:
    ....
    ....
    ....

2. Give examples of Chinese fields/products/services that you are very familiar with:

   ....

3. What Chinese personalities do you know in the political, economic and/ or cultural field?

   ....

4. What Chinese personalities do you know in other areas than those already mentioned?

   ....

5. Do you think that there are typical Chinese values?
   Yes ☐ No ☐
   Which? ....

6. Do you use/have used any Chinese products?
   Yes ☐ No ☐
   Which? ....

7. Choose 2 of the following phrases that best describe your opinion about China:

   communist country ☐ developing country ☐ developed country☐
   market economy ☐ centralized economy ☐ mixed economy☐
   pluralist society ☐ state-civilization ☐ nation-state☐

8. Have you ever visited China? Yes ☐ No☐

9. Do you wish to visit it in the future? Yes ☐ No☐

10. If you had the opportunity would you do business with Chinese businesspeople?

11. What is the Confucius Institute?

    ....

12. Do you know any useful Chinese words (thanks, greetings, etc.)? Yes ☐ No☐

13. Do you think it is useful to learn the language? Yes ☐ No☐

14. Please tick one of the answers to the statements in the table below:

In my opinion:	strongly disagree	disagree	indifferent	agree	strongly agree
	1	2	3	4	5

14.1. China has been and is a danger to Europe/Romania and, therefore, it is best to keep economic relations with it to a minimum.

14.2. China's imperial or communist ideology has been and continues to be influenced by the desire for domination – it therefore poses a threat to Europe/ Romania or any other state in the world.

14.3. In the relations with China ideology is, obviously, an influencing factor, but it should not influence Romania's economic pragmatism.

14.4. China is a huge consumer market with relatively low quality standards. Romania needs to take advantage of that fact and businesspeople need to focus on this area.

In my opinion:	strongly disagree	disagree	indifferent	agree	strongly agree
	1	2	3	4	5

14.5. The Romanian state does not encourage economic relations with China, but Romanian businesspeople know their economic priorities and invest in the relationship with the Chinese.

14.6. China is the symbol of communism, but the Chinese, as individuals, are generally very hardworking people, respectful, good employees and colleagues.

14.7 China is aware of its imperial heritage and its present statute, and acts as any great power – widening its sphere of influence, without any sentimentality towards its partners or opponents.

In my opinion:	strongly disagree	disagree	indifferent	agree	strongly agree
	1	2	3	4	5
14.8 China is the symbol of arrogant power and of communism, and the Chinese, as individuals, are generally a miniature image of China – arrogant, aggressive, taking advantage of any kind of situation.					
14.9 China has managed to bring more people out of poverty than any other country in the world.					
14.10 China is the second largest country in the world generating foreign direct investments (FDI) and the first beneficiary country of this type investments (FDI).					

Thank you for your time!

CHAPTER 12

China's Public Diplomacy versus Mainstream Media's Narrative

A Challenge in Image and Reputation Management

Greg Simons

1   Introduction

China is a rapidly rising global economic, political and military power. This rise has been assisted in part through a global information and communication programme that supports the strategic policy goals of the government. The manner in which China communicates its global message has undergone rapid transformation in terms of form and content.[1] Internet and social media based communication has also undergone significant reconsideration and use as a means that renders the 'old' geopolitical constraints of space and time as a less effective barrier of the official message.[2] Entman[3] speaks of the role and significance of mass media communication as a means to relay foreign policy directions and goals. However, this present article understands that the official voice of public diplomacy is not the sole voice and needs to compete with other, often contradictory or opposing messages by other actors.

This article seeks to address the issue of the national image and reputation of a country as communicated through a foreign national media system. News and mass media content is the source of information and knowledge that provides the public with remote access to places and events that they do not experience personally, which in turn can shape public opinions and perceptions

---

1 Yang, A., Klyueva, A. & Taylor, M. (2012), Beyond a Dyadic Approach to Public Diplomacy: Understanding Relationships in Multipolar World, Public Relations Review, 38, pp. 652–664; Chang, T-K. & Lin, F. (2014), From Propaganda to Public Diplomacy: Assessing China's International Practice and Image, 1950–2009, Public Relations Review, 40, pp. 450–458.

2 Chang, T-K. & Lin, F. (2014), From Propaganda to Public Diplomacy: Assessing China's International Practice and Image, 1950–2009, Public Relations Review, 40, pp. 450–458; Simons, G. (2015), Taking New Public Diplomacy Online: China and Russia, Journal of Place Branding and Public Diplomacy, 11, pp. 111–124.

3 Entman, R. M. (2004), Projections of Power: Framing News, Public Opinion, and U.S. Foreign Policy, Chicago: The University of Chicago Press.

of the country being covered. The situation of foreign coverage of a country is mostly beyond the ability to control the publication of material. As such, there can be a significant clash between what is being communicated through the official public diplomacy message of a country and what is being communicated via the national media coverage of that same country in a foreign setting.

In particular this article seeks to understand the official Chinese public diplomacy message to global audiences. Then with these message narratives being understood, it will seek to identify and understand whether this message comes through in original or as an interpreted form in the main national Swedish newspapers. Thus, the research question stands as follows, does Swedish media coverage of China confirm or contradict the official public diplomacy message of China?

In order to investigate and give an informed answer to the question posed, the paper shall begin the theoretical and conceptual understanding and definition of public diplomacy. Once this foundation is laid, the paper then moves to understanding and analysing the Chinese approach to public diplomacy. The next issue is how the image of China in Sweden is communicated within the context of the wider world. All of the preceding sections provide the background to the next section that concerns the survey of articles on China that have been appearing in the Swedish newspapers *Dagens Nyheter*, *Dagens Industri*, Svenska *Dagbladet* and *Aftonbladet*. The subjects and narratives are broken down into categories and compared with the official strategic narratives of Chinese public diplomacy.

2   Public Diplomacy and Reputation Management

There is a need to utilise a means for projecting a country's attractiveness internationally. Public diplomacy (PD) is something that has been in existence for a long time in practice,[4] but is still very much in vogue. The term, at times, is used inter-changeably with propaganda or nation branding, which tends to add confusion as to its purpose.[5] Propaganda is the use of emotions to a mass audience in order to achieve a political or economic goal. It does not involve the creation of mutually beneficial relationships through word and deed

---

4   Jowett, G. S. & O'Donnell, V. (2012), Propaganda and Persuasion, 5th edition, Thousand Oaks (CA): Sage, p. 287.

5   Szondi, G. (October 2008), Public Diplomacy and Nation Branding: Conceptual Similarities and Differences, Discussion Papers in Diplomacy: Netherlands Institute of International Relations Clingendael.

between messenger and the target audience. PD is a term that is often uttered, but what does it mean and entail? One possible explanation for its purpose is given below.

> Public diplomacy [...] deals with the influence of public attitudes on the formation and execution of foreign policies. It encompasses dimensions of international relations beyond traditional diplomacy; the cultivation by governments of public opinion in other countries; the interaction of private groups and interests in one country with another; the reporting of foreign affairs and its impact on policy; communication between those whose job is communication, as diplomats and foreign correspondents; and the process of intercultural communications.[6]

The above mentioned quote dovetails with the hierarchy of impacts that public diplomacy can potentially achieve – increasing peoples' familiarity with one's country, increasing peoples' appreciation of one's country, getting people engaged with one's country and influencing people.[7] L'Etang[8] says that this can involve offering a nation's cultural capital to target countries in order to generate goodwill with younger generations. Others, such as Seib,[9] note that "public diplomacy is a process, but it cannot be separated from policy". This has implications for the underlying reasons for engaging in public diplomacy (PD), other than the superficial aspect of making a country more 'likeable'. Common objectives for PD include increasing awareness, managing reputations, changing legislation or altering attitudes.[10]

There are five elements of public diplomacy, which are identified by Nicholas Cull. Listening: collecting the opinions and data from the target audience through listening, rather than speaking to them; advocacy: an active function where the messenger attempts to promote a certain idea or policy that benefits them; cultural diplomacy: making known and promoting a country's cultural resources and accomplishments. In effect, an exporting of culture; exchange diplomacy: to send abroad and to receive people for a period of study

---

6   Jowett & O'Donnell, op cit, p. 287.

7   Leonard, M., Stead, C. & Smewing, C. (2002), Public Diplomacy, London: The Foreign Policy Centre, pp. 9–10.

8   L'Etang, J. (2011), Public Relations: Concepts, Practice and Critique, London: Sage Publishing, p. 241.

9   Seib, P. (2012), Real-Time Diplomacy: Politics and Power in the Social Media Era, New York: Palgrave-MacMillan, p. 122.

10   Coombs, W. T & Holladay, S. J. (2010), PR Strategy and Application: Managing Influence, Singapore: Wiley-Blackwell, p. 299.

and/or acculturation, thereby exporting ideas and ways of doing things; international broadcasting (news): an attempt to manage the international environment through mass media assets, in order to engage the foreign publics.[11] These require an understanding of the various elements in order to create an effective approach.

Seib[12] notes that "public diplomacy is related to media accessibility and influence." The message must be seen and heard in the public information space. However, other considerations also need to be taken into account. There are three elements to public diplomacy – news management, strategic communication and relationship building.[13] This paper's primary focus is on the element of relationship building, which is a product of not only what China communicates about herself, but what other actors communicate about China. Thus, in the current political and global information environment there needs to be a more proactive and continuous form of communication within public diplomacy in order to stand a chance of being able to generate a successful effect.

Nancy Snow distinguishes between what she terms as being *Traditional Public Diplomacy* and *New Public Diplomacy*. The listed features of *Traditional Public Diplomacy* include: Government to Publics (G2P); official in nature; "necessary evil" as technology and new media democratised international relations; linked to foreign policy/national security outcomes; one-way informational and two-way asymmetric (unequal partners in communication); give us your best and brightest future players; passive public role; and crisis driven and reactive.[14]

The *New Public Diplomacy* formula has a number of significant changes over the old non-interactive and reactive model, including Public to Publics communication (P2P); unofficial actors present (NGOs, practitioners and private citizens); "everyone's doing it"; active and participatory public; dialogue and exchange oriented, two-way symmetric; generally more reference to behavioural change; based upon relationship, systems and network theories.[15] The political and information environment in the new model is much more

---

11   Jowett & O'Donnell, op cit, pp. 287–288.

12   Seib, P. (editor) (2009), Towards a New Public Diplomacy: Re-directing U.S. Foreign Policy, New York: Palgrave-MacMillan, p. 112.

13   Leonard, Stead, Smewing, op cit.

14   Snow, N. (2010), Public Diplomacy: New Dimensions and Implications, in McPhail, T. L., Global Communication: Theories, Stakeholders and Trends, 3rd edition, Chichester: Wiley-Blackwell, pp. 84–102, p. 89.

15   Snow op cit., pp. 91–92; Melissen, J. (editor) (2005), The New Public Diplomacy: Soft Power in International Relations, New York: Palgrave-MacMillan, pp. 11–16.

dynamic – and involves a greater range of actors. Developments in information technology and politics has not only enabled, but pushed these changes as the information and political environment has evolved. This enables foreign governments to engage foreign audiences with political marketing within their public diplomacy programmes. How does China conceive and manage its public diplomacy programmes?

3   The Chinese Approach to Public Diplomacy

China is a relatively new entrant in the world of modern public diplomacy,[16] but is very active in developing this tool. D'Hooghe[17] gives an excellent and in-depth account of the foundations and practice of public diplomacy in China. This section seeks to build on the understanding in the narrow context of China's on-line public diplomacy efforts. There is a great deal of importance attached to public diplomacy by the Chinese government, which has sought to integrate and bring about mutual enhancement between government diplomacy and public diplomacy. As China engages increasingly in the international political and economic spheres, it feels the need to use an information strategy that will pave the way for the state to achieve its set of goals and objectives. China's soft power and hard power potential are simultaneously developed. Public diplomacy is seen as the instrumentalisation of soft power, which involves the use of values, cultural influence, social systems and ideologies.[18,19] Qui Yuanping, Deputy Director of the Foreign Affairs Office of the Communist Party of China Central Committee summarised the motivation and the challenge.

> Amid remarkable rise of its national strength, China has leapt to be the second largest country in terms of economic production in the world. China has been watched closely and discussed extensively by the international community. Different countries have different opinions about

16   D'Hooghe, I. (July 2007), The Rise of China's Public Diplomacy, Discussion Papers in Diplomacy (The Hague, Netherlands Institute of International Relations Clingendael).

17   D'Hooghe, I. (October 2014) China's Public Diplomacy, Diplomatic Series volume 10 (Lieden, Brill).

18   Kallio, J. (2012) Watching a Dragon's Egg Hatch: The Makings of a Sinocentric World? Working Paper 74 (Helsinki, The Finnish Institute of International Affairs).

19   Yang Jiechi, China's Public Diplomacy, Qiushi Journal: Organ of the Central Committee of the Communist Party of China, Vol. 3, No. 3, http://english.qstheory.cn/international/201109/t20110924_112601.htm, 1 July 2011 (accessed 3 February 2012).

China. In such an international environment, China should offer to explain its growth pattern, long-term development strategy, and development concepts to soothe concerns aired by the sceptics in the world, better integrate to the world and nourish a good image.[20]

From the above comments, Chinese public diplomacy is geared towards economic goals and objectives, taking care of any political or image problems that may adversely affect economic growth.[21] This requires careful and considered approach in terms of conceptual and practical development of public diplomacy. Research and development is conducted by research institutes that are located within the structures associated with the Foreign Ministry. One of these is the Centre for Public Diplomacy Studies at the Beijing Foreign Studies University, which recently produced the *Report on Chinese Public Diplomacy Research*. A conference was held at this university in September 2011, the Forum on Public Diplomacy and 4th Diplomats Forum, with the theme of challenges and opportunities. The event was divided in to three sessions: 1) government and public diplomacy: innovation of traditional diplomatic policies; 2) culture going global and public diplomacy: dialogue between civilisations and international discourse power; 3) enterprises going global and public diplomacy: brand shaping and national image.[22] These discussions, research and reports tend to demonstrate that thinking is along Snow's concept of *New Public Diplomacy*, although the organisational structure is not yet in place to properly support this concept.

In terms of organisational structure and responsibility, a Public Diplomacy Office has been established under the Information Department of the Ministry for Foreign Affairs. There have been efforts to rectify the problem of coordination and initiatives within and external to the Foreign Ministry. There has also been an Advisory Committee on Public Diplomacy established, this serves the function as a publicity body that provides information on China's conditions, development concepts, and

---

20   Public Diplomacy to Improve China's Image in the World, People's Daily Online, http://english.peopledaily.com.cn/90882/7599052.html, 19 September 2011 (accessed 3 February 2012).

21   Zhang, J. (2008). Making Sense of the Changes in China's Public Diplomacy: Direction of Information Flow and Messages. Place Branding and Public Diplomacy 4(4): 303–316; D'Hooghe, 2007, op. cit.

22   Public Diplomacy to Improve China's Image in the World, People's Daily Online, http://english.peopledaily.com.cn/90882/7599052.html, 19 September 2011 (accessed 3 February 2012).

policies.[23] Such a constellation of the organisational arrangement of public diplomacy in China demonstrates that this is perceived as a foreign policy issue, which involves the use of channels of information in order to gain the desired effect.

China in 2003 began to communicate its "peaceful rise" in the global arena narrative, only to drop it a short time later, fearing that it would upset the global geopolitical status quo where the United States was the sole remaining superpower. As such, the implication was that its source of power was to be from soft power rather than hard power.[24] Three developments or trends can be observed within Chinese soft power and public diplomacy. These are: 1) Chinese soft power is growing as its culture does, the economic-political model also, is becoming more attractive to different parts of the world; 2) a rapid expansion and improvement of Chinese public diplomacy is taking place; 3) the involvement of non-state actors is increasingly taking place.[25] A great deal of importance and faith in the ability of public diplomacy to deliver results is witnessed, which accounts for the great deal of attention and discussion on the issue. These developments and trends in Chinese PD seem to support the idea that the New Public Diplomacy model is being adhered to.

The Chinese public diplomacy programme is rooted in its historical tradition. It is guided by "socialist theories with Chinese characteristics". Those characteristics are the Deng Xiaoping Theory, the Three Represents, Scientific Outlook on Development, and the notions of bringing harmony, lasting peace and prosperity. The tasks and priorities are designated by the Party.[26] Leaders are also considering and developing strategy for public diplomacy in new areas, such as cyberspace. There was a call in mid-2011 to formulate a public diplomacy strategy for cyberspace as a means of proactively creating a national brand. The idea behind this was to utilise China's "Internet users-based reporters" as a means to target Internet communities around the world with the official message through social networking sites in order to change opinions and perceptions. The very large Chinese Internet community could

---

23   Yang Jiechi, *China's Public Diplomacy,* Qiushi Journal: Organ of the Central Committee of the Communist Party of China, Vol. 3, No. 3, http://english.qstheory.cn/international/201109/t20110924_112601.htm, 1 July 2011 (accessed 3 February 2012).

24   Chang, T-K. & Lin, F. (2014), From Propaganda to Public Diplomacy: Assessing China's International Practice and Image, 1950–2009, Public Relations Review, 40, pp. 450–458, p. 450.

25   D'Hooghe, 2007, op. cit., p. 7.

26   Yang Jiechi, China's Public Diplomacy, Qiushi Journal: Organ of the Central Committee of the Communist Party of China, Vol. 3, No. 3, http://english.qstheory.cn/international/201109/t20110924_112601.htm, 1 July 2011 (accessed 3 February 2012).

be a potential means with which to flood cyberspace with the official message. There are also other reasons that motivate this move. This could be a potential avenue to gain information dominance in cyberspace through the sheer number of Chinese Internet users and to attempt to crowd out competing messages from other actors.

> With the Internet gradually overtaking newspapers, more and more people are relying on the Internet as a trusted and timely news source. People tend to spread news among friends, relatives, colleagues and other intimate groups via the Internet. They established close relations before spreading the news, so they tend to find the news more trustworthy than those on traditional media.[27]

A number of points of exploitation are clear in this brief quote. Firstly is the issue of exploiting increasing public distrust of the traditional mass media. Next, means of exploitation is found in the peer to peer dissemination of news, which comes back to the point made earlier that individuals are trusted more than organisations. This would appear to be an attempt at mass media reputation management on a very broad and large scale. The value therefore is not in the raw news per se, but in the relationships that spread the news among individuals and thereby spread the alternative Chinese spin on news and information. The assessment is that publicity through traditional media has become increasingly ineffective and expensive in the era of Internet-based information and communication. Thus the Internet is seen as providing a quick, cheap and influential means of delivering the Chinese government message.

The institutional structure of Chinese PD is very hierarchical and under the responsibility of the Foreign Ministry. In terms of managing messages and directing the work of PD, such an arrangement makes matters easier. However, this is going to be a possible problem in the event of managing a crisis where speed and accuracy of information and communications are paramount to defending the national reputation. A great deal of work has been done on establishing the theoretical and conceptual aspects of PD, with various conferences and events that have included different stakeholders to discuss the issues of development and direction. There is also, unlike Russia, an established and communicated Chinese idea and message for the outside world (whether or not this is believed or resonates is another matter). Chinese attention seems to

---

27   China Needs Public Diplomacy Strategy for Cyberspace, People's Daily Online, http://
     english.peopledaily.com.cn/90001/90780/91342/7396388.html, 31 May 2011 (accessed 3
     February 2012).

be directed at ensuring economic growth and overcoming any obstacles that may impede this goal.

More recently the Chinese approach to public diplomacy includes the aspects of image building and relationship management.[28] The system of international relations, and consequently the practice of public diplomacy communication and competition are getting more complex as the global system of international relations gradually shifts from unipolar form (after the Soviet Union's collapse) to a multipolar world. Media coverage in Chinese party publications characterise China as a responsible nation that actively engages in international affairs, where China positions itself in relation to other global actors, such as the United States and Russia. This is the basis for the creation and maintenance of a relationship between China and foreign publics. Public diplomacy and relationship management is used to position China in a wider context and strategically uses the relationships to accomplish foreign policy goals.[29] China has taken the approach of increasing its footprint in the sphere of international broadcasting and communication in order to try and counter the negative reputation and brand of the country, in order to transform communication and soft power in to strategic political and economic power.[30] This requires careful consideration and approach in terms of managing issues through organisational structures.

One of the current instruments that are used for the realisation of Chinese soft power is the United Front Work Department of the Chinese Communist Party based in Beijing (http://www.zytzb.gov.cn/tzb2010/index.shtml). The organisational structure consists of nine bureaux that relate to different perceived sources of informational threat – 1) the Parties Work Bureau, 2) Minorities and Religious Bureau, 3) Hong Kong, Macau, Taiwan and Overseas Liaison Bureau, 4) Cadre Bureau, 5) Economics Bureau, 6) Non-Party Members, Non-Party Intellectuals Bureau, 7) Tibet Bureau, 8) New Social Classes Work Bureau, and 9) Xinjiang Bureau. Its goal is to win global hearts and minds through what President Xi stresses as the "great rejuvenation of the Chinese people". In the strategic context, its aims and goals are "to win support for China's political

---

28   Yang, A., Klyueva, A. & Taylor, M. (2012), Beyond a Dyadic Approach to Public Diplomacy: Understanding Relationships in Multipolar World, Public Relations Review, 38, pp. 652–664; Rawnsley, G. D. (2015), To Know is to Love Us: Public Diplomacy and International Broadcasting in Contemporary Russia and China, Politics, 35(3–4), pp. 273–286.
29   Yang, Klyueva & Taylor, op cit., p. 662.
30   Rawnsley, op cit., p. 284.

agenda, accumulate influence overseas and to gather key information."[31] There is a certain dilemma in the effectiveness of the work of such institutions owing to the nature of the image of China that is projected in the global information space, which counters and competes with the positive image projected by Chinese public diplomacy.

4   Image of China in Sweden in the Context of the Wider World

From the previous section, Chinese public diplomacy emphasizes China's peaceful global rise and various opportunities of mutually beneficial cooperation between China and other countries. Sweden certainly does see some economic prospects and opportunities with its interaction with China. However, certain ideological threats are also simultaneously perceived that contradict the messaging of Chinese public diplomacy. China's image in Sweden is to an extent determined by the manner in which the global liberal democratic system, of which Sweden is considered a part, characterises the country in the wider geopolitical context.

China is seen simultaneously as being an opportunity and a threat. On the one hand, China's policy of normalising global relations (especially with the United States), its economic reforms and desire for stability in the international order. "Yet this has not stopped U.S. analysts from hand-wringing over whether China will continue to uphold the order's existing institutions and values as its economy and military capabilities continue to grow".[32] In this regard, an economically and militarily weakened China is seen as less of a threat. This is seen further on in the RAND report. "The short answer is that China supports international institutions but contests the Western liberal democratic value system and the U.S. system of military alliances that undergird the *US-led world order*".[33] American analysts argue that there has been a break in Chinese policy since 2012 with President Xi coming to power. In some cases–for example, Australia–countries are being urged to

---

31   Kynge, J. & Anderlini, L., Inside China's Secret 'Magic Weapon' for Worldwide Influence, The Financial Times, https://www.ft.com/content/fb2b3934-b004-11e7-beba -5521c713abf4?segmentId=778a3b31-0eac-c57a-a529-d296f5da8125, 26 October 2017 (accessed 30 October 2017).

32   Mazarr, M. J., Struth Cevallos, A., Priebe, M., Radin, A., Reedy, K., Rothenberg, A. D., Thompson, J. A. & Willcox, J. (2017), Measuring the Health of the Liberal International Order, Santa Monica (CA): RAND Corporation, p. 105.

33   Idid.

join the United States in resisting and countering China's rise in the Indo-Pacific region.[34] There is an element of fearful projection in forecasting China's global role. The Chinese approach of non-interference in the domestic affairs of other countries was seen as something that originated in 1954 when China was much weaker economically and politically, but increasingly China is engaging in a more active global role. "While Beijing remains rhetorically committed to the stance, it is now a very different power, boasting the world's largest standing army and the second biggest economy". In addition, the US$1 trillion in investments in the One Belt, One Road initiative is seen as a potentially menacing spectre of China's increasing global footprint.[35] Different issues carry different perceptions when it comes to the formation and issue of opinion and perception of China's national and foreign policy issues.

Sweden established diplomatic relations with the People's Republic of China in May 1950, which was some six months after the country was founded. The first Western country to sever ties with the Republic of China was Sweden, after the Nationalist government fled to Taiwan. Bilateral relations between the countries for the first decades were very limited, until Deng Xiaoping initiated economic reforms that increased international trade. In 1981, the Swedish royal family and the Prime Minister at the time, Thorbjörn Fälldin visited China, and in return China's Prime Minister at the time Zhao Ziyang made an official visit to Sweden in 1984. By the late 1980s, regular political and trade delegations were visiting China, which was interrupted in 1989.[36] Protests in Beijing in 1989 saw a freezing of diplomatic relations.[37] The 1990s witnessed a period of normalising relations that saw increased exchanges and contacts between Sweden and China. There are also cultural links between Sweden and China involving organisations such as the Nordic Confucius Institute which was active from 2005 to 2015. In 2010, a celebration was held to mark the 60th anniversary of the establishment of diplomatic relations between Sweden and China. The emphasis in the celebration

---

34   Smyth, J., Australia Looks to US to Counter China's Strength, Financial Times, https://www.ft.com/content/0f4d147c-d009-11e7-b781-794ce08b24dc?segmentId=778a3b31-0eac-c57a-a529-d296f5da8125, 23 November 2017 (accessed 24 November 2017).

35   Davis, B., From Myanmar to Zimbabwe, China's Global Footprint Grows, AFP in Space War, http://www.spacewar.com/reports/From_Myanmar_to_Zimbabwe_Chinas_global_footprint_grows_999.html, 24 November 2017 (accessed 27 November 2017).

36   Hellström, J. (2010), The EU Arms Embargo on China: A Swedish Perspective, FOI-R-2946-SE, Stockholm: Swedish Defence Research Agency, pp. 11–12.

37   Ibid., pp. 12–14.

was on the history of trade and culture.[38] An emphasis on people to people
contacts and interactions was stressed, and to be deduced from this was the
history of positive and constructive relations between the Chinese and Swedish
peoples. Hard politics is potentially a more problematic issue to engage in than
the soft issues such as culture, however it should not be neglected in the bigger
picture of building image, reputation and relationships.

When looking through the various governmental reports, debate articles by
government ministers and press releases from the Government Chancellery
Office, a clear number of official viewpoints and priorities emerge with
regards to the official Swedish government perspective of China and the bilateral relationship. These governmental communications tend to form around
three primary clusters of subjects: 1) the development of government to government cooperation and collaboration; 2) the development of business and
investment ties between China and Sweden; and 3) critique of Chinese policy along value and normative lines. A number of communications involved
the attempted projection of a proactive and competent Swedish government
working in partnership with China, therefore aligned with the first cluster of
subjects. This was demonstrated by announcing upcoming meetings and the
aims of those events[39] or cooperation at governmental level on specific concerns as energy[40] or climate.[41] An example of a report in the third category is
*Human Rights, Democracy and the Principles of the Rule of Law in China 2015–
2016.*[42] The 19-page long report takes a very critical tone of the current state of
these issues in China from a perspective of liberal notions of human rights,

38   Chen, X., A Long History of China-Sweden Relationship, People's Daily Online, http://
      en.people.cn/90001/90776/90883/7001796.html, 27 May 2010 (accessed 23 November
      2017).
39   Statsminister   Stefan   Löfven   Besöker   Kina,   Regeringskansliet,   http://www
      .regeringen.se/pressmeddelanden/2017/06/statsminister-stefan-lofven-besoker-kina/
      , 5 June 2017 (accessed 27 November 2017); *Anna Johansson Deltar i Kinesiskt Toppmöte
      om Infrastruktursatsningar*, Regeringskansliet, http://www.regeringen.se/artiklar/2017/
      06/starkta-samarbeten-under-energiministermote-i-kina/, 12 May 2017 (accessed 27
      November 2017).
40   *Stärka Samarbeten Under Energiministermöte i Kina*, Regeringskansliet, http://www
      .regeringen.se/artiklar/2017/06/starkta-samarbeten-under-energiministermote-i-kina/,
      14 June 2017 (accessed 27 November 2017).
41   *Sverige och Kina Ingår Avtal om Klimatsamarbete*, Regeringskansliet, http://www
      .regeringen.se/pressmeddelanden/2015/04/sverige-och-kina-ingar-avtal-om
      -klimatsamarbete/, 8 April 2015 (accessed 27 November 2017).
42   Ministry of Foreign Affairs, Human Rights, Democracy and the Principles of the Rule
      of Law in China 2015–2016, State Chancellery, http://www.regeringen.se/498ee9/
      contentassets/f8f0525faeaf4673affbb62159c57189/kina---manskliga-rattigheter
      -demokrati-och-rattsstatens-principer-2015-2016.pdf, nd (accessed 27 November 2017) It

freedom of expression and the rule of law. The negative and idealistic tone of this particular topic contrasts vividly with communications concerning the second subject cluster. Various reports speak of Chinese investors visiting Sweden,[43] another communication involved the issue of Sweden wanting to help the Chinese become sustainable and to deepen cooperation between sustainable companies in China and Sweden,[44] other communications featured the development[45] and the tightening[46] of business relations between the two countries. Although these were sometimes framed within the ideological sets of value and norm-based principles, the overall tone was positive and upbeat. This also corresponds to one of Sweden's policy interests and priorities, namely the development of trade relations with China.

When it comes to economic matters and especially financial potential, the reporting and observations can seem somewhat contradictory. This is seen with the One Belt, One Road initiative that was launched by President Xi in 2013. The plan envisages China linking with Africa, Asia and Europe through a network of ports, railways, roads and industrial parks. This has been described as being "central to his (Xi's) goal of extending Beijing's economic and geo-political clout".[47] This is in keeping with the threat potential assessment of RAND above. There is the narrative that the One Belt, One Road initiative will bring only lop-sided gains in China's favour at the expense of the partner countries.[48] Other articles are much more positive concerning the One Belt,

---

should be noted that Sweden writes such reports on all countries, and uses Sweden's situation as a base-line for other countries.

43   Chinese Investors Visit Sweden, State Chancellery, http://www.regeringen.se/artiklar/ 2016/09/kinesiska-investerare-pa-besok-i-sverige2, 16 September 2016 (accessed 27 November 2017).

44   Så vill vi göra Kina hållbart, State Chancellery, http://www.regeringen.se/debattartiklar/ 2015/09/debatt-sa-vill-vi-gora-kina-hallbart/, 8 September 2015 (accessed 27 November 2017).

45   Linde, A., *Jag vill Utveckla Samarbetet med Kina Kring Hållbart Företagande för att Förbättra Arbetsvillkor, Bekämpa Miljöförstöring, Motverka Korruption och Stärka Kvinnors Ställning,* State Chancellery, http://www.regeringen.se/debattartiklar/2017/06/jag-vill-utveckla -samarbetet-med-kina-kring-hallbart-foretagande-for-att-forbattra-arbetsvillkor -bekampa-miljoforstoring-motverka-korruption-och-starka-kvinnors-stallning/, 29 June 2017 (accessed 27 November 2017).

46   Johansson, A., *Tätare Samarbete Mellan Sverige och Kina,* State Chancellery, http://www .regeringen.se/artiklar/2016/04/tatare-samarbete-mellan-sverige-och-kina/, 3 October 2014 (accessed 27 November 2017).

47   Reeves, S. & Sagita, D., China's Silk Road Revival Hits the Buffers, AFP in Space War, http://www.spacedaily.com/reports/Chinas_Silk_Road_revival_hits_the_buffers_999 .html, 12 November 2017 (accessed 17 November 2017).

48   Ibid.

One Road initiative, "this ambitious posture of China raises the fundamental question of as to whether it will be United States or China who will ultimately determine the rules of trade and investment".[49] There seems to be a different perception and view in Sweden when it comes to the Belt and Road Initiative.

How exactly is the BRI viewed by Sweden? In order to answer this question adequately, there needs to be some context given to Sweden's trade with China. Firstly, China is Sweden's largest trading partner in Asia and is therefore a priority country with regards to Sweden's export strategy.[50] Therefore, China is seen as an economic opportunity for Sweden. But Sweden's approach has been one that is characterised by the exercise of caution. This may be a result of the highly marginal impact of the initiative on Sweden. Although the plan has received more publicity in Sweden recently, the Swedish Foreign Ministry was unable to identify any parts of the projects associated with it in Sweden.[51] This has in turn created a number of ambiguities and uncertainties for Sweden's potential involvement. The situation is compounded by the lack of any formal agreements between China and Sweden and a lack of national strategy on the One Belt One Road initiative.[52] The current situation means that Sweden's policy makers have adopted a cautious wait and see approach on the issue, whereas the Swedish business community is "cautiously optimistic".[53] From 13–16 May 2017, Anna Johansson the Minister for Infrastructure visited Beijing to participate in the Belt and Road Forum for International Cooperation,[54] which represents an official move to improve communication and understanding of the issue, plus its relevance and potential for Sweden. The impression seems to be that the Swedish political and business communities are waiting for a clear signal from Beijing in order to move from the cautious wait and see position that they have adopted.

---

49   Aftab Ali, Y., *China's Belt and Road Initiative Inspiring Regional Partnerships*, CRSS Blog, https://crssblog.com/2017/11/23/chinas-belt-and-road-initiative-inspiring-regional-partnerships/, 23 November 2017 (accessed 23 November 2017).

50   *Sweden's Export Strategy*, Swedish Government Chancellery, http://www.regeringen.se/contentassets/e2b2f540107143e99907cbe604a87ce2/sveriges-exportstrategi.pdf, September 2015 (accessed 27 November 2017).

51   Weissmann, M. & Rappe, E. (2017), *Sweden's Approach to China's Belt and Road Initiative*, No. 1, UI Paper: Stockholm, p. 5.

52   Ibid., p. 7.

53   Ibid., pp. 8–10.

54   *Anna Johansson Deltar I Kinesiskt Toppmöte om Infrastruktursatsningar*, Regeringskansliet, http://www.regeringen.se/pressmeddelanden/2017/05/anna-johansson-deltar-i-kinesiskt-toppmote-om-infrastruktursatsningar/, 12 May 2017 (accessed 27 November 2017).

For many people with no direct contact with China, mass media is their connection to gain information and knowledge in order to shape opinions and perception. Just how reliable is Western media in relaying an 'accurate' image and impression of China? The answer to this question depends upon to whom you ask this question. Wang Qiu, a member of China's legislature and head of the state-owned broadcaster China National Radio had a clear answer, where he claimed 60% of all Western mainstream media reports "smear" China. This view is reflected and shared among many Chinese that "Western media plays up China's weaknesses, exaggerates its potential as a regional threat, and ignores its successes".[55] Do Swedish mass media follow this pattern or do they have a more nuanced style of reporting on China?

5   China in Swedish Media

5.1   *Method*

This article is the offshoot of a conference that was held at Sun Yat-Sen University in China in December 2017 on the issue of EU countries' relations with China. The author of this study was asked to give an account of the Swedish perspective and a mass media approach was considered as the best way to generate an understanding of the popular perception being generated. Four Swedish national newspapers were selected for a qualitative reviewing of articles on and about China in November 2017. These newspapers were: *Dagens Nyheter, Dagens Industri, Svenska Dagbladet* and *Aftonbladet.* They were selected owing to their national coverage, accessibility of materials via the Internet and differing market positions. *Dagens Nyheter* (www.dn.se) was published in December 1864. The newspaper describes itself as being an "independent liberal" publication. It has a circulation of 793, 100 copies and 1.5 million unique web visitors every week.[56] *Dagens Industri* (www.di.se) was founded in 1976 and is the largest business newspaper in the Nordic region with a circulation of 328, 000 readers per day. It covers Swedish and international business news.[57] The first issue of *Svenska Dagbladet* (www.svd.se) was published in December 1884, the newspaper describes itself as being

55   Allen-Ebrahimian, B., How China Won the War Against Western Media, Foreign Policy, http://foreignpolicy.com/2016/03/04/china-won-war-western-media-censorship -propaganda-communist-party/#, 4 March 2016 (accessed 23 November 2017).

56   *About Us*, Dagens Nyheter, http://info.dn.se/info/om-oss/, nd (accessed 24 November 2017).

57   *Om oss*, Dagens Industri, https://www.di.se/om-oss/om-oss/, nd (accessed 28 November 2017).

editorially "independently conservative". It has the second largest circulation in Sweden with 150, 000 copies per day.[58] The final newspaper to be examined and analysed is *Aftonbaldet* (www.aftonbladet.se) which was founded in 1830 and is editorially left-leaning in its political framing and sense. It has a circulation of approximately 150, 000 copies per day.[59] These particular newspapers were chosen owing to their size, periodicity of publication (all dailies), influence and diversity of stated editorial line. All translations from Swedish to English have been done by the author, unless otherwise stated.

In November-December 2017, the author conducted a search on the websites of *Dagens Nyheter, Dagens Industri, Svenska Dagbladet* and *Aftonbladet*. The key search word used was "Kina" (China) in the search engines of each of these Swedish national newspapers. Only relevant articles from the months of July-November 2017 will be analysed. The results of each of the searches yielded the following tally of articles (as hits from each search):

- Dagens Nyheter – ca. 58, 000;
- Dagens Industri – 33, 749;
- Svenska Dagbladet – 33, 139;
- Aftonbladet – 12, 219.

The resulting searches were manually checked for relevance, such as China being the primary subject of the article, old articles were excluded and the content examined. In order to make sense of patterns and trends, these articles were subjected to interrogation from the perspective of rhetoric and frames. Rhetoric is to be understood as "the art of public speaking with persuasive intention".[60] Within rhetoric, there are three possible types of appeal: *logos* (logic, including false logic), *ethos* (credibility and position of the speaker), and *pathos* (the use of emotions to persuade, either positive or negative).[61] There are two potential meanings with regards to the definition of framing. One is in reference to the manner in which news content is usually shaped and contextualised by journalists within a familiar framework of reference that bestows meaning. The second meaning concerns the process of subjecting an audience

---

58   *SvD in Brief*, Svenska Dagbladet, https://kundservice.svd.se/omsvd/, nd (accessed 24 November 2017).

59   *Media Report for Aftonbladet*, Price Waterhouse Coopers, https://www.pwc.se/sv/media/ assets/pwcs-medieintyg-april-14-aftonbladet.pdf, April 2014 (accessed 24 November 2017).

60   McQuail, D. (2010), McQuail's Mass Communication Theory, 6th Edition, London: Sage, p. 569.

61   Aristotle (translated with an introduction by Lawson-Tancred, H. C.) (1991), The Art of Rhetoric, London: Penguin Books.

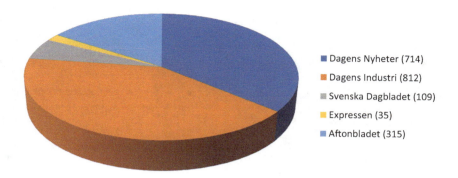

FIGURE 12.1 China in Swedish media

to specific frames of reference in order to prime them and to set the agenda.[62] The first meaning of framing shall be used within the context of this article.

5.2   China Narratives in Swedish Press

After sorting for relevance in terms of the above-mentioned criterion, the following sample sizes were derived: Dagens Nyheter – 714 articles; Dagens Industri – 812 articles; Svenska Dagbladet – 833 articles; and Aftonbladet – 315 articles. These articles covered very broad and diverse themes and subjects from hard topics as politics, economics and security issues to soft topics such as sport and culture. The established categories for the types of information were: 1) world news; 2) economy; 3) editorials and debates; 4) news (taking place in Sweden with a Chinese 'connection'); 5) sport; and 6) culture and science. Figure 12.1 graphically illustrates the relative weight given by the various media outlets to coverage of China.

The first of four Swedish newspapers to be examined and analysed was Dagens Nyheter, which had an article count of 714 in the months of July–November 2017. Please see figure 12.2 for a breakdown of the type of content featured on China. World news tended to be negative in nature when concerning China's engagement in international relations, stressing ties with supporting 'non-democratic' regimes, such as in Syria or even Burma. One article from the November 23rd cast moral judgement: "When the greater part of the world is outraged over the Burmese Army's violence against the Muslim Rohingya [...], China signals the country wishes closer ties with Burma's

---

62   McQuail, op. cit., p. 557.

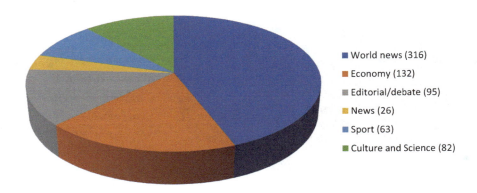

FIGURE 12.2 Dagens Nyheter content[a]
   [a] The search link for Dagens Nyheter: https://www.dn.se/sok/
   ?q=Kina&page=1&sort=newest&date=

military.[63] This confirms the use of a system of idealistic values and norms to criticise Chinese foreign policy, which is often projected in terms of regime support or geopolitical competition or the abuse of human rights. In addition, stories also included news such as accidents (fires, explosions and so forth) or other crises (earthquakes and natural disasters). Logos and pathos are the primary rhetorical means used to influence the audience, where often the logic of threat and the spectre of human rights violations are stressed. The most positive and upbeat type of information content came from the theme of economy, where China's potential as a market for Swedish goods and services, and as a source of foreign investment in Sweden is emphasized. Logos and ethos is the main appeal of the writer in this type of media content, where the logic of financial potential is supported by quotes from experts.

When the total aggregated result is broken down into the individual months of news content reveals different periods of intensity and focus, please see graph 12.1.

The second Swedish media outlet to be examined and analysed was Dagens Industri, which yielded a tally of 812 articles. On the issue of world news, this particular source was much less inclined to make value or norm-based judgements of China's foreign policy and actions. The primary rhetorical

---

63   *Torbjörn Petersson: Storpolitiskt spel när Kina vill närma sig Burma igen,* Dagens Nyheter,
      https://www.dn.se/nyheter/varlden/torbjorn-petersson-storpolitiskt-spel-nar-kina-vill
      -narma-sig-burma-igen/, 23 November 2017 (accessed 28 November 2017).

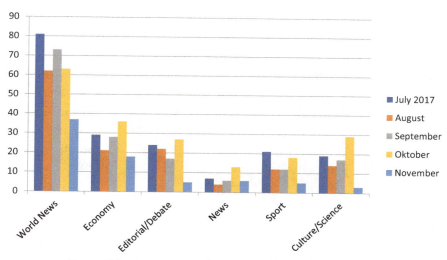

GRAPH 12.1   Dagens Nyheter news content by type – July–November 2017

mechanisms of persuading the audiences were through logos and ethos. As seen in figure 12.3, the bulk of the information content of the media outlet related to issues pertaining to the economy. The monthly tally of information genres is given in graph 12.2. China was variously presented as being both a potential opportunity and a potential threat to the Swedish business community. The opportunity angle related to China as a large consumer market for Swedish goods and services, Chinese investment in the Swedish economy as well as business and research development collaboration between the countries. Economy was by far the most covered category of this newspaper, which is unsurprising given that it is a business daily.

Svenska Dagbladet was the third paper to have its content examined and categorised, there were a total of 833 articles included in the analysis. For a breakdown of the nature of the information that appeared in the given time frame, please see figure 12.4. Graph 12.3 shows the monthly fluctuations in news type content. The articles concerning the world news category were alarmist in nature at times, such as a headline concerning Chinese investments in Eastern Europe – "Chinese offensive in Eastern Europe", which gives a militaristic and threatening overtone.[64] There were a wide range of topics in this category from climate change politics to disasters and crises

---

64   TT, Kinesisk offensiv i Östeuropa, Svenska Dagbladet, https://www.svd.se/kinesisk -offensiv-i-osteuropa, 27 November 2017 (accessed 28 November 2017).

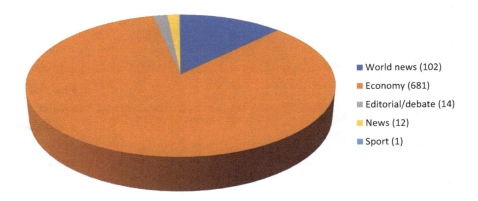

FIGURE 12.3 Dagens Industri content[a]

    [a] The search link for Dagens Industri: https://www.di.se/search?ArticlePage
=1&ArticleSort= RELEVANCE&Query= Kina&ArticlePageSize=
10&FilterArticle=ArticleOnly

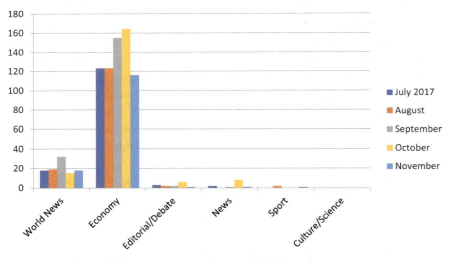

GRAPH 12.2 Dagens Industri news content by type – July–November 2017

to China's involvement in events taking place in Burma and Zimbabwe. In addition to the alarmist articles, others tended to focus on negative news and geopolitics. An article within the editorial/debate category used highly emotionally charged and value-norm loaded words in order to persuade its

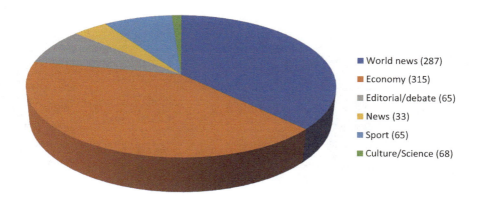

FIGURE 12.4 Svenska Dagbladet content[a]
    [a] The search link for Svenska Dagbladet: https://www.svd.se/
    sok?q=Kina&sortering=datum-fallande

readers – "Gunnar Hökmark: Environmental literature relativizes human hell."[65] Articles that fell under the category of economy tended to be more positive and optimistic in nature, tending to identify economic developments and opportunities. This is in line with the Swedish government's policy directions and priorities. However, there were occasionally alarmist pieces appearing too, such as a quote from an American security adviser that stated Sweden was threatened by China's desire to dominate the global economy.[66] Such content is in line with views being expressed from the US-led Western world that support the continued hegemony of the global liberal political system.

The final newspaper that was examined was Aftonbladet, which yielded a sample of some 315 articles in total. Please see figure 12.5 for the specifics of the nature of Aftonbladet's coverage of China for the months of July-November 2017. When the total aggregated result is broken down into the individual months of news content reveals different periods of intensity and focus, please see graph four below. Qualitatively, the information does not differ greatly from the nature and tone of the previous media outlets' content.

---

65   Hökmark, G., *Gunnar Hökmark: Miljödiktatur relativiserar det mänskliga helvetet*, Svenska Dagbladet, https://www.svd.se/miljodiktatur-relativiserar-det-manskliga-helvetet, 18 November 2017 (accessed 28 November 2017).

66   Törnwall, M., *Säkerhetsrådgivare i USA: Sverige hotas av Kina*, Svenska Dagbladet, https://www.svd.se/sakerhetsradgivare-sverige-hotas-av-ryssland-och-kina, 16 November 2017 (accessed 28 November 2017).

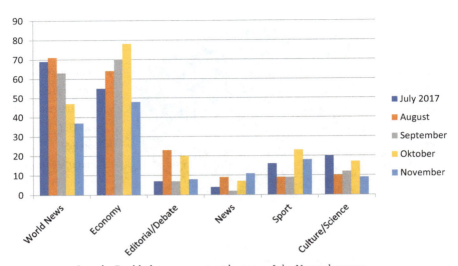

GRAPH 12.3   Svenska Dagbladet news content by type – July–November 2017

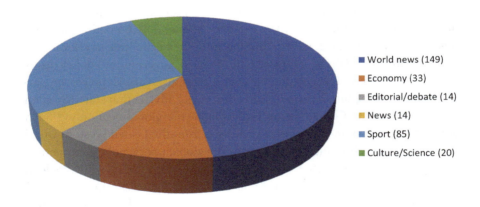

FIGURE 12.5 Aftonbladet content[a]
        [a] The search link for Aftonbladet: https://sok.aftonbladet.se/?q=Kina&&start=0

Although there is an overwhelming focus on world news, and the economy news is generally negative in nature, which diverges from the official government line and the editorial line of the other four named media outlets.

All of the newspapers observed covered the XIX Congress of the Chinese Communist Party in October 2017. Interestingly, they took a common approach to reporting on it. This was that it was a grab for power by President Xi, who

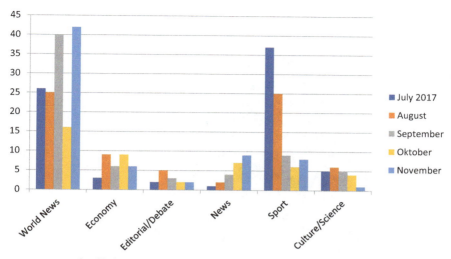

GRAPH 12.4   Aftonbladet News Content by type – July–November 2017

became framed as being a "new Mao". In terms of the interaction and inter-play between Swedish Government policy goals and interests, Swedish mass media reporting and Chinese public diplomacy, there are some clearly observ-able points. Please see figure 12.6 for a graphical representation of the relation-ships between these actors. An important first observation and statement is that measure of activity does not automatically translate to measure of effect, which needs to be clearly understood by those actors engaged in public diplo-macy. Actions as exemplified in words and deeds of public diplomacy will have a positive effect (and maybe the intended one) so long as the promised rela-tionship has a positive outcome for all parties, not only in terms of pragmatic considerations (such as economic cooperation), but also ideologically speak-ing (as shown in the geopolitical dimensions of the perceived Chinese 'threat' to the hegemony of liberal democracy). The influences, effects, reactions and counter-actions are a two-way and not a one-way process. Mass media seem-ingly take their cue from the Government's policy priorities, and echo those in their coverage. Sometimes this coincides with Chinese public diplomacy, but at other times it is in opposition to it.

6   Conclusion

The total sample of articles drawn from the four Swedish national daily news-papers amounted to 386 selected from the massive pool. In spite of the diverse

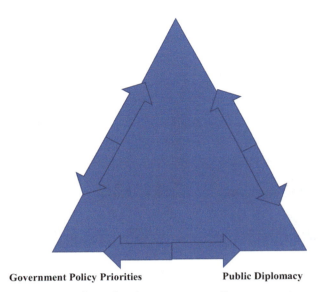

Government Policy Priorities   **Public Diplomacy**

FIGURE 12.6 Relationships between mass media, government
           policy priorities and PD mass media

nature of the market positioning of the media outlets analysed, and the diversity of the information types, there were some clear patterns and trends that were observed. The following question was posed in the introduction of this paper, does Swedish media coverage of China confirm or contradict the official public diplomacy message of China? In order to answer this question clearly and consistently, it is necessary to recap the official Swedish government position on different issues concerning relations with the People's Republic of China. Although, initially there should first be a brief recap of China's public diplomacy messages to the world, which are intended to set the tone for the intended resulting relationships between China and global publics.

The official Chinese message of communicated public diplomacy is clear. Namely that China is an ancient civilisation, which hundreds of years ago used to be a world power, and now is currently returning to the position of a significant global actor in an increasingly multipolar world. What was initially expressed as a peaceful rise is now characterised as creating a harmonious world. A lot of emphasis is placed upon the soft power potential of China's cultural heritage. China is also able to make use of its significant economic power as a source of attraction, such as President Xi's One Belt, One Road initiative.

The Swedish government is not consistent in the management and communication across the primary policy and diplomatic relations with China. This is evident in the narratives and rhetoric that is used in communicating its point of view, which often establishes Sweden as setting the benchmark of what is to be expected in terms of policy, word and deed in the management of these relations. The particular rhetoric and framing used in managing the communication of the issues of business relations and international relations signal the audience as to the tone and expectations. These two sets of key issues are envisaged and communicated very differently. State to state diplomatic relations within the sphere of international relations is somewhat awkward and bound in the larger geopolitical picture. That is, Sweden is more aligned to the global liberal political order and a United States-centric global world order. It may not be officially allied, but it is aligned, which accounts for the framing of China's military and geopolitical rise as a threat to the current global hegemony. Hence the criticism of such aspects as human rights, which takes Sweden rather idealistically as the "benchmark" for how rights and freedoms should be construed. A deeply utopian and ideologically idealistic set of values and norms are used to convey the criticism. On the other hand, business and investment relations are handled very differently. A much more pragmatic and expectant tone is signalled concerning the deepening of trade and business relations between China and Sweden, instead of the emotionally based logic used in the previous issue, a much more pragmatic, sometime cautious, but reasoned logic is applied. This is seen at the policy level too, where Sweden prioritises trade and business relations with China in the Asia region. In this issue, China is seen and communicated as an opportunity and not a potential threat. This can be seen in the official Swedish response to the One Belt, One Road initiative, where the government is unsure of how much role is reserved for Swedish businesses and government, which prompts it to take a wait and see approach in order to receive a clear signal from Beijing.

Reporting and the editorial line of the four identified Swedish newspapers on the issues of international relations (via world news and editorial/debates) and business/trade relations (via economy) tends to closely follow the policy line and officially communicated government position. When international relations were reported there was a tendency to stress Weaknesses and Threats (such as crises and disasters or the geopolitical 'threat' posed by China). On the issue of economic news, the tendency was to emphasize Strengths and Opportunities (such as the strong business and economic relations between the countries and the potential for further business and financial cooperation). There may be some evident tactical and operational differences in terms of approach and focus – Svenska Dagbladet and Dagens Industri produced more stories on China than the other media outlets whilst Dagens Nyheter's focus on world news contrasted with Dagens Industri's focus on economy. However, there was no significant observable difference and divergence from the Swedish government's officially stated position on those issues, excepting Aftonbladet's scant coverage of economic news. Therefore, the mass media reporting in this paper tends to demonstrate that they performed a reinforcing message of the official viewpoint and were to an extent an echo chamber of the government line.

The final part of the question relates to the issue, whether the Swedish government, and by extension the mass media outlets observed in this paper, converge or diverge from the Chinese public diplomacy narratives? As it stands, the answer is divided as it is both yes and no. In terms of the communication and reaction to the economic and business relationships between Sweden and China tended to reinforce the message of a mutually beneficial relationship between the two countries, which seems to be based on Sweden as the junior partner wanting benefits from it and therefore playing a more diplomatic and careful communication game based upon pragmatism. This contrasts with international relations, where China is seen as a rival and a challenger to the global liberal political order of which Sweden is part. Therefore, the situation is not viewed as being harmonious, but rather as a threat to the continued hegemony of global liberalism. The view of China as a rival and a challenger is likely a product of both a need to cater to certain voter groups, and due to normative perceptions within institutions related to preferences regarding form of government and constitutional rights and freedoms.

Bibliography

Aristotle (translated with an introduction by Lawson-Tancred, H. C.) (1991), The Art of Rhetoric, London: Penguin Books.

Chang, T-K. & Lin, F. (2014), From Propaganda to Public Diplomacy: Assessing China's International Practice and Image, 1950–2009, Public Relations Review, 40, pp. 450–458.

Coombs, W. T & Holladay, S. J. (2010), PR Strategy and Application: Managing Influence, Singapore: Wiley-Blackwell.

Entman, R. M. (2004), Projections of Power: Framing News, Public Opinion, and U.S. Foreign Policy, Chicago: The University of Chicago Press.

D'Hooghe, I. (October 2014) China's Public Diplomacy, Diplomatic Series volume 10 (Lieden, Brill).

D'Hooghe, I. (July 2007), The Rise of China's Public Diplomacy, Discussion Papers in Diplomacy (The Hague, Netherlands Institute of International Relations Clingendael).

Hellström, J. (2010), The EU Arms Embargo on China: A Swedish Perspective, FOI-R-2946-SE, Stockholm: Swedish Defence Research Agency.

Jowett, G. S. & O'Donnell, V. (2012), Propaganda and Persuasion, 5th edition, Thousand Oaks (CA): Sage.

Kallio, J. (2012) Watching a Dragon's Egg Hatch: The Makings of a Sinocentric World? Working Paper 74 (Helsinki, The Finnish Institute of International Affairs).

L'Etang, J. (2011), Public Relations: Concepts, Practice and Critique, London: Sage Publishing.

Leonard, M., Stead, C. & Smewing, C. (2002), Public Diplomacy, London: The Foreign Policy Centre.

McQuail, D. (2010), McQuail's Mass Communication Theory, 6th Edition, London: Sage.

Mazarr, M. J., Struth Cevallos, A., Priebe, M., Radin, A., Reedy, K., Rothenberg, A. D., Thompson, J. A. & Willcox, J. (2017), Measuring the Health of the Liberal International Order, Santa Monica (CA): RAND Corporation.

Melissen, J. (editor) (2005), The New Public Diplomacy: Soft Power in International Relations, New York: Palgrave-MacMillan.

Rawnsley, G. D. (2015), To Know is to Love Us: Public Diplomacy and International Broadcasting in Contemporary Russia and China, Politics, 35(3–4), pp. 273–286.

Seib, P. (2012), Real-Time Diplomacy: Politics and Power in the Social Media Era, New York: Palgrave-MacMillan.

Seib, P. (editor) (2009), Towards a New Public Diplomacy: Re-directing U.S. Foreign Policy, New York: Palgrave-MacMillan.

Simons, G. (2015), Taking New Public Diplomacy Online: China and Russia, Journal of Place Branding and Public Diplomacy, 11, pp. 111–124.

Snow, N. (2010), Public Diplomacy: New Dimensions and Implications, in McPhail, T. L., Global Communication: Theories, Stakeholders and Trends, 3rd edition, Chichester: Wiley-Blackwell, pp. 84–102.

Szondi, G. (October 2008), Public Diplomacy and Nation Branding: Conceptual Similarities and Differences, Discussion Papers in Diplomacy: Netherlands Institute of International Relations Clingendael.

Weissmann, M. & Rappe, E. (2017), Sweden's Approach to China's Belt and Road Initiative, No. 1, UI Paper: Stockholm.

Yang, A., Klyueva, A. & Taylor, M. (2012), Beyond a Dyadic Approach to Public Diplomacy: Understanding Relationships in Multipolar World, Public Relations Review, 38, pp. 652–664.

Zhang, J. (2008). Making Sense of the Changes in China's Public Diplomacy: Direction of Information Flow and Messages. Place Branding and Public Diplomacy 4(4): 303–316.

CHAPTER 13

The Spiritual Roots of Typical European (and Western) Evaluations of China

Kaspars Klavins

1   Introduction

We cannot use one culture as a measure for another. Unfortunately, that is what human beings have been doing for thousands of years, and Europeans are not an exception in this process. For the evaluation of China and Chinese civilization, Europeans have been using their own traditions, society, religion, way of life and system of values. As a result, many of the evaluations of China, which have changed through time, whether positive or negative, have not been objective reflections of China and Chinese culture, but rather diagnoses of the spiritual situation of Europe and the Western World itself. From a comparative point of view, intercultural relations are prospective provided their motivation follows from a serious immersion into the specifics of the other culture – even to the point of integration. An outstanding example of this is Jesuit activities in China in the 16th–17th centuries. At that time catholic missionaries actively translated compositions of ancient Chinese philosophers and familiarised Europe with them, whilst at the same time bringing certain technological achievements from Europe to China. Yet we should not forget that the true purpose of these fruitful missionary activities was to achieve the absolute monopoly of "our own religion" through the elimination of all others.[1] Certainly, intercultural studies are meaningful, provided they help to direct a society into a context of new values. Nowadays, the energy of Western society and its readiness for innovation and extraordinary problem solving have diminished, gradually giving way to China and other Asian countries. From an essentially spiritual aspect, the problem is that Europe lacks a deeper ethically-philosophical concept, which applies to other cultures. In China for example, the link between government ideology and ancient Chinese spiritual-philosophical teachings is supported anew, which is easily noticeable in the

---

1   Zhang Xiping. Following The Steps Of Matteo Ricci To China. Beijing: China Intercontinental Press, 2006, p. 129.

paper on culture-historical essays by China's Economic Reform Foundation Trustee Huang Yongshan "Being of Tao".[2] Also, the Chinese leadership's concept of *harmonious society* (*hexie shehui*) which gained importance after 2004, along with the concept of building a *"harmonious world"*, which became one of China's main foreign policy trends after 2005, were not understood in the West in the context of a revival of traditional Chinese political philosophy (the doctrine of non-offense by Mo Zi (470–390 BC) or the consideration of all wars as fundamentally unjust by Mencius (372–289 BC), etc.).[3] Rather, these approaches were interpreted within the context of a typical Western understanding of international competition and geopolitics.[4]

Of course, China is continuously changing while, at the same time, keeping many of its old traditions alive. In today's world, this co-exists surprisingly well with its extremely fast socioeconomic and technological transformation, as has been typical also for other East Asian nations, such as Korea during its comprehensive industrialisation in the 20th century. The use of ancient cultural beliefs in the modern Chinese spiritual revival cannot be adequately evaluated in the light of the permanent confrontation of civilizations. The recent demonization campaign of China in the Western media in connection with the outbreak of the Coronavirus disease (COVID-19), with references to the age of "Cultural Revolution" (1966–1976), is just another attempt to generate myths, as is the attempt to look at China's foreign policy in the light of an analogy with major Western powers.

This situation calls for a reassessment of the typical European (and Western) evaluations of China, whilst simultaneously looking for a way to change one's own intellectual paradigm which is no longer capable of presenting an alternative in the context of modern social, ecological, medical and psycho-emotional risk factors.

2   Heritage of the Distant Past

It is very difficult to assess the spiritual roots of typical Western attitudes to one or other phenomena, because the culture-historical genesis of Western civilisation itself largely differs from the official historical interpretations or the

---

2   Huang Yongshan (2015). Being of Tao. Beijing: China Intercontinental Press.

3   Ding, S. To Build A "Harmonious World"//Guo, S., and Blanchard, J-M. F., (editors) (2010). "Harmonious World" and China's New Foreign Policy. Lanham: Lexington Books, pp. 107–108.

4   Guo, S., and Blanchard, J-M. F. Introduction//Guo, S., and Blanchard, J-M. F., (editors) (2010). "Harmonious World" and China's New Foreign Policy. Lanham: Lexington Books, p. 2.

average European or American perceptions of it. For example, there was already interaction between Hellenistic culture and China – starting with the expansion led by Alexander the Great – when the ancient Greeks reached Central Asia and India, merged with local traditions, quickly learned about Buddhism and readily accepted it. However, some very important principles of the world outlook of Ancient Greeks, which are similar to the life-understanding elements which paradoxically continue to exist in China, completely disappeared from Europe from as early as the Middle Ages. Just as in Chinese medicine and philosophy, the ancient Greeks featured the unity of human intellect and physical body[5] – in contrast to later Western civilization, which increasingly differentiated these areas. The same can be said of the term *ataraxia* ("tranquillity of soul") and so on. And still – according to some thinkers – already at that time there were differences between the Chinese society of *'gardeners'*, whose main leaders did not interfere with the life of the people but simply controlled the latter in order to maintain peace and consensus – and the Greek society of *'sailors'*, where everyone was in continual polemics with everyone else.[6] In any case, Europe, and Western civilisation born there, is much more an heir to the Middle Ages than to the ancient world.

3   **Searching for the Unexplored Orient**

The interest Europeans took in China in the Middle Ages and Early Modern Period was related to the understanding of reality as the interpreter of God's or the Devil's mystical will. Anything that was *unusual* was perceived as evidence of the works of either God or Satan (a *'wonder'*), which implied *'wondering'* as an act confirming belief. In this context, China became a target for the exotic search for wonders, which was coupled with an accumulation of jewellery, ceramics and silk, in itself related to the appetite for collecting which emerged during the Renaissance.[7] The colonial expansions of the 15th and 16th centuries, along with the seeking of wonders during the overseas trade period of the 17th century, turned into the invention of exoticism. In the itineraries of this period, information about China appeared chaotically, from the perspective of European colonialists, mixing in one pot all the 'curiosities' of the faraway,

---

5   Already the pre-Socratic philosopher Thales (c. 624 – c. 546 BC) spoke about unity of spiritual and physical development.

6   Vernant, J.-P. (1987). Mythos und Gesellschaft im alten Griechenland. Frankfurt am Main: Suhrkamp, pp. 73–80.

7   Schaer, R. (2007). L'invention des musées. Paris: Gallimard.

mysterious lands which they of course 'discovered', to a greater or lesser extent. A perfect example of this is the Dutch traveller Johan Nieuhof's (1618–1672) description of Brazil,[8] where "Brazilian flora segue to Chinese fauna". The eclectic narrative has an ambitious objective: to provide information on lands "from China to Peru".[9] Another example of a typical European narrative of this period is the description of China by the Dutch physician and writer, Olfert Dapper (1636–1689) where "... engravings of 'races' tend naturally to collapse the different continents ..." and "... the term 'Indian' is applied to Chinese and American indigenes alike ... ".[10] It does not matter whether the authors of the abovementioned depictions were themselves travellers or, like Olfert Dapper, who never went outside the Netherlands – transcribe it all from other sources, because their goal was not an accurate, systematic and analytical study of cultures, but rather a search for "fabulous exotica".[11]

This trend continued for a very long time, reaching even into the 18th and 19th centuries (in certain cases even into the 20th century). It is interesting that a certain inertia regarding the highlighting of problems and traditions of non-Western populations has remained to this day in international observations by European (and Western) politicians and journalists: 'they' are often perceived as something common and homogenously strange, following the division of 'them and us', which in turn leads to a higher degree of indifference with regard to the sufferings of (those) people during catastrophes, epidemics or military conflicts.[12] The inhabitants of China fully experienced such attitudes already at the beginning of the 20th century, which is vividly evidenced in the itineraries of that time. Sometimes, even the European travellers themselves expressed their indignation at the self-satisfied Western conclusions that "only Chinese" suffered from plague epidemics which were not therefore of much concern.[13]

8   Nieuhof, J. (1682). Gedenkweerdige Brasiliaense Zee- en Lant-Reise und Zee- en Lant-Reize door verscheide Gewesten van Oostindien. Amsterdam: Jacob van Meurs.

9   Smith, P., and Findlen, P., (editors) (2001). Merchants and Marvels: Commerce and the Representation of Nature in Early Modern Europe. New York: Routledge, 2001, p. 357.

10   Ibid., p. 358.

11   Ibid., p. 361.

12   In this aspect one can agree with the criticism of Western Orientalism by Edward Wadie Said (1935–2003) regardless of the numerous mistakes permitted by this author in analysing historical events. The cynical attitudes to civilian deaths in Iraq and Syria dominating the US mass media were criticised by Rainer Mausfeld (1949 -): https://www.uni-kiel.de/psychologie/mausfeld/pubs/Mausfeld_Die_Angst_der_Machteliten_vor_dem_Volk.pdf

13   Rummel, W. v. Ertse Klasse und Zwischendeck. Eine Weltumsegelung durch Zufall. Berlin: Heimat und Welt, 1911, p. 300.

Specialisations in individual studies of the Middle East and East Asia, like Arab Studies, Sinology or Japanese Studies, are phenomena of the modern period. For a long time, the Arab, Islamic or Jewish civilizations of the Near East were more familiar to the Europeans. In the early modern period, the entire European "secret knowledge"[14] in its attempts to accumulate Egyptian, Chaldean, Persian, Greek and Arab wisdom, was based on studies of the history of ancient civilisations of the Middle East. A German scientist of the 17th century, named Athanasius Kircher (1602–1680), was very close to understanding the ancient Egyptian hieroglyphs even before Jean-François Champollion (1790–1832).[15] Of course, China as a country with secret knowledge, was an image that spread across Europe via the Near East, part of the stereotype of the Middle East as the cradle of civilisation, rooted in the Bible and which sometimes prevented Europeans from understanding China's different, specific cultural-historical heritage. For example, the same Athanasius Kircher, whose contribution to Egyptology cannot be doubted, undertook to quickly and easily disclose the essence of Chinese civilisation by identifying Confucius with Moses and stating that Chinese characters were the abstracted hieroglyphs of Egypt. Interestingly enough, stereotypically fusing the Middle East and East Asia under the single notion of 'Orient', with no consideration of the chasm separating the religiously-philosophical, social and mental traditions of those regions, is also characteristic to modern westerners, both in the areas of daily consciousness and professional evaluation. In fact, the mentality of Islamic society is closer to that of European or American than to the world outlooks of, say, China or Korea. The life understanding presented by Daoism or Buddhism does not provide for emotionally justified 'sacrificing' in the name of a religious idea. Neither does it provide room for 'heroism' or 'ambition for fame' which are dictated by a personal ego, especially where such is rooted in irrational, historically or eschatologically chosen arguments, which are common to the Middle East and the West. Likewise, the appetite of the inhabitants of the West and Middle East to put forward their immediate cravings for the 'improvement' of their financial or social status, is different from the instructions of Confucianism, suited more to rational co-habitation and the long-term existence of the community, which are still today of high importance in China. The ability to implement the single child policy is a great example. We can find similar moments in the thinking of Arabs, Turks, Iranians and Europeans

---

14   Magic, Alchemy and Hermeticism.
15   He, for example, correctly classifies the language of Copts as the last degree of evolution of the Ancient Egyptian language. Unfortunately Kircher did not manage to decode the Egyptian hieroglyphs.

even in the works of Islamic writers when they discuss East Asian cultures (for example, Nazim Hikmet).[16] One can find there as much incomprehension and stereotypes regarding the Chinese life outlook, as in European or American fiction and cinema.

4   The 'Foreign' as the Projected Space of One's Own Problems

In the 16th and 17th centuries, Europe was still standing at a crossroads – in social, as well as cultural, scientific and religious terms. Its medieval foundation had been shattered and many of its traditions (both in positive and negative senses) respected over centuries, were put into question. The later stage of Renaissance which saw disappointment in social reforms; the fight against injustice and usury; the Reformation and Counter-Reformation; The 30-years war, followed by a breakup of Central Europe; obscurantism as regards the official science; and the flourishing of alternative knowledge – all of these were part of the diagnosis of the European mind at a time when the Jesuits developed a new methodology and philosophy of cross-cultural understanding. The missions of the Jesuits in China during the 16th and 17th centuries were mutually transferring technologies, science, philosophy, arts and religion between China and the West. China's image was positive as long as the Jesuits were able to see a connection between Confucian ethics and Christianity. In this respect, one can fully agree with Umberto Eco's conclusions that "China was presented not as an unknown barbarian to be defeated but as a prodigal son who should return to the home of the common father."[17] The Jesuits began translating Confucius's works into European languages and communicating information concerning the various fields of Chinese science, medicine, and philosophy, including information about Yin/Yang principles, etc. According to Robert Irwin, that is how Chinese studies and European *Chinoiserie* started: "A literary cult of the Chinese sage developed, English landowners had their gardens landscaped in the Chinese manner, French *philosophes* brooded on the supposed merits of Chinese imperial order, and the German philosopher Leibniz studied *I Ching*".[18] At the same time, it should be taken into account that the real motive of Jesuits was 'missionising', and contacts in the area of science were only a means of increasing the impact of Catholicism. As stressed by Zhang

---

16   Hikmet, N. (1982). Les romantiques. Paris: Temps actuels.

17   Eco, U. (1998). Serendipities: Language and Lunacy. New York: Columbia University Press, p. 69.

18   Irwin, R. (2007). The Lust of Knowing. The Orientalists and their Enemies. London: Penguin Books, p. 129.

Xiping: "... when studying western culture introduced by the missionaries, we should not rest on the lay of science. What we should do is to analyze their ideology and religious concepts. Thus we may understand the core of western learning introduced by the missionaries".[19]

From the West's point of view, religious doctrine was, and remained, the dominating aspect of building European-Chinese relations at that time, and as a result, all positive additional advantages soon lost their effect. Unfortunately, the less flexible, but more powerful Dominicans, were not able to understand the culture represented by Chinese farmers in their villages and they prohibited Chinese Christians to pay worship to their ancestors and Confucius. So, from a great, charming "Europe-like" country (as the Jesuits called it) – the image of China changed to a land of "idol-worshipers".[20]

Western evaluations of China do not coincide with the idea of progression, propagated in the West, according to which the accepted worldview is that the human race is developing towards wisdom and understanding. Sometimes, evaluations made a long time ago (16th–17th Centuries) may be more objective than later ones. This shows just how complicated and difficult is the evolution of the European mind, and the Western mind in general. As the further reports of missionaries show, the image of "idol-worshippers" continued further into the 19th century and even to the beginning of the 20th century.[21] Many factors have dictated the incomprehension of European (and Western) missionaries on familiarising themselves with the Chinese religious mentality, which is more based on the practical and persistent improvement of one's own ethical and psycho-physical qualities, rather than the eschatological doctrine of the "sinfulness of this world" and its ensuing "reward". From this standpoint, it may be said that Chinese religions focus on this life, while Christianity holds the afterlife to be more important. Moreover, the original sin theory of Christianity denies happiness in this life, which is not the case of Chinese thought.[22] These differences account for the large proportion of melancholy and depression even in economically rich and socially secured Western societies, while a cardinally different attitude to life has enabled the Chinese to retain the principal characteristics of their lifestyle and the stability of social relations even

---

19   Zhang Xiping. (2006). Following The Steps Of Matteo Ricci To China. Beijing: China Intercontinental Press, p. 129.

20   Ibid., pp. 144–145.

21   Hesse, J. (1906). Die Heiden und wir: 275 Geschichten und Beispiele aus der Heidenmission. Calw Stuttgart: Verlag der Vereinsbuchhandlung, p. 122–156.

22   Li Qingben, Cui Lianrui (2008). Comparison of Chinese and Western Literature. Beijing: China Intercontinental Press, p. 40.

during the most difficult periods involving modern catastrophes. For example, according to 2011 statistics, France and the USA were at the very top of the list as regards the prevalence of depression.[23] For more than 400 years, sadness has been an integral part of European society, and in 2020, depression will be the second most widespread cause of disability in the world![24] Among others, one cause of this is the estrangement found in Western families, which has grown with the development of capitalism in the 18th century, the deterioration of rural communities and the loosening of social ties among kin. In the process of the modernisation of China, the social-psychological ties in the family, community and among work colleagues, have generally remained in place regardless of the challenges that have been encountered. The activities of European missionaries in China both in the 19th century and at the beginning of the 20th century – where the preachers of Christianity also highlighted the problems of their own society, which were strikingly different from the principles planted by Confucianism and the Chinese understanding of a physically and psychically sound member of society – could only facilitate mutual estrangement. This came to the fore during the Boxer Rebellion (1899–1901).

5   Between Admiration and Demonization

Certainly, European *Chinoiserie*, founded in the 16th-17th centuries as a cultural phenomenon, continued well through the Early Modern and Late Modern Periods, to a certain extent, marking its presence in Western *belles-lettres*, art, design, interior design, gardens and the park culture of the 20th century. One could certainly refer to "Chinese fashion" in the 18th century. One can fully agree with Zhang Xiping that "In daily life, Europeans were proud of using Chinese commodities, including Chinese furniture, Chinese wallpaper, Chinese porcelain and Chinese tea".[25] China was admired by leading European intellectuals, including the "king of thought" François-Marie Arouet Voltaire (1694–1778), who believed that China was the best-governed nation in the world.[26] In the works of European thinkers of the time, Confucius was as

23   http://www.empowher.com/mental-health/content/which-countries-have
      -highest-and-lowest-rates-depression

24   http://www.clinical-depression.co.uk/dlp/depression-information/major-depression
      -facts/

25   Zhang Xiping. (2006). Following The Steps Of Matteo Ricci To China. Beijing: China
      Intercontinental Press, p. 171.

26   Ibid, p. 172.

renowned an authority in issues related to correct public administration, as the Persian-Arab physician Avicenna (*Ibn-Sinâ*) (980–1037) was once in the area of medicine. For example, a German Enlightenment writer – the "German Voltaire": Christoph Martin Wieland (1733–1813) refers to Confucius in the same context in his didactic work *The Golden Mirror* (*Der goldene Spiegel oder die Könige van Scheschian*). Moreover, he presents his book, written in allegorical parables, as the retelling of a Chinese composition.[27] Such a publication was nothing new in the European Enlightenment where, alongside "Persian", "Arab", "Ancient Greek" or "Roman" authorities, "the wise Chinese" held a stable place in the Western Pantheon of "symbols of wisdom".

If we analyse the evaluations of China as they occurred in Europe from the 18th century onwards (and later in the 20th and 21st centuries in the US), we see that they cyclothymically alternated between admiration and demonization, which is in line with the dualism of thought forged in medieval Europe ("God's children/servants"), historically changing with the level of secularisation but continuing today in the evaluation of other traditions in the categories of polarity: "good/evil", "beautiful/ugly", etc. Western thinking did not allow for the harmony of opposites, as was accepted in classical Chinese philosophy. Furthermore, the colonial, and later economic expansion, developed an enormous potential in European and American societies for mastering the technologies of other cultures, foreign languages and purely external attributes of civilization, without a more serious exploration of the internal philosophical and ethical messages of these cultures. As a result, many evaluations of China have been dominated by purely formal, external, technological and economic criteria, leading to the belittling of that country during the times when it was classified as "economically backward" and to praising it when the Chinese economic boom started. The Chinese ecological, medical and other kindred forms of knowledge, which had been well preserved under the conditions of traditional economy, have often been left out of the focus of evaluators.

Tao yin, Qigong or Kung fu methodologies for reaching health, internal peace and harmony, along with traditional Chinese medicine and image therapy, combined with Feng shui philosophy concerning the surrounding environment (which has been recently winning over Western audiences to an ever larger extent, in literature, cinema and activity clubs), did not stimulate any interest in Europeans at all for a long time, regardless of the fact that they constituted the basis of numerous Asian life-teachings and martial arts. From the

---

27   Wieland, Ch. M. (1772). Der goldene Spiegel oder die Könige van Scheschian, eine wahre Geschichte. Lepzig: M. G. Weidmanns Erben und Reich, p. 47–48.

end of the 19th century to the middle of the 20th century, writings about China only slightly touched upon these areas without stimulating deeper analysis, stereotypically treating them as "mystic", "superstition", "worship of spirits, ghosts, demons and amulets" – to use the terminology of missionaries. The renowned book by John Otway Percy Bland and Sir Edmund Backhouse *China Under the Empress Dowager* (1910),[28] which was published also in German in 1913 in Berlin, is a convincing example of this.[29] Eugen Lehnhoff expresses himself in a similar manner in his compilation *Secret Political Organisations* (1930) when speaking about the Chinese psychical and physical mobilisation skills which were revealed to European colonists during the Boxer Rebellion, seeing them merely as "magic swords" with "belief in supernatural forces", "obsession", "epileptics", "visionaries" and "demons".[30]

Whilst Chan Buddhism, thanks to its wide dissemination, became popular among Western intellectuals earlier (at least theoretically), other significant Chinese ways to spiritual-physical improvement have still not been fully understood in Europe and North America, and this is due to the different perception of life and ethics by westerners.

Interest in Chan Buddhism,[31] Taoism and "secret Chinese knowledge" flourished in Europe in relation to esotericism and theosophy (see Helena Blavatsky, etc.), which was popular in the 19th century. Unfortunately, this interest too turned into an appetite for quick achievement as regards this "secret knowledge", often understanding it as the justification for romanticised, pseudo-scientific expeditions to India, China, Japan or South Eastern Asia in attempts to enter the "mythical kingdom of Tibetan Buddhism – *Shambala*", or simply the publication of sensational articles and possible itineraries instead of the patient development of psychically-physical and ethical qualities. All this does not differ much from looking for exoticism during the era of colonialism.

Assessment of traditional Chinese medicine may be also perceived as a certain Western criterion of the perception of China. Of course, each medical tradition has its advantages and disadvantages, which urgently calls for cooperation between different cultures and schools in this sector today. What is implied here is the ability of the West to accept Chinese medicine per se, understanding both its unique and universal aspects. Already at the beginning of the

28   Bland, J. O. P., and Backhouse, E. (1910).China under the empress dowager. Philadelphia: J. B. Lipincott Company.
29   Ibid., pp. 314–315.
30   Lennhoff, E. (1930). Politische Geheimbünde. Zürich; Leipzig; Wien: Amalthea-Verlag, pp. 439–444.
31   https://plato.stanford.edu/entries/buddhism-chan/

20th century, European Christian missionaries had the possibility to become familiar with Chinese healing, yet their conclusions were unfortunately based upon an argumentation dictated by religion, which accepted only one path – treatment practices under the auspices of Western Christianity.[32] Regardless of the increase in diverse scientific and specialised literature, Western mass media still do not provide sufficient publications about traditional Chinese medicine. Yet the Chinese government is set to "promote the use of TCM remedies globally, while upping its investment in an already extensive domestic network of TCM clinics and hospitals. …"[33] The issue is not actually about the "scientific" or "non-scientific" knowledge of ancient Chinese medicine, practices of energy management or spiritually-meditative therapy, but rather it is about insufficient intercultural knowledge. This situation is well described by Xie Zhuan and Xie Fang in their summarising study:

> Chinese medicine is a unique system of holistic medicine established on philosophical bases instead of biological sciences. It views the various parts of the human body as an organic whole, closely related to one another. It also views the human and the environment as an organic whole, in which the human reacts to the changes of environment. Therefore, the analytical approaches commonly used in biological sciences may not always be applicable to the study of Chinese medicine. This makes one wonder whether Chinese medicine is scientific, a question that Westerners often raise.[34]

The difficulties of Western medicine also stem from the world outlook inherited from the Middle Ages. In Western tradition, a disease is not understood in interaction with a person's spiritual and physical being but taken outside its context and demonised as "evil", which is rooted in the global confrontation of "God and Satan". Today, the terms "good" and "evil" are replaced by others, while the essence of treatment remains the same. The still frequently practiced neutralisation of "evil" symptoms by means of tablets and injections without looking for the cause of the illness, is the same old demonization tactic. A completely opposite approach was characteristic to traditional Chinese medicine where mental diseases were perceived as problems of a person's

---

32   Leuschner, F. W. Aus dem Leben und der Arbeit eines China-Missionars. Berlin: Buchhandlung der Berliner evangelischen Missionsgesellschaft, 1902.

33   https://wddty.com/community/blogs/bryan-hubbard/2017/10/25/chinese-delivery.html.

34   Xie Zhufan, Xie Fang. (2010). Contemporary Introduction to Chinese Medicine in Comparison with Western Medicine. Beijing Foreign Languages Press, p.14.

physical health and vice versa.[35] Additional problems in the contacts between European/American and Chinese scientists are due to the fact that Chinese science studies the human being as an indivisible whole while Western science has taken him to pieces in order to study each piece separately. The essentially different understanding of medicine, along with different treating of 'illness' and 'health', most accurately show the huge gap between the world outlook of westerners and Chinese. Active and radical, generalising a separate moment tendency of evaluating foreign cultures, is specific to the West, following on from the inability to accept the unity of phenomena in nature and society and placing "religion versus material, logos versus mythos, sensation versus intellect, metaphorical versus literal, inner versus outer, object versus subject, spiritual versus supernatural, nature versus culture, and humans versus the Divine" (Amira El-Zein).[36] The enormous interest in martial arts in China frequently stems from westerners seeking "physical victory", fame, respect and other problems related to the ego, sometimes without understanding that a demonstration of fighting is only one of the by-products of energy management. Films, such as *Peaceful Warrior*, a 2006 drama directed by Victor Salva and written by Kevin Bernhardt, which excellently highlights the essence of Qigong, is an outstanding exception in the Western film industry.

6   Achievements in Civilisation Judged as a *Procrustean Bed*

Measuring the degree of industrial and technological development has been an important factor in the evaluations of China by the West, stretching from the itineraries of the 20th century which stressed a "lack of civilisation",[37] to the current premonitory mass media news on China as a superpower which should today be increasingly "taken into consideration". The extensive, quantitative indicators of such an approach do not allow an understanding of the true capacity of China, which is first and foremost rooted in the heritage of spiritual culture. Technology can be quickly mastered. The same cannot be said about the tremendously multifaceted and smart methodology of education, pedagogy and training, which has continued to exist in Asia even during "economic stagnation", including the practice of the effective psychological mobilisation

---

35   Liao Yuqun. La Médicine Traditionelle Chinoise. Beijing: China Intercontinental Press, 2010, p. 56.

36   El-Zein, A. (2009). Islam, Arabs, and the Intelligent World of the Jinn. New York: Syracuse University Press, pp. XVI–XVII.

37   Dittmar, J. (1912). Im neuen China. Köln a. Rh. Schaffstein.

of human capacities which is still intensively applied there. When facing these capacities, a Western person, estranged from family, community and finally even, from himself, is helpless, unprepared, confused and inadequate. The latter oscillates between undefined "borderless" integration and philistine aggression, making "different social values" absolute. At the beginning of the 20th century, when comparing Europe and China, a German Baltic thinker – Hermann von Samson – called on us not to overestimate the importance of Western technological and other "achievements", stressing their temporality.[38]

A considerable diversity of explanation as regards China's "backwardness" is found in the publications of the 1930s, which coincide with a complicated period in the history of China, both in areas of foreign and domestic policy. Western European experts attempted to compare China's inertia, "unable to combat a great battle" environment, with Japan's "achievements in civilisation" (judging by Western standards, of course).[39] The 'friendly' representatives of the USSR in their turn explained the "backwardness" by "remains of feudalism" and the "pressure of international imperialism".[40] Both cases lack any attempt to explore, even in the slightest manner, the social traditions inherited by China and the attitude towards phenomena of formal "development" dictated by the specific local culture. In its situation of nervous existence full of constant breakdowns, Western society has never been completely ready to accept a gradual evolution based on the interpretation of ancient customs, philosophical and literary heritage. Rather, it has related modernisation to sudden breaks and denials of history. China's success did not come in this way. On the contrary, many inherited phenomena have given rise to the rapid advancement of modern China and set forth government priorities in areas associated in the West with completely different approaches. A vivid example of this can be found in recently published articles concerning the failure of functionality of the Chinese education system which present the argument of its too tight links with liberal arts – including literature, philosophy and history – and its hulking, "non-flexible" university administration system.[41] However, according to the ancient experience of Chinese intelligentsia and beliefs based in Confucianism, it is exactly the preservation of an organic link with the cultural heritage of the past which ensures respect for authorities, at the same time

---

38   Helmersen, G. v. (1908). Hermann von Samson. Riga: Verlag von Jonck and Poliewsky, p. 300.

39   Anonymous (1932). Betrachtungen zur Mandschurei-Frage. Berlin: No publication guide, p. 19.

40   Avarin, V. (1934). "Nezavisimaja" Mandzurija. Leningrad: Partizdat.

41   Abrami, R. B. (2014). Why China can not innovate. The Gulf Times. 10. 03. 2017, p. 7.

avoiding the trap of short-term gain (modern financial bubbles) and the possibility of manipulating the younger generation – which has recently finished so tragically in Arab countries.

7   On the Eve of a New Paradigm for Intercultural Understanding

Western 'dynamic' understanding of 'achievement' and 'loss' in the context of both an individual's life and society, which treats long-term and gradual evolution as a "lack of development" – does not coincide with the traditional East Asian understanding of the principles of synergy between man and environment. Slogans, such as "Win or die", "All or nothing", "To be or not to be" are not characteristic of the Chinese perception of existence which allocates sense and meaning to every activity, even the most apparently small if it has been performed with a positive intention. The saying "Do no evil things, however insignificant they may be, and do not give up doing good things, however minor they are" is rooted in the ideas presented in the oldest Chinese classic "I Ching" ("Book of Changes").[42] This attitude has provided all strata of Chinese society with motivation not to lose the capacity for work or joy in circumstances, which from a European point of view, are hopeless and "unacceptable". The dramatic history of China in the 20th century, despite all the tragedies of modernisation, is rather a confirmation than a denial of the surprising continuity and viability of a Chinese life-philosophy over an extremely long period of time. The recent renaissance of classical philosophy, literature, arts and crafts, that have survived despite Western colonialism, Japanese occupation and economic modernisation, are testimony to this. Contemporary Europe's increasing interest in Chinese spirituality, which facilitates comparisons between the intangible cultural heritage of Europe itself and China, and includes folklore, ethnography and traditional medicine, revealing paradoxical similarities, marks a hope for a new stage in the mutual dialogue between Europeans and Chinese today. Over the years, the societies of East Asia and the West have had, and still have, numerous opportunities to enrichen each other by combining the best in both intellectual traditions.

---

42   Tang Wenhui, Liu Zhiqiang (editors) (2016). Book of Changes (Selections). Guilin: Guangxi Normal University Press, p. 49.

Bibliography

Abrami, R. B. (2014). Why China Cannot Innovate. The Gulf Times, March 10, p. 7.

Avarin, V. (1934). "Nezavisimaja" Mandzurija. Leningrad: Partizdat.

Betrachtungen zur Mandschurei-Frage (1932). Berlin: No publication guide, p. 19.

Bland, J. O. P., and Backhouse, E. (1910). China Under the Empress Dowager. Philadelphia: J. B. Lipincott Company.

Dittmar, J. (1912). Im neuen China. Köln a. Rh. Schaffstein.

Eco, U. (1998). Serendipities: Language and Lunacy. New York: Columbia University Press, p. 69.

El-Zein, A. (2009). Islam, Arabs, and the Intelligent World of the Jinn. New York: Syracuse University Press, pp. XVI–XVII.

Guo, S., and Blanchard, J-M. F., (editors) (2010). "Harmonious World" and China's New Foreign Policy. Lanham: Lexington Books.

Helmersen, G. V. (1908). Hermann von Samson. Riga: Verlag von Jonck and Poliewsky, p. 300.

Hesse, J. (1906). Die Heiden und wir: 275 Geschichten und Beispiele aus der Heidenmission. Calw Stuttgart: Verlag der Vereinsbuchhandlung, pp. 122–156.

Hikmet, N. (1982). Les romantiques. Paris: Temps actuels.

Irwin, R. (2007). The Lust of Knowing. The Orientalists and their Enemies. London: Penguin Books, p. 129.

Lennhoff, E. (1930). Politische Geheimbünde. Zürich, Leipzig, Wien: Amalthea-Verlag, pp. 439–444.

Leuschner, F. W. (1902). Aus dem Leben und der Arbeit eines China-Missionars. Berlin: Buchhandlung der Berliner evangelischen Missionsgesellschaft.

Li, Q., Cui, L. (2008). Comparison of Chinese and Western Literature. Beijing: China Intercontinental Press, p. 40.

Mausfeld, R. (2015). Neoliberal Indoctrination: Why do the Lambs Remain Silent? https://cognitive-liberty.online/prof-rainer-mausfeld-why-do-the-lambs-remain -silent/.

Nieuhof, J. (1682). Gedenkweerdige Brasiliaense Zee- en Lant-Reise und Zee- en Lant-Reize door verscheide Gewesten van Oostindien. Amsterdam: Jacob van Meurs.

Rummel, W. v. Ertse Klasse und Zwischendeck. Eine Weltumsegelung durch Zufall. Berlin: Heimat und Welt, 1911, p. 300.

Schaer, R. (2007). L'invention des musées. Paris: Gallimard.

Smith, P., and Findlen, P., (editors) (2001). Merchants and Marvels: Commerce and the Representation of Nature in Early Modern Europe. New York: Routledge, p. 357.

Tang, W., Liu, Z., (editors) (2016). Book of Changes (Selections). Guilin: Guangxi Normal University Press, p. 49.

Vargas, Ph. De (1922). Some Elements in the Chinese Renaissance. Shanghai: The New China Review.

Vernant, J.-P. (1987). Mythos und Gesellschaft im alten Griechenland. Frankfurt am Main: Suhrkamp, pp. 73–80.

Wieland, Ch. M. (1772). Der goldene Spiegel oder die Könige van Scheschian, eine wahre Geschichte. Lepzig: M. G. Weidmanns Erben und Reich, pp. 47–48.

Xie, Z., Xie, Fang. (2010). Contemporary Introduction to Chinese Medicine in Comparison with Western Medicine. Beijing: Beijing Foreign Languages Press, p. 14.

Yongshan, H. (2015). Being of Tao. Beijing: China Intercontinental Press.

Yuqun, L. (2010). La Médicine Traditionelle Chinoise. Beijing: China Intercontinental Press, p. 56.

Zhang, X. (2006). Following the Steps of Matteo Ricci to China. Beijing: China Intercontinental Press, pp. 129; 171.

CHAPTER 14

The Historical Foundation for a Speculative BRI as the Best Route to a Renewed Self

Jean-Paul Rosaye

The main objective of this article, originally composed for a conference in Zhuhai, PRC and entitled *China: a European Perspective*, was to put together a consistent French view of China today, within the context of the current European economic and cultural uncertainties. The obvious way of doing this was to start first with an analysis of several recent books, written by eminent French intellectuals who generally set the tone of French thinking on the situation of France and Europe in the world. The next step was to proceed to some synthetic commentary within the broader historical and philosophical view of intercultural and transcultural relations.

The main conclusion that can be drawn is that Europe, and France more particularly, is at a crossroads regarding its position on the global scene, and that it must find a solution to confront the issues of the postmodern, post-industrial and post-cultural whirlpool in which it has been placed since the 1970s. Europeans, in other words, have to produce a decent answer to the triumph of economics, to the spectacular rise of the individuals' rights, to the demise of national institutions and to the increasing governance of Big Data.

As a response to what the French historian Pascal Ory has called the "Revolution of 1975",[1] Anglo-Saxon countries (and Britain more particularly) have opted for a civilizational regression to the classical liberalism that had made their countries rich and powerful, rather than for the continuation and amendment of the Keynesian social-democratic polity. Donald Trump's election to the US Presidency and the victory of Brexit (for the moment) in Britain have reinforced a doctrinal parochialism and an insular spirit that has spread since the time of Margaret Thatcher and Ronald Reagan. However, such redirection has not been totally accepted by the Europeans, and so far, there has been no real convergence regarding the strategic choices to be made. But

---

1 Cf. Pascal Ory, "Trente Glorieuses, Trente Critiques: et maintenant?", in *Le Débat*, n° 160, 2010/ 3, p. 64–70.

no procrastination is acceptable any longer, and it is in that context that the European perspective on China is a most important issue.

Since the subprime crisis of 2008, globalization has been brought to a stand-still; if not to some form of de-globalization,[2] according to some analysts who emphasize the rise of nationalism and religious sentiment everywhere. In the meantime, as if responding to this pause in the Western neo-liberal globaliz-ing thrust, the General Secretary of the Communist Party of China, Xi Jinping, announced in 2013 the launching of the *One Belt One Road* project (OBOR, now called the *Belt and Road Initiative* or BRI) with a view to involving China in a gigantic economic scheme that would stretch to Europe and Africa. This has led some important French thinkers to insist that Europeans would do well to embrace the Anglo-Saxon scheme and fuse with their civilizational model, while others have judged that China remains a possible option for regaining some driving force, while keeping American "soft power" at some distance.

European civilization might well have totally collapsed after the two world wars, and the wave of decolonisation brought by the twentieth century. Politically, economically and morally exhausted, Europe has nevertheless remained active, due to major intellectual resources. It might therefore be hoped that Europe can still produce an effort to atone with the world and solve the main issues to which it is now confronted, without indulging in intellectual isolationism or lapsing into some romantic nostalgia for the ideological mod-els of its former worldwide dominance. And it is in this respect that China and Europe can entertain a fruitful cooperation.

The economic aspects of international relations are as a rule widely studied, if only because of the hegemony of economics in world affairs, and the recent BRI project is accordingly envisaged almost solely within this perspective. But this article aims at focusing on the necessity to explore a speculative BRI, one which is more philosophical or transcultural rather than economic in nature. China can, in this respect and because it is a very old civilization, help Europe towards a theoretical refoundation of its intellectual powers. An auxiliary con-tention is that the idea of an intellectual collaboration is not new, as a num-ber of historical precedents tend to show. Indeed, it has often been the rule in the past, and it has followed a pattern which is well known and has proved its worth.

This topic of European perspectives on China will be dealt with in two main parts. Part one will analyze several reactions to Europe's most crucial current

---

2   See Walden Bello, *Deglobalization, Ideas for a New World Economy*, London and New-York, 2002, Peter A.G. van Bergeijk, *On the Brink of Deglobalization*, Edward Elgar, 2010, Jacques Sapir, *La démondialisation*, Paris, Seuil, 2011.

predicaments, suggesting either its final resolution in the Anglo-Saxon civiliza-tional model or a reconfiguration with the help of Chinese thinking. Part two will explore the second path, showing the underlying presuppositions and its *modus operandi*.

1   Europe at a Crossroads

The 2008 mortgage crisis generated a historiographic turn among some European scholars studying contemporary history. As they were trying to understand the sources of the crash and more generally the context in which it had taken place (see notes 2 and 3), they were led to view retrospectively the decade of the Seventies as a period in which the matrix of our present world was constituted. Until the beginning of the twenty-first century, the 1970s had been the Bermuda triangle of historical analysis. Everyone was satisfied with its denigration as a "lost" decade of crisis, failure, doom and gloom, and with the general belief that the crisis had been overcome by the advent of neo-liberalis[3] But the current financial and economic crisis, which is not abating in Europe, has led thinkers to reconsider this interpretation and admit that a multi-faceted revolution had taken place during the Seventies, causing a par-adigmatic shift in European civilization that required more than a neo-liberal answer. A short list of the main characteristics of this shift would include the liberal renaissance in Anglo-Saxon countries and the third industrial revolu-tion due to ICT s, but also the considerable upheavals brought by the counter-cultural movements of the sixties and the seventies, bringing more autonomy to the individual selves in Western societies, and placing traditional European values under stress.

Up to the present day, Europe has been reluctant to accept completely the neo-liberal materialistic vision of the world. Revolutionary times require no easy expedient, and neo-liberalism cannot be the sole answer to the postmod-ern revolution. Britain's response consisted of ideologizing the traditional lib-eral model that helped her build a large Empire in the 19th century, but this is by no means a final choice for Europeans, and this explains partly perhaps why Brexit was a logical outcome after all.

Following Pascal Ory's idea that this revolution started in 1975, after the thirty golden years that followed the second world war, Marcel Gauchet, a leading

---

3   For an enlightening study of this historiographic turn, see Lawrence Black, Hugh Pemberton and Pat Thane, *Reassessing 1970s Britain*, Manchester University Press, 2013.

French thinker, has argued in a book published in 2017[4] that a New World had emerged with the first oil shock in 1973, challenging the Europeans with the necessity to invent new values in a postmodern context, without resorting now to the Christian religious inclinations that were formerly instrumental in this regard. As liberalism has a long-standing significance as the ideology that provoked the demise of the Christian tradition (through which European culture had blossomed), its endorsement as the sole cultural framework for Europe is simply out of the question. Edgar Morin, yet another famous French philosopher, also concurred in a book published in 2017 that the time had come for a new civilization.[5] According to him, culture is not a superfluous luxury: it conveys meanings, produces a context and helps through the making of choices, while the neo-liberal search for profit and markets through competition and financial speculation is a makeshift often generating burn-outs and suicides.

2008 has therefore led to reconsidering the 1970s, but the world has changed in the meantime. The mutations incurred have had a ratchet effect. Western societies are now integrating more individual rights every year (from the removal of the death penalty to the rights of abortion and contraception, same-sex marriage, gender reconsideration, etc.). And this has been enlarged to the whole world thanks to virtual globalization, causing all the while contradictory movements threatening the continuation of this globalization. In a nutshell, no business plan creating a world market of de-spiritualised societies can solve the social upheavals that have been generated, and Europe is now facing a fundamental cultural challenge – seeking the intellectual response that will transcend this predicament and bring a cultural renaissance.

Two other French thinkers, Régis Debray and Emmanuel Todd, both in their recent writings and during the marketing process of promotion of their books, have underlined that the future of Europe lay in adopting the Anglo-Saxon cultural model. For Debray, a former companion of Che Guevarra and advisor of French socialist President François Mitterand, the USA is the only real hegemonic civilization today and France is now already Americanized.[6] As for Todd, who provided in a large volume the synthesis of a lifelong study of family types in the world and their links to social policy, Anglo-Saxon civilization is the repository for cultural values closer to the European worldview.[7]

---

4   Marcel Gauchet, *Le nouveau monde* (*l'avènement de la démocratie, tome IV*), Gallimard, Bibl. des sciences humaines, 2017.

5   Edgar Morin, Denis Lafay, *Le temps est venu de changer de civilisation : dialogue avec Denis Lafay*, Editions de l'Aube, 2017, p. 27–30.

6   Regis Debray, *Civilisation : Comment nous sommes devenus américains*, Paris, Gallimard, 2017.

7   Emmanuel Todd, *Où en sommes-nous : une esquisse de l'histoire humaine*, Paris, Seuil, 2017.

Both consider Chinese civilization as profoundly different from Western civilization, whether for political or for sociological reasons. Todd also insists that China has to overcome too many serious demographic, political and economic difficulties to be of any help to Europeans. For these two thinkers, notwithstanding their genuine respect for the venerable Chinese civilization, there is no way the latter could deliver the old European continent from its cultural predicament.

This is not the case of François Jullien, a French philosopher and Sinologist, who for decades has militated for a closer interaction between the European and Chinese modes of thinking.[8] It is precisely the great differences between the European and Chinese modes of thought that makes China so essential to Europe.

As the French philosopher Paul Ricœur expressed in his famous dictum, "To say self is not to say I", and its corollary that "the shortest route from self to self is through the other".[9] In other words, the best route to a renewed identity implies the contact with the otherness, or in Ricœur's words again: "[...] the selfhood of oneself implies otherness to such an intimate degree that one cannot be thought of without the other, that instead one passes into the other, as we might say in Hegelian terms".[10] And in the workings of the human psyche, the greater the otherness the deeper will be the awareness of the identity of self.

The reference here to Hegel is important as this German philosopher represents the acme of European thought, encapsulating in his philosophical system the whole metaphysical tradition of Europe. And as Jullien wrote, alluding to Hegel's most famous work, "It is time to write a 'phenomenology of mind' that is no longer European".[11] In François Jullien's vision of China, only a speculatively intellectual *Silk Road* makes sense:

It is not only China's importance today, and above all its economic importance, that compels us; and all the hybridizations and superimpositions of globalization will not let us avoid the great disentangling that has

---

8   See for example, *Chemin faisant. Connaître la Chine, relancer la philosophie. Réplique à ****, Le Seuil, 2007, and *De l'universel, de l'uniforme, du commun et du dialogue entre les cultures*, Fayard; rééd. « Points », Seuil, 2010.

9   Paul Ricœur, *Oneself as Another*, translated by Kathleen Blamey, Chicago, University of Chicago Press, 1992, See the author's Preface.

10   *Ibid.*, p. 3.

11   François Jullien, *The Book of Beginnings*, Transl. Jody Gladding, New Haven & London, Yale University Press, 2015, p. viii.

become necessary. We must indeed *enter* into Chinese thought, actually enter, in order to exit that ideological outlet that threatens and allows European reasoning to examine itself, both its rich and its exhausted resources.[12]

Only a speculative and intellectual exploration can reconfigure thought genuinely and discard debilitating prejudices, as is adroitly expressed in the following remark by Jullien:

> We explore the resources of thought as they can reconfigure, from one side as from another, the field of the thinkable. It is true that we will no longer lapse into the commonplaces of humanism, so easy to keep repeating, which have as ardent a hold on us as our prejudices do. Rather, we will provide humanism with the tool for constructing and developing itself.[13]

Examining our own culture through the lenses of another is not meant, according to Jullien, to lead to relativization, but to take stock of the typologies, narratives, dramatizations and stereotypes that have been produced so far, and see how they can develop from there. At least, this will eschew the uniformization that has been imposed with the idea of a global world with its gigantic market of languages and folklores that can be redeemed through an impoverished transcultural scheme.

2   The Wealth of Intellectual Influence

François Jullien honestly admits that the presuppositions of his intellectual enterprise of enlarging the possibilities of mind through his study of Chinese thought partake to the rediscovery and rejuvenation of what is essential in European thought.[14] His idea of the wealth of intellectual influence articulates

---

12   *Ibid.*, p. 17.
13   *Ibid.*, p. 121.
14   "I went into China first of all to be able to finally enter into the Greek thought that I probably felt, if confusedly, I had inherited: this connivance through familiarity (atavism) is not knowledge. To make these possibilities of mind emerge, on the contrary, simultaneously emancipates and impassions: emancipates us by desolidarizing us from the adherences we have been subject to; impassions us (the philosophical eros) because these possibilities rekindle one another respectively by clarifying each other in their choices and by discovering each other engaged". *Ibid.*, p. 130–31.

a rationale of influence disclosing an everlasting pattern, profoundly integrated in the history of mankind, and revealing as to the operations of consciousness, i.e. disclosing some enlightening episode in the phenomenology of mind.

Several modern authors have pointed to the specificity of influence and its power – or faculty – to awaken or arouse forgotten elements of consciousness. William Butler Yeats, the first Nobelized Irish poet, considered that "we do not seek truth in arguments or in books, but clarification of what we already believe",[15] and this idea echoed an almost similar statement made by Friedrich Nietzsche when he gave the subtitle "How we become what we are" to *Ecce Homo*, a book listing the influences in the shaping of his mind. The same could also be said of Sigmund Freud's famous "*wo es war, soll ich werden*", giving the gist of his own idea of consciousness and psychoanalysis. The mechanism of influence turns out to work as a reminder, clarifying and reviving ideas too complex or too confused to be grasped fully and emerge in the mind. It is often said, for instance, that civilizations crumble when they have become too complex: a return to common speech, to traditional forms renewed and adapted to new situations is thus regularly needed. As Stéphane Mallarmé and T.S. Eliot after him insisted, it is imperative to "purify the dialect of the tribe". Something new is necessary for something deeply-rooted to emerge.

This pattern has been historically significant, and the whole story of intercultural exchange tells the same tale of the constant cross-fertilization and fecundity of cultures. With this consideration in mind, it is indeed always difficult to explain clearly what is the true identity of cultures.[16]

Two famous instances can be briefly evoked as conspicuous examples where Chinese thought had real impact on European art, politics and economics: the cases of English landscape gardening, and European liberal economic thought.

In 17th and 18th century England, gardening reflected political principles. The Stuarts had borrowed from the French an art of gardening that symbolised the principles of the Absolute Monarchy, personified at the time by Louis XIV, the Sun King. In Hampton Court for example, the three main alleys, like rays of the sun, converge towards the Royal Palace, very much in the same way as in the Château de Versailles. But after the Glorious Revolution of 1688 that marked the end of the Stuart era, gardening could no longer follow the same rules, and the English looked for new models for their gardens that would oppose the geometric and artificial displays favoured by the French. Their speculation drove them to a type of gardening that would follow the randomness of nature

15   W. B. Yeats, *Explorations*, New York, Macmillan, 1962, p. 130.
16   François Jullien, *Il n'y a pas d'identité culturelle*, L'Herne, 2016.

while maintaining some degree of man-made design and contrivance. Blurred exotic concepts meant to come from China, like the famous *"Sharawadgi"* concept introduced by Sir William Temple,[17] were cited to justify the intro-duction of some irregularity in gardening, and this was reinforced when the *Yuanye*, a garden treatise of the late Ming dynasty, was put to use, transform-ing English gardens into places of meditation and harmony with nature. The Anglo-Chinese garden was born.

The real ambassador of Chinese influence was William Chambers, famous for his work in Kew Gardens (West London) and his main theoretical books[18] that were very soon translated into French and knew some European fame. With Chambers, Chinese influence reached a pinnacle, but this fame was its *nemesis*. The sardonic and denigrating French characterized English garden-ing as the Anglo-Chinese garden, putting much stress on the Chinese imports. In a context of almost continuous opposition and colonial warfare between England and France during the 18th century, the English resorted accordingly to minimizing the Chinese influence on their gardening style. This was done first with a pamphlet ridiculing the Chinese fashion, and accusing it of tor-turing nature,[19] and then with the introduction of the *picturesque* fashion,[20] revealing a desired return to traditional forms behind the appeal of Oriental design. After some contortion, the *picturesque* became therefore the definitive version of the art of English gardening thanks to a Chinese catalyst.

The second case is even more edifying, insofar as economic liberalism, that helped Europeans conquer the world, is generally presented as a strictly European creation. But here again, Chinese influence was instrumental in bringing out its main theoretical aspects.

The Chinese notions of the *Tao* and *Wu-Wei* can be tentatively used to explain Smith's concepts of the 'invisible hand', the 'principle of natural lib-erty', or his plea for the removal of regulations and custom duties so as to favour competition and free trade in his famous work *The Wealth of Nations*. But in fact, the idea of a formal link between Smith and Chinese thought is not simply an idea in the air for it was presented in a research paper entitled

---

17   *Upon the gardens of Epicurus* (1685), London, Chatto and Windus, 1908, p. 54.

18   *Designs of Chinese buildings, furniture, dresses, machines, and utensils: to which is annexed a description of their temples, houses, gardens, &c* (1757), and *A Dissertation on Oriental Gardening* (1772).

19   William Mason, *An Heroic Epistle to Sir William Chambers*, 1773.

20   Uvedale Price, *Essay on the Picturesque*, 1794.

Wu-Wei in Europe: A Study of Eurasian Economic Thought, published by the London School of Economics in 2005.[21]

The French supporters of the *laissez-faire, laissez-passer* ideology, especially the Physiocrats, whom Adam Smith had read and emulated in his own economic works, had themselves been influenced by classical Chinese thought. These ideas had transited via the French Jesuits' translations of several classical Chinese texts.

China had been tremendously popular in 18th century France, leading to what was called an 'Oriental Renaissance' by Edgar Quinet in 1848.[22] But this craze receded in the 19th century, in the wake of industrialisation, and particularly after the two Opium Wars that almost pictured Chinese civilization as outdated. Chinese thought fell out of fashion in Europe, as it was replaced by the new values of industrial strength and imperial prestige, which of course forgot all about the important Chinese impulse. Eventually, economic theory placed the emphasis on Jean-Baptiste Say and Adam Smith's writings, vastly discussed and amended in 19th century books of political economy.

3   Conclusion

As the Slovenian philosopher Slavoj Žižek wrote and said repeatedly, contradicting Marx's famous 11th thesis on Feuerbach,[23] the objective of philosophy now is no longer to change the world but to re-interpret it. Time has come to "enact a 'materialist reversal' of Marx himself and return to Hegel".[24] And this may coincide with François Jullien's project of writing a "phenomenology of mind that is no longer European". At any rate, even if one is not required to agree with Žižek's enforcement of the class struggle concept to oppose cultural tolerance and relativity in postmodern societies, there is some consensus on the fact that Europeans have to think the world again.

---

21   Christian Gerlach, *Wu-Wei in Europe. A study of Eurasian economic thought,* Working Papers of the Global Economic History Network (GEHN), Department of Economic History, London School of Economics and Political Science, London, 2005.

22   Edgar Quinet, "De la renaissance orientale", in *Revue des Deux Mondes,* Tome 28, 1841; see also Raymond Schwab, *La renaissance orientale,* Paris, Payot, 1951.

23   "Philosophers have hitherto only interpreted the world in various ways; the point is to change it".

24   Slavoj Žižek, *Less Than Nothing: Hegel and the Shadow of Dialectical Materialism,* Verso Books, 2012, p. 207.

Yet, Europe is caught between two civilizations aspiring to regulate the world, and it has to decide upon its future now. While the Anglo-Saxon world is in fact one realization of the potentialities inscribed in the European spirit, it may be advisable to re-adjust European perspectives on China today, at least in favour of a new intellectually exploratory path – a speculative silk road – to propitiate a European renaissance And this does not necessarily require any formalization of a purely economic trade agreement with the Chinese Belt and Road Initiative.

Bibliography

Bello, W. (2002). Deglobalization, ideas for a New World Economy. London: Zed Books.

Bergeijk, P. A.G. van. (2011). On the brink of Deglobalization. UK and USA: Edward Elgar Pub.

Black, L., Pemberton, H., and Thane, P. (2013). Reassessing 1970 s Britain. Manchester: Manchester University Press.

Debray, R. (2017). Civilisation : Comment nous sommes devenus américains. Paris: Gallimard.

Elgar,E., and Sapir, J. (2011). La démondialisation. Paris: Seuil.

Gauchet, M. (2017). Le nouveau monde (l'avènement de la démocratie, tome IV). Gallimard, Bibliothèque des sciences humaines.

Gerlach, C. (2005). Wu-Wei in Europe. A study of Eurasian economic thought, Working Papers of the Global Economic History Network, Department of Economic History, London School of Economics and Political Science.

Mason, W. (1773). A Heroic Epistle to Sir William Chambers. London: J. Almon.

Morin, E., and Lafay, D. (2017). Le temps est venu de changer de civilisation: dialogue avec Denis Lafay. Editions de l'Aube, pp. 27–30.

Jullien, F. (2016). Il n'y a pas d'identité culturelle. Paris: L'Herne.

Jullien, F. (2015). The Book of Beginnings. Translated by J. Gladding. New Haven & London: Yale University Press, pp. viii.

Ory, P. (2010/3). Trente Glorieuses, Trente Critiques: et maintenant? Le Débat 160, pp. 64–70.

Price,U. (1794). Essay on the Picturesque.

Quinet,E. (1841). De la renaissance orientale. Revue des Deux Mondes 28.

Ricœur, P. (1992). Oneself as Another. Translated by K. Blamey. Chicago: University of Chicago Press.

Schwab, R.(1951). La renaissance orientale. Paris: Payot.

Todd, E.(2017). Où en sommes-nous : une esquisse de l'histoire humaine. Paris: Seuil.

Upon the gardens of Epicurus 1685 (1908). London: Chatto and Windus, pp. 54.

Yeats, W. B. (1962). Explorations. New York: Macmillan, pp. 130.

Žižek, S. (2012). Less Than Nothing: Hegel and the Shadow of Dialectical Materialism. London: Verso Books, pp. 207.

Index

Printed in the United States
by Baker & Taylor Publisher Services